D0759836

# Unnatural Rebellion

JEFFERSONIAN AMERICA

*Jan Ellen Lewis, Peter S. Onuf, and
Andrew O'Shaughnessy, Editors*

# Unnatural Rebellion

*Loyalists in New York City during the Revolution*

Ruma Chopra

University of Virginia Press    Charlottesville & London

University of Virginia Press

© 2011 by the Rector and Visitors of the University of Virginia

All rights reserved

Printed in the United States of America

ISBN 978-0-8139-3109-8

Book Club Edition

*To Prem and Hans, Kusum and Jia*

# Contents

# ACKNOWLEDGMENTS

When I was a doctoral student at the University of California, Davis, Clarence Walker, in passing, observed that African Americans who chose enslavement over freedom in the antebellum period were neither irrational nor fearful. The slaves' attachment to their masters required an alternate and deeper explanation. Alan Taylor emphasized the same with regard to the Euro-American loyalists' allegiance to Britain during the era of the American Revolution. In a letter written from New York to her cousin in Scotland in May of 1785, the loyalist Nancy Jean Cameron acknowledged the compelling emotions that drove colonists to choose British patriotism over rebellion: "Patriot or rebel we are what we see is right to each of us, conscience may make cowards." I am thankful to Clarence, Alan, Mrs. Cameron, and to other voices that echo from the archives, all of which have taught me to consider how people make sense of their lives.

Alan is brilliant. His deep commitment to scholarship and to his students is unsurpassed. If mentors indeed lead by example, there is no higher standard. Clarence attends to the entire world without missing a single nuance. His friendship—his loyalty—has meant everything. From the beginning, other members of my graduate committee, John Smolenski and Caroline Cox, offered their guidance. John showed a cultural studies student how to read history, and Caroline taught that student how to feel less intimidated writing it.

Other scholars provided friendship and also perspective. I am flattered when I am asked to place my work in relation to Judith Van Buskirk's *Generous Enemies*. Her warmth and goodness are, of course, legendary. Ronald Hoffman of the Omohundro Institute inspired much-needed confidence with his kindness and sustained interest in the project. I could not have begun learning about colonial New York without Edward Countryman's established corpus. For the ice cream cake, and their incredible warmth, I thank my very good friends, Carol Lasser and Gary Kornblith of Oberlin College.

For making the world of archives less overwhelming to a beginning student of history, I want to acknowledge Barbara DeWolfe and Janet Bloom at the Clements Library, Caroline Sloat at the American Antiquarian Society, Richard Ryerson at the David Library of the American Revolution, and many others at the New York Historical Society, the New York City Museum, the New York Public Library, the New York State Library, the Gilder Lehrman Society, the National Archives in Kew, and McGill University.

In its final stages, the book benefited from the detailed and thorough commentary of Robert M. Calhoon and Robert Middlekauff. Without judgment, they allowed me to pose any question and to ask it as often as I wished. My department chair at San Jose State University, Patricia Evridge Hill, provided scholarly feedback, unearthed mysterious sums for research, and through her stories and talents, sustains a remarkable department. Richard Holway and Raennah Mitchell of the University of Virginia Press are wonderful.

With their own noise, and in the best of all ways, Zoey and Ahab tuned down loyalist clamor. For Rahul, I have no words. To his parents and mine, I dedicate this book.

# Unnatural Rebellion

# INTRODUCTION

When thousands of British regulars and Hessian soldiers entered New York City on September 15, 1776, a diverse group of Americans—officeholders, merchants, artisans, and shopkeepers—welcomed them. As the *New-York Gazette and Weekly Mercury* recorded, they "expressed the Feelings of their Hearts by loud Acclamations and Shouts of Applause."[1] Envisioning their future within the stability of the British Empire, these loyalists trusted the British military forces to quickly crush the unprovoked, unnecessary, and ultimately "unnatural rebellion." No less patriotic than the revolutionaries, the glorious cause they promoted was reunion with the empire and not American independence.

Almost four decades ago, Winthrop D. Jordan drew attention to the suddenness of the American break with the empire. He addressed how the mainland American provinces, in January 1776, through the words of Thomas Paine, vicariously killed George III, "the royal brute of Great Britain." *Common Sense,* he observed, subliminally prepared Americans to overthrow a paternal father defined as a tyrant who treated his children as slaves. Jordan emphasized the affective and symbolic moment when bitterness and suspicion replaced affection and comity, when many Americans turned from feeling filial to fraternal, and imagined a government without a monarchical head.[2]

The abruptness of the break explains, in part, why a significant minority of Euro-Americans in the mainland colonies emotionally distanced themselves from the upheaval. Indeed, just months before choosing overt resistance, John Jay expressed his dread of the "unnatural convulsions" rent within the empire.[3] Although Jay emerged as one of the leaders of the rebellion, his sentiments—the recoil from rebellion—persisted among those who saw the conflict as resolvable, the tension as healable, and the shattering consequences as avoidable. To these Americans, the rebellion symbolized a sudden reversal, a turning back on the positive consequences of tighter integration with Britain. Surprisingly cosmopolitan in their understanding of the integral relationship between colonial and imperial commerce, they refused to shun a connection that had made the colonies the richest and freest people in the Western world. In their eyes, American slavery was synonymous with American independence.[4]

If the movement for American independence mandates an understanding of Whig ideology, the opposing pull for reunion with the empire requires consideration of loyalists' shared apprehension of a rebellion they variously considered sinful, squalid, and selfish.[5] If the rebels imagined the British as enemies of their cherished rights as Englishmen, the loyalists dismissed the rebels as hypocritical schemers who showed a greater infidelity to American liberty by resorting to vigilantism to suppress political disagreement. Promoted by an ambitious minority who tolerated neither debate nor discussion, the rebel "spirit," in loyalist eyes, represented persecution, vindictiveness, and wantonness.[6] It was inherently tyrannical.

Like the rebel leaders, the loyalists recognized that public authority must rest on the consent of the governed and therefore resented the arrogance that drove British measures between 1765 and 1775. Yet in the end, the Americans who opposed independence felt a deeper threat from rebel leaders who justified the legality of revolution than from the restrictive legislation imposed by the British ministry. Although the loyalists differed in the strength of their convictions, in the timing of their loyalty, and in their methods of opposing the rebellion, they shared similar fears about the unleashing of violence that threatened to annihilate any sense of reason, about the blindness and provincialism of rebel leaders who awoke the passions of the mob on a utopian vision that had no successful historical precedent, and about the appalling prospect of an unbalanced society. In short, they feared the rebellion would lead to the anguish and miseries associated with a state of nature, one in which might makes right.

John Shy emphasizes that historians, ensnared by the "lure of relevance," tend to efface the social uncertainties that shaped and reshaped affiliations during the Revolution. One misconception has been to imagine a teeter-totter: if the revolutionaries were rising, the loyalists must have been declining. Beyond doubt, the rebels played an increasing role through the years of the imperial crisis. They assembled as a congressional body, passed punitive measures against opponents, and chose selected elites as military and civil leaders. Forced to the defensive by rebel accusations of cowardice and treason, the dissenters, by necessity, came to occupy a narrower discursive ground. Represented as naive and misguided or worse, disloyal and dangerous to American liberty, loyalist persuasions went underground but did not disappear. Instead, on one hand, they reemerged in a tide of incomprehension and rage directed at the rebels and, on the other, in a surge of affection expressing longstanding ties of blood, kinship, habits, and affection to the parent country.

What the loyalists wanted to defend was comprehensive—their privileged and free lives under the benevolent empire. But as the revolutionaries regulated the press and punished neutrality, the loyalists, backed into a corner, responded to rebel discourse in a shrill and discordant voice. Through the use of extravagant rhetoric, they hoped to bridge the gap between their ideal of reunion and the reality of growing rebel power. Separation from Great Britain represented more than the symbolic severing of the monarchical head. Killing the sovereign meant simultaneously killing the body politic.[7]

The defensive metaphor of the "unnatural rebellion" moored the loyalist refugees who envisioned a terrifying future outside the empire. Inherently flexible, it generated structures of feeling around which multiple emotions could cluster and set other ideas as almost inconceivable. New York councillor and future loyalist William Smith Jr. hoped desperately for a political solution that would obviate the possibility of an "unnatural contest," one he feared would lead to mobocracy.[8] In June 1775, he urged his more ardent rebel friends to consider reconciliation with the British Empire, to "ponder well upon the strange look of this tremendous roar."[9] Three months earlier, fellow councillor and merchant Henry Cruger had worried about the vanishing prospects of conciliating the "unnatural breach."[10] New York's assistant rector of Trinity Church, Anglican Reverend Charles Inglis, expressed the widespread loyalist rage at the rebel turn to violence. In October 1776, Inglis damned the rebellion as "certainly one of the most causeless, provoked and unnatural that ever disgraced any country."[11]

Not a product of a single loyalist spokesman, the phrase "unnatural rebellion" emerged as a collective denunciation. It signified alarm, horror, revulsion. It carried a "unitive potency" that encompassed and communicated a host of otherwise isolated and refractory impressions about the consequences of breaking with the British system.[12] It created a provisional place from which to dismiss rebel claims of British tyranny, to criticize rebel violence as not only illegal and unconstitutional but wanton and barbaric, and most fundamentally, to reject a fratricidal war between two branches of the same family.[13] As Georgia's loyalist governor James Wright cautioned his state's assembly in 1775, "Don't catch at the shadow and lose the substance."[14]

The loyalist aversion to the unnatural war bears closer scrutiny because it did not prevail only among lawyers, merchants, and ministers. It reveals a subconscious social strand that tinged common loyalist discourse and grounded the dissenters' understanding of the conflict. A few examples from various loyalist refugees who crowded into New York City between 1776 and 1783 illustrate the meaningfulness and wide circulation of this shorthand. In October 1776, New York's loyalists welcomed the British presence because they hoped to suppress the "inevitable ruin" that would result from the "present destructive and unnatural Rebellion," a war "inexcusable in the sight of God and Man."[15] In 1778, upon news of the rebel alliance with the French government, a loyalist essay shunned the "unnatural alliance with Perfidious Frenchmen" and boasted the "natural one" the colonists shared with British Empire.[16] In July 1779, Mary Price, a loyalist refugee from New Brunswick, New Jersey, wrote that she was among the "numerous unhappy persons who have suffered by the unnatural rebellion of this country."[17] A year later, in June 1780, when the New York City loyalists celebrated British success in Charleston, South Carolina, they expressed their desire for a "speedy suppression of the present unnatural rebellion and of the re-establishment of peace."[18] Later in 1780, when some loyalists volunteered to serve in the British military, they made use of the same powerful expression: "From the commencement of the present unnatural rebellion it has been often wished that some regular and efficient system was adopted for employing the zeal of that class of His Majesty's loyal subjects in North America."[19] In October 1781, when loyalists in Bergen Neck, New Jersey, welcomed Prince William Henry to the city, they explained that the "unnatural contest" led by a designing and base set of men had compelled them to defend "that which every man at the risk of his life ought to defend."[20] In 1783, John Huyek of Kinderhook in Albany County wanted British aid to move to Canada because he had served since early 1777 in the "unnatural war."[21]

The revolutionaries understood the changeability of people's allegiance and the interestedness that drove allegiance. The punishments used to sup-

press neutrality, as much as opposition—tarring and feathering, imprisonment, and banishment—reveal the revolutionaries' anxiety. In a period of
narrowing possibilities and sharpening political distinctions, they understood the fragility of their own coalition and hence deemed it necessary
to exclude zealously those perceived as traitors. Yet our dominant understanding of the war homogenizes and narrows the political world of the
late eighteenth century. Unlike the rebels, we have discounted the substantive threat of loyalist persuasions to revolutionary ideals.

During the 1970s, historians approached the question of loyalism
through biographical studies of prominent loyalists. Without reducing motivation to political or economic interests, they wanted to understand—
and explain—why colonists who shared the same imperial world took opposing sides. The impulse that guided this approach was an implicit belief
that loyalism was extraordinary—perhaps abnormal—in an eighteenth-
century mainland society that moved steadily toward what Robert Middlekauff calls "Congregational democracy." Some of these studies emphasized that Euro-Americans who opposed the call to revolution suffered
from personal insecurities and lacked the boldness to imagine a new society outside the British fold.[22]

Recent works turn away from the personality and psychology of elites
to examine ordinary people's pragmatic considerations for choosing allegiance. They demonstrate how colonists made political choices within
specific regional, racial, religious, and economic contexts. Of course,
unless the outcome is obvious, political decision making is not a simple
choice but an amalgam of practical calculations, high expectations, and
deep-rooted, perhaps irrational beliefs. And the outcome was by no means
evident. During the years of the war, many colonists—white and black—
switched political allegiances readily. Some measured the odds and waged
their future variously on long-term British or rebel success. Others were
most concerned about their earnings or their families' safety. Yet in the
end, loyalism, as the rebels understood more intuitively than we have
since, was more than a set of thousands of discrete choices: it held the
potential to build a competing solidarity.[23]

The present volume explores the commitment and resilience of Euro-
Americans who asserted allegiance to the British Empire. Indebted to
studies that conceptualize the eighteenth-century mainland societies as
politically heterogeneous and that highlight the volatility of colonists' allegiances, it offers a full-scale study of loyalism in the port where it had the

greatest chance of success, New York City.[24] Located halfway between the Royal Navy bases at Halifax, Nova Scotia, and St. John's, Antigua, New York City occupied a strategic position on the North American coast. It was also the second-most populous city in North America, a leading commercial seaport, and the most polyglot metropolis in the colonies. During the American Revolution, the British army governed in various periods and for varying lengths of time the North American ports of Boston, New York City, Newport, Philadelphia, Savannah, and Charleston. Recognized for its harbor on the East Coast and the Hudson River, which provided easy communication with Canada, New York was the longest-held North American city under British rule: it served as British headquarters and the center of loyalist activity for seven years. Protected from the rebel threat by British military forces, New Yorkers were in the best position to widen the loyalist appeal. However, the antagonistic relationship between loyalist civilians and the British military curbed loyalist reach. The imposition of military rule over New York City limited the civil capacity available to loyalists.[25] It tempered their ability to discredit the hated rebellion or to dispute rebel allegations of British tyranny. In preserving their military authority, the British sacrificed the legitimacy of the loyalist alternative. The collapse of the New Yorkers' coalition reveals, in miniature, the loyalists' chief handicap as they competed with the revolutionaries for the hearts and minds of undecided colonists.

# 1 ❦ NATURAL RIGHTS AND NATURAL TIES

*Britons in New York City*

> *We (colonies and England) grew rich together. She immensely so by the monopoly of our commerce; and we flourished by her credit; by the fertility of our soil, our natural advantages, and our own labour.*
>
> —William Smith, "Notes for Mr. Hamilton on the American Dispute," November 1775

The royal colony of New York protected British interests in mainland North America. Governor Bellomont's 1699 reflections on the strategic position occupied by New York still held sway six decades into the eighteenth century: he declared that New York "ought to be looked upon as the Capital Province or the Citadel to all the others; for secure but this and you secure all the English colonies, not only against the French but also against any insurrections or rebellions against the Crown of England, if any such should happen, which God forbid."[1] Located astride the Hudson River–Lake Champlain water route toward Canada, New York provided a barrier against French invasion from the north. It served as a vantage point from which the empire could monitor the political pulse of other colonies. In 1755, the British established their central post office in North America in New York City. Prior to 1763, the only British regular troops stationed in the mainland colonies in peacetime garrisoned New York, which attests to Whitehall's recognition of the strategic importance of the colony to the British empire in North America.[2]

An energized point in the British North Atlantic trading network, New York City served as the royal and economic center of New York province. Located at the southern tip of Manhattan Island, the city was compact, about a mile in length and on average, a half mile in width. It enjoyed vigorous growth from the second quarter of the eighteenth century and became the commercial entrepôt and cultural nexus for Manhattan Island, western Long Island, southern Westchester, Staten Island, and eastern New Jersey. A network of roads and waterways connected these communities and provided markets for merchants, farmers, importers, and artisans.

In 1756, New York Councillor William Smith Jr. observed that "our Merchants are compared to a Hive of Bees who Industriously gather Honey for others."[3] Although the city's trade was smaller than that of Philadelphia, diverse entrepôt activities allowed New York merchants to maintain a favorable balance of trade with the mother country. Most significantly, the nearly continuous state of war between Britain and France provided New York merchants with valuable contracts from the British government. During the eighteenth century, New York's overseas trade superseded its intercolonial trade. Involved in the redistribution of imports and the warehousing of goods for overseas shipment, New York City served as the entrepreneurial center of the province and boasted a local merchant and artisan community of skill and ambition.[4]

As the political center of the colony, New York City was home to the royal governor and his entourage of royal officials. Fort George, at the southern tip of Manhattan Island, included the governor's residence as well as barracks that could accommodate two hundred soldiers. Fort George rendered the city imperial as much as colonial and reminded New Yorkers of the protection the empire gave them. The governor administered the colony with the advice of an appointed council and the consent of an elected provincial assembly. He had authority to prorogue the assembly and to veto bills, to command the colony's militia and enforce the navigation acts, and to preside over chancery courts and review fraudulent land titles. In addition to naming the attorney general, receiver general, and surveyor general, the governor also chose the mayor, recorder, and common clerk for New York City's common council.[5]

Leading New Yorkers knew they had much to gain from the governor's favors. But the governor also needed the support of provincial leaders to enforce British policies. He could not directly control the elected legislative bodies in the colony or the city: the provincial assembly and the city council, respectively. The assembly had acquired the means of hampering and sometimes obstructing the king's government in the colony because the salary of the governor and chief justice, as well as funds for other civil officers, depended on the assembly's appropriation.[6]

The selective adoption of British legal culture illustrates New Yorkers' understanding of their strategic position in the periphery of the empire. They used the flexibility of British constitutional culture to aggrandize their position within the colony. Key to maintaining autonomy was limiting His Majesty's prerogative in the colony. In 1749, in response to the question, "What is the constitution of the Government?" New York's governor George Clinton replied that the constitution "is founded on His Majesty's Commission & Instructions to his Governor." However, under advisement of his closest advisor, Cadwallader Colden, Clinton complained that New York's assembly "have made such Encroachments on his Majesty's Prerogative by their having the power of the purse that they in effect assume the whole executive powers into their own hands & particularly claim the sole right of Judging of and rewarding all Services, as well as fixing Sallaries on the Officers annually, and by rewarding particular contingent Services."[7] New York's elite jealously guarded against Crown encroachment over the governance of the city and the colony. Yet they well understood that association with the royal governor and council, and thereby with the London ministry, signified social and political prestige.

Other than the position of governor and lieutenant governor, the council was the highest colonial office. Compared with New York's governors, who on average served for only three years, the councillors served almost ten years. They amassed political capital, learned an imperial vocabulary, and gained the respect of New Yorkers and governors. Their role as unofficial advisors to newly arriving governors assured them an incomparable recognition, both at home and abroad. Placed in a position to benefit from and influence the governor's distribution of patronage, New York councillors gained high standing. Assemblymen stood when a councillor entered a meeting, and New Yorkers honored councillors with glorified obituary notices in the New York newspapers. Awarded lucrative government contracts during the eighteenth-century wars, the councillors used their position to strengthen the clients beholden to them for employment, land, and positions. The majority guided policies favoring commercial interests. Their overseas ties gave them a keen sense of English politics, and their urban residence made them sensitive to transatlantic trading interests.[8]

James DeLancey typifies the imperial connections required for appointment to the exclusive council. The son of the late seventeenth-century Huguenot immigrant to New York Stephen DeLancey, who had amassed a fortune in commerce, James DeLancey was groomed for success. Sent to Corpus Christi, Cambridge, and Lincoln's Inn in the 1720s, DeLancey became one of a handful of New Yorkers who was professionally trained in law and had powerful connections in England. Upon his return, DeLancey became a member of the New York Council in 1729 at the age of twenty-six, chief justice of the New York Supreme Court in 1733, and served as lieutenant governor from 1753 to his death in 1760. After James DeLancey's death, his brother, Oliver DeLancey, occupied his seat on the New York Council. These men served as middlemen of an energetic and prosperous empire.[9]

Like other colonists, New Yorkers generally saw themselves as British subjects and treasured the British constitution as a guarantee of public order. Indeed, they believed that the constitution of the colony mimicked in miniature the constitution of Great Britain. They trusted the conservatism of the British constitution because it rested on the revered Magna Carta and because it had long protected the rights of Englishmen. They believed that American liberty rested on the supremacy of the British Crown, the maintenance of the English system of government, the particular glory of which was its perfect balance of monarchy, aristocracy, and democracy. Sovereignty did not reside only with the king but within a mixed structure that included the king, the House of Lords, and the House of Commons. New Yorkers insisted that government in New York was congruent to Great Britain's because the governor represented the king, the council the House of Lords, and the assembly the House of Commons. The distribution of power among three branches served as a bulwark against tyranny by any one branch.[10]

New Yorkers believed the empire's fluid constitutional framework, with its mixture of common-law traditions, written statutes, and customary liberties such as trial by jury and representative government, permitted an ideal relationship between the colonies and the British government. They could maintain their local autonomy while participating fully in the empire's transatlantic trade and culture. Their belief in the integrative quality of the constitutional relationship with the empire created the confidence they needed to sustain an autonomous political culture within the colony.

In general, New York's legislative procedures followed the precedents set by the English Parliament. The assembly initiated bills, which required the consent of the council and the governor. But there were divergences. Although modeled after Parliament, New York's legislative structure dispersed local power at the county level. For example, New York's assembly had no dedicated home but shared City Hall with the common council of the city. Likewise, judicial power in New York emanated from a single supreme court instead of the three high courts of England (the King's Bench, Common Pleas, and Exchequer).[11]

In comparison with Boston or Philadelphia, a higher number of New Yorkers were eligible to vote in the city. At least two out of every three free adult males had the franchise in New York City, compared with less than half in Boston and Philadelphia. Both freeholders (men who owned at least 50 acres in the city) and freemen qualified to vote, but freemen made up the majority of the New York electorate. Bricklayers, masons, blacksmiths, gunsmiths, weavers, bakers, sailmakers and rope makers, goldsmiths and silversmiths, and other artisans of highly specialized crafts tended to be freeholders.[12] Most freemen were artisans, cartmen, porters, boatmen, mariners, and others who bought political privileges for a few shillings.

Because of the widespread franchise, members of the elected legislative bodies required popular support to maintain political influence and authority. New Yorkers elected twenty-seven members to the provincial assembly, four of whom came from New York City. The city's voters also annually elected fourteen aldermen and assistants, seven assessors, and sixteen constables to the city's common council.[13]

Of those elected to the municipal government between 1761 and 1771, over 57 percent were mechanics.[14] But this number is deceptive because the number of mechanic officeholders declined in proportion to the importance of the position to be filled. New Yorkers needed more than ability and ambition to gain the most eminent positions. Merchants and landholders with close ties to the royal government or transatlantic commerce dominated the New York assembly and council.[15]

The ethnic and religious diversity in the city prevented any overriding sense of identity comparable to that of Boston. Residents of New York City included diverse immigrants from western and northern Europe, grandchildren of the immigrants wooed to settle in Dutch New Amsterdam during the mid-seventeenth century. By 1664, when the English conquered the city and renamed it New York, the Dutch West Indies Company had attracted a diverse and cosmopolitan society of Dutch, German, French, English, Scandinavians, and at least 375 Africans.[16]

By midcentury, slaves and free black people comprised 20 percent of the population, a larger proportion than in any other city in the northern colonies of British America. Most of New York City's slaves came from the sugar islands of Barbados, Antigua, and above all, Jamaica. The slaves came in very small numbers, just a handful on any given ship, almost always on the return leg of voyages made by New York–based trading vessels.[17] In 1750, 30 to 40 percent of all white households in the city owned one or two slaves.[18] In addition to royal officials, shopkeepers, and professionals, prosperous bakers, bolters, brewers, and butchers also owned slaves.[19] Slaves worked predominantly in the maritime sectors of the New York economy, toiling with mechanics as wagoners, dockers, and cartmen. They also performed general domestic services.[20]

Changing patterns of immigration affected the ethnic composition of New Yorkers by the middle of the eighteenth century. Between 1700 and 1775, about 585,000 immigrants entered the thirteen North American colonies, with just under half entering from Africa as slaves. The 1707 Act of Union encouraged Scots to take advantage of opportunities for career advancement in the colonies.[21] Approximately 35,000 Scots entered the mainland colonies in the eighteenth century, of whom 20,000 came between 1768 and 1775.[22] Administrators, ministers, and merchants crossed from Scotland to take advantage of opportunities in the port of New York City. Born of a Presbyterian minister in southeastern Scotland, Dr. Cadwallader Colden arrived in New York in 1718 under the patronage of Governor Robert Hunter, converted to Anglicanism, and served in prominent political positions in New York for almost four decades, until 1776.[23] An important member of the American scientific community, Colden corresponded regularly with associates such as Benjamin Franklin.[24] Colden would serve as the most royalist of Crown officeholders in New York for five decades prior to the American rebellion. Born of Scottish descent in Ireland, Anglican Reverend Charles Inglis immigrated to the colonies at the age of twenty-one and become assistant rector of New York City's Trinity Church by 1765.[25] As a member of the Society for the Propagation of the Gospel in Foreign Parts, Inglis swore loyalty both to the Anglican Church and to the British constitution. Andrew Elliot typifies the many Scots seeking a mercantile career in the North American colonies. The brother of an English baronet, Elliot immigrated to Philadelphia at the age of eighteen; married Elizabeth Plumsted, the daughter of a wealthy Philadelphian; and used his family's political connections to gain a post as a collector of customs in the port of New York in 1764 upon the death of another Scotsman, Archibald Kennedy.[26] In November 1750, Elliot observed cynically that people came to America "to get Money and then return."[27] The rebellion would highlight his considerable influence within the New York mercantile community and set up his political career.

Although they shared with the colonists of English origin an allegiance to Protestantism and faith in British constitutionalism, the Scots and the English did not share a uniform set of assumptions. The Scots brought with them their own blend of culture, tradition, education, and outlook on the empire. They consistently regarded the empire as a whole and not only from the perspective of the metropolis or their local communities. Historian Ned Landsman notes that the Scots' vision of the British Empire, rooted in their political tradition, imagined the connection between the peripheries and the center as an "expansive commercial union." These Enlightenment men imagined a mutually advantageous trade relationship between the provinces and the metropole. Trade and culture, they believed, bound the union more strongly than coercive political power.[28] They established and consolidated both intercolonial and transatlantic networks and promoted the causes of colonial union and imperial reform. New Yorkers of Scottish descent such as Colden, Inglis, and Elliot imagined their security and advancement within an expansionist and integrative empire.[29] They did not fundamentally question the desirability of union but rather pushed proposals for the kind of union that would best protect colonial interests from metropolitan interference.[30]

As residents of one of the larger colonies that did not have a predominant religious group in control, New Yorkers tolerated religious diversity. The colony included people of Dutch Reformed, Presbyterian, Anglican, Huguenot, Moravian, Anabaptist, Lutheran, Quaker, Jewish, and Catholic faiths. The Dutch Reformed and Presbyterian congregations prevailed in the city. In addition to ethnic identities or birthplace, faith revealed social class, education, and family connections.[31]

Only about 10 percent of the colony's churches were Anglican. In 1750, 20 out of 164, and in 1776, 26 out of 239 of New York's churches were Anglican.[32] Despite their small numbers, the Anglicans enjoyed the favor of the royal governors and financial assistance from the Society for the Propagation of the Gospel in Foreign Parts. Consequently, they wielded considerable influence in the city. With its fashionable association with status and empire, Anglicanism increasingly appealed to the elite. In 1760, the critic William Livingston wryly observed: "Whatever is modish captivates juvenile understandings; and the Church of England might, for that reason, expect a further accession of the Dutch Youth."[33]

New York's merchant elite made up about 10 percent of the city's population. New York was a trading town, and New Yorkers flourished with the growing commercial possibilities of the empire.[34] Ships carried merchandise into the city from ports throughout the British Empire and left loaded with produce from the Hudson Valley, Long Island, New Jersey, and Connecticut. By midcentury, the city had surpassed Boston in volume of trade and competed successfully with the nearby port of Philadelphia. New Yorkers developed far-flung trading networks within the empire and relied heavily on English credit. They traded primarily with the West Indies and secondarily with the British Isles. According to Bruce Wilkenfeld, in 1764, 48 percent of the tonnage departing from the port went to the West Indies, 27 percent to Great Britain, 11 percent to other countries in Europe, and 13 percent to other mainland colonies along the Atlantic coast. New York merchants exported timber, wheat, corn, and meat to the West Indies in exchange for sugar and slaves, and they imported finished goods such as refined sugar, wine, indigo, and cloth from Britain. Not only did these goods satisfy colonial demands, but their shipping, distribution, and marketing shaped the commerce in the city.[35]

The city economically depended on Britain. In 1750, the port cleared over £42,000 in exports to Britain and imported more than five times that amount. Since New Yorkers consistently imported more than they exported, they incurred a chronic trade deficit. To maintain and expand their trading network without a sufficient supply of coined money, these merchants relied on British wholesalers to extend favorable terms of credit. As early as 1724, Colden lamented: "Whatever advantage we have with the West Indies it is hard to make it even with England, so that the money imported from the West Indies seldom remains six months in the Province before it is exported to England." Yet despite the endemic imbalance of trade, New Yorkers became adept at warehousing and reshipping commodities such as rice from South Carolina, wheat and flour from Maryland, and flaxseed from Connecticut and Pennsylvania to maintain a favorable balance of trade.[36]

Influenced profoundly by English etiquette, dress, and architecture, New York merchants embraced the markers of gentility.[37] In 1756, a British naval officer commented, "I had no idea of finding a place in America, consisting of near 2,000 houses, elegantly built on brick, raised on an eminence and the streets paved and spacious, furnished with commodious quays and warehouses, and employing some hundreds of vessels in foreign trade and fisheries. . . . Such is this city that a very few in England can rival it in its show, gentility, and hospitality."[38] The wealthiest lived in elaborate mansions on Broadway, which also featured two elegant Anglican churches and the governor's mansion at its foot. They bought fancy four-wheeled coaches and carriages from London and provided business for wig makers, silk dyers, and retailers of expensive furniture. They beautified their homes and gardens, staged grand balls for each other, and separated themselves from all those who had no entry into the gentry class. As Richard Bushman states eloquently, an appearance of "dirty hands, slovenly clothes [and] ungainly speech marked off the coarse and rude from the refined and polite."[39]

The middling people who worked in trading enterprises predominated in numbers and influence in the city. The majority of New Yorkers worked as carters, tailors, blacksmiths, silversmiths, brick makers, joiners, carpenters, mariners, coopers, and cordwainers. Many New Yorkers divided their time between skilled work and commercial enterprise, relying on credit to expand their businesses. Instead of exclusively mastering and practicing a single trade, they participated in a variety of enterprises that had the potential of a good return. For example, some raised livestock for local and export markets and purchased imported cloth and household goods for resale in the city and its environs. As innkeepers, they provided food, drink, and lodging to paying guests. Relying on their wives, slaves, and servants for labor and patrons for credit, they benefited from New York City's location as an expanding trade entrepôt.[40]

Despite a population increase of four to six thousand newcomers—Scottish merchants as well as mariners, the seasonally unemployed, the indigent immigrants from Europe, and migrants from the hinterland seeking work in the city—the boundaries of New York City expanded slowly between 1760 and 1775. Most New Yorkers continued to live within a mile of Fort George at the southern tip of Manhattan Island. Although the city grew with the construction of the new King's College and the Bridewell, the new jail, this expansion did not sharply shift the city's center of population. The clustering of the population along the southern portion of Manhattan had resulted in semidistinct residential areas by the 1730s. The six wards of the city contained varying portions of artisans, merchants, farmers, and mariners, but the commercial heart of the city was concentrated about a block or so inland from the East River along Queen Street, Dock Street, Smith Street, and Wall Street, with its center at prestigious Hanover Square.[41]

New York merchants joined the landed elite to dominate provincial and city governments. While the merchants' status rose as they made fortunes in trade, the power of the landed gentlemen was long-standing. Their influence came from the continuation of the manorial system inherited from the Dutch in the late seventeenth century and supported by English Crown officials in New York colony. The granting of hundreds of thousands of acres to favored gentlemen ensured that a few families owned much of the land in the colony of New York. Although these large landholdings discouraged immigration into the colony, they accrued considerable prestige and power to the landowners. In 1700, fewer than a dozen men owned three-quarters of the granted land in New York colony. Comprising more than a million acres, the Rensselaerwyck manor covered most of Albany County.[42]

New York's governors ignored the 1756 restriction from the lords of trade that limited land grant awards to one thousand acres. Bribed by New York's speculators, the governors found ways to award larger grants of land to themselves and to the speculators. The New York Council, required to pass the land grants, happily complied, for they received favors in turn. In 1773, Governor William Tryon "promised to give the Council 10,000 acres without fees" for their concurrence.[43] Tryon asserted that the judicious granting of land to "Gentlemen of weight and consideration" served as a "counterpoise" to the "leveling spirit" that prevailed in many of His Majesty's colonies.[44] An added benefit for governors like Tryon was the cultivation of the aristocracy that they believed stabilized political society.

By the late 1750s, two competing interests under the family names of DeLancey and Livingston had emerged in New York. Although the two interests did not divide strictly by religion, New Yorkers associated the DeLanceys with Anglicanism and the Livingstons with religious dissent, especially Presbyterianism. The Livingstons usually resided in country estates, and they derived their fortunes from the possession of large landed estates in Albany, Dutchess, and Ulster counties. The DeLanceys had also accumulated large landholdings, but commerce had led to their eminence, and therefore they centered their lives and activities in urban New York City. Commerce and landownership did not stay neatly separated but spilled over, one into the other.[45]

Both families based their political power on a combination of political charm, strong organization in the provincial assembly, and the cultivation of connections with powerful patrons in Britain. For example, James DeLancey's familial link with Sir Gilbert Heathcote, director of the Bank of England, and his connections with his former tutor, Thomas Herring, who became the archbishop of Canterbury, helped him secure his position as royal governor of New York for most of the years between 1753 and 1760.[46]

The two families shared similar wealth and prestige, and both upheld British rule. Both families believed the colony and the Crown benefited from the imperial relationship. The colony enjoyed political liberties and gained economic and military protection, while the empire gained loyal subjects who consumed British manufactures. In the mid-eighteenth century, these two interests did not divide fundamentally over political concerns: they competed only to govern New York.[47]

The Seven Years' War enhanced the wealth and status of New York's elites. The conflict began in 1754 when the British determined to drive the French from Canada, a determination that generated the largest war ever waged between European nations in North America. New York City's proximity to French Canada made it the logical British supply base and communications center for the British army. Between 1755 and 1758, twenty-five thousand British troops arrived in the northern ports of Boston, New York, and Philadelphia. A huge fleet manned by fourteen thousand mariners carried them to the ports of New York and Boston.[48]

The growing scope of military activities as a result of intensified Anglo-French rivalry increased the financial and political rewards of victualing. Foodstuffs—bread, meat, peas, and beer—could be sold at a 100–percent markup. The bills of exchange drawn from London in return for services provided the best and safest remittances. In contrast to the dangers of transatlantic crossings, which resulted in a loss if the vessel foundered or arrived late, bills of exchange were safe from all perils.[49]

The army's demand for food, alcohol, and other supplies made fortunes for favored war contractors and created employment. The frenzied shipyard activity enlarged the city's merchant fleet from 157 vessels in 1749 to 477 in 1762 and increased the combined tonnage from 6,406 to 19,514. Imports from England jumped during the war years. For example, James Beekman, who had imported English goods worth £1,622 between 1753 and 1755, imported £4,183 worth of goods in 1756 and £10,904 worth in 1757, and between 1756 and 1760 he averaged £7,219. Others who received lucrative contracts because of their political connections included provincial councillors Henry White, Charles Ward Apthorpe, William Bayard, Oliver DeLancey, and his brother-in-law John Watts.[50]

Thomas Greg and Waddell Cunningham benefited from the transformation of New York City into the center of British military operations in North America during the Seven Years' War. In 1756, the two Irishmen pooled resources to form a trading house in New York City. Born in northeast Ulster, Cunningham belonged to an Irish merchant community in New York that included the successful merchant George Folliot and Councillor Hugh Wallace as well as non-Irish merchants such as Gerard R. Beekman. The merchants aggressively imported dry goods, bought and sold ships, invested in New York privateers, and conducted a lucrative trade with the French enemy in the Caribbean. In 1762, Cunningham bought a sugar plantation in Dominica, a newly acquired island in the growing British Caribbean. In partnership with fellow Irish merchant James Duane, Cunningham purchased twenty thousand acres in Ulster and Albany counties.[51]

Other New York merchants profited from privateering. When news of war reached the city in 1756, merchants bombarded the royal governor, James DeLancey, with applications for letters of marque. In two years, the number of privateers cruising against French shipping increased from 24 to 224. New Yorkers recognized the potential for profit as one group of seven prizes brought a return of £100,000 to the local economy. In 1757, as increasing numbers of sailors deserted the Royal Navy to participate in privateering expeditions, the royal governor had houses searched to find enough sailors to man the royal vessels.[52]

A 1770 map of the city, drawn by Bernard Ratzer, a British officer, reveals the city's expanding affluent class. It shows a line of new country estates that ranged north of the city, some fronting on the Hudson or the East River, some at the end of long, tree-lined avenues. Owners of the estates included men like Oliver DeLancey, who built his share of a family fortune during the Seven Years' War, and Andrew Elliot, who used his familial and mercantile connections to climb to the higher levels of imperial placemanship.[53]

Along with merchants, New York's artisans, mariners, and laborers found their earning power enhanced as a result of the war. The demand for shipbuilding craftsmen drove wages up to a level not exceeded in any of the port towns before the American rebellion. For example, in 1758, ship carpenters earned eight shillings and laborers four shillings, double the prewar rate. Similarly, as privateering lured mariners to sea, the demand for maritime labor drove up mariners' wages to five shillings per day, triple the peacetime rate.[54]

In 1763, the Treaty of Paris confirmed the British conquest of French Canada and ended the war. Britain controlled an enormous expanse of land in North America, from the Atlantic Ocean to the Mississippi River and from Florida to Hudson Bay. Before the Seven Years' War, the British had posted only a few hundred troops in America. At the close of the war in 1763, confronted with defending the huge expanses of western territory it had newly acquired, the Crown decided to maintain nearly ten thousand men in the colonies. The new garrisons served under British commander in chief Thomas Gage, headquartered in New York City.[55]

The imperial presence in the city hardly troubled New Yorkers, who were long accustomed to the sight of redcoats. Residents joined soldiers in festively celebrating the king's birthday and watched as the troops paraded for review by the commander. Regarding the troops as an unfortunate expedient, New York merchants took advantage of the British military presence in the city. When these gentlemen hosted a dinner, they invited not only the governor and other civil officers but the general and his suite, along with the captains of His Majesty's ships. Indeed, the presence of the imperial officers affirmed that New York had close and profitable ties to the British Empire.[56]

## Resistance to British Policies, 1763–1773

During the Seven Years' War, the British had doubled their debt from a prewar £73 million to a postwar £146 million. The British Crown tried to require the colonists to share the expenses of a standing army in North America. The colonists, the London ministry believed, should contribute to funding the troops stationed for their defense in North America. In 1764 and 1765, the ministry drafted proposals to draw revenue from the colonies.[57]

Parliament's decision to levy taxes on the colonists came during the most serious economic crisis in the history of New York City. Because New York was the center of military provisioning in the Seven Years' War, the departure of most of the British troops created a recession. New York merchants received the last contracts from the British military in May 1761, when the main British fleet left for the West Indies. By withdrawing 18,000 sailors and 22,000 troops from the mainland colonies, the British drastically reduced specie and employment in the city. The wartime boom came to an abrupt halt. In January 1762, Councillor John Watts remarked, "The Tipling Soldiery that use to help us out at a dead lift are gone to drink in a warmer Region, the place of its production." Two years later, Watts lamented the dismal state of the mercantile community: "Commerce is so stagnated here that little or nothing sells, and payment for what does sell keeps the same dull pace."[58]

By 1760, New York's privateers and the Royal Navy had so well swept the French ships from the Atlantic that further privateering opportunities diminished. New Yorkers immediately felt the loss in earnings. The increase in cases filed for debt between 1760 and 1763 indicates the plight of the inhabitants. Before 1760, the city's mayor court had never exceeded sixteen actions for debt. By 1763, there were forty-six, and in 1766, the number had climbed to eighty. In 1765, one New Yorker worried: "Trade in this part of the world is come to so wretched a pass that you should imagine the plague had been here, the grass growing in most trading streets; and the best traders so far from wanting the assistance of a clerk, rather want employment for themselves."[59]

Like other urbanites in North America, New Yorkers experienced frustrated ambition and stagnating fortunes. The greatest hardships imposed by the post-1760 slump fell upon New York's laborers, those who had the smallest savings to cushion the economic downturn. The British military's wartime demand for food compounded by food shortages in the British Isles had raised grain and meat prices to 29 percent above prewar levels. The price of milk rose from the wartime eight pence per gallon to twelve pence in the mid-1760s. Some New Yorkers believed that the cost of living had doubled during the war years.[60]

The rapid growth of an impoverished class attests to the overall economic decline in the city. In the decades prior to the war, New York City had its share of poor, as attested by colonial poor laws, restrictive immigration policies, and crowded almshouses. In 1736, New York built an almshouse and distributed relief for forty persons, most of whom were sick, crippled, old, or orphaned.[61] Beginning in 1760, however, the number of poor soared. In January 1760, church wardens made special collections in each ward to supplement tax funds for the poor, and in 1762, the editor of the *Weekly Post-Boy* complained about the growing "number of beggary and wandering poor" in the streets of New York.[62] The churchwardens informed the common council of the shortage in funds. Without more money, the impoverished would perish for want of food and fuel. In 1765, a group of wealthy New Yorkers organized the Society for the Encouragement of Arts, Agriculture, and Economy, which sponsored a linen manufactory to employ three hundred poor people. In 1769, other merchants organized a Marine Society both to improve maritime knowledge and to alleviate the needs of seamen and their families. By 1771, 360 people were confined to the almshouse. Two years later, as over 425 people jostled for space in the cramped building, the city established more stringent procedures for removing paupers who were not native New Yorkers.[63]

In 1765, Parliament proposed unprecedented taxes in the colonies. Prior to 1763, the major instrument of imperial governance came in the form of instructions issued to royal governors. Until enactment by the colonial legislature, royal instructions carried no sanctions. However, because Parliament directly levied the taxes in 1765, the assemblymen had no recourse. To challenge the policies was to challenge parliamentary sovereignty over the colonies.[64]

Most New Yorkers resented the 1765 Stamp Act, which required additional duties on printed material, including newspapers, broadsides, pamphlets, and business and legal documents. Tensions between the British government and New Yorkers rose to a high pitch. In the fall of 1764, New Yorkers explained their reasons for resisting British taxation in a petition submitted to the House of Commons. The petition began by asserting that the right of self-taxation belonged only to the legislature in the colony, consisting of the "Representatives chosen by the People, who, besides the Power of making laws for the Colony, have enjoyed the Right of Taxing the Subject for the Support of the Government." Without an exclusive right to tax themselves, they argued, they could have no liberty, happiness, or security, for this right was inseparable from the idea of property. Who, they asked, "can call that his own, which may be taken away at the Pleasure of another?" Because the right of property was the "Natural Right of Mankind," no one should pay a tax unless levied by a representative.[65]

In October, twenty-seven men from nine continental colonies met in New York to organize a response to the Stamp Act. They insisted that Parliament did not have the right to levy duties and taxes that violated the colonists' fundamental constitutional rights. Their argument rested on the core belief that only the colonists' representatives could exercise the power of taxation. The ministry's assertion that the colonies, like many boroughs in Britain, remained virtually represented in Parliament, did not convince them. They argued that their geographical distance from the seat of Parliament negated true representation. They should not bear a share of the empire's burden because they did not share in the control of its administration. Accustomed to regularly electing local delegates to represent their particular interests, they did not believe that representatives living three thousand miles away could understand or satisfy their concerns.[66]

In the fall of 1765, economically distressed New Yorkers launched a citywide protest against the Stamp Act. Their severe economic context led them to urban protest and violence. Under the leadership of three middling merchants, Alexander McDougall, Isaac Sears, and John Lamb, a coalition called the Sons of Liberty (or Liberty Boys) united artisans, sailors, and laborers in the city.[67] The Liberty Boys advocated militant measures against the Stamp Act. On October 24, when troops housed the hated stamps at Fort George, handwritten placards signed by "Vox Populi" warned that "the first Man that either distributes or makes use of Stampt Paper let him take Care of his House, Person, and Effects. We dare."[68] On October 31, several thousand artisans, mariners, and laborers marched down Broadway to Fort George to protest the Stamp Act. The same night, the crowd threatened the homes of those who supported British policy. The next day, two thousand New Yorkers marched to Fort George and, after hanging effigies of the devil and Governor Colden, gutted the house of Major Thomas James, scorned for his defense of the Stamp Act. In December 1765, Watts observed that the "ill-boding aspect of things . . . rendered people so poor, cross, and desperate that they don't seem to care who are their masters or indeed for any masters."[69]

The Stamp Act Congress and the stamp act riots followed the English tradition of protest based on the righteous justification of a moral economy; neither represented protorepublican activities. The crowds protested to draw attention to a specific grievance, not to overturn the social hierarchy. They did not seek to topple the economic structure or redistribute social wealth. Colonists believed extralegal, irregular action was necessary when issues could not be dealt with through established institutions. The Liberty Boys responded not only to high principles in rebel newspapers and pamphlets but to the worsening conditions of their lives in the aftermath of the Seven Years' War. They believed purifying a corrupt imperial order would improve their lives. In 1765 and 1766, they, like most colonists, believed they lived in the freest system in the world and felt a source of pride in their association with the empire.[70]

The Stamp Act generated opposition from both the DeLancey and Livingston political factions as well as people of all religious denominations and all occupational categories. Very few in New York supported Lieutenant Governor Cadwallader Colden in upholding the tax. He believed that the colonists should submit to the will of the Crown and Parliament. Colden equated opposition to the tax with subversion and treason.[71]

The two political factions in New York jockeyed for political power. Both understood that the Liberty Boys' destruction of the property of imperial officers could threaten the entire local governing class. Like the Livingstons, the DeLancey faction favored conservative and constitutionally sanctioned protest against British taxation. However, in a bid to win the votes of New York's volatile electorate, the DeLanceys allied with the Liberty Boys in 1765 and 1766. In the 1768 and 1769 assembly elections, the DeLanceys won a majority in the provincial assembly. By siding with the radicals who had supported stringent measures against British taxation, the DeLanceyites won a fleeting political advantage in the colony. Patricia Bonomi explains that the DeLancey victory in the elections of 1768 and 1769 represented a symbolic opposition of merchants to the "most tradition-bound and elitist segment of colonial society, variously called the lawyer party, landlord party, Presbyterian or dissenter party and occasionally, Livingston party."[72]

However, in 1770 the DeLanceys lost popular support from suspicious New York voters after the assembly funded redcoats stationed in the city. The Liberty Boys cried treason. Colden observed the volatile political situation: "The grant of money for the troops is unpopular. We have two parties in violent opposition to each other. One is careful to preserve their popularity in order to secure their seats in the assembly [the DeLanceys], and the other [the Livingstons], takes every method to gain popularity in hopes of a dissolution of the assembly on the arrival of a new governor."[73] The Liberty Boys argued that the assembly had betrayed New Yorkers' constitutional rights by complying with arbitrary quartering laws. The DeLanceyite assembly had agreed to abide by the stipulations in the Quartering Act in return for the restoration of paper money as legal tender in New York. Five years prior, Parliament had stipulated that the colonists could not use paper money for the payment of debts. Members of Parlia-

ment believed that colonists artificially inflated their currency and manip-
ulated exchange rates to defraud English merchants. However, the dearth
of paper money had limited commercial transactions and severely jeopardized New York colony's financial position. The DeLanceys thus sacrificed
their common constituents' immediate concerns about funding a standing army to promote the merchants' interests in greater liquidity.[74]

Between 1765 and 1768, the quartering issue had haunted the Livings-
ton-dominated assembly, which had extended goods and services to troops
without, however, explicitly complying with the tenor of the Quartering
Act. The Livingston leaders had recognized that providing funds for a
standing army would alienate some constituents. In the charged political
climate created by the new Parliamentary taxes, the standing army provoked a new kind of resentment. In contrast to a militia of local amateurs,
a standing army represented a corrupt centralized power with the potential to strike arbitrarily against the people. In addition, in a depressed context of unemployment and high food prices, soldiers competed for scarce
jobs. In 1767, one New Yorker, a "Tradesman," lamented about unemployment, the cost of firewood, and the rise in rent. As British soldiers supple-
mented their low rations by working at cut-rate wages, they provoked
civilians' resentment.[75]

British officers and New York leaders managed the tension between
civilians and the 130 redcoats stationed in the city in 1766. In August, when
civilians publicly jeered in contempt of British soldiers, the soldiers retaliated by cutting down the symbolic Liberty Pole. British officers promptly
punished the soldiers' misconduct. When one soldier tried to resume the
quarrel by attacking a civilian in the street, a court-martial sentenced him
to four hundred lashes.[76]

But royal and local leaders failed to fully contain the explosive situation
between civilians and soldiers. Under Isaac Sears, the radicals retaliated by
leading a crowd of two thousand to erect another pole. The Liberty Boys
also heckled troops who paraded on the nearby fields. In September 1766
and again in March 1767, the redcoats took the pole down. The Liberty
Boys erected it again, the third time encasing the pole in iron. In January
1770, when the soldiers sawed the Liberty Pole into pieces and taunted
civilians, a riot broke out between them in what later came to be called
the Battle of Golden Hill. Although the brawl did not result in any casual-
ties, Gage and his officers decided to ship the most belligerent regiment

to Pensacola in Florida. They sought to quiet the crisis before the people turned against elite leaders as they had done in 1765.[77]

As the DeLanceys had capitalized upon the Stamp Act disturbances in 1765, the Livingston elites exploited the Golden Hill incident to embarrass the DeLanceys and to win over the radicals in the city. In both cases, New York's leaders addressed the demands of their electorate without openly defying the Crown. Their measured stance also guided their response in 1767 to the Townshend Acts by which Parliament levied taxes on paper, glass, lead, paint, and tea. In response, New York's merchants boycotted those goods. Their boycott, however, was more pragmatic than passionate. The colonists' consistent demand for high-quality manufactured items had ensured that New York imported more from Britain than it exported. As New York's leaders waited for Britain to rescind the duties in 1768 and 1769, they expected the boycott to benefit local manufacturing and reduce the trade imbalance with the mother country.[78]

When Britain repealed duties on all items except tea in April 1770, most New Yorkers embraced what they regarded as a reasonable compromise. Patricians and merchants wanted to strengthen the imperial relationship, not to undermine it. Shopkeepers in the city had cleared out old stock and, faced with a dearth of supplies, welcomed a fresh stock of imports. In May 1770, over the protests of some Liberty Boys, New York's merchants rescinded the city's boycott against the Townshend goods. Without jeopardizing their financial standing, the leading men of New York had defied the radical elements in the city. The peace that prevailed during the next months, and indeed years, demonstrates that New York's traditional leaders had effectively handled the protests against the latest British demands.[79]

Merchandise taxed by the Townshend Act arrived several months later without disturbance. No Liberty Boys gathered to prevent the unloading of the goods. In addition, the DeLancey merchants who had led the movement to rescind the Townshend duties continued to win popular support. In the municipal elections of October 1770, they won a majority. One observer, New York City printer James Rivington, celebrated the DeLanceyite victory, declaring: "Last Saturday, a struggle was made by the McDougall party to get the better in city Elections, of the Royalists but the latter prevailed and established an everlasting and invincible superiority."[80]

In a concerted effort to consolidate their interests and guard them from imperial demands and local disturbances, New York merchants founded the Chamber of Commerce in April 1768, the first of such mercantile institutions. The Chamber formed for "encouraging commerce, supporting industry, adjusting disputes relative to trade and navigation and procuring such laws and regulation as may be found necessary for the benefit of trade in general." Composed of twenty-four merchant-politicians of English, Irish, and Dutch ancestry, the Chamber exemplified the cosmopolitan character of New York City. Having served as alderman, mayor, and assemblyman, Councillor John E. Cruger became its first president. Another New York councillor, Irish-born Hugh Wallace, an importer of European goods, became the second president. Of Huguenot descent, alderman, vestryman of Trinity Church, and governor of New York Hospital Elias Desbrosses served as treasurer. Former clerk of the New York Insurance Office Anthony Van Dam became secretary. In the midst of political turbulence, these men strove for a disinterested stance that would protect their economic gains. They hoped their political moderation would translate into increased influence over the city. The Chamber received royal recognition when the governor issued a charter of incorporation in March 1770.[81]

Between 1763 and 1773, New Yorkers' resistance to British policies signified their opposition to political infringements in a climate of economic distress. New Yorkers were Americans with the constitutional rights of Britons. Arbitrary taxation, they believed, threatened to consign them to become the slaves of a distant government. The New York elites were moderates, fearful of losing their social standing and severing their profitable imperial connections. Only in retrospect do the Liberty Boys appear as protorevolutionaries. Prior to 1774, neither the elites nor the common people imagined eliminating the bonds between the mother country and the colonies. In 1767, most hoped with Councillor Smith that the constitution should "bend" to accommodate colonial economic and political growth.[82]

Outside of the Anglican clergy, whose lives and careers indebted them to the empire, New Yorkers failed to divide clearly along ethnic, class, or religious lines during the crises of the mid-1760s and the early 1770s. The diversity of the population—made up of people with multiple interests, faiths, ethnicities, and origins—prevented New Yorkers from speaking with one voice. Michael Kammen emphasizes that the New Yorkers' "striking heterogeneity" made "firm allegiance . . . hard to make and harder to hold together." No overriding sense of loyalty united them.[83]

New York City's mechanics did not form a discrete political bloc. Gary Nash suggests that the lack of a secret ballot in New York City may have prevented the formation of a cohesive artisan electorate. By allowing patrons to witness their clients' political preferences, oral and public voting weakened the formation of autonomous interest groups and deepened the dependency of clients on their economic patrons. As Nash elaborates, many mechanics beholden to merchants, lawyers, or urban landlords feared offending the men who controlled their "rent, job opportunities, credit, and even personal affairs."[84] Satisfied with the established patronage networks, New Yorkers had little desire to form opposing (and weaker) coalitions based on other solidarities.

Like other eighteenth-century colonists, New Yorkers voted for leaders who promised them occupational security and economic opportunity. Because many DeLanceyites made their fortune from the shipping and shipbuilding industry, they employed large numbers of cartmen. Consequently, in the 1768 and 1769 elections, the DeLanceys received enormous support from the city's numerous cartmen. However, the volatility of New York's electorate indicates that patrons could not dictate the political choices of their clients. They consistently had to woo and win over the electorate. Politicians developed a practical tolerance to accommodate New Yorkers' diverse interests.

New York's heterogeneity cut through the ranks to the elite. For example, although many associated the DeLancey party with Anglicanism, Anglicanism with imperial presence, and the imperial presence with loyalism, some Livingstonites, such as William Smith Jr., eventually rejected independence, while some prominent Anglicans, such as John Jay, chose independence. And some non-Anglican DeLanceyites became loyalists. They included James Jauncey, a Presbyterian, and John Cruger of the Dutch Reformed faith. There were also royal non-Anglican placemen in New York City who remained loyal, such as Andrew Elliot, who was Presbyterian.[85]

Between 1763 and 1773, leading New Yorkers favored a moderate path that fell between the radicalism of the Liberty Boys and the unquestioning obedience of royalists like Colden. During this decade, New York's two factions barely differed in their stance on imperial taxation. Both believed that constitutional monarchy protected its subjects and allowed them a voice over matters concerning their lives. They understood that arbitrary taxes levied by the distant Parliament violated their political liberties as British subjects. They also agreed that the British government had the right to tax the colonies externally to regulate trade but not to tax them internally to raise revenue.

Until 1773, New York's leaders strategically maneuvered local support and negotiated with the imperial government to win and retain political ascendancy in the city. Less committed to constitutional principles than local politics, these politicians followed a middle path. Above all, politicians feared any sudden or dramatic changes that threatened to overturn the fragile accommodation of diverse interests within New York.

Living in a commercial city blessed by the profits of empire, the leaders avoided taking positions that would jeopardize their well-established connections to the empire. They had forged their identity in the wake of empire, and they focused on what they had in common with one another and with the empire: culture, language, constitutional liberty, trading interests, Protestantism. Most New Yorkers hoped the constitution would adapt to changing colonial circumstances, on terms that retained the British king as sovereign while rejecting the authority of Parliament. They extended simultaneously their allegiance to New York, to the American colonies, and to Britain. Most had no reason to imagine a world without imperial ties.

# 2 ᛒ "Uncommon Phrenzy"
## Rebel Usurpation, 1774–1776

> It is with affliction we behold a nation as renowned for wisdom as for valor
> involved in a civil war, in which disloyalty of His Majesty's American sub-
> jects to their Prince or want of affection to their Mother Country constitute
> no part of the Unnatural Controversy . . . and we trust, under a merciful
> God, in the aid of your intercession with His Majesty, for a speedy termina-
> tion of those hostile animosities of his contending subjects, which under-
> mine the power and threaten the destruction of the empire.
>
> —Humble Address of Mayor, Aldermen, & Commonalty of the City of
>  New York to Governor William Tryon, July 7, 1775

Not until 1774 did British coercive measures against the port of Boston
incite some New Yorkers toward rebellion. Nothing had alerted them to
the fact that the colonies were about to depart from the normal practices
of traditional politics. The difficulties of the decade came from the aftermath of a global war and the expected dislocations of an economy read-
justing to peacetime conditions. The New Yorkers had no way to foresee
the crisis that would engulf them. While many believed that the colonies
would eventually outgrow their dependent status, they did not believe
that moment had yet arrived.

Although reluctant to offer submission to British policies, many New
Yorkers were hesitant to move toward aggressive resistance. Some with
mercantile interests who would reject rebellion had closer connections to
empire, and better informed of British policies, they felt more confident
about an American future within its protective realm. Their attraction to
the ideal of empire permitted them to see British efforts at taxation as
disturbing infringements, not as enslavement.

The Boston Tea Party in 1773 led to British retaliation in the form of the

Coercive Acts in 1774. The battles of Lexington and Concord followed in 1775. The latter created a sense of urgency and forced a *crise de conscience* for New Yorkers. Between 1774 and 1776, many gradually realized that they faced a growing and irreconcilable conflict between imperial sovereignty and colonial aspirations for greater autonomy.

The passage of the Coercive Acts, or Intolerable Acts, as they came to be know in America, temporarily united most New Yorkers. Passed in retaliation for Boston residents' dumping the East India Company's tea into Boston Harbor in December 1773, the acts closed the port of Boston and provided for the billeting of troops within Boston. These measures alienated an overwhelming majority of colonists and thus provided the broadest possible base on which an opposition could be erected. Designed to punish and humble the city of Boston, they aroused fears that a similar fate awaited New York City. In May 1774, New York Councillor William Smith Jr. worried that these policies would cause colonists to "lose all the Attachmt. we once had to so great a Degree for the Parent Country."[1]

Moderate leaders in the colonies worried about the escalation of the conflict caused by Britain's hard stance against Boston. Like the radicals, they considered the British government's reaction to the Boston Tea Party excessive and unjustified. They were also concerned about the brittle and uncompromising tone that had crept into the imperial debate. In February 1774, Pennsylvania assemblyman Joseph Galloway, a longtime protégé of Benjamin Franklin, expressed his anxiety about the future of the colonies if cast outside the unifying influence of the empire. Galloway worried that the various colonies acted as independent communities that shared nothing in common. They had "different forms of government, productions of soil, and views of commerce; different religions, tempers, and private interests." Their only hope of mutual harmony and stability lay within the empire.[2]

Galloway and other conciliators drew on the Albany Plan of Union first advocated in 1754 as a system of defense against the French and their Amerindian allies along the northern borders of New York. Benjamin Franklin of Pennsylvania, William Smith Sr. of New York, and other promoters of the Albany Plan supported the formation an intercolonial government that could raise taxes to pay for soldiers, build fortifications, and equip vessels. Although this plan did not receive intercolonial or imperial support, the idea of a union under the Crown remained a source of inspiration for those involved twenty years earlier. These included Joseph Galloway and Franklin's son, Governor William Franklin of New Jersey, as well as William Smith's son, Councillor William Smith Jr. of New York. These moderates continued to believe that an American supergovernment could act as an ideal intermediary between the colonies and London and provide a constitutional solution to imperial conflicts.[3]

In a letter to William Franklin, Galloway proposed a written constitution to define more clearly the colonies' relationship to Parliament: "I wish most sincerely with you that a Constitution was formed and settled for America, that we might know what we are and what we have, what our Rights and what our Duties are, in the Judgment of this country as well as our own. Till such a Constitution is settled, different sentiments will ever occasion Misunderstanding."[4] Galloway called for a Crown-appointed president-general to serve as the chief executive for the colonies. He would govern with a grand council chosen by the colonial assemblies for a period of three years. The grand council would exercise "all the legislative rights, powers and authorities necessary for regulating and administering all the general police & affairs of the colonies." Together, the president-general and grand council would constitute "an inferior branch of the British legislature."[5] To mediate potentially conflicting interests among the colonies, the president-general could veto any acts passed by the grand council. Galloway's proposal gave the colonies veto power over imperial taxes but preserved the ultimate sovereignty of the Crown and Parliament. To deny the supreme authority of Parliament over the colonies, he believed, would be a "manifest contradiction while we confess that we are subjects of the British Government."[6]

In September 1774, Galloway presented his "plan of union" to the members of the First Continental Congress assembled in Philadelphia. Formed in response to the Intolerable Acts, the First Continental Congress consisted of delegates from twelve mainland colonies. Many representatives believed it was the duty of the colonial assemblies to present Britain with proposals to promote a return to peace.[7]

New Yorkers had nominated Isaac Low, Philip Livingston, John Alsop, James Duane, and John Jay to represent the colony in the First Continental Congress. The five New York representatives voted in favor of Galloway's plan. None of the five wished to increase the tension afflicting the relationship between Great Britain and the colonies, and in the congressional debates they were part of the conciliatory minority. According to William Franklin, Galloway's plan was "much handed about in New York and greatly approved of by some of the most sensible men of that city."[8] Duane explained that the New York delegates had come to the congress to support Massachusetts but also to agree upon some lasting plan of accommodation with Britain. Duane hoped the king would repeal the Intolerable Acts and propose a compromise to reconcile the colonies. Jay reminded the delegates that "the measure of arbitrary power is not full, and I think it must run over, before we undertake to frame a new constitution." Rather, he argued, the task was "to correct faults in an old one."[9]

However, Galloway's plan failed to pass in the First Continental Congress. Unlike New York's representatives, most of the other delegates balked at conceding the legislative powers of the colonial assemblies to one common and centralized legislature. They claimed that they lacked the authority to approve the far-reaching constitutional changes that Galloway proposed. Although they still wanted the empire united by a sovereign king, they opposed a unifying legislature for all British subjects in the colonies.[10]

To compel the British ministry to rescind the Coercive Acts, the First Continental Congress adopted a detailed program of economic resistance known as the Continental Association. The congress agreed to stop imports from Great Britain, Ireland, and the West Indies by December 1, 1774, and if needed, to bar exports to Britain after September 10, 1775. The congress also encouraged the formation of local committees to enforce the Association's program.[11]

The Association began the process of sorting out loyalists and rebels based on opposition to or support for the boycott. Upon his return to New York City, John Jay inched closer to the radicals by leading the Committee of Inspection, charged with policing compliance. The Intolerable Acts allowed the Liberty Boys to enter the political arena after a three-year absence. In the spring of 1775, they enforced the Association in New York City. They also intimidated and punished common people for speaking against the Association. In January, in a tavern on Long Island, Isaac Sears and Alexander McDougall humiliated John Case, a sixty-year-old resident of Suffolk County, New York, when he denounced resistance to Britain. They forced Case to sit on a corner beside a black servant, deeming him "only fit to sit in the company of slaves." Sears declared that Case was lucky to have escaped a branding with a red-hot gridiron. In February 1775, when British ships loaded with boycotted merchandise arrived in the city, New York radicals gathered to prevent the ships from unloading. A

Captain Watson fled promptly from the harbor. When he returned, the radicals seized him and drew crowds as they paraded him through the streets. In March, two hundred men assaulted suspected loyalist William Cunningham. They demanded that Cunningham go on his knees in front of the Liberty Pole and damn King George. An Irishman who had immigrated to New York in August 1774, Cunningham did not forget the insult. When British commander in chief General William Howe appointed him provost marshal in 1776, Cunningham showed similar cruelty to captured rebel prisoners in the city.[12]

The radicals' extremism troubled New York's leading men, who hoped the troubles would quickly subside and the city's normal operations promptly resume. Prominent elites such as Oliver DeLancey dreaded the loss of valuable contracts if the city's upheavals persisted. In April, General James Robertson, barrack master general for North America, asserted that although he had already spent £260,000 in New York, he would buy military provisions elsewhere if the city government did not restrain the radicals. DeLancey turned his fury against the British and Captain Watson, demanding: "What does that damn'd Rascal come up here again for? Why don't he quit the Port?"[13]

Anxious to preserve their own place within the British Atlantic, New York's elite tried valiantly to maintain the collapsing middle ground between the empire and the colonies. To imperial authorities, they wished to appear as men of substance who could suppress colonial disturbances and maintain a loyal empire. To their constituents, they wished to seem to have enough influence to protect the locals from imperial interference. At all costs, they wished to avoid responsibility for an unpalatable decision. Although this Janus-faced ambivalence had reached a new height, New York's leaders knew their role as an enduring aspect of eighteenth-century colonial life.

Many who had protested British policies between 1765 and 1774 now dreaded the consequences of rebel despotism and social anarchy more than they worried about British taxes. New Yorkers refused to participate in politics with upstarts who dismantled the established legal hierarchy and attacked core constitutional principles. They displayed their unwillingness to join the likes of the Liberty Boys by crafting proposals sent privately to London authorities and by penning encouraging pamphlets targeted to the colonial populace.[14]

The core group of New York writers who protested the vigilantism of the Liberty Boys between 1774 and 1776 were Anglican clergyman. They objected to the extremist demands for ideological conformity, asserted their right to dissent from popular opinion, and emphasized the need for tolerance. Under the leadership of Samuel Seabury, Charles Inglis, and Thomas Bradbury Chandler, New York and New Jersey Anglican clergy attacked the Association during the late fall of 1774. Between November 1774 and January 1775, printer James Rivington published four pamphlets authored by Seabury that assailed the Continental Congress's economic boycott of British goods. Scion of an old New England family, a Yale graduate, and an ardent pamphleteer, Seabury posed as a simple farmer to lash out against the Continental Congress. Like other Anglican clergy, Seabury's loyalism reflected his church's conviction that society should be hierarchic, that ordinary human beings required the supervision of kings and bishops, and that Presbyterianism would lead to revolution. He condemned the congress for rending the bonds of civil society and threatening the rule of the king with a "parcel of upstart, lawless, committee-men." In the fourth pamphlet, entitled *An Alarm to the Legislature of the Province of New York,* Seabury warned that the Association and its boycott would set up a "a new sovereign power in the province and plunge it into all the horrors of rebellion & civil war."[15]

Moderates from New Jersey and Pennsylvania joined New York's Anglican leaders in opposing the committees' violence. On January 3, 1775, Governor Franklin urged his assembly to suppress the violent measures that threatened to culminate in "Anarchy, Misery, and all the Horrors of a Civil War." Another New Jersey loyalist denounced the radical committees in a letter published in the *New York Gazette:* "I had rather submit to acts of Parliament implicitly, nay to the *will* of a King, than to the *Caprice* of Committee-Men."[16] In February, a New Yorker lamented that the Association had taken "Government out of the hands of the Governor, Council, and General Assembly; and the execution of laws out of the hands of the Civil Magistrates and Juries."[17] In March, Rivington printed Galloway's essay *Candid Examination of the Mutual Claim of Great Britain and the Colonies.* Galloway denounced the "American demagogues" who only wanted the "ill-shapen, diminutive brat, INDEPENDENCY." He insisted there must be "union between two great countries whose interest and welfare are inseparable."[18]

General Thomas Gage, governor of Massachusetts and commander in

chief of the British army in America before General Howe, also continued to hope for a peaceful accommodation until the early summer of
1775. Married to an American woman, Gage shrank from the thought
of a trial by battle. But under orders from an impatient London ministry
determined to teach the rebellious colonists a lesson, Gage dispatched a
column of infantry to seize arms hidden by the rebels. However, in April
1775, when armed conflict erupted between the empire and the colonies
at Lexington and Concord, the heavy British losses only strengthened the
resolve of the radicals. Fearing the violence of the rebellious, many leading Massachusetts loyalists from the countryside sought haven with the
British army in Boston.[19]

The battles in Massachusetts inspired radicals to seize power in New
York. The British had precipitated a military engagement from which
many colonists emerged convinced that the onus of aggression lay in the
tyranny of the empire. They believed that the British ministry had violated
the constitutional contract between the king and his people by sanctioning
a military attack against civilians in Massachusetts. But most New Yorkers
did not reject George III. Unwilling to break free from the old constitution,
they demanded that the king recognize the ministers' abuses, repeal the
Intolerable Acts, and restore the privileges of the people. Few imagined a
legitimate alternative to the king's unifying authority.[20]

An uprising began in New York City on April 23, 1775, when the Liberty
Boys broke open City Hall and seized five hundred muskets and quantities of gunpowder.[21] For nearly a week, the Liberty Boys upended the
city's routine, disrupting commercial transactions and halting judicial
procedures. Backed by more than three hundred armed men, Isaac Sears
marched to customs officer Andrew Elliot's house and demanded that he
neither enter nor clear any ships. Sears's men also compelled Elliot to hand
over the keys to the customhouse. By July, Elliot feared the insolence of
the Liberty Boys, whom he described as "very ignorant awkward lazy well
looking young men."[22]

On April 29, Councillor Smith described the turmoil in the city, the
drafting of the militia, the closing of civil courts, the customhouse, and the
port. He also noted the New York merchants' "dread" of rebel violence:

> It is impossible fully to describe the agitated State of the Town
> since last Sunday, when the News first arrived of the Skirmish

between Concord and Boston. At all corners People inquisitive for News. . . . Tales of all kinds invented, believed, denied, discredited. . . . Little business done in the day—few Jurors and Witnesses attend the Courts. Armed Parties summon the Town publicly to come and take Arms and learn the Manual exercise. They are publicly delivered out and armed Individuals shew themselves at all hours in the street, consternation in the Face of the Principal Inhabitants. . . . Sears yesterday afternoon with 360 Armed men waited on Eliot the collector and got the Keys of the Custom House to shut up the Port. The Merchants are amazed and yet so humbled as only to sigh or complain in whispers. They now dread Sears's Train of armed Men.[23]

On May 27, Lieutenant Governor Colden expressed shock at the dramatic escalation of rebel militancy after the bloodshed at Lexington: "You will be surprised . . . to find how entirely the legal authority of Government is now superseded in this Place, where only a few Months ago the prospect of public affairs gave so much satisfaction to the Friends of Government."[24] In June, Colden mourned that the city had lacked a sufficient number of troops and that the man-of-war *Asia* had not arrived in New York until late May. The presence of substantial troops or the threat of naval retaliation, he believed, would have deterred the "rash designs" of the people, who, governed only by their "own wild and dangerous passions," ignored the advice of New York's leaders.[25] New York merchant John Wetherhead later recalled that the "affair" at Lexington "hurried people into violences tenfold greater than ever." Triggered by their "secret hatred" against "men of well known loyal principles," the mob "dragged" people to the Liberty Pole, where they were "insulted and beaten in a Cruel manner, if they refused to kneel down and Curse the King and his Government."[26]

Some leading New Yorkers had long feared dreadful consequences if common people gained power. In May 1774, when the Sons of Liberty elected a committee of correspondence to organize their protest against the Coercive Acts, Gouverneur Morris worried: "The mob begins to think and to reason. . . . I see, and I see it with fear and trembling, that if the disputes with Britain continue, we shall be under the domination of a riotous mob."[27] In mid-1774, the leaders who had taken control of the radical movement included politicians from both political interests in the city. Moderates such as Morris, John Jay, and Peter Van Schaack tried to temper the radicals' violence and demands. Although many of these moderates supported the Association, they denounced violence against royal and elite authority.[28]

Only after the armed clashes at Lexington and Concord did New York's Livingston leaders lead the protest movement initiated by the city's radicals. When the British attacks against the Massachusetts colonists hardened the radicals' profound mistrust of power and corrupt government, the Livingston interests took control of New York's growing radical movement. Deprived of political power in the provincial assembly and the provincial council, the Livingston interests dominated the extralegal committees, snatching popular power from the moderate DeLanceyites. In the process, the Livingstons cast aside the radical spokesmen and assumed command over the alternative government that formed in the city. The criticism of British policy catapulted their status in local politics.

In a fateful election held on April 29, 1775, eighty-four of the one hundred newly elected committee members consisted of prominent merchants and lawyers, of whom only nine would become loyalists. In May, this Committee of One Hundred inventoried the city's ammunition, forbade the sale of arms to suspected loyalists, organized militia companies in each ward of the city, and established a military watch. Under the leadership of James Duane, John Jay, and Peter Van Schaack, the committee also approved a city-specific "association," which vowed to contain the violence of the Liberty Boys.[29]

At the Second Continental Congress meeting in May 1775, Jay proposed the motion to send a final petition to the king. In the original draft of the Olive Branch Petition, Jay offered concessions withdrawn from the final draft crafted by John Dickinson. He proposed that the king "commission some good and great men to enquire into the grievances of her faithful subjects" to achieve reconciliation. Jay's draft downplayed the status of the Continental Congress, asserted the assemblies' willingness to negotiate with Britain, and disavowed independence as a goal.[30]

The leaders who prevailed in New York's extralegal committees continued to hope for an imperial settlement that would return order to the city. Although they supported the Association, they rejected radical measures toward independence. Caught between the extremes of those who opposed the Association ardently and those who trusted the Liberty Boys' direction, these moderate leaders navigated a middle course to keep open the possibility of reconciliation. For example, in August 1775, they avoided confronting the loyalists in Westchester and Albany counties, in New York

City, and on Long Island who prevented rebel committees from collecting arms, supplied the British fleets with provisions and information, and criticized revolutionary measures.[31]

Facing British fleets off New York harbor, New York City's leaders also recognized the port's vulnerability to attack. On August 23, an exchange of fire between New York's committee members and British warships confirmed New York's weakness. Under the moderates' direction, when John Lamb and his men tried to seize royal artillery from the city, a small boat from HMS *Asia* volleyed musket balls at the radicals, and a sailor died. When Lamb regrouped to seize British arms, British naval captain George Vandeput opened fire. Fearing the dreadful consequences of a British attack, the moderate leaders compelled Lamb to retreat. Later that day, when Governor William Tryon called an unprecedented meeting with New York's extralegal committees, the latter agreed not to seize any British cannons or supplies in the city and to provision British ships in New York harbor. Hence a curious military situation existed in New York. While a colonial army blockaded British troops in Boston, New Yorkers supplied British ships in New York harbor as part of Tryon's deal with the Provincial Congress.[32] In November, when the Continental Congress suggested the seizure of royal military stores in New York City, the moderate leaders informed the delegates that they had no intention of so risking the city's safety. In December 1775, McDougall explained the contingencies that dictated the leaders' caution: "Our neighbours are not sufficiently informed of the condition of the colony, and some of our zealous friends in it, were urging to measures without the necessary means to carry them into execution in all their extent, regardless of the most probable and dangerous consequences."[33]

New York's moderate leaders avoided a precipitous move toward independence. They sought reconciliation within a revised constitutional framework. They insisted that the British government should regard the colonies not as subordinate but as a critical and coordinate component of the empire. In a determined effort to establish a middle ground, Councillor Smith sent memoranda and expounded his views privately to radicals in the colonies and hard-liners in Britain. In June 1775, Smith denounced the Crown's uncompromising stance. "It was the error of the parent state," he complained, "and a part of pride to assert a principle that was not worth a farthing unless she had power to carry it into execution and if she had this power needed no declaration of it upon paper for its support."

He pressed the British ministry to observe the bitter opposition to its policies, to "ponder well upon the strange look of this tremendous roar." The ultimate issue, he asserted, was "not what the Constitution was, or is, but what present circumstances considered, it ought to be." In place of fruitless debates about constitutional rights, both sides should seek a common ground. The present, he declared, is "the precise moment for attempting this good work."[34] In November 1775, Smith carefully untangled American claims of liberty from the assertion of independence from Britain: "Every American wants liberty. . . . The incautious observer thinks it is independency. This is bad logic."[35]

One of the strongest advocates of reconciliation, Smith occupied a prominent and influential position in New York colonial government by 1775. The son of New York's chief justice, Smith graduated from Yale College in 1745. Upon graduation, Smith clerked in his father's law office and at the chancery court, and at the age of twenty-three, he became a licensed attorney at law in New York. At the age of forty, Smith, of Presbyterian faith, became a member of the Anglican-dominated New York Council.[36]

His biographer, L. F. S. Upton, astutely describes Smith as "distinctively colonial, aristocratic and yet dissenting in his assumptions." Although Smith shared the privileges and the conservatism of many of New York's leaders, he hardly fits within the group of New York's royal sycophants. A codifier of New York's laws and a historian of the colony, Smith wrote multiple essays defending the colonists' constitutional rights against any form of arbitrary authority. For example, he regarded suspiciously the Anglican Church as a repressive institution that threatened the civil liberties of New Yorkers. In the 1750s, he opposed Anglican control over New York City's newly established King's College because he feared that the Anglicans would permit only their own members to receive higher education. Smith argued that the provincial assembly should have sole authority to name the college's trustees and president, and confirm the college's bylaws.[37]

Smith believed the colonies' peace and prosperity hinged on the capacity of politicians on both sides of the Atlantic to reconstruct imperial administration in light of growing American maturity. He dreaded the consequences of a rupture with the mother country. Aristocratic in his distrust of power in the hands of common people, Smith, like other New York moderates, feared republicanism as mob rule.

Smith blamed both Great Britain and the colonies for their uncompromising stance. In fact, he resented defending parliamentary sovereignty. In passing the Stamp Act and asserting her authority to tax the colonies, the mother country had advanced a new principle that Americans had every right to protest. Likewise, in passing the Coercive Acts, Britain had betrayed her obligations to nurture her colonies. But Smith believed that American assemblies remained duty-bound to present Britain with proposals to restore peace. The ultimate blame lay not with Britain but with those who wished to dismember the empire.

An ardent defender of colonial liberties, Smith sought an improvised and pragmatic accommodation with Britain. In the summer of 1775, Smith urged New Yorkers to send a petition that expressed their abhorrence of the "unnatural contest" and then "without a word about rights, proceed to state the line of conduct that will calm the stormy, troubled sea of discontent." First, the colonists should assert their willingness to contribute revenue as long as Britain sought funds "in the way of requisition." The colonial assemblies would decide how best to collect the needed funds. Second, the petition should assert that, in exchange for the colonists' liberal support of government, the Crown would not interfere in the ecclesiastical and civil affairs in the colonies. But Smith acknowledged that his sentiments "run in a line not popular on either side of the water."[38] Indeed, Smith steered a delicate course in denying Parliament's right to tax the colonies while upholding its legislative supremacy.

Between 1765 and 1775, Smith had consistently urged Britain to redefine its relationship with the colonies. The readjustment, he asserted, needed a formal constitution acceptable both to Parliament and to the colonial assemblies. Smith's 1767 proposal resembled Galloway's 1774 "plan of union." But, more akin to Britain's legislative structure, Smith's plan called for a bicameral legislature with a nominated upper house. Smith imagined two Crown-appointed governing bodies: a twenty-four-member American council and a lord lieutenant. He also suggested the creation of an American parliament based in New York City that would supersede the various colonial assemblies. The parliament would comprise 141 members chosen by the colonial assemblies: the two Floridas, Rhode Island, Nova Scotia, and Georgia would have five representatives each; New Hampshire, Maryland, North Carolina, and Quebec, seven; South Carolina and New Jersey, eleven; New York, Pennsylvania, and Connecticut, twelve; and finally, Massachusetts Bay and Virginia would each have seventeen members. The American parliament would deal directly with the Crown and not with the British Parliament in fiscal concerns. In all other matters, the American parliament would acknowledge the superiority of the British Parliament.[39]

In November 1775, Smith deplored the British officials' misunderstanding of the colonial situation. He echoed John Watts's complaints in 1765 and Galloway's grievances in 1774. In a December 1765 letter to New York's former governor Robert Monckton, Watts had expressed his frustration: "If internal Taxes are to be laid by fellow Subjects who know Nothing of their Circumstances & whose Interest it will be to make them beasts of burthen, . . . it is a meer mercy if they do not [rebel]." Galloway had warned that if Britain meant to retain the colonies, "it will be wisdom in her to restore to her American subjects the enjoyment of the right of assenting to, and differing from, such bills as shall be proposed to regulate their conduct." By failing to gauge the depth of the colonists' devotion to a particular conception of legality, Smith argued, the British government had exacerbated the crisis. They had permanently "opened Pandora's box" by denying the colonists their rightful constitutional heritage. "To tax the colonies by act of Parliament," Smith observed shrewdly, "was totally to disanglify them."[40]

During 1775, New York's radicals continued to snub the counsel of the city's merchants, the Anglican ministers, the royalist officials, and the moderate leaders. On July 12 and 13, they looted an ordnance warehouse and burned a royal barge. After the moderates approved construction of another barge, the radicals sawed it to pieces. On November 23, Sears with eighty mounted volunteers attacked the printing press of loyalist James Rivington. They hoped the example of Rivington would serve as a warning to potential sympathizers of the empire.[41]

Rivington, who traced his lineage to the British gentry, had begun his career in the colonies in 1760 with an ambitious bookselling business in Philadelphia and New York City. He had hoped to offload overstocked books to a colonial clientele. In 1773, Rivington had started printing his newspaper in New York City. The debates between Anglican clergymen and the city's dissenters had raised the circulation of his paper to 3,600 by 1774. It had earned Rivington's appointment to the post of His Majesty's printer for the province of New York in March 1775 at £100 per annum. It had also won him the hatred of the Liberty Boys.[42]

As Rivington's press prepared to reissue Galloway's *Candid Examination*, Sears and his men stormed into Rivington's shop, destroyed his press, and left to the tune of "Yankee Doodle."[43] They also stopped at Westchester and seized the Anglican propagandist Samuel Seabury. They accused him of writing pamphlets "against the liberties of America." Seabury bitterly complained that the mob was "unjust, cruel, arbitrary, and tyrannical." He also protested the treatment of one of his daughters, who was "abused and insulted" by Sears's men.[44] In his own defense he stated: "My ancestors were among the first Englishmen who settled in America. I have no interest but in America. I have not a relation out of it that I know of. . . . I had rather be reduced to the last shilling, than that the imperial dignity of Great Britain should sink, or be controlled, by any people or power on earth."[45]

In December 1775, as Governor Tryon observed the growing upheaval in the city, he embraced a harder line. Six months earlier, when he had returned to New York City after a brief sojourn in England, he grieved over the collapse of royal authority in the city.[46] In a letter to General Gage, just one day after his return, Tryon lamented, "I . . . find the Lieutenant Governor has little authority to transfer to me."[47] His return to New York coincided with a visit from George Washington. Ironically, just hours after greeting Washington, many of the same New York militiamen and civilians saluted and welcomed Tryon. Even in mid-1775, most New Yorkers balked at overtly breaking with the empire. If there was a glaring contradiction in greeting the extralegal continental commander in the afternoon and the legal royal governor in the evening, New Yorkers refused to admit it.

To avert a radical revolution, Tryon urged the London ministry to yield on the question of taxing the colonies. On July 4, 1775, Tryon wrote, "Oceans of blood may be spilt but in my opinion America will never receive Parliamentary taxation." Yet neither King George III nor Parliament would budge. After observing the colonists' insult of imperial authority during the Boston Tea Party in 1773, the king had decided to demonstrate the empire's military might to discipline colonies deemed ungrateful and recalcitrant.[48]

In December 1775 and January 1776, Tryon bitterly reported that loyalists endured tarring and feathering, plundering, imprisonment, and banishment at the hands of extralegal committees. He pleaded for five to six thousand regulars to restore order in New York, and he promised to raise additional regiments of loyalist militia to aid the British troops. Without military aid, he feared that loyalists would "through despair be drove to abandon their allegiance and become soldiers by necessity, at once against their principles and their lawful sovereign." Only a large body of royal troops could destroy "the influences of committees and Congresses." Tryon had served as governor of North Carolina from 1765 to 1771 and had suppressed militarily the 1771 Regulator Rebellion in that colony. He understood well the need for immediate armed action against crowds of belligerent colonists. But General Howe declined Tryon's request. In his tactful reply to Tryon, Howe explained that he expected to be in New York in the spring and anticipated military advantages if, until then, Tryon could "lull the Rebels" into a false sense of security.[49]

In January 1776, Thomas Paine's publication of a pro-independence tract, *Common Sense*, galvanized public opinion and transformed the debate in the colonies. After struggling to make a living as a staymaker, shopkeeper, and petty excise official in England, Paine had arrived in Philadelphia in November 1774 at the age of thirty-nine. Writing in the language of the people, Paine set out to change the colonists' paradigm of political belief. In his famous tract, he discredited monarchy and aristocracy as always brutal and corrupt and made the case for a republic as immensely preferable. Monarchy, he argued, had ruined American trade by embroiling the colonies in numerous wars, created a world of "blood and ashes," and opened the door to "the foolish, the wicked, and the improper."[50] He urged the colonists to unite against the British monarchical government and immediately assert their absolute political freedom as a free republic. He denounced as tyranny any government that failed to represent its citizenry.

The British betrayal at Lexington in April 1775, Paine argued in *Common Sense*, rendered colonial plans and proposals for redress useless. Indeed, he railed, "reconciliation and ruin are related."[51] He encouraged the colonists to claim immediately their natural rights by uniting under a new republican government. The colonies had the right number of inhabitants and possessed natural resources such as hemp, timber, iron, and grains to create a powerful commercial structure and to manufacture gunpowder and cannon to create their own defensive navy. The continental colonies should create a charter of the United States that would replace the Magna Carta of England. Freed from the evil of a king and hereditary succession, a republican society based on people's natural interests would establish a harmonious society.

Paine encapsulated perfectly the radicals' hostility to aristocratic privilege and social deference and provided a utopian vision of the future, a harmonious republican society devoid of political corruption and economic oppression. By showing faith in people's ability to create their own government and providing some hints for the establishment of a republic, Paine's comprehensive argument solidified the radicals' opposition to reunion. At a time when most pamphlets in the colonies sold in the hundreds or a few thousand, *Common Sense* went through twenty-five editions and sold 150,000 copies in a single year.[52]

In March 1776, Revered Inglis responded directly to *Common Sense*. Addressing himself to the "passions of the populace," Inglis warned that Paine's "scheme" of a republican empire was "new as it is destructive." It invited "uncommon phrenzy" and would prove ruinous to America. By rashly inviting the Continental Congress to move toward a "romantic and untried scheme," argued Inglis, Paine furthered the breach between Great Britain and the colonies. Instead of proposing reconciliation with Britain on "solid constitutional principles," the fanatical Paine proposed "cutting off a leg because the toe happened to ache." Insisting that he belonged to no party and cared only about the welfare of America, Inglis pleaded for the avoidance of "blood and slaughter."[53]

However, by the spring of 1776, rebel committees suppressed moderate voices. Before Tryon could issue orders to distribute Inglis's essay, forty Liberty Boys burned the fifteen hundred copies. New York's extralegal committees warned printer Samuel Loudon not to print the pamphlet. A loyalist lamented, "A pamphlet called Common Sense, has carried off its thousands; an answer thereto has come out, but instantly seized in the printer's shop, and burnt in the street, as unfit to be read at this time."[54]

In February 1776, with the arrival of rebel general Charles Lee in New York City, political allegiance suddenly became locked. The forty-three-year-old Lee had an impressive and unusual military record in the British army. In his early twenties, he had served as a lieutenant in a British regiment sent to America in 1755 under the command of Major General Edward Braddock. In 1762, Lee served under Brigadier General John Burgoyne in a successful raid against the Spanish on the Iberian Peninsula. During the civil war in Poland that lasted from 1765 to 1770, he served as royal aide-de-camp and as major general. Lee's decision to fight with the Continental Army may have resulted from George III's unwillingness to promote him for his military accomplishments. But Lee also joined the rebel side because he distrusted what he considered arbitrary and corrupt monarchical authority.[55]

Lee's political activity in the spring strengthened the rebel cause in New York City. He immediately set a new uncompromising tone in the city. His troops suppressed the neutral position. Historian John Shy describes Lee as a ruthless commander who "moved through this murky world of indecision like a flame." Deriding New Yorkers' moderation, Lee reported that the people breathed a "spirit of procrastination, timidity, and hysteria," and that he expected "little cooperation."[56]

New York's leaders had to decide whether to support rebellion or reunion. Already poised as chiefs in the committee movement in New York, many in the Livingston interest asserted themselves as leaders of the radical coalition for independence. As the revolution came to New York, Lee's military presence transformed "wishy-washy appeasers" into "hardline insurgents."[57] Lee ordered the extralegal committees to disarm suspected loyalists. He demanded also that the inhabitants cease provisioning His Majesty's ships and break off all communication with Tryon. He observed that the committees needed to take the "last and decisive step."[58] The New Yorkers who refused to renounce their loyalty to the empire found themselves cast as traitors inimical to colonial liberties. Lee also appointed Isaac Sears as lieutenant colonel. Sears forced New York City's residents to take an oath of allegiance to the Association, and he identified and published the names of those who refused. Alexander McDougall regarded approvingly Sears's efforts to compel the moderates to act more assertively. On March 20 McDougal wrote, "It will be the last instance of their passivity on the point of so much importance to the liberty of a freeman."[59]

More than General George Washington, Lee believed in the use of the militia forces. He thought the British and Americans had won the Seven Years' War only because they had abandoned conventional tactics and engaged willingly in guerrilla warfare. A military radical for his time, Lee believed that a successful revolution required a powerful grassroots movement. Unlike Washington, who focused attention on expanding the Continental Army, Lee believed that an organized group of militiamen could provide effective resistance to the British troops. When he did not find the civil alertness and zeal he expected in New York, he moved against those who resisted.[60]

Lee's crackdown accelerated a massive exodus from New York City by the moderate and fearful. Dreading both rebel persecution and the consequences of an impending British invasion of New York, over ten thousand additional New Yorkers left the city by August 1776.[61] A year earlier, rumors about a massive British attack on the city had led eight thousand New Yorkers to leave the city.[62] Many moved to farms and houses in the New York hinterlands or to nearby towns in New Jersey. In February, Tryon lamented the "unabated vigour and desperate excesses" carried out by the rebels as they identified and abused those loyalists who persisted in the city.[63] Meanwhile, the rebel militia disarmed over a thousand loyalists on Long Island.[64]

In early 1776, General Washington worried that the British seizure of New York would split the colonies: "Should they get that Town and the Command of the North River, they can stop the intercourse between the northern and southern Colonies, upon which depends the Safety of America." General Gage had conveyed exactly the same information to the British secretary of state the previous year. Indeed, Gage proposed the "foundations of the War should be laid" in New York City for four reasons. First, like Washington, he noted that that the possession of New York was "advantageous" because it would render communication difficult between the northern and southern provinces. Second, the British army could maintain easy communications with Canada and launch expeditions to the southern provinces. Third, the "commodious" Hudson River, large and navigable, could easily transport the supplies available in New York's hinterlands to the King's troops. Finally, Gage believed many New Yorkers were friends of the British government who when "freed from the oppression they are under the rebel party," could reestablish constitutional government.[65]

The court-martial and hanging of a Continental Army soldier, Thomas Hickey, on June 28, 1776, in the presence of thousands of New Yorkers culminated a year's violence against dissenters and hardened the line between supporters and opponents of Great Britain.[66] Hoping Hickey's betrayal would provide a valuable lesson to opponents of American independence, Washington wrote: "I am hopeful that this example will produce many salutary consequences and deter others from entering into the line traitorous practices."[67]

The violence in the city shocked some of New York's moderate leaders, who saw the fulfillment of their deep fears about mob rule. They worried that dramatic changes would threaten the fragile accommodation of diverse interests within the province. Active participants in colonial politics, they knew firsthand the centrifugal impulses that threatened colonial stability: the volatility of colonial political institutions, the economic dependencies of the colonial system, the lack of disciplined military experience in the colonies, and the anarchic potential of the leveling principle. They conceptualized society as composed of unequal and imperfect creatures who were malleable and volatile and would destroy society without an aristocratic hand. Out of the unnatural rebellion, they did not have reason to expect a stable body politic.[68]

They worried about a society ruled by self-interested factions who ruled without a shared commitment to political ideals or stability. These moderates saw conflict as inevitable and trusted the experience of the imperial government to resolve issues that rent the fabric of colonial society. They saw the colonial future within an expanding, commercial, and transatlantic empire. Participating within a global trading network protected by the Royal Navy opened opportunities for apprenticeship and career advancement and meant lucrative appointments for family members. The British government, restrained by its own internal traditions of constitutional and common-law traditions, seemed less threatening to liberty than the violently enforced conformity so pervasive within the colonies.[69]

The most articulate Anglican cleric in New York, Reverend Charles Inglis, abiding by his duty to the King and his oath to the Church, supported inseparably both the Church of England and the King-in-Parliament. For Inglis, Anglicanism represented a necessary aspect of political stability. After the Continental Congress issued the Declaration of Independence, Inglis sent his family seventy miles up the Hudson River but stayed in the city himself to visit the sick, baptize the children, and offer support to the poor. On the death Dr. Samuel Auchmuty in March 1777, Inglis became rector of Trinity Church in New York City and continued in this role until 1783.[70]

Although an Anglican like Revered Inglis, Peter Van Schaack's did not support reunion based on the same principles. A graduate of King's College, the twenty-eight-year old lawyer finally remained loyal based on his legal understanding of the binding contract between the empire and the colonies. In 1774, Van Schaack served in New York's extralegal committees. He supported the First Continental Congress, deeming its import and export boycotts a "peaceable mode of obtaining redress" that "should have a fair trial." In the spring of 1776, however, Van Schaack refused to sign a pledge to take up arms against Great Britain. Van Schaack was willing to support the congress when it defended the rights of the colonies upon "the firmest foundation." However, he balked when the "views and designs" of the leaders sought nothing "short of a dissolution of the union between Great Britain and her colonies." Van Schaack rejected the notion that Britain conspired to enslave the colonies. In 1776, he still believed that most of the British acts "seem[ed] to have sprung out of particular occasions, and [were] unconnected with one another." In 1775, Van Schaack left New York City for his home in Kinderhook, Albany County, almost a hundred miles to the north.[71]

Unlike the vocal clergy or the extraordinarily legalistic Van Schaack, most New Yorkers did not leave behind detailed ideological justification for their stance or their decisions during the rebellion. New York Councillor John Watts's decision to leave the city depended, no doubt, on his faith in patronage networks established across the Atlantic. A merchant of Scottish descent, Watts held a position on the New York Council for almost two decades. Like those of other merchant-councillors, Watts's political connections brought him lucrative contracts for food, clothing, boots, and other items during the Seven Years' War.[72] He attributed New York's disturbances to the worsening economic conditions in the city. Committed to the supremacy of the British government, he belittled the "rash conceited priggs and printers [who] meddled with question of Parliament."[73] Alarmed by the increased political activity of the unenfranchised after the battles of Lexington and Concord, Watts, along with fellow councillors Colonel Roger Morris and Henry White, sought safety in London in May 1775. Unlike Morris and White, Watts did not return home.[74]

Isaac Low did not leave the colonies during the rebellion. Born in New Brunswick, New Jersey, Low entered into public life when he became a founding member of the Chamber of Commerce in 1768. During the 1760s, he headed committees of merchants in support of the boycott on importation and exportation. Between 1774 and 1776, he, along with Van Schaack, chaired extralegal committees organized to enforce the Continental Association.[75] In May 1775, Rivington commended Low's moderate leadership over the committees: "The power over our crowd is no longer in the hands of Sears, Lamb, and such unimportant persons, who have for six years past been the demagogues of a very turbulent faction in the city."[76] Low was one of the five New York delegates to the First Continental

Congress in the fall of 1774. After the battles of Lexington and Concord, on April 29, 1775, Low assailed George III as "a Roman Catholic, nay, a Roman Catholic tyrant; . . . he had broken his coronation oath."[77] Between the summer and fall of 1775, however, Low struggled to find a compromise to repair the divide between the colonies and the empire. In the spring of 1776, when it was impossible to remain neutral, he chose to remain loyal. Fearing the bloody consequences of a British invasion of New York City, he sought haven in Raritan, New Jersey. He would return to New York in 1777, after the British government reestablished control, and play a minor civil role in the city. Most important, he would reinstitute the Chamber of Commerce in 1779 and preside as president.[78]

Landowners such as Frederick Philipse, who turned their country estates into complex economic enterprises, do not fit any one-dimensional profile of merchants. Frederick Philipse III possessed a settled, well-developed estate, Philipsburgh, in Westchester County.[79] Intimately involved in the money economy, Philipse also imported sugar, cotton, and ginger from the West Indies and exported flour, lumber, and horses to the West Indies and to the other mainland colonies. He served as a militia colonel and as a member of New York assembly beginning in 1751. In January 1774, Philipse joined the extralegal New York Committee of Correspondence. In April 1775, however, he refused to support the establishment of the Second Continental Congress because he balked at the violence unleashed after the meeting of the First Continental Congress. In early 1776, he also refused to sign an oath of allegiance to the revolutionary cause. In August 1776, he wrote resolutely to his wife: "I have done nothing (upon the Strictest Examination) Inimical to the Liberty's of my Country or ever would, let the Consequences be what it will."[80] Imprisoned and held in Connecticut until December 1776, Philipse was released when he swore not to bear arms against the United States of America. Although Philipse played no role in British administration during the years of the rebellion, he received an annual allowance for his support.[81] His son-in-law, Roger Morris, won an appointment in the British civil administration during the rebellion. In January 1779, the British authorities appointed Morris as inspector of loyalist refugees, responsible for weighing and granting claims to those who suffered for their persistent loyalty to reunion.[82]

Caught between their loyalty to two competing states, uncertain of which one to renounce, New Yorkers struggled in these crucial years to identify only one as home.[83] The rebellion imposed upon Euro-American colonists an unwanted and unnatural choice. Both sides—only later called patriots and loyalists—shared language, political traditions, mores and culture, a degree of common descent, and religion. In an ethnic sense, both sides emerged from the larger British Atlantic state and shared an underlying nationalism. What divided them ultimately was their response to the dissolution of the empire. Whereas the rebels turned to aggressive resistance, the loyal Americans remained unwilling to sever ties with the political state that had nourished them. They found the rebellion not only unlawful but incomprehensible. They agreed that the Parliament had legislated inconsistently, but they did not conclude that the acts represented Parliament's insincerity. In the end, they preferred the will of a remote British ministry over the will of New York's committees: the violent clamor from below represented a greater threat than the illegal tyranny of British government.[84]

The revolutionary divisions in the city materialized gradually. Between August 1775 and August 1776, as the rebels took control of New York City, more than eighteen thousand people fled the city in panic. Many who stayed hoped for British victory. Their churches forcibly shut, the Anglican clergy, along with faithful parishioners, longed for British forces to liberate the city. Their power snatched, the DeLanceys and their constituency hoped that a British victory would restore their leadership. Oliver DeLancey's cousin, New Jersey attorney Cortlandt Skinner, expressed the hopes of many of the New York loyalists. In December 1775, he anticipated that the dispatch of a "few Regiments and fleets to different provinces will sett us Right, at least bring us to our Senses and support the friends of Government."[85] Skinner believed that war, not ideological arguments, would settle the conflict.

# 3 ❧ "Quicken Others by Our Example"

## New Yorkers Welcome the British

> It is most devoutly to be wished that the Continent may follow the example
> of this city—that the Americans in general may avail themselves of his Maj-
> esty's Clemency, and paternal Goodness in offering to restore them to His
> Royal Protection and Peace.
>
> —Loyalist Petition, *New-York Gazette and Weekly Mercury,* October 21, 1776

General William Howe and his elder brother Admiral Richard Howe were
the British commanders in chief of land and naval forces in North America, respectively. In June 1776, they secured Staten Island and assembled
the largest expeditionary force ever seen in North America. In addition
to over 32,000 well-armed professional British and Hessian soldiers, their
force included 10 ships of line, 20 frigates, and nearly 170 transports. The
British army landed troops on Long Island on August 22, 1776, and five
days later defeated the Continental Army under General George Washington in the Battle of Long Island. Thereafter, on September 15, 1776, the
British defeated rebel troops at Kip's Bay on the East River and took possession of New York City on Manhattan Island.[1]

The British commanders felt confident in their ability to suppress the
rebellion. Convinced about the superiority of their well-disciplined troops
in contrast to Washington's ragamuffin soldiers, they anticipated a decisive end to the resistance by winter. Colonel Charles Stuart fondly recalled
the British triumph on Long Island: "The thunder of the ships, the appearance of the enemy, the ardor of our troops, the whole army drawn up on
Long Island ready to support us, surpassed everything of magnificence."[2]
Another officer, Major Hugh Percy, confidently asserted that the capture
of New York meant that rebels would "never again" stand against British
imperial power.[3] In a private letter to his sister-in-law in London, Major

General Henry Clinton, second in command to General Howe, confided that he did not "despair of eating Christmas dinner at Haybridge" in England.[4]

As New York loyalists witnessed the arrival of the British army and naval forces, they felt secure that British military power would quell the opposition to reunion. Five months before British arrival in the city, the royal governor, William Tryon, believed that "a great number would join the King's troops as soon as they saw them land, particularly if they saw the Rebels once defeated."[5] From his refuge in New Jersey, New York Councillor William Smith Jr., detected a "daily declension of the power of Congress."[6] On October 31, 1776, Reverend Charles Inglis encouraged ministers to defer soliciting funds from the Society for the Propagation of the Gospel in London for the losses the Anglican churches had suffered at the hand of the rebels. He urged the ministry to wait until the "city & country are restored to his majesty's peace and protection."[7] Confident of the imminent restoration of civil order in the city, Inglis saw no need to safeguard the clerics' interests.

The loyalists' enthusiasm for the British arrival extended beyond the elite through the ranks. Common people also expected professional well-armed British soldiers to defeat the unorganized and untrained rebel troops. When British forces assembled on Staten Island in July 1776, loyalists from Long Island and New York City fled the turmoil in their communities. They welcomed the British with a ship full of provisions. These New Yorkers expected not only to supply provisions but to assist militarily in aiding the British effort. One officer particularly commented on the arrival of three riflemen from Long Island, "an English, Scotch, and Irishman."[8] Two months later, on September 4, after British forces occupied Long Island, forty-nine men from Oyster Bay appeared before the troops, carrying on "a long pole, a white shirt, by way of truce."[9] Risking their personal safety, these armed loyalists crossed to the British side and eagerly offered their services.[10]

When British forces entered New York City, loyalists assembled in large numbers to express jubilation. They carried officers on their shoulders and raised His Majesty's colors with loud acclamations. Many showed their allegiance by placing red ribbons in their hats.[11] One woman hoisted His Majesty's flag while trampling on the rebel colors.[12] Bolstered by the presence of British might, these loyalists anticipated an immediate return to peace and prosperity.[13] One British officer observed that the people had felt so much of "real tyranny" that they did not know how to express their "release."[14] A Moravian minister, Ewald Gustav Schaukirk, described the utopian moment: "Joy and gladness seemed to appear in all countenances, and persons who had been strangers one to the other formerly, were now very sociable together, and friendly."[15]

Clearly expecting to profit from British victory, merchants in New York City solicited business from the newly arrived military clientele. Broker and merchant William Tongue assured the "gentlemen of the army and navy" that their desire for wines, Jamaican spirits, brandy, and any other items "will be accommodated." John McKenny, a tailor, promised that he would serve the gentlemen of the army and navy "on reasonable terms." McKenny sought to employ journeymen tailors to assist him in help-ing clothe the troops. Thomas Brownejohn, a druggist and apothecary, announced his willingness to supply the army and navy "at the shortest notice, with all kinds of medicines, on the most reasonable terms." Valen-tine Nutter, a bookseller and stationer, assured his uniformed customers that he had account books "fit for the navy" and "orderly books of various sorts."[16]

Loyalists cooperated with the British military by enlisting in militias, joining provincial units, and supplying provisions and services. They re-duced British expenditures.[17] The British received assistance from conduc-tors, smiths, carpenters, collar makers, and drivers. Farmers cut firewood for fuel, cartmen transported supplies, tavern keepers served rum and spirits, and shopkeepers sold sundry items.[18]

Loyalist enthusiasm and voluntary assistance reinforced the British com-manders' belief that most of the colonists were loyal. After landing on Staten Island in July 1776, Howe reported to Secretary of State Lord George Germain that the inhabitants only "wait for opportunities to give proofs of their loyalty and their zeal to government."[19] Major General James Rob-ertson reassured his troops that they were among friends: "The troops who may do duty in, and about New York, are hereby informed that not only the best, but the greatest number of inhabitants of this province, are Loyal, good Subjects; lately, they have been persecuted for publishing their sentiments, and the fear of death has forced many to disguise them."[20]

British officials believed that the rebellion was the work of an ambi-tious and determined minority who had compelled the king's supporters to remain silent. Fearful of rebel persecution, the colonists out of "pru-dence and safety" concealed their "sentiments and determinations."[21] Major General Clinton supposed that the "people in general are inclined but a few desperate chiefs hold out."[22] When British forces offered protection and displayed goodwill, the colonists would declare their loyalty. The rebel leaders would lose popular support, and the colonies would once again enjoy the prosperity and constitutional liberties guaranteed under the empire.[23]

The Howes understood that their primary goal was to win the allegiance of the rebellious colonies. If they adopted a strategy of unlimited destruction, they risked alienating the colonists and destroying any chance of restoring harmony and concord with the mother country. A violent strategy would strengthen rebel cohesion and determination. A strategy of conciliation would best demonstrate British willingness to forgive her recalcitrant subjects and once again welcome them as members of the powerful empire.[24]

On July 14, 1776, the Howes jointly issued a proclamation promising a free and general pardon to all those "deluded subjects" who agreed to a "speedy return of their duty." Hoping to kill the obstinate plans of those who prolonged the "unnatural rebellion" between Britain and her colonies, they promised to "promote such measures as shall be conducive to the establishment of legal government and peace." They promised that colonists would suffer no reprisals for past actions if they took an oath of loyalty to the king and constitution. Targeted at colonists who remained hesitant or fearful, the proclamation strove to broaden the "great middle ground" between active loyalism and active rebellion and encouraged covert loyalists to declare their allegiance.[25]

After landing on Long Island, the Howes issued a second proclamation on August 23, 1776, promising "faithful" subjects who delivered themselves at the headquarters of the army "full protection for their persons and property." The notice stated that rebel leaders had "compelled" the loyal inhabitants of the island to take up arms against His Majesty's government. British forces would therefore bestow mercy on subjects who returned to their duty.[26]

On September 19, 1776, four days after British forces entered New York City, the Howes circulated a third proclamation to encourage colonists to accept British protection and enjoy the blessings of "liberty and propertys upon the true principles of the Constitution." Significantly, this notice also invited His Majesty's "well-affected" subjects to "confer" with British authorities on the "means of restoring the public tranquility."[27] The

Howes anticipated that prominent loyalists within the city would welcome the conciliatory overtures and serve as intermediaries in winning the allegiance of the wavering populace.

But the proclamations disappointed many loyalists who resented British lenity toward the rebels who had treated the king's friends harshly. Hard-liners frowned upon all talk of concessions, pardons, or moderation. They believed British conciliatory gestures cast the empire as weak and further fuelled the rebel cause. They did not think British victory was possible until the rebels feared the British more than they feared rebels.[28] Comprising a minority of leading loyalists, these hard-liners were royal officeholders who had already paid a high price for their allegiance. From his precarious refuge in a warship, Governor Tryon had witnessed the ferocity of the rebel assault against the king's friends. In January 1776, he had vainly asked Germain for "arms, ammunition and clothing" to equip a loyalist corps that could check the "unabated vigour and desperate excesses" in the city.[29] Tryon believed the British should reciprocate rebel "excesses" by systematically destroying rebel property and capturing rebel leaders.[30] Reverend Inglis echoed Tryon's frustration at British moderation toward the rebels. He advised Lord Howe's secretary, Ambrose Serle, that "firmness and dignity" would alone compel obedience. To "temporize," Inglis asserted, "is to strengthen the hands of the faction by the ruin of her own friends."[31] Inglis had received severe treatment from the rebels. He had chosen to remain in the city to safeguard his property and serve the church. But he could not keep open the church or stop rebel committees from plundering his house. Angered by the "guilt and ingratitude" expressed by the scale of rebel violence, Inglis denounced the numerous afflictions endured by the king's friends: "I could fill a Volume with such instances."[32] Councillor Henry White, who had earlier left for England to escape rebel condemnation, also stressed the "absolute necessity" for "greater coercion" to restore the colonies to subordination.[33] Ironically, these hard-liners defended the use of violent tactics while simultaneously promoting the constitutional glories that would follow reunion. They insisted that displaying ruthless power toward rebels was sounder strategy than displaying indiscriminate British humanity.

Jockeying for the military commanders' favors, moderates were unhappy with pardons that allowed other gentlemen to come inside British lines at any time without suffering adverse consequences. The loyalist gentlemen who had declared their allegiance by September 1776 expected to receive greater benefits from military commanders. In their view, gentlemen who were slower to declare allegiance did not merit the same rewards. Loyalists complained when the British extended their proclamation of pardons beyond the initial sixty days.[34] They lamented that the British government "frowned" on the "first friends of government" but "caressed" those who came in later to take the oaths of loyalty."[35]

The benevolence or, as Adjutant General Frederick Mackenzie expressed it, "extraordinary lenity" offered to rebels in general and especially to American officers on parole gave "great disgust" to the king's friends.[36] The loyalists accused the commissioners of paying insufficient attention to the chameleonlike character of rebels who declared allegiance solely for reasons of safety and self-interest rather than from ideological commitment. They feared that rebel prisoners would secretly act in concert with rebel outlaws to destroy grain and forage and carry off friends of government. Many who took the oath of allegiance, Schaukirk observed privately, later showed "insincerity and bad principles, going back again to the rebels."[37]

Both British officers on the scene and the London ministry recognized the antagonism generated among loyalists by the indiscriminate pardons of former rebels. Mackenzie warned that the pardons would "provide bad policy in the end."[38] From London, Germain empathized with the loyalists' complaints but without advancing another approach: "It is poor encouragement for the friends of Government . . . to see their oppressors without distinction put upon the same footing with themselves . . . this sentimental manner of making war will, I fear, not have the desired effect."[39]

Primarily concerned to maximize supporters, the British refused to distinguish between early and belated loyalists. In a letter to the London ministry, the Howes indicated that they were "unwilling" to "exclude" any of the rebels from the "benefit of the King's mercy." They insisted that any "exceptions from his majesty's pardon . . . will be a matter of future consideration."[40] The exclusions would create needless divisions between British subjects. Reestablishment of peace and tranquility, they believed, meant pardoning the greatest number of people. Any person who took the oath of loyalty, regardless of any "posterior" acts he may have perpetrated, counted as a loyal British subject and deserved similar protection.[41]

While protesting the widespread pardons, loyalist leaders also questioned the proclamations as offering too scant a political vision of the American future. If the commissioners lacked the power to conclude a final treaty, the loyalists argued, they could still have communicated "such overtures as might be a foundation for reconciliation."[42] Yet the proclamations proposed no specific terms for reconciliation, no tangible rewards for reunification. They vacuously promised mercy without spelling out how the British would govern the restored empire. Smith feared that the proclamations failed to appease colonial fears of British domination: "What egregious blundering to publish an address in such general terms! How much more they might have promised themselves, from an explicit intimidation of the benefits they had authority to confer and secure! Every new discovery of illiberality is oil to the popular jealousy. This paper confirms the assertion of the committees that his lordship had nothing to offer."[43] As Colonel Stuart observed the loyalists' disappointment, he speculated that the Howes were unfamiliar with colonial expectations. He remarked that the proclamations seemed "more calculated to impress the minds of the people than to give them information."[44]

Along with the London ministry, the Howes clearly underestimated the colonial expectation of a political settlement that affirmed extensive self-rule. In July 1776, the rebels had issued the Declaration of Independence to spell out their grievances against the king and to assert their right to rebel. New York loyalists awaited parliamentary proposals that would respond directly to rebel allegations and grant the colonies' specific concessions.

In the fall of 1776, the ministry had sent the commissioners to New York City with specific political instructions. The commissioners had permission to call for a new legislature in a province after they had dissolved all rebel-organized committees and disbanded the rebel armies. When the legislature formally accepted His Majesty's pardon and renewed its allegiance to the king, it could petition to resume normal trade. Any "colony, town, port, district, or place" could resume unrestricted trade following the restoration of constitutional governance. The British expected one colony after another to submit in this fashion until all again acknowledged the supreme power of Parliament.[45]

After British troops had defeated the rebels on Long Island on August 27, the Howes had invited the Continental Congress to confer on terms of peace. On September 11, their negotiations failed because the rebel leaders refused to consider anything short of independence. Thereafter, in the proclamation issued on September 19, the Howes underscored that the congress had "disavowed every purpose of reconciliation." They directly asked the "inhabitants at large" to consider their circumstances and to determine whether it is "more consistent with their honor and happiness" to "sacrifice" their lives for an "unjust" cause or to return to a "free enjoyment of their Liberty and Properties, upon the true Principles of the Constitution." The proclamations issued by the Howes in July and August 1776 had also offered pardons to subjects who deviated from their duty to the king. However, the proclamation issued on September 19 established a more aggressive tone: it named the rebel congress as the enemy and actively sought to convince colonists of the political merits of reunion with Great Britain. It asked the colonists to choose between an uncertain and illegal revolt and a just and lasting reunion with the mother country. The commanders believed their individual offers of pardon would encourage thousands of colonists to oppose the tyranny of the congress.[46]

Loyalist spokesmen, however, feared that this piecemeal strategy of inviting the loyalty of individual colonists without offering substantive concessions to the colonies as a whole would not suffice to quell the rebellion. Although the London ministry stubbornly awaited rebel submission to the British Parliament, loyalists hoped for an alternative that would satisfy American moderates. Many, like Councillor Smith, disagreed with the empire's "haughty attachment to the principle of unlimited submission."[47] Instead, they sought a "middle way" that would redress American grievances within the imperial edifice, a path between American independence and American subordination. In January 1776, Peter Van Schaack expressed the search for a loyalist compromise: "To obviate the ill effects of either extreme some middle way should be found out, by which the benefits to the empire should be secured arising from the doctrine of a supreme power, while the abuses of that power to the prejudice of the colonists should be guarded against; and this, I hope will be the happy effect of the present struggle."[48]

Although these loyalists feared that independence from the mother country would result in political anarchy and social chaos, they did not believe that colonists should blindly surrender to the mother country. Like the rebels, they thought that the colonial contribution in the Seven Years' War and the colonies' growing maturity entitled them to an enhanced status within the empire. But unlike the rebels, the loyalists advocated legal and constitutional means to achieve their ends. Both sides should seek mutual understanding on the policies needed to achieve a permanent connection that would benefit the colonies and the empire. The "only foundation of all legitimate governments," argued Van Schaack, was a "compact between the rulers and the people" that obliged both parties to fulfill their respective duties. Ideally, the colonies gained from political stability and military protection from the empire, while the mother country benefited from growing trade with the colonies.[49]

More than mere pardons, the loyalists wanted the British to propose a comprehensive plan as an inducement to reunion. Joseph Galloway was a prominent Philadelphia lawyer who entered the British lines in New York City in December 1776. In 1774, the Continental Congress had rejected his plan for a revised relationship between the colonies and Great Britain. Now, two years later, he thought the rebellion presented an opening for Great Britain to "rectify her former errors in administering the colonies."[50] He urged Parliament to propose a solution that permanently placed the colonies in a beneficial but subordinate relationship to the mother country. He well understood that Parliament could not rectify the crisis quickly: "I do not mean that the Constitution which is to unite the two countries should be settled in a hurry. I well know the task will be difficult."[51]

Unlike the rebels with their Declaration of Independence, the loyalists did not think it was in their legal power to frame a declaration of loyalty. They believed the rebel leaders had forced their minority position upon the populace using violent and illegal means. In contrast, the loyalists wanted to redress American grievances against the mother country using legal and proper methods. They wanted Parliament to propose new terms, which the colonies could then negotiate toward a final settlement. Galloway insisted that a plan for a revised relationship between the colonies and the mother country could not originate in the colonies but "must be done by Parliament alone."[52]

Two assumptions dictated loyalists' refusal to issue their own alternative to the Declaration of Independence. First, they believed the colonies were subordinate to the supreme power of the Parliament and could not initiate "legal and constitutional" proposals to Parliament. A meeting of Americans to propose an alternative to the impasse would be illegal without an explicit commission from Great Britain. Second, even if a general colonial body convened, the colonists would not reach a general settlement. Riven by competition and self-interest, the colonies' "dissimilar and inconsistent" interests would render it impossible to create any "just and permanent system." Galloway concluded that Parliament should "establish, by its own authority, a system as shall give the same constitution, laws, manners, & freedom or *nearly the same as may be* to the people in America as possessed and enjoy'd by their brethren in Britain."[53]

The core of the loyalist analysis was that the union between Great Britain and the colonies was a covenant that neither party had a right to dissolve. Since society comprised imperfect and self-interested people, difficulties were inevitable. However, negotiation, not arms, should be the primary method to address any conflicts.

## Toward Military Rule

The rebellion had interrupted legal procedures and civil institutions the leading New Yorkers cherished. The colonists had long adopted the customary English practice of using the writ of habeas corpus to protect their personal liberties. The free inhabitants lived under the system of "Anglo-Saxon justice," which permitted them to appeal decisions and defend their liberties using a combination of British common-law procedures, the mayor's court, and, for final appeal, New York province's Supreme Court.[54]

Aldermen and their assistants with the mayor and recorder formed the municipal legislature of the city. The city council assembled every fortnight in City Hall to discuss and decide upon issues that affected the markets, hygiene, and safety of the city. They issued rules for prevention of fires; regulated nuisances and filth in the streets; prohibited peddlers; granted liquor licenses; supervised the sale of wood, hay, and other necessaries; and managed docks, slaughterhouses, and public markets. They appointed inspectors of bread, chimney inspectors, city wardens, constables, and the like.[55]

When the British entered the city, New Yorkers anticipated the immediate revival of the organs of civil administration. Having endured rebel occupation, they hoped to use the protection of British troops to reestablish constitutional government. They saw the restoration of civil rule in New York City as a necessary step to winning the hearts and minds of the larger colonial populace. In contrast to the tyranny imposed by extralegal rebel committees, the restitution of the legal edifice in New York City would demonstrate the benefits of balanced government promised by reunion. The loyalists wanted the British to reconvene the provincial assembly and the New York Council, open the courts, and reactivate the posts of city government. They wanted normal politics and trade to resume.

Instead, on September 16, 1776, one day after British possession, General Howe appointed a military commandant who replaced the legislative functions of the municipal government. Howe refused to summon either the provincial assembly or the council. He did not appoint a mayor, nor did a city council protect the civilians' interests. Instead, a Board of General Officers convened regularly to administer the city. No civilians participated in the Board of General Officers in an official capacity.[56]

Those who had held posts in the provincial and city governments retained their titles, but their offices were subordinated to the military. The commandant regulated in minute detail the business, the wharves, and the police of the community. Tavern masters, cartmen, auctioneers, and almost anyone else who wanted to do business in town had to obtain licenses from the commandant.[57]

Military courts assumed the judicial authority formerly exercised by civil courts. Courts-martial presided over by two military officers, a president and a judge-advocate, replaced a civilian judge and jury and tried civilians and soldiers alike. No warrants were necessary for arrest, and civilians lacked any civil means of redressing grievances.[58]

Sir James Robertson, anonymously described as a man "unconnected with provincial party and uncontaminated with rebellion" was the first military commandant of New York City.[59] One British officer referred to Robertson as the "cleverest fellow in the army and the most sensible man." Of Scottish descent, Robertson was a fifty-nine-year-old veteran of the British army. He had already served in North America for twenty years and commanded a brigade during the Battle of Long Island.

During the Seven Years' War, Robertson served as principal supply officer and as inspector general for the British army. He secured ships and wagons; arranged for boats, barracks, and bedding; purchased clothing; and examined all public accounts. Between 1765 and 1774, he served as barrack master general under Sir Thomas Gage. In New York alone, he dispensed £260,000 in royal funds to purchase military supplies. During his ten-year tenure, his duties brought him powerful connections and gave him enormous influence within the mercantile communities that supplied the British troops. His acquaintances in New York included Governor Tryon and councillors Cadwallader Colden, John Watts, and William Smith Jr., as well as customs collector Andrew Elliot. The outbreak of hostilities between the rebels and the British created yet another opportunity for Robertson's advancement.[60]

Robertson was confident that over two-thirds of the colonists favored reconciliation with Great Britain. In his previous experience as quartermaster, he had known colonists to feel "reverence and affection" for Great Britain." In fact, he believed, they were "more jealous of each other than of Britons."[61] Like the Howes, Robertson favored a conciliatory policy to woo support from the largest number of colonists. He trusted that the widely circulated pardons demonstrated Great Britain's good intentions toward its wayward subjects. They exhibited "Pity and Humanity," even to "ungrateful Rebels," and proved to the colonists that the British "were their friends." In contrast to rebel leaders, who compelled submission with threats, the British would invite colonists' allegiance by showcasing their paternal benevolence.[62]

But British benevolence toward the undecided did not protect New Yorkers from the abuses of martial rule in the city. The inhabitants did not experience the British foothold as the sanctuary conceived by Robertson. Their abiding faith in the empire did not protect them from the severe effects of living in a garrison with thousands of troops. Within days of British rule, Ambrose Serle noted that "complaints are made" of the Hessians who plundered both friends and foes of government "indiscriminately."[63] In mid-September 1776, another British officer commiserated with the misery of the inhabitants who could not protect their "poor effects" from soldiers and sailors.[64] Within two weeks, a general court-martial ordered the execution of two British soldiers, John Dunn and John Husty, accused of raping a Long Island widow, Elizabeth Johnstone.[65] Colonel John Peebles observed many other "shocking abuses of that nature" that were outside public notice.[66] In October, Lieutenant Colonel Stephen Kemble decried the "ravages" committed by the soldiers on the "poor inhabitants" in the city. The troops destroyed "all the fruits of the Earth" and regarded the property of rebels and loyalists as "equally a prey." In November, Kemble reported the "scandalous behavior" of British and Hessian troops who threatened with death those who obstructed their attacks.[67]

British orderly books provide instances of the commanders' attempts to curtail soldiers' violence against civilians. General Howe's orderly book contains numerous directives asking soldiers to remain in specified areas and respect loyalist homes, property, and farms. On July 5, 1776, Howe mandated that "soldiers shall on no account straggle from their Quarters after Sunset." Four days later, he warned: "The Commanding Officers of

Corps are desired to attend to the behaviour of their Guards and Sentries particularly at night." Upon landing on Long Island on August 22, Howe implored the soldiers to restrain from plundering from the loyalists: "It is strongly recommended to the Army to preserve Good Order & Discipline, and upon no account to molest or commit any depredations upon the Inhabitants of the Island." British and Hessian soldiers continued to receive disciplinary orders after they landed in New York City. In September, officer Loftus Cliffe observed that general orders were "positively against moroding [sic]" even though fresh provisions had already begun to fall "very short." In December, Robertson ordered soldiers "not to pull down House, Fence, or injure the Property of any person whatsoever."[68]

However, there is evidence that some British officers, with tacit approval from the commanders, did not enforce the disciplinary orders. Officer Kemble noticed officers who "licensed" soldiers' violence against the city's civilians. Colonel Stuart observed that soldiers "disregarded" repeated warnings because they knew they would not bear the fullest punishment for their crimes. British officers looked the other way when soldiers misbehaved toward civilians or their property. Although aware of the officers' latitude toward the soldiers, Tryon did not curse the relaxation of discipline. In his letter to Germain, he explained that General Howe did not strongly penalize troops for their misconduct because he feared that punishments could instigate "a general mutiny."[69] Howe preferred that soldiers release their "insolence" in small-scale violence against civilians rather than rise in opposition to their superiors in an act of direct disobedience.

Nevertheless, British commanders worried about New Yorkers' intolerance for the outrages committed by the troops. In November 1776, General Howe fruitlessly solicited Germain to send additional officers for the companies operating around New York City. He explained that "the temptation for plunder was so great that it was not in the power of a few officers to keep the men under proper restraint."[70] The commanders tried to issue written directives to protect the loyalist elite. On December 23, 1776, Clinton specified that the estates of Mr. Henry Lloyd and Dr. James Lloyd "may not to be molested by any of His Majesty's troops."[71] But officer Kemble dismissed the commanders' warnings as insufficient because the soldiers "pay no attention to them." The soldiers did not care to distinguish between the king's friends, active rebels, and neutrals. Assembled from diverse social origins, the soldiers included many penniless bachelors who regarded pillaging as a "quasi-legitimate supplement" to their squalid conditions and meager pay. Unlike British officers, who scrupulously guarded their reputations, these soldiers knew their good character did not earn them political position, social status, or a higher military rank.[72]

Martial rule shook the loyalists' confidence in the legal edifice of the empire. They desired reconciliation because they believed they were part of an empire made up of particularly blessed people. They trusted in the benefits that would accrue with "British law, British protection and British union."[73] They expected British governance, based on long-standing principles, to stand apart from the rebel mob rule that "violated all the sacred ties of civil society," including "personal liberty and freedom of speech."[74] Yet British rule in the city did not revive the revered institutions and basic civil liberties of their British heritage such as trial by jury.

Constitutional thinking was embedded in the colonists' worldview. Like other colonists, New Yorkers believed that legal institutions such as the jury protected them from arbitrary and unlawful government. They regarded the jury as part of the ancient constitution and common-law tradition inherited from the Magna Carta (1215), the Petition of Right (1628), and the Bill of Rights (1689). In the fall of 1776, they found themselves confronting a situation that defied their fundamental expectations of British government.[75] A military rule that suspended civil authority and offered no civil redress confounded loyalist expectations.

## Loyalist Petitions

Loyalist leaders worried that military rule reinforced rebel accusations of British despotism and boosted fears about the empire's "illiberal" intentions toward the colonies.[76] Steadfastly dedicated to reconciliation and peace, these gentlemen promoted the restoration of civil governance to reinforce the natural linkage of colonial rights with loyalty to the Crown. They believed the revival of civil law in New York City was fundamental to the larger cause of the colonies' reunion with the empire.

After living under military rule for nearly a month, New York City loyalists gathered to petition the Howes to revive civil government in the city. In contrast to the rebel hinterland, where colonists suffered under the rule of extralegal committees, the city should set an example of legal and proper government to encourage the restoration of allegiance by both undecided colonists and deluded rebels. The return of civil rule in the city would dispute rebel allegations of British tyranny and demonstrate that the king intended his loyal subjects to have all the rights to which Britons were entitled.

New York City provided a perfect stage to demonstrate the benefits of belonging to the British empire. The city had many loyalists and enjoyed British military protection and a thriving commercial port. The city could demonstrate the freedom and prosperity possible under the orderly governance of conservative elites who remained loyal to the constitution. The loyalists anticipated that other colonies would soon "follow the example of this city," turn away from the "present destructive and unnatural rebellion," and return to their former deference.[77]

A month after the British assumed governance of New York City, loyalist elites assembled their constituents to prepare a petition that requested restoration of civil rule in the city. The gathering of the loyalists to present the petition was not a spontaneous event. The city elite sought to assemble a political interest that would restore the imperial edifice that had promised them commercial and political benefits. On October 14, 1776, a notice in the newspaper formally invited all "his Majesty's loyal and well-affected subjects" to assemble for a meeting of "utmost importance."[78] Two days later, the concourse of people gathered at City Hall included hundreds of common people as well as members of His Majesty's council, judges, and other "well-affected citizens."[79]

On October 21, 1776, 948 loyalists gathered in New York City to deliver a "decent and respectful" address to the Howes, "the King's Commissioners for restoring Peace to his Majesty's Colonies in North-America." This petition responded directly to the proclamations issued by the Howes.[80] The loyalists returned the "tenderest emotions of gratitude" for the "paternal goodness" and "shining character" of His Majesty. They pledged to bear "true allegiance" to the king and to uphold the constitutional supremacy of Great Britain. In return, they awaited the city's and the colony's restoration to "His Majesty's protection and peace."[81]

The loyalist leaders had solicited wide support from the community. However, the numbers that gathered to demand the restoration of civil peace exceeded their expectations. The numbers being "too great," they set up another mechanism to obtain the signatures of the ardent supporters. They agreed to meet at a "Public House" adjoining City Hall "from

10 o'clock a.m. to 2 o'clock p.m. every day, to take subscription till all had signed."[82] Loyalist leaders strove to maximize the number of signatures to legitimize themselves as representatives of the entire community.

Following the example of New York City, in November and December 1776, the three counties on Long Island offered an oath of loyalty and a plea for resumption of civil order. From Suffolk County, 614 loyalists signed and had published their oath of allegiance. Two weeks later, 1,184 Queen's County loyalists embraced the invitation of His Majesty's commissioners and vowed to "quicken others by Our Example." Finally, on December 9, over seven hundred loyalists from King's County anticipated a return of His Majesty's "auspicious government and protections" and a revival to the "blessings" enjoyed under His Excellency's "just and mild administration."[83] All four petitions appeared in the *New-York Gazette and Weekly Mercury* between November 4 and December 9, 1776.

An examination of the first few signers in the New York City petition reveals the leadership of that loyalist community. The name of each loyalist appeared in order of social and political prominence. In New York City, Chief Justice Daniel Horsmanden signed first, followed by New York councillor Brigadier General Oliver DeLancey. Next followed the signatures of his son-in-law, John Harris Cruger, and five other members of the New York Council or New York Assembly including Henry White, Charles Ward Apthorpe, William Axtell, George Duncan Ludlow, and Jacob Walton.[84] A leading lawyer, Benjamin Kissam, also expressed his fidelity to the empire. The Anglican Reverends Samuel Auchmuty and Charles Inglis swore their allegiance following the signatures of the leading merchants Jacob Walton, George Folliot, John Wetherhead, and William and Samuel Bayard. Merchants who had advertised their goods to the British military, such as William Tongue, Valentine Nutter, Thomas Brownejohn, William Hauxhurst, and Jacob Watson, also joined this loyalist coalition.[85]

The order of names reveals the pattern of loyalist leadership in New York City and the counties in Long Island. The leading signers included those filling or tapped to fill the governorship, chief justiceships, and other prestigious political positions in the colony. There were also colonial veterans who had fought in the Seven Years' War and Anglican clergy sent by an ambitious Society for the Propagation of the Gospel in Foreign Parts to pave the way for a bishopric in America. They were merchants who had profited as middlemen of an integrated British Empire, which they refused to leave when the rebellion erupted.[86] These men intensified their commitment to the British as they transformed from loyal subjects to loy-alist leaders.[87] Their stake in the empire matched their high aspirations for America. They wanted to link the institutional strength of Britain with the talents and resources of North America.[88]

Less than 2 percent of the loyalist signers were officeholders. A close examination of the later names reveals the social diversity of loyalists. Most of the signers were united not by birth, profession, or class but rather by their common desire to preserve their connection to their patrons and thereby to the British Empire. Further down the list, the signers included apothecaries, farmers, shopkeepers, artisans, tavern owners, and cartmen. A substantial portion of the signers were those of middling stature, people who won no special favors and achieved no prominence under British mili-tary government. The list also suggests that masters enlisted their depen-dents in the signing of the petition. For example, Rynier Hopper, foreman of the carters in the city, signed the petition, along with cartmen John Steel, Paulus Banta, Abraham Brower, Elias Bailey, and Stephen Allen.[89]

The demand for civil restoration unified many people who claimed loyalty for diverse reasons. These people sought a redress of their griev-ances within the imperial structure. As Richard Bushman observes, the eighteenth-century petition represented a complaint to the king, a roy-ally sanctioned method of "releasing resentments and identifying abuses and injustices." These loyal subjects had endured a month of military rule under the direction of a military commandant. They petitioned the Howes because they expected royal power to protect, not suppress, their liberty.[90]

In *Inventing the People,* Edmund S. Morgan explains that petitions implic-itly told the king or his representatives what they "must or must not do to his subjects." He argues that petitions represented the possibility of "influencing" policy and not merely pleading for redress.[91] The petition appealed and requested simultaneously. Within the petition, the loyalists adopted a deferential tone that affirmed the bounties of British patronage but simultaneously sought their rights as British subjects: they wanted the military authorities to restore civil law within the city promptly.

The humble tone adopted in the petition affirmed the petitioners' abso-lute loyalty and gratitude to the king. They made it clear that their loyalty arose from their unshaken faith in the king's protection. Yet their obedi-ence also came from their full expectation that their request would be granted. They promised submission to the protector king in return for his protection of their constitutional rights. They asked that the covenant between the king and his subjects be upheld.

By displaying the strength of their numbers and the example of their loyalty, loyalist leaders hoped to persuade the undecided or fearful colonists to support reunion. These prominent gentlemen offered to rally loyalists to serve in the militias and provincial units, to provide services and supplies to British troops and horses, and to volunteer homes, hospitals, and churches to meet British military needs. To common people within the city, they offered patronage and protection and a commitment to restore peace.

The gathering of the thousands of supporters who favored reunion represented a unique political moment. It presented the British with an opportunity to use this base of supporters to begin the restoration of civil rule. Administered by civilian leaders, the city would symbolize the blessings of reunion. In response to each of the loyalists' four petitions, Tryon assured the inhabitants that he would support their wishes "although the completion of them must be left to the decision of his Majesty's commissioners."[92] Tryon expected that British strength would soon subdue the province of New York and he would reestablish his dominion within civil institutions. In November 1776, he confidently put together a list of officers and magistrates so "that the civil government may have its full operation as soon as it is judged proper to reestablish it with all its powers."[93]

From London, Germain expressed his satisfaction at the "warm expressions of duty and affection" and vaguely trusted that the "time is at no great distance" when the province would return to "His Majesty's peace and to all its former commercial advantages."[94] The Howes promised to take the "earliest opportunity" to consider the loyalists' request. In a private letter written on November 30, however, they explained that it was not "proper to return any other answer."[95] With tacit agreement from London, the Howes quickly tabled the loyalists' petitions. Immediate restoration of civil rule in the city did not figure in their plans to quell the rebellion. Waging war clearly took precedence over securing peace in the commissioners' mindset. Nothing in the Prohibitory Act that granted them their powers prevented them from restoring civil rule in the city. The act actually empowered them to restore any district to His Majesty's peace. However, it did not require that they do so.

Writing to Germain after five days in New York City, the Howes had explained the contingencies that mandated the establishment of martial rule "in the present moment." Their letter indicates their understanding of the constitutional breach signified by martial law. Military rule was not the customary law imposed on British subjects anywhere within the empire. Still, they believed local exigencies in the city rendered the abeyance of civil rule necessary: "I have only to add that as the rebel army remains strongly posted at the north part of the island of New-York, and the inhabitants who had fled or been compelled to leave the city, before the King's troops took possession of it, are not returned; we have it not yet in our power, even were it expedient in the present moment, to effect the compleat re-establishment of the Civil Government of this district."[96]

The commanders had suspended civil rule because the stubborn persistence of rebel forces in the surrounding countryside compelled them to prioritize military security over civilian concerns.[97] On September 24, 1776, the Howes directed Tryon "to postpone any executive acts of Government" until the colony "is more liberated from the control of the Rebels." Expecting British forces to quell the rebellion in a few months, Tryon readily agreed to "keep the executive powers of Civil Government dormant, leaving every thing to the direction of the Military."[98]

In their explanation to Germain, the Howes also emphasized the dearth of inhabitants in the city because many had "been compelled to leave" and had not returned to the city. The British had entered a city ravaged by war. Only five thousand civilians, less than 20 percent of the city's previous population, remained in the city in September 1776. Along with merchants, the inhabitants of New York City comprised hundreds of farmers, artisans, tavern keepers, shopkeepers, cartmen, abandoned slaves, and the very poor.[99] Tryon bleakly observed the "wretched and miserable inhabitants" who had lost their all, "many in want for their families of the necessaries of life."[100] These inhabitants lived among the "plague-stricken" streets in New York City, where houses previously filled with luxuries and valuables now stood vacant. Returning New Yorkers often found their "dwellings empty, furniture smashed, and not a window left whole and their cattle gone forever."[101] One loyalist complained that his former residence was a "dirty, desolate, and a wretched place."[102] The wharves were empty save for the ships of war, supply, and transport. The courts were closed. Since administrative branches of local government did not function, litigation was impossible. Supervision of the docks, the markets, and the poor remained confused.[103]

The revival of civil authority did not merely mean the restoration of a previous government but the creation of a new civil regime made up of the most trustworthy of the king's friends. In mid-September 1776, the British found too few gentlemen of proven loyalty to govern the city. Many of the Crown's most dependable subjects had fled the city or remained rebel prisoners. The rebels had captured key political men including Supreme Court Justice Thomas Jones and David Mathews, mayor of the city. Of the twelve New York Council members, only five were available to attend to the king's affairs in the city. The eighty-eight-year-old councillor Cadwallader Colden was dead, and Daniel Horsmanden's "infirmities" prevented his full attendance on the commanders. Two councillors, Hugh Wallace and James Jauncey, were rebel prisoners. Two others, Colonel Roger Morris and John Watts, had left the city for England. Finally, William Smith Jr. had withdrawn to the hinterlands and showed no sign of returning.[104]

Aristocratic British officers were uncomfortable relying on the middling classes of merchants, tavern keepers, and shopkeepers who prevailed among the New York City loyalists. These officers came from the upper layer of English society and viewed the colonists as socially inferior and without refinement. Lieutenant John Peebles mildly dismissed all "Yankees" as greedy and cunning in nature. Major Percy, a member of the Board of General Officers appointed by General Howe, denounced all colonists as "a set of sly, artful, hypocritical rascalls, cruel, & cowards. I must own I cannot but despise them compleately." Accustomed to a patronage network in which men of rank recommended those less familiar, British officers did not know how to assess the character of unfamiliar colonists. It was safer to dismiss them all as unworthy and place British officers in key positions because people with mercantile interests lacked the honor of British gentlemen.[105]

Ironically, the many deserters who streamed into British lines to receive the pardons offered by the Howes may have persuaded British commanders that they could not, in fact, depend on the inhabitants' loyalty. On September 24, 1776, Clinton observed that rebels were deserting "by the twenties." On the same day, Mackenzie noted that "80 deserters came one day lately." Five days later, he noted that "scarce a day passes that several deserters do not come in from rebels." From the commanders' viewpoint, colonists who shifted loyalties so casually did not merit their trust. The rebel deserters confirmed British officers' suspicions that the "poor simple country people" were, in the colorful prose of Ambrose Serle, "impudent, base, & hypocritical characters," unworthy of being "descendants of Britons."[106]

One week after the British possession, a suspicious fire destroyed a quarter of the houses in the city.[107] This fire created a fear of rebel incendiaries that lasted throughout the years of the war. Although the authorities could not prove that rebels had set the fire, they recognized that it was impossible to determine who was truly loyal. One officer shrewdly observed that "as the Rebels have changed their dress, it is extremely difficult to discover them."[108] Later, Serle cynically observed the presence of "many pretended friends in New York who are ready to do any mischief, if they dared."[109] Given the extent of disloyalty possible in New York, the revival of civil rule was premature.

The British did not have to hunt for reasons to mistrust the embittered inhabitants. The September 21 fire revealed the intense animosity between rebels and loyalists in the city. The bitterness between the two had reached an alarming intensity by the time British troops entered the city. The loyalists had suffered immeasurably under rebel control of New York City. One resident reported the punishment inflicted on those who refused to support American independence: "On Monday night, some men called Tories were carried and hauled about through the streets with candles forced to be held by them or pushed in their faces, and their heads burned; but on Wed, in the open day, the scene was by far worse; several and among them gentlemen were carried on rails; some stripped naked and dreadfully abused."[110]

Bolstered by British armed presence, the loyalists sought their turn for vengeance against those who had abused them. Robertson attended the scene of the fire when the infuriated crowd "instantly hung" Wright White, a carpenter who had cut the handles of the leather water buckets used to stop the fire. No civil or military trial preceded his punishment. Robertson and his troops also rescued two people from the "enraged populace who had otherwise consigned them to the flames." As Tryon had reported to Germain on September 24, 1776, the city was "too much convulsed for civil government to act with any good effect." Although the British arrested two hundred people, they soon discharged them.[111]

British authorities had no straightforward way to single out the trustworthy among the New Yorkers. They had entered a city in the midst of a civil war where inhabitants railed not at the king or the Continental Congress but at neighbors who had punished them for their allegiance or neutrality. Whereas the British offered proclamations of pardon indiscriminately, many of the New Yorkers who had suffered severely were less merciful. When British officials entered the city, they marked rebel homes with "G.R." (George Rex) to indicate that the space was available for His Majesty's troops. The suspicious fire exacerbated the grave housing shortage in the city and required British officials to confiscate rebel property for military use. However, Pastor Ewald Gustav Schaukirk noted that officers were not the only ones marking abandoned homes: civilians marked homes "from personal resentment" although they "had no order to do so." The British could not rely on vengeful civilians to govern their headquarters. Establishing civil rule necessitated distinguishing not only between true and "pretended" friends but also between hard-liners who determinedly sought vengeance and reliable moderates.[112]

The British imposition of military rule was also inseparable from the empire's growing consolidation following the Seven Years' War. In other words, the establishment of military rule resulted from the centralizing bureaucratic mentality of the empire as well as local contingencies. The empire did not act in a capricious manner in rejecting civil government but followed its post–Seven Years' War practice of aggressively pursuing increased control over its new Atlantic territories and its multiethnic population. Unfortunately for the loyalists, the Americans fell in the same category as the coalition of minority subjects the British inherited after 1763. Instead of being associated with Britons in Great Britain, the loyalists came to be associated with Native Americans and French Canadians. While the British were happy to witness loyalist participation, they were unprepared to empower suspicious subjects in the peripheries.[113]

## Winter 1776–1777

Between August and December, British troops forced the rebels to give up Long Island and New York City, withdraw into Westchester County, surrender northern Manhattan, and abandon much of New Jersey and Rhode Island. With each success, the Howe brothers issued proclamations of pardon. This combination of force and persuasion proved successful initially. On November 30, the commissioners reported the good news to London:

A very considerable number of persons who had been active in the rebellion, particularly in this province, and in that of the Jerseys, have already subscribed the declaration of allegiance. The whole of the Jerseys, except a very inconsiderable part which we think must of course, follow, has submitted; and of the province of Pennsylvania, which his majesty's forces have not yet entered, several persons of property . . . have subscribed the declaration.[114]

British expansion broke up rebel committees and dispersed rebel leaders, which encouraged the undecided to stand up for the king. Optimistic about an imminent end to the rebellion, Tryon explained "to the people (having formed them in circles)" that they had fulfilled their duty and protected their interests by renewing their "proper" allegiance. He reported the confidence of the loyalists around the city, as he heard not "the least murmur of discontent."[115]

In December 1776, the rebels faced a crisis. The period for which Washington's regular troops had enlisted would end on January 1, 1777, and enlisting additional men seemed unlikely. Crowds of colonists had taken advantage of the Howes' amnesty. In December 1776, almost five thousand colonists accepted pardons and took an oath of loyalty to the king. General Howe's aide bragged that the British witnessed the disintegration of the "American rope of sand."[116]

Yet British officers were overly sanguine. On December 26, Washington took the Hessian cantonments in Trenton, New Jersey, by surprise: only about two hundred Hessian soldiers escaped, leaving close to a thousand as rebel prisoners. A week later, Washington defeated British forces in Princeton. By mid-January 1777, Washington's forces compelled the British to evacuate western New Jersey and withdraw into Brunswick and Amboy on the Raritan River in eastern New Jersey.[117]

Leading New Yorkers pushed aside the significance of the two rebel victories. Tryon expressed "chagrin" at the "tarnish" but expected that the British would soon "wipe away the insult." Loyalist essays dismissed Trenton as a mere "skirmish" and emphasized the "sickly" condition of Washington's soldiers, allegedly dying of smallpox in great numbers and facing the "scourge of famine." Ragged, hungry, and diseased, Washington's troops, they believed, posed no threat to the large numbers of well-equipped British troops.[118]

Galloway and Smith also minimized the military setbacks. On March

20, 1777, Galloway optimistically anticipated that another campaign would end the rebellion.[119] In February 1777, Smith bemoaned the "narrowness" of people who became "elevated or depressed" upon their "little losses and advantages." He dismissed the likelihood of American victory despite Trenton and Princeton. The rebels, he opined, could not hope to secure independence "without men, without money, without ships, without cloths, without allies, and sans Every Thing." He advised rebel leaders to take advantage of the moment to negotiate as a "cunning debtor does"— when he has an advantage.[120]

But loyalist efforts to minimize the defeats rang hollow. Both British officers and some loyalists recognized that the defeats were significant. On January 20, 1777, General Howe privately confessed that the "unfortunate and untimely defeat at Trenton has thrown us farther back than was at first apprehended, from the great encouragement it has given to the rebels." A New Yorker echoed his sentiments: "The rebels are again in high spirits since the attack and defeat which the Hessians sustained near Trenton."[121]

While New York City provided an ideal harbor for British ships and its location strategically divided New England from the middle and southern colonies, to fully exploit the city's advantages, the British needed also to control the surrounding areas. For the security of New York City, the British relied on friends on Long Island and Staten Island, on the Jersey shore, and toward the Hudson Highlands to the north. If the British did not control a larger area around the city, the town and its harbor became unusable as a loyalist haven and British headquarters. As Piers Mackesy observes, New York City was large enough to be "provocative" yet too small to be "effective" by itself. Indeed, the city would become a "heavy defensive liability."[122]

Washington's victory at Trenton shrank British control, bringing deadly skirmishes into the suburbs of New York City. Repeated incidents of kidnapping, pillaging, and harassment by rebel outlaws alarmed the inhabitants. In December 1776, Pastor Schaukirk wearily noted that "it is at present unsafe in the evening to be out, on account of several late robberies and persons been having knocked down besides." He also noted some former residents' returning to town to "distress the inhabitants greatly."[123]

Rebel depredations led General Howe to question the British policy of conciliation, which offered pardons to all colonists regardless of their prior acts or behavior. Clearly, many had not embraced the pardons and continued to attack unprotected loyalists. In a March 25, 1777, secret letter to Germain, Howe explained that the "the partial effect of the proclamation is an irrefragable proof that a continuance of the violence of the leaders proceeded from other motives than a despair of the royal mercy." Howe asked Germain if British pardons should be withheld from those who remained violently opposed to British efforts at conciliation. Did a "speedy termination of the war" depend on offering pardons to all colonists, even leaders who flouted His Majesty's protection?[124] In May 1777, Germain turned the question back to Howe. If Howe believed that pardoning the rebel leaders would lead to "the general good," His Majesty would "graciously condescend to receive even those criminals to his mercy."[125] Aspiring to regain the allegiance of rebellious colonists, Germain worried that withholding pardons from selected rebels would further estrange wayward Americans from Great Britain. Germain did not take a stance.

Along with the daily violence inflicted by makeshift rebel bands, British regulars faced relentless attacks by rebel militia. In November 1776, Tryon had reported that the "marauding" operations of both armies resulted in "great distress" to people living in Westchester County, north of the city. As these skirmishes escalated through the winter, they consumed the time and energy of hundreds of British soldiers. Indeed, rebel raids against loyalists and British soldiers became so common that one British officer marveled when he could return to New York City "without any molestation."[126]

The rebel militia gained confidence from harassing and beating British soldiers in the countryside. In February 1777, officer Allan Maclean observed the remarkable success of the rebel militia as it pursued a "very prudent plan of constantly harassing our quarters." The rebels had "tossed and kicked" the British "most amazingly." Maclean concluded that this form of unending small-scale warfare gradually accustomed the rebels "to look us in the face and stand fire." In fact, he pronounced, it made "soldiers of the Americans."[127]

The winter defeats also exposed British reliance on fresh supplies from the countryside. During the fall of 1776, the British troops had eagerly made use of "considerable" fresh provisions from the farms and fields of New Jersey. In fact, General Howe had placed detachments in Trenton and Princeton precisely to ensure that all his soldiers did not draw provisions from the same area. Without British possession of eastern New Jersey, Howe recognized that he would have difficulty finding "covering,

forage & supplies of fresh provisions" for his army. He had widely separated the detachments so the New Jersey and New York detachments
could independently survive off the countryside without competing with
one another.[128]

Although convoys from Great Britain transported dry goods, clothing,
and even horses for the army, the cost was great and delays were common.
In the summer of 1776, Germain had asked Howe to "draw some part" of
the army's supplies locally to minimize expenses. But the city could not
satisfy the demands for provisions, especially hay and fresh meat, required
by an army and navy whose aggregate strength exceeded thirty thousand.
After Washington's victories at Trenton and Princeton, badly needed supplies from New Jersey became unreliable.[129]

British detachments in eastern New Jersey endlessly fought with rebel
troops and plundered the surrounding countryside to acquire provisions.
The two armies, Smith reflected, were like "locusts" and would "consume
every green herb and induce famine and pestilence." In February 1777,
Colonel Stuart agonized at the atrocities committed by the British soldiers: "We now begin to perceive the want of discipline."[130] As British and
Hessian soldiers raided to acquire supplies, they did not care to distinguish
between friends and foes. They thus alienated the neutral civilians, who
despised such indiscriminate depredations. Stuart lamented the effect the
raids had on the country people: "Those poor unhappy wretches who had
remained in their habitation through necessity or loyalty were immediately judged by the soldiers to be Rebels neither their cloathing or property spared but in the most inhuman and barbarous manner torn from
them. . . . Thus we went on persuading to enmity whose minds already
undecided, and inducing our very friends to fly to the opposite party for
protection."[131] Surrounded by armed rebels who gained confidence from
their recent victories and by outraged civilians who resented British foraging expeditions, the loyalist haven of New York City became a city under
siege.

Tryon recognized that the Trenton losses would prolong martial rule
and further restrict his powers. As civil governor, he could grant offices and
land to favored gentlemen. Well-placed loyalists had vied for his patronage and approval. In the British city, however, Tryon was just one more
subordinate administrator, reduced to administering oaths and collecting
donations from wealthy gentlemen for the benefit of the city's poor.[132]
On January 5, 1777, Tryon lamented his fading status: "The shadow of my

government does not remain to me nor am I consulted in any thing relative thereto, therefore can never revive that Sufficience I flattered myself
I once had in it."[133]

If British commanders had refused to restore the city to civil governance after the apparently decisive victory at the Battle of Long Island,
they could not admit civil rule after their retreat from New Jersey. Indeed,
the rebel threat loomed larger not only in the hinterland but also within
the city. As antiloyalist activity grew in intensity, thousands escaped harassment and vengeance from neighboring colonies for safety within British
lines. The influx of unknown people entering the city complicated British
attempts to secure the garrison. In November and again in December 1776,
the British urged "returning inhabitants" to first subscribe their allegiance
at "Scott's Tavern, near City Hall." Fearful of the consequences of another
fire instigated by rebels hidden in the city, Robertson cautioned the "inhabitants of the city" to be "particularly observant of any persons who may
be loitering about their houses in the evening or at night as there is great
reason to believe . . . that our very humane Rebels will do their utmost
to revive the conflagration." In January 1777, Robertson urged "every
householder" to give notice of the arrival of any stranger into his house.
He sternly warned: "All persons who do not comply with the Regulation
before Tuesday morning will be considered as bad subjects and bad Citizens."[134] Robertson's attention to the newcomers was justified. By February 1777, in just five months, the civilian population in the city had more
than doubled to eleven thousand.[135]

New Yorkers returned to the city to seek positions of influence, revive
their businesses, and assist His Majesty's troops in suppressing the rebellion. Councillor White returned from England, as did Anglican Reverend
Samuel Auchmuty from New Jersey. Escaping rebel imprisonment, former mayor David Mathews sought his previous eminence in the city. In
December 1776, Joseph Galloway joined them from Philadelphia.[136] Governor Tryon and Colonel Edmund Fanning left their refuge in the warship
*Duchess of Gordon* and offered their assistance to the British commanders.
Released from captivity, Donald McLean returned to New York City to
resume his retail business. He pledged to serve the "gentlemen of the army
and navy upon every occasion they are pleased to favor him with their
commands."[137] James Hughston, who had left the city in March 1776 when
the rebels set fire to his house in Queen's County, Long Island, returned
in the fall of 1776 and joined His Majesty's troops for the "suppression

of rebellion and reestablishment of the British government in America."
John Hill from Brooklyn, Long Island, had left the city in March 1775 when
he was "severely beat[en]." He had sought safety with the king's troops in
Boston and returned with them to New York City in the fall of 1776.[138]

However, many of the new inhabitants of British-controlled New York
City were not former residents of the city but refugees from country
towns who had to "fly" for their loyalty.[139] They sought housing, employment, protection, and compensation from British authorities. These people comprised those who came to fight with the British army, those who
sought safe employment within British lines, and elites who would vie
with leading New Yorkers to gain favors from the military commanders.
In August 1776, Joshua Hunt of Westchester County entered New York
City with his wife to serve in Captain Andreas Emmerich's loyalist corps.
When he died in September 1777, his wife, Martha, stayed on in the city.
In November 1776, Dr. James Boggs of Shrewsbury, New Jersey, felt the
"dread of being taken up" by the rebels and escaped to New York City,
where he became a surgeon's mate at His Majesty's hospital. In the fall of
1776, the rebels plundered the "farm and house" of Isaac Wilkins, former
assembly representative for Westchester County. After they destroyed his
"cattle, horses, carriages, farming utensils, grain, hay, provisions, liquors,"
Wilkins, who brought his wife, eight children, and seven other dependents
to the city, anticipated compensation inside British lines.[140]

Loyalist merchants left rebel-dominated areas and sought haven in the
city. In November 1776, one resident noted people "daily" entering the city
and "opening shops." Although trading remained restricted in the New
York City port, merchants benefited from the business offered by troops,
who paid them in specie and not in worthless paper bills issued by the
Continental Congress. Artisans such as Isaac Clemens, an engraver from
Boston, and Philip Thomas, a boot and shoemaker from Halifax, as well as
merchants such as John Cruden, a retailer from North Carolina, set up new
businesses in the city. Some New York merchants revived and expanded
their enterprises as they saw fair chances for marketing their goods. Clock-
maker Mervin Perry advertised for an apprentice and a "Negro wench,"
and Henry Ustick sought journeymen blacksmiths and nailers.[141]

Many of these prominent loyalists sought the patronage of high-
ranking British officers and created an active social network in the city.
At balls, concerts, and dinners, loyalist elites socialized with and sought
favors from British officials. The former John Street Theater reopened as

the Theatre Royal, featuring army and naval officers as both actors and audience members opened during the first winter of British rule. Filled with the "brilliant appearance" of the "ladies," and "crowded with company," the theater attracted many inhabitants. Properly balancing entertainment with charity, the theater used its proceeds, according to the *New-York Gazette and Weekly Mercury,* to relieve "widows and orphans of sailors and soldiers who have fallen in support of constitutional rights of Great Britain in America."[142]

In July and August 1776, loyalists in New York City had individually showed support for reunion by offering provisions and assistance to British troops. In September 1776, crowds of New Yorkers had expressed jubilation at the arrival of British troops. They had anticipated that the British would subdue the unnatural rebellion and the colonies would return to peace. In October 1776, an organized loyalist coalition comprised of almost a thousand inhabitants had followed constitutionally sanctioned procedure to voice their opposition to martial law and express their plan for reunion with the empire. They had expected the revival of civil rule in New York City to protect their civil liberties and to showcase the benefits of British constitutional governance to other colonists. They believed just and balanced civil governance in New York City would win the hearts and minds of wavering colonists.

However, by the winter of 1776–77, the loyalists recognized that the rebellion would not soon end. They had received no response to their petition requesting the revival of civil rule. And after British losses at Trenton and Princeton, the commanders were even less likely to grant their request. New Yorkers faced increasing rebel assaults from bordering regions, and they confronted the misconduct of British soldiers residing within the city. Military proclamations restricting soldiers' movements and military declarations promising protection to civilians proliferated each month. Yet British commanders could not fully stem the rebel threat, and military law admitted no civil procedures to protest the soldiers' conduct. Instead of flourishing in a city that invited the envy of rebellious subjects, loyalists inhabited a garrisoned city under siege.

# 4 ❧ "Lord Pity This Poor Country"
## Loyalist Resilience

*That we are involved in a war that threatens ruin to this country, I need not observe; nor need I point out to you the gradual growth of the present wanton and unnatural rebellion: You are well acquainted with it; you saw it rise.*

—Z to "Citizens In and About New York," *Rivington's New-York Loyal Gazette*, November 8, 1777

Printer Hugh Gaine's decision to return to New York City from Newark, New Jersey, in November 1776 indicates the buoyant context of military victory and ideological optimism that persisted for many Americans through the spring of 1777.[1] On September 2, 1776, Gaine reported that New York City "is now invaded by a powerful fleet and army; the inhabitants are obliged to seek a retreat in the Country."[2] Worried by the imminent threat of a British invasion, later that month he abandoned New York City and his *New-York Gazette and Weekly Mercury* and moved to Newark. On September 21, Gaine printed the first issue of the *New-York Gazette and Weekly Mercury* from Newark. Surely he must have been startled when, nine days later, another paper of the same name appeared from New York City with a nameplate that stated that it was "printed by Hugh Gaine." After entering New York City on September 15, the British had taken control of Gaine's printing operations and, in partnership with loyalist leaders, launched the British-loyalist version of his paper.

The most obvious choice of a New York City printer with loyalist persuasions, James Rivington, was missing from the city. Unlike Gaine, who left voluntarily in the fall of 1776 to avoid the dangers of military battle, Rivington fled involuntarily after rebel leaders attacked his printing press the previous year. Those seeking separation from the empire perceived Rivington and his publications as an immediate danger and desperately sought to restrain them; Rivington had proved a perfect target.

In Rivington's absence, Governor William Tryon took over Gaine's abandoned press and launched the publication of the first of four British-sponsored loyalist newspapers in New York City.[3] On September 25, Tryon appointed Ambrose Serle and Reverend Charles Inglis "to undertake the management of the political part in the Newspaper about to be published." Protected by the British military and united in their common respect for the stability of mixed government, these loyalists prepared to respond directly to rebel allegations against the British government.[4]

Ambrose Serle was an English Tory with fixed ideas about the function of the colonies and the criminality of the revolution. He sailed for America convinced that the establishment of the Episcopal Church and the supremacy of the British constitution in America were indispensable. In 1770, he determined that the establishment of an "episcopate upon a proper foundation" was essential to imperial unity. Reminding the Reverend Charles Inglis of the paper Serle had written on this subject, Serle remarked, "The more Wealth & Influence the Church & Bishop could have, the more power wd. result to the Crown." In 1774, he wrote a *Sketch of an Essay on Adjusting our Disputes with the Colonies,* and a year later he published a pamphlet whose title speaks revealingly about his views on the American rebellion, *Americans against Liberty: or an Essay on the Nature and Principles of True Freedom, Shewing that the Designs and Conduct of the Americans Tend only to Tyranny and Slavery.* Prone to emotional exaggeration and Calvinistic extravagance, Serle portrayed the revolution as a religious struggle between good and evil.[5]

Tryon and Inglis were impatient to confront the rebel arguments from their haven in the city. Unlike Serle, they were not prone to righteously elevate the imperial crisis to otherworldly terms. Both had served prominently in the colonies, and were well aware of the magnitude of the rebel attack against British government. In fact, Tryon and Inglis were royal officeholders who had already paid a high price for their allegiance. In October 1775, Tryon was run out of New York City, and the royal government ruled precariously from a warship in New York harbor. In the summer of 1776, in response to the "gathering storm," Inglis had sent his family away from the city. Although he stayed to safeguard his property and serve the church, he could not keep the church open or prevent rebel committees from plundering his house.[6]

Until Gaine's return, the British-loyalist coalition managed the New York City version of *New York Gazette and Weekly Mercury.*[7] Like pre-

Revolutionary newspapers, the paper served as a vehicle for communicating calamities and selling imported merchandise: it included news of the "terrible fire" on September 21 that "consumed about a thousand Houses" and advertisements from merchants such as William Tongue. But the paper also provided the British-loyalist coalition with a regular and respectable mechanism to refute rebel allegations, to criticize rebel ideology as tyrannical and ungrateful, and to remind readers of the harmony and strength enjoyed within the British Empire. Hence, included in the first issue was General Howe's reminder that peace, liberty, and property resided only within the empire. It invited

> inhabitants at large to reflect seriously upon their present Conditions and Expectations, and to judge for themselves whether it be more consistent with their Honor and Happiness to offer up their Lives as a Sacrifice to the unjust and precarious Cause in which they are engaged, or to return to their Allegiance, accept the Blessings of Peace, and be secured in a free Enjoyment of their Liberty and Properties, upon the true Principles of the Constitution.[8]

Howe's notice asked the colonists to choose between an uncertain and illegal revolt and a just and lasting reunion with the mother country.

The first issues of the paper under the management of Tryon and Inglis reveal the British-loyalist hopes in suppressing the unnatural rebellion. Tryon exhorted loyalists "to preserve that constancy of mind which is inherent in the breast of virtuous and loyal citizens" because "a very few months" would relieve them from their "oppressed, injured, and insulted condition." In direct response to rebel accusations that the British tyrannically employed Hessian troops to subdue their own people, an anonymous writer asserted that the employment of German troops was a sign of "true wisdom and good policy" at this juncture, because the deluded colonies who are "running wildly after the shadow of liberty have lost their substance." Similarly, essays by "Benevolus" reminded colonists of the blessings of "British law, British protection, and British union, and those by "Irenicus" differentiated between rebel "ferocity" and loyalist "courage." Significantly, the *New-York Gazette and Weekly Mercury* published the four loyalist petitions from New York City and the counties of Long Island from October to December 1776. These petitions offered effusive allegiance and requested the restoration of civil rule.[9]

New Yorkers' optimism continued in the winter and spring of 1777 as they along with British officers noted the dwindling rebel strength. "The back of the snake is broken," celebrated one letter from New York on January 3.[10] In rebel-controlled Pennsylvania and New Jersey, the *New-York Gazette and Weekly Mercury* reported that people lived without "positive law, and without a Constitution." They suffered "extreme distress" because they lacked provisions and other necessaries and paid exorbitantly high prices for basic goods. Trade was "in a manner entirely stopt." In April, New Jersey loyalist Cortlandt Skinner declared that "another campaign will in all Probability put an end to the rebellion."[11]

The Trenton and Princeton defeats had not won the war for the rebels because Washington's army suffered a debilitating winter encampment at Morristown, New Jersey. In mid-March, General Washington had only 1,200 militia and 2,543 Continental Army soldiers at Morristown, and many of them were unfit for duty.[12] Noting that weakness, the British colonel Charles Stuart predicted British victory: "There is a strong appearance of its being at an end before the autumn." In May, Captain John Peebles noticed that "Americans are becoming discontented with the service." Gaine surmised that Washington's force was too weak to attack the advanced British positions in New Jersey.[13] On May 17, he wrote in his journal that "Washington's Army does not exceed 7000 Men, that very few of the Southern troops had joined them, that the People were very cool."[14] These "cool" people awaited a decisive military turning point before committing their allegiance.

Loyalist spokesmen believed that the British were winning the war. Joseph Galloway, for example, had fled Philadelphia and sought refuge in New York City by December 1776, but in March 1777 Galloway depicted the rebels as growing weaker while His Majesty's cause grew stronger. The British would crush the rebellion in another campaign, he argued, because rebel leaders antagonized colonists with their tyrannical and extralegal measures while rebel soldiers pillaged the civilians. In contrast, the victorious operations of the British fleet and army would produce a "rapid change of disposition of the Americans." Galloway thought that the majority of colonists remained loyal and only awaited decisive British military success to display their allegiance.[15]

By March 1777, William Smith Jr. had decided that the rebels faced collapse as they had difficulty recruiting soldiers, procuring supplies, and controlling the escalating cost of living in war-ravaged regions. People suffered too much misery to tolerate the arbitrary demands of the congress. The rebel leaders recognized they could not long oppose the "power of Great Britain." All their efforts had led to despair and despondency.[16]

From February through April 1777, British authorities and loyalist spokesmen launched an ideological campaign to bolster and solidify loyalist support. They circulated a series of eight commentaries that identified and expanded upon commercial reasons for reunion with the empire. These essays appeared in the *New-York Gazette and Weekly Mercury* under the pseudonym "Integer." Authored by Ambrose Serle and Reverend Charles Inglis, these articles drew on one of the core principles of the loyalist position: the profits of empire.[17]

These "Integer" essays echoed the impassioned tone of essays signed by "Irenicus," "Anglo-Americanus," and "Publicola" published between September and December 1776 in the *New-York Gazette and Weekly Mercury*. These earlier pieces primarily praised the historical stability of the British constitution and faulted rebel leadership as unstable and violent. Whereas the rebels painted a glorious republican future unshackled by imperial demands, the loyalists dwelled on the fearful consequences of a future ruled by the rebel congress. They imagined a "puny divided state," created in a "sea of blood," utterly without order or law. They argued that the threat to colonial freedom came not from external British tyranny or corruption but from the internal anarchy promoted by the selfish schemes of self-interested men who promoted the "unjust and precarious Cause." These "self-created bodies," they asserted, "violated all the sacred ties of civil society," including "personal liberty and freedom of speech." They contrasted the frenzy of the rebel leaders with the rationality and conservatism of the "British law, British protection and British union." Only the British constitution provided the perfect balance of liberty with order.[18]

The 1776 essays also emphasized the natural ties that bound the colonies to the mother country. In October 14, 1776, the *New-York Gazette and Weekly Mercury* published a full-page table itemizing the great expenditures by Great Britain in protecting the colonies of North America. Between 1714 and 1776, Great Britain had spent over £34,696,867. The empire had offered its "opulence and credit" and its "treasury" because the colonists descended from Britons and shared a common culture, religion, and trade. The colonists would lose all this if they heeded the violent schemes of those who opposed their "lawful sovereign, in whose allegiance they were born." Indeed, America would plunge a "dagger" into her own vitals by persisting in a destructive war against the mother country. The colonists should meet their "brethren half-way" to restore mutual happiness.[19]

However, the suspension of civil jurisdiction, civil courts, and civil offices under British military government in New York City undermined the loyalist case for the consistency of British constitutional liberties. In 1777, the loyalists' appeal became less libertarian and more pragmatic. "Integer" cited the long-standing prosperity of the British Empire to critique the economic dangers of American independence. He asked the people to perform a "little common Arithmetic" to recognize that the colonies would not survive independently without the assistance of the British Empire. He mocked rebel attempts to delude the colonists with a currency that was "nothing better than a common piece of paper" and to hire troops with "Paper dollars which can never be paid." The dollars required to fund institutions such as an army and navy and to support courts, ambassadors, Indians, congressional treasurers, deputies, and clerks in an independent United States would "sink" the new government "to the Dogs." As these rebel gentlemen pursued their far-fetched ambitions, they ruined the economic prospects for future colonists. The rebels' lies might "amuse the gaping multitude for a Time, but 'tis vulgar Arithmetic that must satisfy them in the long Run." The mother country, "Integer" argued, could govern the colonies at a twentieth of the cost. Given the "real wealth" offered by the British Empire, he entreated the "people of North America" to abandon their delusions and recognize their duty as subjects.[20]

The loyalists appealed to a largely undecided colonial population. But their overwrought and emotional tone signified their real fears in a violent context they could not control. They wrote obsessively to remind wavering colonists of the stability of British rule and the dangers of rebel rule. Their grandiose language and distraught tone expressed their deep anxiety about the future of the American colonies.[21]

In his final essay on April 7, 1777, "Integer" made a table that synthesized the advantages of reunion while mocking the rebel congress. He deliberately mislabeled the table columns to caricature the rebels' rhetoric. Each of the nine items listed in the table clarified what the colonies would gain from reunification. Great Britain had not only the armed forces to fight the rebels but the economic resources to sustain her ships, soldiers, merchants, territories, and credit.

| Great Britain | America |
|---|---|
| feeble and destitute | strong and well-supported |
| drained of men and money | overflowing with men and money |
| in arrears of her soldiers | army well cloathed and exactly paid |
| her credit sunk | our credit high |
| her inhabitants divided | our inhabitants happy and unanimous |
| overwhelmed with debt | our debt nothing at all |
| her West-India Island starved | we fat and well-liking |
| her ships taken | our own all safe |
| her merchants bankrupt | our merchants, rich and easy[22] |

## Campaigns of 1777

British troops remained largely inactive in their enclaves in New York and New Jersey during the spring of 1777. Howe awaited supplies and troops from Europe before embarking on his campaign to capture Philadelphia. The loss of New Jersey during the winter had not only exhausted British supplies but also prevented the collection of forage required to keep the horses in good condition to mount an offensive campaign.[23] In April 1777, Ambrose Serle noticed that the want of rain had slowed the growth of fodder, which "prevented the motion of the army."[24]

In June 1777, after months of inaction, Howe's move against Washington's army in New Jersey ended in disappointment. When Washington avoided engagement, British forces abandoned their two remaining posts in New Jersey, Brunswick and Amboy, and returned to Staten Island. Colonel Stuart deplored the predicament of the New Jersey loyalists abandoned to rebel persecution. He denounced British policy that left "unprotected and exposed" to a "cruel and implacable enemy" those who "sought [her] protection and served [her]."[25]

Howe's failure in New Jersey released the pent-up frustrations of New Yorkers awaiting a decisive victory. In June, Admiral Howe's aide observed that "rumors are spreading . . . [and] almost everyone blames General Howe." Gaine saw that New Yorkers were "dispirited on the occasion." Another witness, Pastor Schaukirk, wearily commented that "matters go slow and cause concern to all disinterested well-wishers." In July, he noted that the British army was in the same position as a year before, maintaining its jurisdiction only over New York City, Long Island, and Staten Island and Newport, Rhode Island, while the rebels controlled the surrounding countryside. Discouraged, he prayed, "Lord pity this poor country."[26]

Although the British retreat from New Jersey frustrated New York loy-alists, the troops' withdrawal represented a minor misfortune in the eyes of the London ministry, which had designed a grand plan for 1777. Lord Germain's plan focused on capturing the entire Hudson Valley. The High-lands served as the key communications link for rebels in the northern colonies. If the British gained possession of the Highlands, they could block any large shipment of rebel supplies across it. British capture of the Highlands would disturb the communication channel from New England to the rest of the colonies and secure the British an overland route to transfer supplies, horses, and men between their Canadian and northern armies, allowing the two detachments to function as a unified force.[27]

Howe unnecessarily complicated Germain's strategy to crush the rebel-lion. Outlined in November 1776, Germain's strategy included a plan to send one detachment to occupy Boston, another to form a junction with British troops coming down from Canada, and a third column to invade New Jersey. The last detachment would distract Washington's troops from reinforcing rebel soldiers along the Hudson. In accordance with Germain's plan, Howe planned initially to make a movement to Phila-delphia only after these other objectives were met. However, in a subse-quent plan outlined in December 1776, Howe identified an overland route to take Philadelphia as his primary objective for the 1777 campaign. As Howe considered the potential difficulties in maintaining a one-hundred-mile line of supplies and communication between Philadelphia and New York through rebel-controlled New Jersey, he again altered his plans. Four months later, in the second revision to his original plan, Howe resolved to proceed toward Philadelphia by sea, out from New York to the south and up the Delaware. Burgoyne's impending invasion from Canada played only a minor and sporadic role in Howe's plans to secure Philadelphia. Howe did not anticipate a diversionary movement to assist Burgoyne's Canadian expedition. As he had captured New York and blockaded the Hudson River, he wanted to capture Philadelphia and close the Delaware to rebel shipping.[28]

Howe also believed that controlling Philadelphia would summon loy-alist volunteers and free British troops for service elsewhere. Prominent figures such as Joseph Galloway and members of the Allen family pro-vided reassurance of loyalists support in eastern Pennsylvania. Galloway claimed that between 75 and 90 percent of Pennsylvanians were loyal and would affirm their allegiance upon the arrival of the British army. They would offer armed assistance to British troops, relieving British regulars for further field service. Distrustful of finding the same loyalist support in the lower Hudson Valley, Howe relegated Burgoyne's expedition to secondary importance.[29]

In July 1777, Major General Clinton urged Howe to modify his plans. Clinton explained that the success of the Philadelphia expedition would require British forces to remain tied to the area, leaving Burgoyne alone in the upper Hudson Valley. He entreated Howe to send troops up the Hudson to support Burgoyne's advance away from his supply line in Canada. Clinton also expressed doubts about loyalist support in Pennsylvania. He asked Howe to remember his earlier optimism about finding friends in New Jersey, British disappointment, and the resulting retreats from New Jersey, first in 1776 and again in 1777.[30]

Clinton also fretted that Howe's departure would make New York City indefensible. Indeed, in July 1777, when General Howe left for Philadelphia with sixteen thousand troops, he left Clinton with seven thousand soldiers to defend New York City and the surrounding regions. Three thousand of these soldiers were newly raised loyalist regiments. Clinton was concerned that Washington would attack New York City in Howe's absence.[31] In July, Clinton complained to Lord Hugh Percy that his corps stood on the defensive and invited attack by rebel forces. By October, Clinton agonized that he was "left in a most starved defensive as 7 or 8000 men attacked British posts at Staten Island, Long Island and Kingsbridge."[32]

In the summer of 1777, as Howe embarked for Philadelphia and Burgoyne descended from Canada toward Albany, New Yorkers anxiously waited for news of decisive British success. The trickling of rumors from deserters and spies had not reassured them. In August 1777, they began to "speak loudly" against the British commanders. They thought that British actions only protracted the calamities. In September, Gaine noted in his journal: "People much dissatisfied." Lord Howe's aide, Levin von Muenchhausen, noted that "stupid people" criticized Howe's tactics.[33]

In September, Clinton received news of Burgoyne's desperate situation in the upper Hudson Valley. Burgoyne's forces were in poor condition to retreat, he had many wounded and sick, and his transport was short and his supplies even shorter. He urged Clinton to attack the rebel forts in the lower Hudson Valley, as "it will draw away great part of their [rebel] force, and I will follow them close." Burgoyne ended his urgent request, "Do it, my dear friend, directly."[34]

Caught between Burgoyne's alarming situation and his own mandate to protect New York City, Clinton could not risk distancing himself too far from his base. In early October, after the long-anticipated arrival of 1,700 reinforcements from England, Clinton embarked with 3,000 troops to seize the two rebel forts in the lower Hudson, Fort Montgomery and Fort Clinton, about forty miles above the city. Under Major General John Vaughan's command, he sent 2,000 additional troops on a rescue expedition toward Albany. But Clinton's ambitious efforts came too late.[35]

In October 1777, as the British main field army attacked Philadelphia and Vaughan's troops approached forty-five miles south of Albany, Burgoyne surrendered to the Continental Army in Saratoga, forty miles north of Albany. Over five thousand redcoats, Hessians, Canadians, and loyalists became rebel prisoners. On the day of Burgoyne's surrender, Clinton received Howe's orders to abandon the Hudson forts, send four thousand troops to Philadelphia, and withdraw to New York City immediately. The British had lost their chance to control the Hudson gateway. If the British had retained the Highlands, Clinton later wrote, "it would most probably have finished the war."[36]

General Howe knew his career in the colonies had come to an end. Five days after Burgoyne's defeat at Saratoga, he resigned and asked permission to return to England: "I am led to hope that I may be relieved from this very painful service, wherein I have not the good fortune to enjoy the necessary confidence and support of my superiors. . . . I humbly request I may receive His Majesty's permission to resign the command." Disturbed by Howe's handling of the American rebellion, Germain forwarded Howe's resignation to the king, who in February 1778 signaled his approval.[37]

Both before and long after his departure from the colonies, loyalist New Yorkers bitterly complained that Howe's tactical mistakes had given renewed hope to the rebels. In November, one New Yorker wrote to a British minister that "General Howe's conduct ever since he has had the command of the army has been a heap of blunders & ridiculous delays, that have rather tended to encourage the rebels by protracting than to extinguish the rebellion by spirited exertions or utterly destroying the whole rebel army." Another loyalist echoed his sentiments in December 1777: "It is a unanimous sentiment here that our misfortunes this campaign have arisen, not so much from the genius and valor of the rebels, as from the misconduct of a certain person." Galloway complained two years later, "The British General declined an enemy of greatly inferior force" and "undertook this infatuated voyage [to Philadelphia]." In a history of New York written after the Revolution, Thomas Jones castigated the commander, who "cherished, nursed, and fostered" the American rebellion in 1776 and 1777.[38]

Publicly, loyalist leaders shifted rhetoric to cope with the crushing defeat at Saratoga. They sought to divert people by emphasizing the kinship that persisted between the colonies and the mother country and the cordiality shared between New Yorkers and the British military authorities. They no longer promised colonists the substantive rewards of empire: constitutional liberty and economic prosperity. Instead, the redesigned rhetoric recalled the idealized symbols of monarchy: the king, the parade, and the splendor of marching troops. In January 1778, a letter written "To the Printer" asked James Rivington to describe the effusive celebration in honor of her majesty's birthday. The narration would solemnize the commitment of the loyalist community and would "properly encourage" the loyalty of others.[39]

In September 29, 1777, Rivington, newly assigned as His Majesty's printer, returned from London. Residents perceived his return as a sign of the king's commitment to promote the loyalists. When Rivington published the first issue of his paper a month later, Gaine noted the broad loyalist support in the city as "everyone rushed out to the streets to secure copies, clerks, artisans, soldiers, and merchants alike turning aside from their tasks to read it."[40]

Rivington celebrated the British military presence in the city. In February 1778, an essay in the *Royal Gazette* commended the "loud acclamations of joy and other demonstrations" that greeted the parade of one of the provincial units in the city, Emmerich's Chasseurs. One anonymous reader commented: "What a pleasing sensation this must afford to every true friend of their King and Country!" Further, the example of these troops neatly attired and marching through the city would "animate others to imitate this laudable Example." In contrast to the "valour" of the British troops, the loyalists pointed to Washington's "tottering" men who were dying of camp fever, destitute of clothing, and deserting in great numbers.[41]

Yet how could loyalist publications reconcile their glorification of British troops with General Burgoyne's defeat at Saratoga? Loyalist commentaries minimized the significance of Burgoyne's loss and denied that it would transform the nature of the war. They insisted that the "unfortunate miscarriage" under Burgoyne prematurely made the friends of America "exult with insolence." They assured people that Burgoyne's defeat would actually awaken "Britannia" from her "lethargic state." She would now apply "strong and stubborn medicines" to effect a "radical cure." The London ministry would surely abandon moderation in order "to compel America to submission." Loyalists urged the empire to muster its full might to win the war despite the temporary setback at Saratoga.[42]

In the spring of 1778, the *Royal Gazette* optimistically reported that "very large" reinforcements of troops would arrive in America in the spring, as His Majesty used the most "vigorous and effectual exertions for quelling the monstrous rebellion upon this continent." Rivington reassured his readers "that this loyal city is in a state of perfect security, tranquility, and at unity in itself, amply provided with the necessaries, and even luxuries of life; the inhabitants feel no uneasiness from any European intelligence."[43] Rivington hinted that the rebel leaders would not receive assistance from France.

A magnificent meschianza, a medieval tournament staged on the banks of the Delaware River in Philadelphia in May 1778, honored the departure of General Howe from the colonies. It also heralded another loyalist idealization of the war. After three long years of inconclusive conflict, the British sought an escape into a heroic past and the loyalists recorded this escape in glowing terms.[44]

The loyalist writers' desperate wishfulness, verging on fanaticism, betrayed their disappointment in the British, both in their military retreats and in their unwillingness to wage a punitive and destructive war to force the rebels into submission. To rally disappointed loyalists and win over wavering colonists, the loyalists asserted the superiority of British military and naval forces. The king's friends, they declared, would now witness the vigor heretofore applied in only a limited fashion. In June, an anonymous writer in the *Royal Gazette* declared that the British lion would no longer hold forth "ill-timed and unmerited lenitives" but "speedily begin to roar."[45] The loyalist agitators maintained that the British government would move away from compromise and enforce their wishes by using harsher measures to terrify rebel leaders and their followers.

## Franco-American Alliance

The loyalists' animated efforts to rally the people served only as a temporary palliative, as events soon contradicted their idealized expectations.

In February 1778, the French entered a formal treaty of alliance with the rebels. In the spring of 1777, the loyalists had feared the possibility of a French alliance with the American congress. They recognized that France eagerly observed the upheavals in the British colonies. In December 1776, loyalist spokesmen had refuted the "ridiculous" rumor of French intervention that self-interested rebel leaders circulated as the "gospel" to rally their cause. In January 1777, Smith mocked the idea that France would "plunge" into a war on behalf of rebels. In February, he stressed the "improbability" of French intervention. In March, he wrote more cautiously that the rebels needed French assistance to maintain independence. In April, he expressed his deepest fear: "If France abets America . . . then we are ruined."[46]

The French ministers dreamed of exploiting American disaffection and taking revenge against the British for the defeat they had suffered in the Seven Years' War. As early as May 1776, the French had secretly authorized aid of 1 million livres for munitions to the colonies. France carefully observed the progress of the rebellion. If the rebels maintained their tenacious opposition and widened public support for American independence, the French could chance an alliance to weaken the power of the British.[47]

Loyalist spokesmen had consistently denied the possibility of French intervention in the war. In December 1777, the *New-York Gazette and Weekly Mercury* dismissed the "fiction" of French involvement and insisted that the king of France "would never come to a Rupture with England" over the American colonies. In March 1778, an extract from Paris reassured other loyalists that they had "no reason to fear from the House of Bourbon." Even as loyalist leaders acknowledged that the rebel papers were "full with news of a French war swiftly approaching," they insisted that the British government suffered "no apprehensions."[48]

The loyalists dreaded the consequences of French alliance. Symbolically, the rebels' alliance with France revealed the irreparable breach between Protestant Britons. Hardened political interests had superseded the ties of kinship and culture that bound the colonists not only to Great Britain but to one another. Pragmatically, the loyalists understood that the enemy was no longer just rebel farmers in tattered uniforms but now also included a powerful empire, a historically formidable foe. The loyalists feared France as Britain's greatest imperial and commercial rival, with a powerful army and navy.

Shaken by France's alliance with the American congress, the loyalists' renewed rhetoric shifted to attack the menace of French Catholicism. Conceding French power, the loyalists turned it to meet their own ends. They argued that France would transform free American colonists into French dependents.[49] In the summer of 1778, loyalists bitterly crusaded against the "universal establishment of Popery" that would extinguish every "spark" of civil and religious liberty in the world. They contrasted the natural ties of consanguinity, language, manners, and religion that bound the colonies to the British Empire against the "unnatural alliance with perfidious Frenchmen." By allying themselves with the "ambition" and "duplicity" of the "inveterate foes" of Britain, the colonists would enter into league with those who wished to overturn the protestant faith. The Catholic enemy was perfidious, restless, and enterprising. Warning colonists of French cunning, the loyalists constructed the French as a Proteus that entered like a "lamb," transformed into a "fox," and treacherously became the "devouring wolf." The colonies would be sold to a French king and live under "wretched submission" to French despotism and popish superstition.[50]

For the duration of the war, loyalists sought reunion not only in the name of British law and commerce but also in the name of British Protestantism. During the eighteenth century, Britons had increasingly established their political and religious identity as Protestants struggling against the world's foremost Catholic powers. They cited the French expulsion of Protestants in 1685, Spain's persecution of Protestants through the Inquisition, and the anti-Protestant reaction in German Catholic states as examples of Catholic tyranny. Defining France foremost as militarist and unfree, they saw themselves as a people who cherished civil liberties and protected peace. They contrasted the benefits of belonging to the British commercial empire with Catholic despotism that resulted in repeated famines for thousands of peasants in France. Repeatedly, Britons reminded themselves that the struggles of Protestant Reformation persisted.[51]

Despite their calamitous circumstances, many New Yorkers continued to believe that the rebel coalition faced greater difficulties. The loyalists emphasized that the Continental Congress's alliance with Catholic France would cripple the support for independence in America's Protestant colonies. In October, an intelligence report from New England stated that the "French connections [was] disagreeable to all ranks of people," for people feared that France would "next conquer them." The following month,

New Jersey loyalist Isaac Ogden agreed that the majority of inhabitants felt dissatisfied with tyrannical government, detested the French alliance, and lived without necessary provisions.[52]

Multiple intelligence reports spoke of bleak conditions in neighboring counties. In January 1778, another New Jersey exile, Peter Dubois, stated that a "general discontent prevails amongst the most disloyal and disaffected inhabitants in the Jersey counties of Bergen, Essex, Morris, Sussex, and Hunterdon." People grumbled about the exorbitant prices they paid for essential commodities. Indeed, by March 1778, the value of the Continental dollar had fallen to 56 percent of its value in September 1777. A gallon of molasses cost ten times as much in 1778 as it did in 1776. On March 12, Major John Andre reported intelligence that Washington's men were in "ruinous circumstances" for want of adequate clothes for the inclement weather. John Williams, a rebel deserter, confirmed loyalists' suppositions. He admitted scarce provisions and a dearth of meat during the whole summer in Kingsbridge in Westchester County, just north of the city. In December, another New Yorker observed that the rebellion had grown "languid" because of the discontents of the public. In January 1779, Smith emphasized the desperate plight of the rebel army: "Those whose times expire [are] daily leaving it, swearing they will never reenlist. The militia are drafted for recruits into the regiments and lugged away unwillingly to the great dissatisfaction of the farmers in general. No part of the army can stir from their present cantonments for want of cattle, provisions, and forage."[53]

Reverend Charles Inglis drew hope from the disadvantages the rebels faced. In December, he resolved to "forget the past, forbear Recrimination, and in future learn wisdom from former errors and mistakes." He insisted that another two years of the war would reduce the rebel banditti to famine. He cited the depreciation of Continental Congress money, their difficulty in procuring forage and provisions and in recruiting for their army, and their relentless use of imprisonment and banishment to suppress dissension. These "indubitable facts," he asserted, "show that the rebellion is not in a thriving prosperous condition."[54]

As in New York City, the partnership between the rebel congress and the French government brought matters to a crisis in London. Understanding the extensive and expensive demands of waging an international war with France, the British ministry longed to resolve the American crisis amicably. In March 1778, George Germain hoped that a diplomatic initiative would lead to reconciliation between the colonies and Britain and "supersede the necessity of another campaign" in America.[55]

On April 14, 1778, in an attempt to forestall the effects of the French treaty on the American rebels, the British sent the initial peace proposal for publication in New York City. The ministry understood that the "sooner, the more publickly, and the better [the proposals] are authenticated the more effectually Government may hope to draw the proposed advantage." The rebel progress in the war had prompted genuine concessions. Addressed to the Continental Congress, the peace proposal promised that Britain would abandon the taxation program entered upon after 1763. It pledged that Parliament would never tax America in any way except to regulate trade. It assured the return of all the constitutional liberties demanded by the colonists in 1774, the sole right of internal legislation, and the "Irrevocable Enjoyment of every Privilege, that is, short of a total Separation of Interests." In exchange, the colonists would recognize Parliament's power to regulate the trade of the whole empire, abandon the French alliance, and withdraw their pursuit of independence.[56]

In effect, the British offered exactly the concessions New York's moderates had requested in 1774 and 1775 that the British decision makers had then refused to consider. Germain had asserted in 1775 that the colonists had challenged the sovereignty of the mother country, and Britain should answer with "Roman severity." In 1778, however, placed in a compromising predicament by the Continental Congress's alliance with France, Germain sanctioned the peace initiatives.[57]

The peace commissioners, William Eden, George Johnstone, and Frederick Howard, the fifth Earl of Carlisle, known collectively as the Carlisle Commission, arrived in Philadelphia in June 1778, at the most unfavorable moment possible. British troops stood on the verge of evacuating Philadelphia, the capital of the rebellion. News of the French alliance with the United States led to a reappraisal of military strategy toward the rebellious colonies. The British could no longer afford to invest their limited military resources entirely in North America when they faced a threat not only from France but also potentially from its ally Spain. In June, Clinton lamented that it was the "opinion of Government that [North] America may become a secondary object."[58]

The empire's military focus shifted toward the Caribbean Islands, where a mere eighteen hundred British troops guarded the empire's valuable sugar islands. The subtropical products from the West Indian islands were more profitable to the British economy than the products of American farms and fisheries. Furthermore, the empire that controlled the islands would reap enviable profits for years to come. As Piers Mackesy summarizes, the "islands held the lure of compensation for her losses in America, finances to pay for the war, a favorable balance of trade, an economic lever to coerce America."[59]

The new plan sent to Sir Henry Clinton, the new commander in chief, pointed to a policy of "dispersed security." The revised strategy involved not only a shift of resources to defend the profitable sugar colonies in the West Indies but also a shift away from the northern colonies in mainland North America toward a conquest of the southern colonies that had shown greater signs of popular loyalism. Significantly, the new plan entailed an evacuation of Philadelphia. The British aimed to destroy the raw materials that sustained the rebel forces and to mobilize the loyalist population to seize Charlestown in South Carolina. Of the 16,000 British troops removed from Philadelphia, 4,000 would attack St. Lucia, 3,000 would reinforce the Floridas, and the remaining 7,000 would stay in New York to guard the American coast.[60]

New York's leading loyalists recoiled at the French alliance from its inception. The multitude, Smith observed, still "sigh for peace, & the current once turned will be irresistible."[61] In May, he declared: "If a sudden peace is patched up with the colonies, France has much to dread in the West Indies."[62] Another New Yorker who shared Smith's moderation, Peter Van Schaack, urged the Continental Congress to negotiate terms with the commissioners. Pointing to rebel attacks and insults against loyalist civilians, Van Schaack insisted that Great Britain "has not alone trampled upon the rights of mankind."[63] Smith and Van Schaack's steadfast belief in the firmness and elasticity of the British constitution accounts for their confidence. The "perpetual Convulsions," Smith asserted, "whistle among the Branches of the great Tree [the British constitution] without shaking its Roots or even the main trunk."[64]

These New Yorkers hoped desperately that British diplomatic initiatives could still lead to reunion with the empire. On March 12, 1778, Smith observed "joy at New York on the Prospect of Peace."[65] Two days later, he remarked that the "report of Peace flies thro' the lower ranks and brightens up their countenances."[66] Smith predicted that generous overtures from Britain would weaken support for independence and "give a turn to the tide."[67] It would create the middle ground needed to bring in all those caught in the "Spirit of Ambition and Interest and Revenge."[68]

On April 7, 1778, upon reading the details of the peace proposal, Smith expressed approval. A year earlier, he had asserted the importance of an "explicit tender of a liberal constitution" that would encourage America "to barter away her claim to independency for the essential rights of British subjects."[69] He predicted that a few weeks would add thousands to the British side, and the rebel leaders would find it difficult to maintain that authority they had "so lately and so irregularly acquired."[70]

But New Yorkers' optimism concealed their deepest fears. They worried that British idleness since Saratoga promoted the impression of British weakness and reduced potential support for the peace proposal. In April 1778, Daniel Chamier, formerly of Maryland and commissary general in New York City, proposed that the British should launch a campaign before the commissioners arrived from England. The expedition, he suggested, "would rather advance than retard the making of peace." Smith wished also that a party of troops would advance up the Hudson River to "quicken the turn in this province even before the Comrs. Arrive." He knew that the British defeat in Saratoga threatened the success of the diplomatic mission. He hoped for a British victory that would eclipse the loss and demonstrate to colonists the prowess of British arms.[71]

The British peace commissions also worried that Britain's new defensive strategy in the northern colonies doomed the peace initiatives. By evacuating Philadelphia and moving British troops to the West Indies and the southern colonies, the British had, in effect, conceded that they could not suppress the rebels in the northern colonies. In his report to Lord George Germain in June 1778, Johnstone denounced the Philadelphia evacuation as a "fatal, ill concerted and Ill advised Retreat, highly dishonorable to his Majesty's Arms and most prejudicial to the Interest of his Dominions." Henry Clinton suspected also that "it is too late to expect anything from [the commission] without it had been backed with the operations of an army."[72]

In July, the arrival of the French fleet off Sandy Hook, New Jersey, within four miles of New York City, revealed the vulnerable position of the Royal Navy. French fleets had left European waters without confronting a British blockade. On July 11, intelligence reports confirmed twelve warships advancing for New York City. The French fleet had already captured twenty merchant ships. The French admiral, Comte d'Estaing, threatened now to blockade the port of New York City, with Admiral Richard Howe caught inside the bar of the harbor and Clinton's troops trapped inside the city. D'Estaing had six frigates against Howe's three, and his ships of the line mounted 850 guns against Howe's 534. Meanwhile, Washington's troops menaced from White Plains, twenty miles north of the city.[73]

British officials blamed the British ministry for New York's perilous situation. Major Frederick Mackenzie attacked the "unpardonable faults" committed by the government, whose "duty it was to watch the motions of the Enemy in every quarter."[74] Sir Charles Blagden deduced that the "whole continent must view us with contempt; almost all the British force in America is blockaded by sea, & invested by land." Carlisle recognized that the arrival of the French squadron made "every hope of success in our business ridiculous." He believed that "common people hate us in their hearts." Nor was the British and loyalists' predicament lost on Washington, who reflected, "It is not a little pleasing nor less wonderful to contemplate that after two years of Manoeuvring . . . both Armies are brought back to the very point they set out from."[75]

Clinton acted decisively. By July 19, he had stationed eighteen hundred fully equipped troops in Sandy Hook, and they deterred French entry into the harbor. On July 22, the French fleet left Sandy Hook without damaging the British fleet. However, loyalists raged. In November, Isaac Ogden expressed his deep frustration at the passivity of British troops: "24,000 of the best troops in the world were shut up within their lines by 15,000 at most of poor wretches, who were ill paid, badly fed, and worse cloathed, and scarce at best deserved the name of soldiers."[76]

Meanwhile, in the last days of June, the Carlisle peace commissioners had sent their conciliation proposal to the Continental Congress.[77] On July 3, the congress asserted that it would discuss a treaty of peace and commerce with Great Britain only after the king acknowledged American independence or withdrew the British fleet and army from the colonies.[78] Four days later, in a private letter to Germain, the commissioners reported that nothing could be expected from their mission "except through the exertion of His Majesty's arms, or by an appeal to the people at large, or by negotiations with separate bodies of men and individuals."[79] Thus, in July, as the Howe brothers had done in 1776, the commissioners bypassed the congress and broadly circulated the terms of their proposal directly to the American people.

As the British peace proclamations circulated in New York City, the inhabitants confronted another near catastrophe. On August 3, less than three weeks after the French fleet had left the harbor, a fire engulfed the wharf area, consuming more than sixty-four dwellings. When lightning struck a British ordnance shop, 248 barrels of gunpowder exploded. Crowded, heavily built up, and containing numerous homes with wood-shingle roofs, the city stood again in great peril. The city's commandant suspected arson and circulated multiple proclamations promising one hundred guineas for information to convict the incendiaries. The fire made residents jittery, and for the next few months, stories circulated of incendiary plots. Some exploited the mayhem to seize unsupervised military supplies. On September 19, 1778, the commandant demanded that inhabitants return much-needed items such as cloth, hats, shoes, and tents that they had carried off during the fire.[80]

## Loyalists Abandoned

In 1776–77, Joseph Galloway trusted British leadership in the war and had even accepted the suspension of civil rule in New York City. He believed the long-term advantages of reunion with the empire outweighed the temporary inconveniences civilians suffered under martial law. He argued that New Yorkers had already remained under rebel rule and without civil jurisdiction for close to two years. They could endure it for a "few months longer" in return for the promise of "lasting peace and liberty." A revised constitution for the American colonies, which required only "one sitting of Parliament," would restore civil rule immediately in the city. In fact, Galloway declared that loyalists in the city had easier circumstances than their brethren in the rebel-controlled hinterlands. Military governance actually "mended" the situation of the New Yorkers because it guaranteed them protection and allowed them to recover debts and remain "masters" of their own property.[81]

The evacuation of Philadelphia embittered Galloway. Although British governance in Philadelphia failed to fulfill the sanguine wishes of loyalists, Galloway and others vehemently opposed the city's evacuation the following summer. The British had faced many of the same issues that confronted them in New York City. Although they controlled Philadelphia, the hinterland remained in rebel hands. It would take the British over two months to establish a supply line along the Delaware River for the fifty thousand inhabitants—residents, troops, and camp followers—in the city.

The meager provisions that reached the city proved insufficient to feed the residents. The cost of necessary goods such as salt climbed. As British troops foraged desperately and indiscriminately to acquire fuel for the winter, they alienated civilians on the northern perimeter of the city.[82]

As Thomas Gage had promoted New York City three years earlier, Galloway championed the case for Philadelphia. He maintained that the city was the American hub of commercial activity and absolutely crucial to British success in quelling the rebellion. Moreover, he insisted on the prevailing loyalist sentiment in Pennsylvania. In June 1778, he worried that the British evacuation would not only "deprive" the well affected of "all confidence in British protection" but "alienate their minds from the British government and from necessity unite them to the Rebel states."[83]

Despite loyalist supplications, British military forces evacuated Philadelphia in the summer of 1778. Three thousand disappointed Philadelphia loyalists boarded British ships to seek refuge in New York City. One Philadelphia loyalist who fled to New York City, Samuel Shoemaker, expressed the misery of the refugees who feared a rebel "rope around their necks."[84] Galloway reported that the evacuation "struck the inhabitants with great dismay and distress."[85] Like the refugees who entered New York City after each British setback—from New Jersey in 1776 and from upstate New York in 1777—the Philadelphia exiles in the summer of 1778 signified British failure. An anonymous New Yorker expressed loyalists' shock at the evacuation: "As soon as their plan [to evacuate Philadelphia] transpired a universal despondence among the loyal Americans took place; men of moderation were silent and looked stupefied; and men of vigour and penetration, expressed their doubts, sorrow, contempt, and abhorrence." About two weeks later, another New Yorker blamed the 1777 failure on General Howe: "That is no evidence of our weakness or the rebels' strength," he asserted, "but simply a proof of Howe's deficiency in military knowledge."[86]

Abandoned by the British troops in June 1778, two Philadelphia Quaker loyalists, John Roberts and Abraham Carlisle, faced rebel retribution. Both Quakers had assisted the British administration in Philadelphia. As gatekeeper, Carlisle had issued passes to those entering or leaving the city; Roberts had recruited men and furnished supplies for the British. Both men were sentenced to hang.[87]

In October 1778, in a desperate effort to stop the hangings, loyalists petitioned the British government. Philadelphia loyalists Joseph Galloway, Andrew Allen, John Potts, and Samuel Shoemaker and New Jersey loyalist Daniel Coxe expressed their anger at the "unjust outrages against the King's faithful friends for no crime but their fidelity alone." The Quakers' persecution, they predicted, would create dread for others who lived now "in the Rebel power." They received no response.[88]

Two months later, some Philadelphia refugees praised Roberts and Carlisle, mourned their execution, and described the mixed public reaction of apathy and anger that followed their deaths. Over four thousand Philadelphians had attended the burial procession for the two men. Ogden mourned Roberts, who had "suffered with the resolution of a Roman." James Humphreys lamented that "poor Roberts and Carlisle have been cruelly and most wantonly sacrificed." Potts observed that the execution led to further withdrawal and disappointment by the loyalists: "It appears to me that the spirit of our countrymen is too much broken to attempt to relieve themselves from a burthen grievous and disagreeable to them in the highest degree." Discouraged, Potts explained that unless the British employed a greater force, the "game is certainly up, and America lost."[89]

While Potts noted the despondent state of the abandoned loyalists in Philadelphia, other refugees emphasized Philadelphians' indignation at the execution. Charles Stewart, a Philadelphia loyalist, asserted that the hangings had "a great effect on the minds of the people," who believed it was "murder committed on those persons."[90] Coxe believed that the British should turn people's wrath against tyrannical rebel leaders. The execution, he observed, raised the "murmurs of many & give general disgust." The moment, therefore, provided a perfect opportunity for Britain to "fan the latent spark." It "would not want much Fuel to set the whole province in a Flame if advantage was taken of the moment."[91] Despite the refugees' petitions and numerous letters, the two loyalists' execution did not merit official British response. Preoccupied with defending Britain's worldwide interests, the British ministry had no time for two unknown loyalists.

The dismal predicament of the king's friends encouraged an increasing number of loyalist leaders to adopt an uncompromising stance. These hard-liners no longer assumed that their audience was a politically uncommitted population or a deluded group under the grip of demagogic leaders. They counted as enemies deserving of punitive treatment any colonist who had not taken an oath to the British government. The diverse loyalists who adopted a militant stance included colonial politicians such as Joseph Galloway and William Tryon; Anglican ministers such as Charles Inglis; prominent New Jersey refugees such as Isaac Ogden, Daniel Coxe, and

Peter Dubois; and others who had lost vast estates and high status for their allegiance to the empire.[92]

These hard-liners pressed British officials to brutally disperse or destroy those who opposed reunion. Galloway advocated harsher measures to suppress rebel leaders.[93] He argued that Great Britain must prepare to annihilate American rebels before America was "annexed to, & joined with France, in order to annihilate this Empire."[94] He pushed the British to better employ their superior force in New York to pursue and destroy the main force of the Continental Congress. The avoidance of terror against rebel leaders, Galloway believed, only caused a protraction of the rebellion. Peter Dubois asserted the necessity of severe measures against those who committed crimes against the British government and the loyalists. He advocated terrorist tactics against civilians who besieged the king's friends. In December 1777, Dubois supported disarming the rebels, taking hostages, and "punishing the refractory and incorrigible with the severity of military execution." He claimed that the October 1777 destruction of Esopus in upstate New York, where British troops indiscriminately reduced the whole town to ashes, had a "most striking effect" on the minds of the rebels. It had led the rebels to fear the potential damage the British troops could inflict. Dubois explained his rationale for extensively deploying similar tactics: "It seems therefore necessary to make use of such disagreeable expedients to serve the cause of humanity, and to compel . . . rebellious people who cannot be won by clemency or any other consideration."[95]

During the fall of 1778, New York's hard-liners encouraged the growing refugee population to abandon hopes of reconciliation and instead to support a war of desolation.[96] In August, one New Yorker complained bitterly that the conciliatory bills "have been productive of great Evil, and lost us Opportunities not again to be expected."[97] In September, another inhabitant dismissed as foolhardy the commissioners who "entertain[ed] hopes that the people will at length compel the Congress to negotiate." The commissioners, he argued, ignored the "strong Despotism established by these demagogues who have contrived to put all the arms of the country into the hands of their friends."[98] In October, a loyalist essay addressed "To the Americans" announced that the peace proposal should represent Britain's last attempt at lenity. "The horrors of war have hitherto till now been restrained; but should you now refuse the offers of an indulgent mother . . . I

tremble for the consequence."[99] In January 1779, "Britannicus" warned colonists that, although the British had hitherto aimed to reclaim the colonies
through moderation and had displayed restraint by evacuating the cities
of Philadelphia and Boston without setting them aflame, they should now
relentlessly and harshly display their full strength to punish further resistance.[100] A former inhabitant of Maryland, John Goodrich, believed that
a bounty for the capture of active rebels would make every rebel suspect
his neighbors and subvert the rebellion.[101] A Bostonian who had made
his way into New York in the fall of 1776, Edward Winslow, expressed his
disgust at British half measures: "Such a damnable series of treating and
retreating—conciliating—and commissary that fighting (which is the only
remedy for the American disorder) has been totally suspended." He also
observed that "our precious countrymen" who had begun a rebellion os-
tensibly to overthrow the tyranny of a monarchy had willingly subjected
themselves to the power of France's absolute monarch. Winslow mocked
the rebel leaders who saw no contradiction in allying themselves with one
monarch to overthrow another.[102]

The hard-line propagandists urged New York's refugees to take independent military action against civilians and military rebels who had
humiliated them. In April 1778, an address in the Royal Gazette implored
refugees to rise from their current state of "indolence and languid inactivity" in order to "embody themselves into companies of volunteers."
The rebels plundered, insulted, and persecuted them in a "most barbarous
and brutal manner." Unless they took up arms energetically against their
enemies, they could bid adieu to their homes and "be dispersed through
the most remote parts of the globe, to shift for a wretched subsistence."
In June 1778, another essay bemoaned the rebels' rejection of the "mild
and equitable terms of peace" held out by the Parliament. The "Citizen"
announced that Britain's numerous fleets, disciplined armies, and brave
soldiers were prepared for the growing conflict, and he encouraged loyalists to assist British military forces: "We, the friends of her government,
are many in every province. . . . We must now lend a helping hand."[103]

New York's refugees urged prominent gentlemen to provide money
that would equip existing loyalist regiments and motivate the formation
of new loyalist regiments. "It is not sufficient," argued the "Citizen" in
June 1778, that "we stand prepared to rebel an attack." Rather, it is necessary that refugees assist by providing funds, which would "induce many

more to inlist than do at present." Although shielded from the cruel persecution of rebels within the peaceful asylum of New York City, the refugees
should help rescue the loyalists still trapped behind rebel lines.[104]

In 1778, New York's hard-liners began to petition directly to Lord Germain. Governor Tryon believed that the British government failed to
understand the reach and violence of the colonial rebellion. In September,
he asserted that "British forces on the continent were never in so good a
condition as at present to reconcile America to the dependency on Great
Britain." He argued that Manhattan, Staten Island, Long Island, and Rhode
Island provided ideal bases from which to launch "vigorous and hostile
depredations on the continent as would oblige America to call aloud for
the settlement offered by the King's commissioners."[105]

Tryon believed his "nearer view of His Majesty's affairs" offered him
a strategic vantage point, and in December, he recommended specific
retaliatory measures. He asked Germain to issue a reward of £1,000 for
every member of congress seized and delivered to the king's troops. He
also urged the British to send every American prisoner to England and
to require the rebels to pay for each prisoner's passage back to America.
He claimed that "one hundred men thus sent home would make more
impression than one thousand killed in the field of battle."[106]

These refugees pressed the British to launch a final decisive military
operation in the northern colonies. They maintained that the British could
crush the rebellion if the troops exerted themselves fully.[107] In November, New Jersey's Daniel Coxe supposed that a final campaign, "early and
properly reinforced and conducted with Vigor & Activity" would quell
the rebellion during the following summer."[108] John Potts observed that
"everybody expresses the greatest eagerness for action and only wishes
that vigorous measures may be adopted to ensure success.[109] In December,
he declared that "nothing but the most vigorous exertion of military force
will ever reduce this country to their dependence on Great Britain."[110]

Like the hard-liners, many regimental British officers advocated a more
punitive and indiscriminate war against rebel-centered communities. Sylvia Frey suggests that the majority of the three to four thousand officers
who served in America supported a program of "violent pacification."[111]
They disagreed vehemently with Clinton's official conciliatory policy,
which had gained the British neither the respect of the rebels nor additional territory. After the British defeat at Saratoga, Lieutenant Colonel
Thomas Sterling argued that "one more Spirited campaign may do yet,

but we must change our method. . . . Lenity has been tried without effect & I am sure had we burnt & destroyed Rebel property as we moved on the Rebellion would have been over." In July 1778, Major Patrick Campbell denounced moderation. He stated categorically that "nothing but the Bayonet & Torch will ever bring this country['s] People to reason. . . . Every offer of grace from Great Britain serves but to Heighten their insolence and augment their army as their leaders take care to instill in them that it proceeds from fear and not from love."[112] Because the Continental Congress had allied with Britain's natural enemy and treated the "most ample concessions with the most insolent contempt," Major Patrick Ferguson reasoned in August 1778, the British should abandon leniency and devise such a plan as would "disable an irreconcilable enemy."[113]

Despite loyalists' entreaties and their endorsements of British tenacity, the British army remained unprepared to parade its invincibility. Imperiled by the French fleet and surrounded by Washington's army, Clinton planned no major offensives except in the South. Just to hold the city, Clinton believed he needed at least 15,000 troops. He asked Germain for reinforcements to expand the field army by another 30,000 men, but Germain provided only an additional 6,600, due to arrive in the summer of 1779. Lacking sufficient troops and transports, Clinton explained that he could attempt no military initiative. Only in November did he send an expedition of 5,000 men—but it went to St. Lucia in the distant West Indies rather than to attack the nearby rebels.[114]

The departure of the peace commissioners in November 1778 provoked loyalists' fear of British evacuation from New York City. In fact, David Humphreys believed that the country people in New York had ignored the commission's conciliatory gestures because they dreaded the retaliation that would follow British retreat from New York City. Frightened of displaying their support, they found "it prudent to say little about it." The combination of British setbacks and British neglect along with the prospect of an indefinite war alienated many New York loyalists. In November, Major Ferguson remarked that the city contained a thousand sickly half-clothed men, mostly from New York, New Jersey, and Maryland. They lived "without discipline, precaution or hope" because they believed that the British prepared "to quit the country." One month later, another loyalist found it impossible to "dispel the gloom that prevails amongst the refugees."[115]

Uninformed of British military plans or the government's long-term strategy, even high-ranking loyalists worried about British evacuation. They feared that the British abandonment of Philadelphia signified an intention to surrender the North American colonies. The loyalists impressed upon British officers the sorry state of the rebels, which the British could exploit to their own advantage. In June 1778, Isaac Ogden declared that the rebellion "hangs by a slender thread." He claimed that news of the French alliance did not mean jubilation for all colonists. Many "detested" the French connection.[116]

On September 19, 1778, a mock conversation in the Royal Gazette had sought to quell widespread loyalist anxiety:

> Q: Will the British troops evacuate New York as they have done Philadelphia?
> A: No. As long as Great Britain is at war with France, she will choose the best ports on the Atlantic.[117]

The words said nothing about retrieving the rest of the rebellious colonies and so provided scant comfort to the loyalists. In his letter to Galloway, one loyalist suspected "that there is an intention of evacuating this place, if not immediately, at least, next spring." Ogden observed: "The idea prevails here that this country will be abandoned by the King's troops the next spring but I cannot entertain one so disgraceful & destructive to the British empire." In February 1779, Smith admitted that the idleness of the British troops had reinforced people's supposition that the British would evacuate New York City, which had raised the "universal despondency" of the multitudes.[118]

New York's leading men understood the importance of appeasing loyalists' apprehension. On November 7, Smith advised Tryon against leaving New York "as it would discourage the king's friends in the country and countenance the report of the flight of the army." On November 30, three days after the commissioners left New York, Tryon declared categorically that the "British have not the least intention to abandon their possessions at New York and its dependencies." In the winter and spring of 1779, loyalist essays by "Papinian" and "Clarendon" in the Royal Gazette countered rumors of British evacuation. The British, they argued, had as much intention of evacuating New York City as they had of abandoning London. As Britain's forces historically had caused enemies to shudder in every quarter of the globe, they would "make her domestic and foreign enemies surely rue their ungrateful perfidious conduct in the present contest." In

April 1779 "Britannicus" reminded his readers that Christmas has passed, spring had arrived, and still the British forces had not quit the continent or New York City. Every indication, he contended, "indicates a design permanently to hold it."[119]

In February 1778, the French alliance with the rebels unalterably transformed the scale and stakes of the war. By the summer of 1778, discouraged New Yorkers understood they faced a prolonged suspension of civil rule and a prolonged rebellion. After three major campaigns, the British had failed to suppress the rebellion or resolve the political crisis. The loyalists felt bitterness and shock at the staggering turn of events. They expressed chagrin and puzzlement at their very limited influence over the conduct of the war. Yet they did not repudiate the imperial connection. More then British tyranny, they dreaded the future of the colonies under rebel anarchy or French rule. In 1776, loyalists had warned colonists of the anarchic consequences of rebel victory. In 1778, they forecasted American enslavement under French Catholic despotism. Although the loyalists' appeals stressed British invincibility, their overzealous and frantic tone betrayed the loyalists' dismay at the turn of events. As British efforts shifted south, loyalists faced the miserable prospect of remaining in a permanently besieged city under garrison rule.

# 5 ❧ "DIVERSITY OF SENTIMENTS ON THE FUTURE CONDUCT OF THE WAR"
## Loyalist Clamor

> *I confess it to be the height of my wishes to see the King's troops and the loyalists supported and supporting one another. To see all party and professional distinctions done away—contending only who most shall evince their fidelity to the sovereign and affection to their native country.*
>
> —Scotus Americanus to the King's Printer, *Royal Gazette*, December 19, 1778

In October 1778, William Franklin's arrival in the city raised loyalist hopes and led to the formation of a hard-line coalition headed by prominent refugees. These refugees anticipated that Franklin could leverage his prewar position as royal governor of New Jersey to gain the trust of the British in order to place loyalist concerns at the center of British policy. Isaac Ogden hoped Franklin could revitalize the king's friends by convincing them that "throughout the continent . . . some attention is paid to them."[1]

Born a bastard son of a Philadelphia printer, William Franklin had risen up the political ranks under the tutelage of his father, Benjamin Franklin, and the brilliant lawyer Joseph Galloway. By 1753, he had received the clerkship of the Pennsylvania Assembly and became postmaster and then controller of Philadelphia. During his nearly six years in England, Franklin studied law at the Middle Temple, received an honorary MA degree from Oxford University for assisting with scientific experiments, and most important, cultivated the friendship of Lord Bute, second only to King George III in influence in the British government. On Bute's recommendation, the thirty-two-year-old William Franklin became New Jersey's royal governor in 1762, beginning his tenure just as the postwar recession hit New Jersey as severely as it had New York. As prices for grain, lumber, and other products fell, New Jersey farmers faced higher debts, and the number of debtors sent to prisons grew. When Parliament forbade the issuance of additional currency in 1764, New Jerseyites faced a severe shortage of circulating currency. William Franklin walked a careful line between the concerns of the debt-ridden electorate and the demands of the ministry. In November 1765, he wrote to his father: "I have had a difficult Part to manage so as to steer clear of giving any Umbrage to the People here, or of embarrassing myself with the ministry in England."[2]

Franklin saw the 1773 Boston Tea Party as an open defiance of governmental authority. He believed that if Boston promised to make due restitution and agreed to no longer hinder the landing of legally imported goods, the port could soon be reopened. However, if the Bostonians did not agree to this, they deserved the loss of commerce. The New Jersey Assembly defied his wishes and sent delegates to the Continental Congress in 1774. Hoping to bridge the breach between the colonies and the government, Franklin feared the creation of the congress would compel Britain to use military force to bring the colonies to submission. He worried that the "madness on this side of the water" would endanger the safety of government officials in America. In 1774, Benjamin Franklin unfairly reduced his son's moderate position to one of a sycophant, describing him as "a thorough courtier" who saw "everything with government eyes."[3]

In 1775 and 1776, when Franklin opposed extralegal rebel committees in New Jersey, he believed he supported the winning side. In 1778, Franklin recognized the dismal state of the king's supporters. He dreaded the consequences of rebel victory, as he knew it would compel the dissenters to forfeit their property, their position, and their influence. He determined that the British military could not suppress the rebellion without substantial and active loyalist involvement. With Isaac Ogden, he expressed frustration at Clinton's "delicate ideas of Carrying on the war." Like Governor Tryon, he despised the persistence of royal pardons to rebels. If the British government insisted on circulating the pardons, they should be "accompanied with menaces and warnings and followed by blows, till the Congress called out for negotiations." Franklin supposed that unless British forces followed the example of the rebel leaders and executed those who assisted rebel forces, the rebels would continue to murder the king's loyal subjects.[4]

Franklin's degrading experience of twenty-eight months in rebel prisons in Connecticut contributed to his uncompromising stance toward the leaders of the rebellion. Franklin neither suffered rosy-eyed illusions about rebel leaders nor held high hopes from the British government. In a letter to Germain in November, he expressed bitterness that the British had made no effort to exchange him until September 1778. During his entire imprisonment, he raged, he had not received a single letter from any British official.[5]

Franklin condemned British retreats from New Jersey and Philadelphia. He believed that the British should have emulated the course long taken by the rebels by immediately disarming, banishing, or destroying their enemy. Following conquest, the British should have armed loyalists and established civil rule to stabilize each reclaimed area.[6]

In December 1778, Franklin tried to persuade Clinton to attack Washington's troops in New Jersey so that he could reestablish royal government in the colony. Franklin believed American civilian leaders could better win the affection of colonists who resented rule by military foreigners. Each liberated colony would provide a base for further attacks on rebel strongholds. Franklin also hoped to augment his position by serving as governor of one of the reclaimed colonies.[7] But Clinton rejected Franklin's supplications. He feared he could not control independent loyalist units made up of frustrated civilians, many of whom operated outside established channels. Years later, in his reminiscences of the American rebellion, Clinton expressed his specific opposition to the refugees' coalition. The vengeance of these men who "thirsted for indiscriminate retaliation," he felt, would introduce "a system of war horrid beyond conception." Their actions would preclude reconciliation between Britain and her colonies.[8]

In October, a group of refugees implored William Eden to appoint Franklin as the new royal governor of New York. Eden rejected the "absurd" petition and noted that British troops "must go out and recover a colony . . . before any governor is appointed."[9] The British ministry refused to substitute the English-born Tryon, who retained nominal power, with a militant-minded American who would demand a voice in devising political and military strategy. In the spring of 1779, the British would replace Tryon with a figure who had served as an officer in the British military in North America for over two decades, Sir James Robertson.[10]

Franklin persisted in his efforts to gain an official position in the British government. In November, before the commissioners left for London, Franklin desired an office as spokesperson for the loyalists. He explained that "some sensible, spirited, popular person in whom [loyalists] could confide" would unify loyalists' support and "compel the Congress to a negotiation." But Franklin received no encouragement in response to his second request for an official position. In effect, Franklin demanded authority on par with the British military establishment, but the commissioners refused, unwilling to partner with vengeful loyalists.[11]

Strategically situated within the inner circle of British command, William Smith Jr. probably influenced William Eden's rejection of Franklin's request for governorship. He specifically advised against Franklin because he feared that Franklin would extend the breach between the colonies and Britain and foreclose any possibility of reunion. He distrusted deeply what he called the "diversity of sentiments on the future conduct of the war."[12] Smith predicted that banished loyalists like Franklin would become "vindictive foes" and would launch a war of "undistinguished desolation" to ensure rebel destruction.[13] He disapproved of Franklin as well as other unyielding refugees such as Martin Howard, former chief justice of North Carolina, who denounced Britain's conciliatory gestures and stood, Smith believed, "too much for desolation."[14]

Smith feared that a war of destruction would sabotage the potential for restoring civil government in the colony. He had shunned the meetings of the refugees, for he suspected they would "indelicately interfere with the commander in chief." He believed Franklin and some of his New Jersey supporters such as Isaac Ogden were "very sore and vindictive." He abhorred the idea of a "predatory war under the spirit of revenge." No person informed of the divided, exhausted, and debilitated condition of the revolted colonies would believe it possible to maintain the rebellion. He insisted that the rebel cause approached collapse. Clearly, the conciliatory policy of the British government appeared "too liberal and low toned" for Franklin's militant group.[15]

Many New York loyalists distrusted Smith. His links to high British officials made him suspect to loyalists who remained outside the coveted circle of British government in New York City. Indeed, New York chief justice Thomas Jones revealed his distaste for Smith's maneuvering. Smith, he remarked, was "in all companies, at all times, and upon all occasions with one or the other of the commissioners. . . . He became the favorite, the confidant, the bosom friend of Eden." In fact, Smith's official influence remained limited. When he prepared a proclamation that stipulated that each colony would receive a seat in the British Parliament, the Carlisle commissioners removed the provision. They remained unprepared to grant the colonies such a high level of involvement at the center of the empire. Again, when Smith proposed a prohibition against employing slaves of persons living within British lines, perhaps as a means of regaining his own two runaway slaves, Tryon struck it out of the draft. The garrison's need for laborers and sailors, both black and white, took precedence over loyalist slave owners' anxiety.[16]

In December 1778, the loyalist hard-liners under Franklin formally broke off from the moderates who hoped to reunite the empire by a diplomatic settlement. In a petition addressed to the Carlisle Commission, twenty-three hard-liners expressed their frustration with martial rule in New York City, their demand for greater protection against rebel persecution, and their desire for greater military force to suppress the rebellion. Ogden observed that the petition marked the loyalists' rejection of their subordinate role in the rebellion: "You will perceive by the address to the Commissioners . . . that the Friends of Government dare begin to speak."[17]

New York's refugees concluded their petition to the commissioners by criticizing British treatment of loyalists and rebels alike. The former remained neglected, while the latter received undue consideration. With obvious bitterness, the petitioners observed that "if the same pains had been taken for [loyalists'] support and encouragement which have been employed to reclaim the rebellious," the rebellion would have collapsed. The petitioners emphasized that many faithful and loyal subjects remained dispersed behind rebel lines throughout the colonies. Thousands awaited only encouragement to assist the British troops in ending the rebellion.[18]

As General Clinton faced the hard-liners' criticism in New York, General Howe confronted a heated parliamentary inquiry in London in the spring of 1779. In a bold series of attacks, loyalist exile Joseph Galloway accused Howe of ill-treating the Philadelphia loyalists, despising their help, and thereby missing opportunities to prevail in the colonies. In a pamphlet responding to Galloway's charges, Howe minimized the soldiers' misconduct and justified his unwillingness to depend on American loyalists. Whereas Galloway pointed to soldiers' indiscriminate violence against civilians, Howe minimized the frequency, extent, and impact of such incidents. Howe retorted that there were few, and not of an "enormous nature." In response to Galloway's claim that "wives and daughters were violently polluted by the lustful brutality of the lowest of mankind," Howe answered: "I do not recollect or have heard of more than one imputed to the soldiery, and that was said to have committed in [West] Chester County, in province of New York. The criminal was secured; an enquiry immediately took place; but the accuser refused to prosecute."[19]

Whereas Galloway emphasized the numbers of the loyalists and their readiness to fight with the British, Howe highlighted his suspicion of their motivations. He explained that Galloway's faith in the loyalty of the Americans remained "either ill-founded or so much exaggerated." To Galloway's announcement that Howe had refused "repeated attempts made by bodies of men to form themselves in arms, and to assist him in suppression the Rebellion," Howe answered that the high desertion rate of the loyalist regiments made them untrustworthy. To Galloway's assertion of the inhabitants' willingness to provision British troops during British governance of Philadelphia, Howe rejoined that people's assistance did not arise from allegiance to the Crown but from their desire to receive British pay for their supplies. The Philadelphia loyalists, Howe explained, had not supported the British forces in sufficient numbers. In addition, he added, only a fourth of loyalist volunteers were American-born. Half of the volunteers were Irish and the remainder Scots and Germans. Clearly, the British could not depend upon native-born American colonists' allegiance: "Much might be said upon the state of loyalty, and the principles of loyalty in America. Some are loyal from principle; many from interest; many from resentment; many wish for peace, but are indifferent which side prevails; and there are others who wish success to Great-Britain, from a recollection of the happiness they enjoyed under her government."[20] Until the last days of the war, the British struggled to define—and find— loyal subjects motivated by unselfish interests.

The Seven Years' War had only reinforced the British officer's disdain of the provincial soldier. In 1760, one British officer expressed the prevailing opinion: "The Provincials [are] sufficient to work our Boats, drive our Waggons, to fell Trees, and do the Works that in inhabited Countrys are performed by Peasants." In 1775, a British surgeon in Boston had a laundry list of criticisms about the American colonists: they were "a drunken, canting, lying, praying, hypocritical rabble without order, subjection, discipline, or cleanliness." Many British officers considered loyalist troops poorly trained, inexpertly led, and generally unreliable.[21]

## Arming Loyalists

Without foreign allies to share the burden of war, the British turned not only to white but also black loyalists. For the first time in North America, the British recruited blacks as soldiers.[22] In November 1775, Lord Dunmore's proclamation in Virginia directed all "indented Servants, Negroes, or others . . . that are able or willing to bear Arms" to defect to the British side. Dunmore did not intend a general emancipation of slaves in the American colonies. Indeed, his declaration included servants indentured to rebels as well as slaves. The enormous difficulty in subduing the rebels in Williamsburg, Virginia, had compelled him to issue the dramatic proclamation. Dunmore wanted to weaken the rebel leaders by drawing away their slaves. He hoped the blacks would augment British military manpower in North America, particularly in the West Indies. Like other British officials, he assumed that because of their dark skins and equatorial origins, the blacks could better withstand the heat in the southern colonies and in the Caribbean, and spare the lives of British soldiers.[23]

From the more than 800 blacks who reached the British side, Dunmore formed the "Ethiopian Regiment," made up of 120 slaves owned by rebel masters in Virginia and Maryland, as well as slaves from loyalist households.[24] The majority of the Ethiopian Regiment died of fever and disease when they sought haven from Virginia's rebels aboard the cramped and unsanitary conditions on Dunmore's warship in Chesapeake Bay. In the summer of 1776, Dunmore abandoned the regiment to join General Howe in New York City.[25]

In February 1776, Major General Clinton led British troops on a failed mission in North Carolina. When some slaves sought refuge within British lines, he determined to create a company, employing them as "Pioneers and on working Parties."[26] Clinton provided the slaves with provisions and clothing and ordered the officers to treat them "with tenderness & humanity." However, unlike Dunmore, Clinton never intended to employ blacks in active combat. In the summer of 1776, Clinton left North Carolina to join General Howe in New York City. The seventy-one men from the Black Pioneers who accompanied him would construct fortifications, dig trenches, and maintain the upkeep of barracks and other buildings in the city.[27]

In 1777, black enlistments in New York City's loyalist regiments provoked censure from British officers. On March 14, Alexander Innes, newly assigned inspector general of provincial forces, reporting that "Negroes, Mulattoes, Indians, and Sailors" joined loyalist units, posed a critical question to the commander in chief: "Shall they be discharged and orders given none in future admitted?" Two days later, General Howe issued an order that explicitly forbade "Negroes, Mollatoes, and other Improper Persons" from participating in combat alongside loyalist troops. The requirement that loyalist regiments "be put on the most respectable footing," akin to British regulars, required that "improper persons . . . be Immediately discharged." Howe's low opinion of blacks, inherited from racial attitudes intrinsic to British society, became apparent during the British governance of Philadelphia. In 1778, he expected blacks only to "attend the Scavangers, Assist in Cleaning the Streets & Removing all Newsiances being thrown into the Streets."[28]

After assuming his new role as commander in chief, General Clinton, on June 30, 1779, took another erratic step toward arming blacks. Undoubtedly, black eagerness to serve kept the pressure on the British commanders. Clinton guaranteed "to every Negro who shall desert the rebel standard, full security to follow within these lines any occupation which he may think proper." He promised every rebel-owned slave, man or woman, freedom inside British lines. He did not intend to establish slave regiments. He certainly did not seek to incite a slave uprising. He sought only to teach the southern rebels a lesson without jeopardizing British slaveholding interests in the American colonies or the West Indies.[29]

As much as they did the blacks, the British initially viewed the white loyalists only as an expedient measure in response to a crisis situation. During the summer and winter of 1776, in response to petitions from prominent loyalists, General Howe selectively issued a few warrants to enable them to organize and command loyalist regiments. But Howe limited the extent of loyalist military involvement. He favored New York and New Jersey loyalists, some of whom were veterans of provincial or regular units from the Seven Years' War. In the summer of 1776, New York Councillor Oliver DeLancey raised the New York Loyalists; New Jersey's attorney general, Cortlandt Skinner, recruited the New Jersey Loyalists; and veteran British officer Lieutenant Colonel Robert Rogers from New Hampshire enlisted the Queen's Rangers.[30] In the winter of 1776–77, Howe issued warrants to Governor William Tryon's secretary, New York–born Edmund Fanning, to raise the King's American Regiment. In addition, he gave warrants to influential New York merchant John Bayard for the King's Orange Rangers, to Virginia-born Beverly Robinson for the Loyal American Regiment, and to British veteran Brigadier General Montfort Browne for the Prince of Wales American Regiment.[31] By the spring of 1777, approximately three thousand loyalists had enlisted in these new regiments.[32]

Germain's refusal to send sufficient European reinforcements compelled General Howe to reappraise white colonists' potential to serve with British regulars. In February 1777, he modified the pardons to encourage rebel desertion from the Continental Army. Howe had previously made pardons available to any colonist who agreed to take an oath of allegiance to the king. In exchange, Howe offered hazy assurance of British protection and His Majesty's approbation. The colonists "speedily returning to their just Allegiance were promised a free and general Pardon, and were invited to accept, not only the Blessings of Peace, but a secure Enjoyment of their Liberty and Properties, upon the true Principles of the Constitution." These recruits would stand against the "lawless influence and power" that sustained the unnatural rebellion. The new pardons promised bounties and land to young men ready to fight with British forces. Each man was to serve a period for three years, or "during the present unhappy rebellion in America." American-born colonists could join a loyalist corps, enlist in the British establishment, or return to England. Irish-born Americans had to join the British army or return to Ireland.[33]

Between February and March, the Royal American Volunteers, King's Loyal Orange Rangers, Colonel John Morris, and the Prince of Wales Royal American Volunteers all posted recruitment notices in the *New-York Gazette and Weekly Mercury*. Similar in tone, each notice listed particular rewards for enlistment. Men in Lieutenant Colonel John Bayard's regiment received forty shillings, along with new clothes, arms, and accoutrements. Those serving in Colonel Norris's regiment received five dollars bounty and a new set of clothes with a hat, shirt, shoes, and stockings. In addition, once the rebellion had been suppressed, each man could redeem a deed for fifty acres of land in New York province. In addition to five dollars in bounty, the Prince of Wales Royal American Volunteers were promised "100 acres of valuable land on the Mississippi free from incumbrance." "Bringers," those who brought additional recruits, received an additional two dollars for each one.[34]

White and black men answered British notices in the spring and summer of 1777. Many of these newcomers were single men, some of whom came to assist the British enterprise and others, doubtless, to collect their

bounties. Many came from rebel-controlled New Jersey or from the hinterlands of New York. Those who entered British lines with arms probably
deserted from rebel forces. In March, Colonel Stuart noticed that rebels
deserted to the British side by the "50s and 100s." Gaine observed forty
men from Dutchess County who joined "Beverly Robinson's Battalion,
which fills amazingly." Captain John Peebles saw "deserters and blacks"
coming "in parties with their arms" inside British lines "almost every day."
In April, Gaine commented that nothing was "stirring" in the city with
the notable exception of deserters coming in from the country. On April
17, forty-three men came in from Poughkeepsie, north of the city. The
next day, two hundred more came from Dutchess County. Lord Howe's
aide noticed that, driven by the lack of food and clothing, roughly eight
deserters arrived daily. In May, thirty-two men deserted from New Jersey
and thirty-three from Dutchess County. Lieutenant Loftus Cliffe claimed
that the rebels lost men as quickly as they raised them. Indeed, he avowed,
"this Town swarms with them." In June, Peebles noticed "deserters coming in as usual." In July, Gaine observed "sundry deserters" entering the
city from the surrounding countryside.[35]

By December 1778, British effective forces numbered approximately
33,000, of whom 7,320 were loyalists and 25,659 British and Hessians.[36]
Loyalists urged the government to provide greater incentives for loyalist recruitment and to provision and arm the new regiments adequately.
New Jersey's Isaac Ogden denounced the "scandalous neglect & ill treatment" of the loyalist corps, which had "prevented thousands from joining
the Kings army." When assured of arms, Ogden asserted, "thousands of
oppressed and persecuted friends of government would take refuge here
and very soon form such a body of men that Washington with his whole
force would be afraid to approach." In New York City alone, he claimed,
the British could recruit nearly ten thousand men.[37]

In December 1778, Governor Tryon asked that "higher bounties be
given to provincial recruits and the clothing of provincial regiments (at
least I wish of those raised in this province) be sent from England to the
commanding officers of said corps." Although Tryon did not specify the
amount of bounty loyalist recruits should receive, he clearly believed that
the established bounty of sixpence a day was insufficient. In January, for a
meeting intended to "take into consideration certain provincial matters,"
he prepared a list of regulations to promote loyalist recruitment. In addition to forty pounds annually to each recruit, he requested two nurses for

the hospital, funds for hospital expenses, stationery for the orderly room, and three guineas' bounty for each loyalist recruit. He also requested one guinea as a reward for the apprehension of every deserter.[38]

Reverend Inglis also believed that Britain needed to raise more loyalist troops to win the war. The loyalist regiments simultaneously added to British strength and weakened the enemy by drawing away potential rebel recruits. Inglis hoped that the British would recognize the "expediency of enlisting as many Americans as possible." The government's weak efforts to raise and provision loyalist regiments represented "gross mismanagement" and "should have been attended to from the beginning more than it was."[39]

In response to these repeated exhortations, many of New York's refugees sought warrants to establish loyalist regiments in 1778. Issued by the commander in chief, such warrants gave the recipient authority and funds to organize a military company comprising a requisite number of men. Once the officer had assembled sufficient men to complete the company, he received ammunition, bounties, and provisions from the British military establishment. In March, Captain John Campbell from Staten Island offered to lead an excursion into Bergen County, New Jersey, with a party of a hundred men to "take by surprise that vile pack of robbers and march them prisoners to Paulus Hook." In April, Abraham Woolsey informed Clinton that 160 men were ready to join the king's forces between New Windsor and Tarrytown, New York, if the commander would send a sloop up the Hudson for them. In May, Richard Swanwick wished to "accompany a detachment against Mr. Washington because [he knew] the country & inhabitants from many miles thereabouts and wish[ed] to be of service to the British army." Swanwick hoped also to recover his "unhappy family," trapped behind rebel lines. In September, John Chalmers of Maryland offered a "considerable number of provincial troops" for the king's service. In October, Robert Cooke from New Jersey sought to recruit a company.[40]

But the highest British officials doubted the efficacy of loyalist regiments and issued only a limited number of warrants. Since the funds for loyalist regiments came from the contingent money for "serviceable expenditure" and did not issue directly from Parliament, the British commander in chief hesitated to award warrants without assurance that the troops justified the disbursement.[41]

In January 1778, General Henry Clinton expressed the prevailing sentiment about American soldiers: "Provincials, if not sustained by regular troops are not to be trusted."[42] Clinton felt comfortable only when the loyalists acted as scouts, cut roads, hauled supplies, constructed fortifications, and performed other ancillary tasks. These tasks did not require high levels of training or discipline. He believed that the colonists had performed these services adequately during the Seven Years' War. But employing "provincials" as a "considerable portion of our acting force . . . on services of moment" was another matter entirely. The loyalists would only weaken British regulars. Ironically, Clinton would concede the growing discipline and strength of rebel soldiers, yet he remained dubious of the potential of loyalist regiments.[43]

Clinton also begrudged his limited sway over loyalist recruits. In October 1778, he wanted to send Hessians and loyalists for service to the southern colonies, as their loss to the main army in the North would "not be so much felt." But Massachusetts loyalist Edward Winslow, muster-master general and hence a precise barometer of opinion among the soldiers, cautioned that many loyalists had enlisted on the condition that they would not serve beyond New York and New Jersey. Ambitious loyalist officers eager to receive bounties for enlistments had "seduc'd men" to service by promising them that they would never serve in other areas. Winslow warned the commander that the loyalists would not tolerate British efforts to transfer them to unknown places, as this was "unjust & not consistent with the original compact." Compelled to honor the contractual commitment the British had made to loyalist recruits, Clinton resented his inability to command the loyalist regiments in the same manner that he commanded British units.[44]

Many British officers commonly regarded loyalist regiments as incompetent and unworthy of the same treatment as British regulars. They expressed the professional's disregard for the amateur. Major Frederick Mackenzie's remarks on New Jersey loyalist Cortlandt Skinner were typical. Appointed brigadier general of the New Jersey Volunteers, Skinner had raised 1,101 men from New York, New Jersey, and Pennsylvania by May 1778. Mackenzie observed dismissively: "The Brigadier is a very good man, and a loyal subject, but has no idea of moving even . . . [a] small . . . body of troops, and is therefore a very unfit person to be entrusted with the Command of a thousand men."[45]

The late eighteenth-century British army was a full-time, highly disciplined organization that had matured over a century's worth of warfare. Those who occupied the highest commands, such as major general and lieutenant general, usually came from the upper crust of society. The regimental officers, including the lieutenants, captains, and majors, came from the country gentry and mercantile classes. Accustomed to deference, they understood authority and respected those who commanded it. As a group, they disdained not only the lower orders of society but the American colonists in general.[46]

In contrast, the loyalist officers in New York were military amateurs who had only involved themselves in warfare to defend their homes. They appeared sloppy and awkward and hardly deserving of the same treatment accorded to British regulars. No sharp distinction divided the colonial officers from the rank and file. Typically, the officers lived in the same neighborhoods as their men and commanded their allegiance through ties of familiarity. Unlike the British soldier who served from a sense of duty and the fear of disciplinary punishment, the loyalist served for a contract: for a stated period of time, for a specified purpose, and for a definite rate of pay.[47]

Foremost, British officers continued to suspect that solely self-interest motivated loyalists. In February 1778, one Philadelphian reported that so many officers came in to recruit the new levies that General Howe "was apprehensive of fraud & refused to inlist them." From New York, Clinton lamented repeatedly that the "whole provincial line is over-officered." Later in the month, he complained of a major in Oliver DeLancey's corps who "is now absent and never did any duty as such." In December 1779, Lord Rawdon, commanding the Volunteers of Ireland, complained that the loyalist corps was "loaded with a number of officers, many of them Irish, entirely without interest, without connections, and without money to enable them to raise men."[48]

The disorderly behavior in some loyalist regiments authenticated the suspicions of Howe and Clinton that the colonists were an unruly and undisciplined lot. In 1777, Howe discharged loyalists from the Prince of Wales American Volunteers for harboring deserters from His Majesty's ships of war.[49] In July 1778, a private in Brigadier General DeLancey's regiment, Bartholomew McDonough, suffered death for raping the widow Phebe Coe and her daughter. McDonough laid "violent hands on her, threw her on the bed, and there by force and against her inclination and notwithstanding she urged every thing she could to prevent him, he not only penetrated but she believes emitted in her body." Another soldier,

Jacob Hall, deserted from the First Battalion of New Jersey Volunteers. He had enlisted to serve in western New Jersey, and because the army had left that part of the country, he insisted his oath was not binding. Caleb Boyle of the 2nd Battalion of New Jersey Volunteers enlisted in another corps to receive an additional bounty.[50] In 1779, when suspicions arose about the many rebel deserters who made up Captain John Ferdinand Dalziel Smyth's company, Smyth defended their allegiance: "I conceive a great number of men who have deserted from the Rebels have been loyalists from the beginning, and forced into their service, and who have deserted from them the first opportunity."[51] Local residents accused two soldiers, William Green of the Queen's Rangers and Thomas Salem of the Bucks County Dragoons, of robbing three houses on Long Island and raping Hannah Dray's seventy-year-old mother-in-law.[52] A year later, after repeated complaints from inhabitants in Kingsbridge, Clinton disbanded another loyalist regiment, the Emmerich Chasseurs.[53] The farmers complained that Captain Emmerich's men had not only searched their houses on various pretenses and committed "wanton barefaced robbery" but had also seized young men under pretense of having the authority to press them into the service.[54]

In November 1779, upon protests from esteemed loyalists such as Samuel Seabury, Clinton purged the Queen's Rangers, under the command of Robert Rogers, of "undesirable officers" who had condoned plundering. While an officer in the Rangers, a Mr. Brandon had accepted a bribe of twenty-five guineas from a soldier to grant him a fraudulent discharge. When the captured soldier, apprehended as a deserter, confessed his wrongdoing, Brandon refunded the money. Another officer, Captain Griffith, robbed a man of grain at Newtown on Long Island. According to the inspector general of loyalist forces, Alexander Innes, Captain Eagles cheated several men out of their bounty and behaved like a blackguard, "drinking[,] playing cards & with his men was look'd upon in the regiment as a lyar and coward."[55]

Clinton continued to dismiss the value of loyalist military strength in New York City. In his letters to political statesmen in London in 1780 and 1781, he explained that he lacked sufficient troops to attack General Washington. In September 1780, he complained to William Eden that he had only thirteen thousand troops. "The number I have," he explained, "is by no means adequate to the defense of this post." Clinton discounted the value of the loyalist militia companies to hold New York City if the regulars were sent to attack Washington. In January 1780, General James Pattison had conscripted 2,662 loyalists, formed into 40 militia companies, to guard the city during the severe winter. These militia units served until August 5, 1782. But Clinton doubted their reliability. He supposed that these poorly trained men, "merchants, tradesmen, and persons attached to the different army and navy departments," could not live up to the standards of professional soldiers.[56]

Brigadier General Montfort Browne stood apart in his criticism of British policy toward loyalist recruitment. In January 1778, Browne declared that the colonists, from their numerous connections, have a "very extensive influence and by this means, greatly assist and promote the cause of Government, for it is natural to mankind to think favorable of and become reconciled to such measures as their relations and friends are engaged in supporting." Indeed, if the same number of loyalist soldiers had been raised as there were Hessians in British pay, Browne claimed, "the Rebellion would, most certainly, at this day, not exist." Half the amount spent on the Hessians, he argued, would produce double the number of provincials. Moreover, a recruit raised in the colonies not only added to British forces but detached one from the rebel cause.[57]

## Commercial Compromise

The British military administration was more accustomed—and therefore more receptive—to regarding loyalists as commercial allies than as military partners. Benefitting from their long-standing experience as middlemen of the empire, the loyalist merchants were not ignored when they lobbied on behalf of mercantile interests.

In 1776, the British commanders' reluctance to depend on the loyalty of the New Yorkers had led them to enforce the Prohibitory Act in the city.[58] This meant that the city's merchants could not export merchandise from the port without special export licenses. They could still import goods from England but could not export to Great Britain or her dependencies.

Impatient for the restoration of civil rule, New York's merchants petitioned the Howes through Tryon. They asked that the commanders offer trading concessions to the city, which had clearly demonstrated its allegiance. However, when Tryon presented the merchants' petition to Serle, he patiently replied that it was "more politic to defer presenting the Petition at present." He advised Tryon to postpone presenting the petition to His Majesty's commissioners because a direct refusal would make them "unpopular" in the colony. Familiar with the loyalist expectations, Tryon explained that it was his "civil duty" to present the petition without postponement, even for a day. But Serle stressed that normal operations in the port could only resume after the "Reduction of the Rebel-Army." As he left Tryon's apartment, Serle insisted that he was not opposed to opening the port, asserting that the "Difficulty only rests in the Time."[59]

The Howes' instructions empowered them to suspend the Prohibitory Act only after they had declared the colony at His Majesty's peace and had reconvened the colonial assembly. Once the assembly accepted the legislative supremacy of Parliament, trade restrictions would no longer apply. Since the city remained under martial law and the colony of New York was not yet fully restored to British jurisdiction, the Howes did not consider reopening the port.

In suspending civil rule and enforcing the Prohibitory Act in the city, the Howes did not think they were arbitrarily imposing long-term martial rule upon British subjects. Military rule was only an "expedient" measure that would secure headquarters until the British crushed rebel opposition. Upon receiving the loyalist request to open the city's port, the Howes regretted that they could not yet comply:

> Sorry as we are to disappoint the expectations and zeal of any of His
> Majesty's loyal subjects, when we consider how small though important a part of this extensive province is yet professedly in allegiance,
> we cannot with any degree of propriety declare the whole at peace;
> and to open the trade of this province partially, even could any trade
> be carried on, would in the present situation of affairs be productive
> of no good effect and might introduce such abuses as would defeat
> the intentions of the Prohibitory Act.[60]

Their justification for enforcing the Prohibitory Act resembled their reasons for delaying the restoration of civil government. The Howes worried about opening the port "in the present situation" when the entire colony was not at His Majesty's peace and when such a "small" portion had professed allegiance. Unable to authenticate the loyalty of the inhabitants, they feared the possibility of civilians smuggling precious goods to nearby rebel-controlled areas in New York, New Jersey, and Connecticut. They also worried about the "abuses" that would ensue if seamen deserted the naval forces for the lure of quick profit in mercantile ships. Military requirements for provisions and sailors superseded civilian needs. For the moment, merchants who did not receive special export licenses could only sell their goods to the military and to the large number of loyalist refugees daily flocking to the city.[61]

On July 17, 1777, General William Howe appointed Andrew Elliot as superintendent of New York City to regulate imports and exports between British ports. Upon orders from Howe, Elliot established stringent rules governing the entry and export of goods in the city. The masters of merchantmen had to make a proper entry of their cargo upon arrival in New York City, store the goods in specified warehouses, and dispose of the articles only after receiving permission from Elliot. Only captains favored by a certificate from Elliot could have use of the city's port.[62]

During British rule of Philadelphia in 1777 and 1778, New York's favored merchants worked in collaboration with Philadelphian merchant Tench Coxe to sell all types of items demanded by the army or the city's civilian population. In March 1778, Coxe explained to New York merchant Isaac Low that Howe wanted "to see the Army, Navy, & inhabitants supplied nevertheless, & intends to grant special licenses for that purpose to persons in whom he can confide." These articles included rum, molasses, tea, and salt, as well as woolens, linens, silks, buttons, and looking glasses. Since Coxe charged 5 percent commission on all goods, his profits remained proportional to the size and value of the cargoes consigned him.[63]

Coxe's distant familial connection with important civilians such as Joseph Galloway as well his commercial partnerships in New York City stood him well both during British governance of Philadelphia and after the British evacuation of the city. Galloway, superintendent of customs during British rule, granted to Coxe favors denied to other merchants. When the British abandoned Philadelphia in June 1778, Coxe shed his loyalist leanings and adopted a pragmatic attitude. On June 10, he considered himself "likely if permitted" to become a good American. While Coxe made flush profits under the British and readily compromised his political ideals under the rebel government, most of New York's merchants confronted a different predicament.[64]

The few merchants who received the patronage of well-placed British officials profited handsomely. Like Coxe, New Yorkers Isaac Low and Abraham Cuyler thrived. In November 1777, they shipped a single consignment to British-ruled Philadelphia for the amount of £3,000. Scottish merchant Neil Jamieson benefited from Elliot's patronage. Jamieson, a partner of the Glasgow firm Glassford, Gordon, Monteath and Company, left his properties in Norfolk, Virginia, and fled to New York City in September 1776. In addition to a distillery and goods stores, he lost twenty-six houses, which had brought him an annual rent of £430. In 1777, Jamieson resented his lack of place in the British administration when "he saw people daily arriving over who had been appointed to beneficial employments." None, he claimed, had borne his proportion of losses. But Jamieson soon re-established his mercantile business. By 1778, Jamieson advertised his wares in New York City. In 1779, his confidence led him to try to ship illegally to St. Eustatius. Jamieson appeared unscathed by his brush with illicit trade. In December 1782, he sat with former New York Councillors Henry White and Hugh Wallace to provide recommendations on the economic conditions of the city.[65]

Facing a prolonged military jurisdiction under restrictive trading conditions, New York's merchants imagined economic disaster if not granted more liberal trading terms. Most did not have the proper connections or sufficient stature to receive British concessions and therefore suffered a dramatic decline in their circumstances. These merchants repeatedly asked the peace commissioners for a relaxation of trade restrictions. Their fortunes worsened in July 1778, when the French fleet threatened New York City. All import and export trade ceased for a month. Seeking relief on September 2, 1778, New York's merchants submitted a formal petition to the peace commissioners. Referring to themselves as "royal and dutiful subjects," they expressed formulaic gratitude for "His Majesty's paternal goodness to all his subjects" and made two requests. First, under British auspices, they naturally expected a restoration of "peace, harmony and legal government" in the colonies. They hoped that the government would soon restore "those inestimable blessings to suffering thousands upon so firm and constitutional a basis, as will insure its duration to the remotest period." The merchants hoped civil government would bring stable trading conditions and surer profits. Second, the merchants described their ruinous state on account of the stoppage of shipping and asked for the immediate suspension of the Prohibitory Act. They explained that the embargo had led an immense quantity of valuable merchandise to accumulate and remain wasted in the city. As a result of the Prohibitory Act, there were, in the summer of 1778, 261 merchant ships, with an aggregate cargo of 35,000 tons, lying idle in the harbor, in addition to exportable goods gathered in the city's warehouses. New York merchants wanted permission to export items not required by the garrison to Great Britain and other British-controlled ports.[66]

Merchants Robert Alexander and John Miller submitted wisely that they, as industrious and honest loyalists, did not wish to burden the British government. They wanted to benefit their country by the export of British manufactures and at the same time provide supplies for Britain's "gallant sons" to enable them "to combat and defeat the most inveterate foe." Indeed, by engaging in a "liberal and manly plan of commerce," the merchants would assist the British military forces.[67]

In his reflection on the state of the rebellion, entitled "Observations," Elliot promoted the suspension of the Prohibitory Act as the first step toward the revival of civil rule. He believed in the potential of commerce to draw in many who suffered miserably under the rebels. The resumption of trade in recovered ports, he argued, would "furnish the people at large . . . with the fairest opportunity of abandoning their leaders." He supposed also that an established "mercantile plan" would pacify merchants "who are eager to resume their former stations."[68]

However, Elliot concluded his "Observations" with a word of caution: an "improper enaction" of a mercantile plan, he noted, "might retard the submission of the provinces," as colonists would misunderstand the gesture as British "Relinquishment" of the colonies. Elliot feared the consequences of uncoupling economic privileges and political liberties in New York. Both represented the rewards guaranteed to loyal British subjects. He feared that a liberal economic policy would contrast starkly with British military rule. Some colonists would conclude that the economic concessions granted to merchants signaled Britain's commitment to protect only commercial interests. Although some New Yorkers would gain from increased commercial opportunities, the establishment of economic freedom without the accompanying civil courts and legislative government would alienate many others.[69]

With approval from Germain, in November 1778 the peace commissioners suspended the Prohibitory Act. Germain saw the suspension as a means to encourage wavering Americans to support the king and foster desertion from Washington's army through the lure of prosperity. The commissioners thought that a partial opening of the New York City port would confirm Great Britain's long-term commitment to the colonies. The economic relief allowed to New York merchants, they explained, would create a "strong impression on the royal colonies, as a proof of our having some permanent system."[70]

The commissioners also expected the suspension of the Prohibitory Act to benefit common people in New York. Better supplied with essentials if merchants could trade with the British West Indies and with Canada, the city would lessen its dependence upon food from Cork, Ireland, more than three thousand miles away. New Yorkers could import wheat and flour from Quebec and fish from the Newfoundland coast. The city would thus avoid "very serious and unhappy consequences" if provision fleets from Ireland should be delayed.[71]

The commissioners gratified New York's merchants further by authorizing privateers to seize French vessels. In August 1778, Governor Tryon received the coveted commission that granted him authority to issue additional letters of marque. Between March 1777 and August 1778, he had already authorized 185 privateers to make reprisals against rebel ships. Over six thousand sailors had participated in these operations. Between September 1778 and March 1779, the additional privateers licensed by Tryon brought in bounty valued at £600,000. In February, Isaac Ogden exulted that "upwards of 70 privateers are now cruising out of this port, they have been very successful, & must totally destroy the trade of the United States." In March, Tryon reported the good news to Germain: "Seldom a day passes without a prize by the Privateers."[72]

Tryon thought that people's uneasiness had abated with the potential of acquiring substantial goods from rebel ships. In September, as Tryon administered oaths of allegiance to inhabitants on the eastern end of Long Island, he observed that "acrimony of the opposition is . . . much softened" and attributed the change in attitude directly to "the late concessions of government."[73] In February 1779, Tryon wrote to Germain that the "adventurers in the letters of Marque derive great comfort and encouragement" from the expressions of His Majesty's satisfaction. The following month, Tryon promised generous bounties for "seamen, shipcarpenters and other landsmen," who wished to participate "in short and successful cruises against his Majesty's enemies."[74]

The influx of consumer goods from captured cargoes had a dual impact upon business in New York City. It created further opportunities for the well-placed of New York's captains and merchants. Owners of privateers, such as John Watts, John Amory, and Theophylact Bache, and captains, such as William Bayard's son, Samuel, must have profited from the large volume of goods in circulation, as did others who, by January 1779, used privateering as an excuse to sell stolen property as privateering loot. In March 1779, Tryon declared that the city had "become an immense magazine of all kinds of supplies, for a very extensive commerce."[75]

However, as some merchants sought to profit by charging exorbitant prices, they distressed residents of lesser means. By 1778, the cost of essentials in the city had climbed. In September, Commissioner Carlisle observed that "all the necessaries of life [were] dear beyond conception." The price of bread in the city, William Eden heard, had doubled in just six days. In November 1778, as prices spiraled out of control, James Rivington's journeyman printers petitioned Rivington for an additional three dollars per week. Since the "necessaries of life are raised to such an enormous price," they argued, "it cannot be expected that we should continue to work at the wages now given."[76]

The merchants' profiteering drew British attention. In January 1779, British officials mandated that auctioneers could operate only if granted a license. They further tried to curb the rising inflation in the city by appointing William Bayard as vendue master, in charge of regulating all auctions in the city. The fifty-year-old wealthy merchant was deemed a true subject. The British trusted Bayard for his known commercial connections with England, the Caribbean, and South America. By 1774, Bayard had acquired real estate holdings that included eight houses, two storehouses, and a pier, a property valued at £17,000. In 1776, Bayard also raised a loyalist regiment, the King's Orange Rangers, in which his two sons served as officers. In 1778, Bayard used his considerable income and influence to raise money for and provision soldiers from New Jersey. After 1779, he profited further by establishing monopolistic control over public auctions.[77]

As New York merchants prospered from trade and privateering, they sought to reestablish their earlier authority in the city. In June 1779, twenty-three merchants met in the "Upper long room at the Coffy House" and drew up a petition to revive the Chamber of Commerce. Addressing themselves to the new commandant, Lieutenant General Daniel Jones, they emphasized their authority in the city's trading concerns before the "present unnatural rebellion." They explained that the "increase of Commerce encouraged by the Proclamations of his Majesty's Commissioners, together with the success of Private Ships of War has induced the Merchants in general to solicit a renewal of our Meetings in order that the many mercantile differences which so frequently happen may be adjusted." Since British military oversight over the city's administration remained uncontested, British officials happily parceled out commercial and administrative matters to the Chamber. The commandant consulted the Chamber on matters such as setting prices for goods, and establishing rates for cartmen. In June 1779, Major General James Pattison solicited the Chamber's advice on the ways and means "for the better Cleansing the City, and for raising a Fund for defraying the Expense thereof."[78]

Notwithstanding the Chamber's assistance in managing the civil affairs of the city, the British navy paid a heavy price for encouraging privateering. In 1776, Admiral Richard Howe had opposed privateering because he feared it would deprive the navy of regular seamen. In the spring of 1778, British authorities had forbidden seamen to enlist in loyalist regiments. In the fall of 1778, when sailors deserted British ships to join privateering excursions, British naval commanders confronted precisely the dilemma they had feared. The profits earned from serving in private vessels lured sailors from the toil and low pay of British transports. Countless announcements in New York's newspapers expressed the frantic efforts of British captains to retain their seamen. A notice in a December issue of the *Royal Gazette* typified the plight of His Majesty's naval forces. From aboard the *Perseus,* five seamen in their late twenties and early thirties had deserted: Samuel Harris; James Harris of Essex, England; and William Elliot, Thomas Hays, and Patrick Duffy of Ireland. The ship's captain offered a five-pound reward "to any person who [would] inform upon any masters of owners or privateers who have inveigled, concealed, or any ways entertained the above persons." In January, when the British charged tailor Thomas Courtney with enticing and concealing seamen to desert from the army victualler *Polly,* Courtney insisted, unperturbed, that "if men comes to me and tells me they do not belong" with a British naval ship, he cannot be liable.[79]

Privateering attracted both seamen and slaves. Ironically, merchant loyalists who expected only profits from privateering lost valued property to privateers. In October, a loyalist demanded the return of a "runaway Negro, a boy named Sam, between 14 and 15 years of age, as it is supposed he will enter on board any privateer." In December, Smith reported that his black servants Jack, worth £75, and Tom, valued at £100, had fled with their chest, bedding, and clothes to join a privateer. In May 1779, another loyalist hoped to recover a "Negro wench named Hager, about 18 years of age" as "she is supposed to be gone on board the fleet."[80]

On April 16, 1779, the commander in chief of His Majesty's ships in North America, Commodore Sir George Collier, published a warning to British sailors. Many seamen, he announced, "have lately inveigled from His Majesty's service into privateers, letters of marque, and merchant-men." If a vessel harbored a deserter, he warned, each man in the vessel would be impressed for His Majesty's service.[81] Five months later, Vice Admiral Marriott Arbuthnot accused New York's privateers of enticing royal seamen to desert. "No boat can come on shore," he complained, "but that every art likely to prevail with them is practiced, and often with success." He warned that he would "press man for man, out of the privateers and merchant vessels" any seafaring man who deserted the king's ships.[82]

But the steady number of "Runaway" and "Deserted" announcements in the newspapers demonstrates that his threats had little effect. Both seamen and servants continued to desert their masters to join privateers. In February 1780, Henry Vandenham, a native of New York, deserted from a man-of-war and changed his name to Henry Ginkins. The captain, Isaac Amory, claimed he was "distressing his Majesty's service" and offered five guineas in reward for his return.[83] Two years later, another master offered a reward for a runaway apprentice by the name of John Abbot, who "intend[ed] to go on board some privateer."[84]

## Military Concession

In 1779, Lord Germain adopted a new strategy toward white loyalists as a result of the advice he received from loyalist exiles in London, trusted British officials in the colonies, and the peace commissioners who had lived with New York City's loyalists for five months. All three groups reinforced Germain's conviction that the majority of colonists remained committed to reunion. Galloway, who had arrived in London in December 1778, declared that if the British regulars drove away Washington's army, the loyalists would disarm the rebel minority by their own efforts. General James Robertson endorsed Galloway's assertion that most Americans opposed the rebellion.[85]

During the summer and fall of 1778, the commissioners had advised the British government to retain North America as the center of war. William Eden implored the ministry to modify its previous orders so that the St. Lucia task force could act instead in North America. He emphasized that only an aggressive British military offensive would convince rebels to abandon independence. Influenced by embittered loyalists, the commissioners believed that further "pacific advances" would expose Britain to rebel insults. In October, dreading the fate of the city's loyalists, Eden lamented that "the poor old island hangs at present on the balance between total ruin, or, complete recovery, and exertion would still do the business."[86]

Predisposed by the prevailing temper in New York City, Carlisle and Eden presented their plan for the gradual revival of civil government in the province of New York. Although the lower county around New York was ready for the reinstitution of royal government, they explained that most of the colony of New York was "not ripe for such a measure." The British should also engage the Continental Army in the Highlands so that more counties in New York, free from rebel forces, would be at liberty to send members to the colonial assembly. After the restoration of civil rule in New York, British troops should raid the coasts of New England and the Chesapeake Bay, disperse rebel troops and militia, and restore loyalist rule over the middle colonies.[87]

Germain recognized, in principle, that the revival of civil rule would remove people's ill-founded apprehensions "of being ruled by military laws in all time to come should they submit to His Majesty's government." In fact, both moderates and hard-liners supported the restoration of civil rule. The hard-liners no longer expected the empire to reach a diplomatic settlement with the rebel leaders. They believed the war would and should end only with their military victory. Less concerned about healing the divide, they focused on the expediency of civil government to facilitate a renewed British offensive. They expected that the restoration of civil rule by loyalists in recovered areas would free British regulars to fight the Continental Army elsewhere. Peter Dubois believed civil government gave the opposition a clear advantage. The rebels, he said, had the support of a "regularly organized civil government with its laws, its judges, and justices, and subordinate officers, ready and disposed to crush whoever dared to attempt an opposition." Ironically, they had established their government by suppressing the "free communication of sentiments" among the king's good subjects.[88]

Loyalist moderates supported civil government because they were determined to maintain their transatlantic allegiance peacefully, regardless of revolutionary blandishments and harsh treatment from friends and foes alike. They resisted brutal retaliation in kind. They remained committed to pursuing the least destructive means of reconciling the colonists to the empire. The revival of civil rule would pave the way for the British and loyalists to showcase their peaceful and constitutional state to deluded colonists.

Moderates were concerned that the persistence of martial rule could alienate colonists permanently. Maryland loyalist Daniel Chamier believed that the pattern of military rule served as a deterrent to those who would otherwise favor reunion with the British Empire. In March 1778, he had criticized the abeyance of civil rule in Philadelphia. The "new government" established in Philadelphia, he observed, appeared "too extensive to be a military one." Chamier believed the British authorities could not successfully control all the civil domains of the city. He suggested the appointment of a deputy governor who could restore civil rule in Maryland until former royal governor Sir Robert Eden saw fit to return to the colony. When the colonists returned to "happiness" under their old form of government, which Chamier called the "best on the whole continent," their situation would be "more envied and their example soonest followed by others."[89]

Smith echoed Chamier. He distrusted the judicial control held by the military commandant. In November 1778, he suggested that "the General might establish a police that would be good substitute till we could form a legislature." He also despaired of the violence advocated by British officers. In October, Smith agonized about those who "have long been for desolation" and who spoke wantonly about creating the office of "conflagrator general." He denounced Sir Robert Pigot's excursions of August 1778, which devastated the towns of Bristol Neck and Warren in Rhode Island. He feared that the petite guerre would prolong the rebellion and waste "the men and wealth for which the reunion is desired." In December, Smith stressed the importance of involving loyalists in the executive role. The "harshness of military government," he urged, "must be mitigated by the establishment of a council neither perfectly military nor totally dependent upon the concurrence of an assembly." If all conquered territories in America become garrison towns, Smith warned the British government in 1779, "she is not worth your attention."[90]

In 1778, when British troops dispersed from the mainland colonies to protect other precious territories from French conquest, Germain confronted a serious shortage of manpower. He responded to the crisis by reassessing the potential of loyalist soldiers. In November 1776, when

General Howe asked for 15,000 troops from Europe, Germain wrote that he could spare only 6,100 men. Germain had described the expense and time involved in recruiting additional thousands and urged Howe to raise American loyalists "for particular parts of the service." In 1776–77, Germain hardly expected loyalists to serve on a par with British regulars. Rather, he hoped loyalists would release British regulars by performing auxiliary and subordinate jobs such as hauling provisions, cutting hay to feed the army's livestock, and reconnaissance. Like others who formed British policies, Germain regarded American colonists as farmers who lacked the bearing and professionalism of British regulars.[91]

Between 1776 and 1778, prominent loyalists who became military officers received the same pay as officers in regular regiments but enjoyed lesser benefits than British regulars. First, because British regulars resisted serving under the command of provincials, loyalists in provincial units were subordinate to officers of the same grade in the British regulars. Thus, a lieutenant in a provincial regiment ranked under a lieutenant in the British regular regiment. Second, reluctant to expand the list of reduced officers under British pay, the ministry refused to offer permanent half-pay to provincial officers once the regiment disbanded at war's end. The promise of perpetual half-pay had induced many Americans to enlist as officers during the Seven Years' War. These officers also benefited because they had first opportunity to fill any vacancies within the army. Finally, the British denied gratuity pay to maimed and wounded loyalist officers and allocated no funds to provide hospital or nursing care for them.[92]

In 1779, Germain anticipated that loyalist military protection of reclaimed colonies would free British regulars to attack the Continental Army. He pressed Clinton to "embody the loyal inhabitants of this country and put them in a condition to defend themselves." Indeed, British efforts would fail if they could not "find means to engage the people of America in support of a cause which is equally their own." He promoted the recruitment of more loyalist regiments officered by their own countrymen who would act in concert with the king's troops or defend a post in the absence of the army. This, he recognized, "is what rebels do." He granted to loyalists the same status that American colonists had carried in the Seven Years' War. The officers' rank would be permanent, and they would receive half-pay upon the reduction of the regiments, in the same manner as afforded to British officers. Widows and children of officered loyalists would "partake in royal bounty." To fill the lower ranks, Germain promised one hundred acres to every private and two hundred to each noncommissioned officer.[93]

But Germain's concessions came too late. In the winter of 1778, Edward Winslow wryly observed that the "flush of romantic military ardor" that had induced loyalists to enlist had dissipated, as had the "pleasures of gratifying revenge for recent persecutions." If the enlisted provincials remained inactive and in the vicinity of their homes, Winslow remarked, "desertions woul'd be frequent." Silvester Fuller, a loyalist arrested for helping Hessians desert, further reveals New Yorkers' sentiments about British soldiers. In the court-martial trial of 1779, he damned "the king, ministry and Parliament for sending over a set of damned rascals to deprive people of their Liberties and Properties."[94]

In 1778, William Franklin hoped to reanimate New York's despondent loyalists. But his efforts to create a powerful and parallel alternative to the British establishment antagonized General Clinton and alienated New York's moderates. Hoping for a reunion with the empire, they worried that Franklin's militancy would create a permanent divide between American colonists. Despite their disappointment with British setbacks and their criticism of British military rule, they continued to believe that the British government remained best situated to mediate the colonial conflict. As some of these moderates had rejected extralegal rebel aggression in 1775 and 1776, they rejected the hard-liners' militancy in 1778.

Rejecting the hard-liners' divisive proposal, the British offered trading concessions to loyalist merchants. In contrast to William Franklin and William Smith, who tried to influence British strategy, the merchants wished only to expand their trading privileges. Their limited aims allowed them to speak to the British administration in a unified voice. Intending to preserve and promote loyalist sentiments, the British did not anticipate that the looser trade restrictions and especially, privateering, would undermine their oversight over the city. The British sailors expected loyalist self-interest to protect them from recapture by their captains, and runaway slaves anticipated that British dependence on black labor could shield them from reenslavement.

In 1776, the British government had assumed the silent allegiance of most of the American people. By 1778, however, the British sensed the growing sharpness in diverse loyalist voices and recognized the heavy cost of loyalist alienation. They also worried that the French and Spanish fleets would combine to challenge Britain's superiority in the seas. In November, Germain observed "that great armaments in Spain give us too just reason to apprehend that the court of Madrid will soon depart from that neutrality which it now professes."[95] Compelled to heed loyalists' concerns, the British belatedly resolved to address loyalist resentment and to fortify loyalists' support by reviving civil rule in New York City. In 1779, the British took the first tentative steps toward transforming British New York into loyalist New York.

# 6 ❦ "A Certificate of Their Necessity"
## A Mix of Refugees and Rules

*With good policy the neighborhood of an army may be really advantageous to the inhabitants and the industry of the inhabitants excited by security may supply most of the demands and lessen the expense of the army.*
—Sir Henry Clinton to James Robertson, June 27, 1780

Between 1777 and 1781, New York City's civilian population more than doubled to twenty-five thousand.[1] Many who crowded into the city were not men of influence or affluence but those of humbler means. The colonists who clamored for British attention and overwhelmed leading loyalists included slaves who sought freedom and opportunity within British lines and a growing white underclass from rebel-controlled areas who viewed temporary exile in the British-led city as a means to avoid the rebel draft, to acquire hard currency, or to find favorable employment.

In January 1779 and two years later in December 1780, the British army in New York City comprised 16,611 men, including 15,780 effectives.[2] To the extent possible in a city filled at times with an almost equal number of British soldiers and loyalist civilians, the British authorities regulated soldiers' infringement on civilian spaces. Yet their consistent prioritization of military over civilian needs led to scattered measures calculated to quiet refugees' concerns and not to reward or expand loyalist allegiance. The growing ad hoc military regulations did not build loyalist goodwill or invite loyalist confidence.

Despite British attempts at instituting order, the city's inhabitants endured desperate circumstances: a severe shortage of housing, insufficient quantities of wood, unhealthy conditions, and a spiraling cost of living. Flour, which had sold for twenty shillings a barrel in 1775, cost seventy shillings by 1781. The price of beef soared from sixty-five shillings to eight

pounds a barrel. Even gentlemen of means found it difficult to obtain necessaries and maintain their previous high standard of living. In September
1778, William Smith Jr., likened the daily cost of living in New York City
with the expense of living in the most extravagant castle in Yorkshire, England. Regular weekly bills came to him "as much as the house-account at
Castle Howard when we have the most company."[3]

The largest numbers of white refugees in New York City came from
the hinterlands around the city and from upstate New York, followed by
New Jersey, Massachusetts, Connecticut, Pennsylvania, Rhode Island, Virginia, and Maryland. The smallest numbers came from North Carolina,
Georgia, and Florida. By 1782, the British allocated over £8,000 to support
refugees from New York province, compared with £4,000 to support refugees who came from New Jersey.[4]

The fallout from Saratoga exacerbated New Yorkers' distressed predicament. Just as British abandonment of New Jersey had swelled New York
City's population in 1776, the British retreat from the Highlands in 1777
pushed a new group of exiles into the city. In October, Gaine reported
the conspicuous arrival of Mrs. Cuyler, the mayor of Albany's wife, with
her children.[5] But most of the refugees from the New York hinterlands
did not augment the distinguished set of gentlemen and their families already present in the city. In December 1777 "three to four hundred women
and children," the wives and children of friends of government from
Poughkeepsie, Newburgh, and other towns in rural New York, entered
the city.[6]

The diverse group of newcomers placed formidable demands on the
British administration. Joshua Gidney of Dutchess County had lost his
property because of his allegiance. Since 1777, he and his nine children had
struggled to survive in New York.[7] Alida Armstrong's husband had assisted
General Burgoyne's campaign in 1777. When the British troops left, rebel
officers "threatened [the Armstrongs] with prosecution for high treason,"
and obliged them to leave their estate near Fort Edward, New York. She,
her husband, and four small children could not survive on her husband's
meager earnings in New York.[8] Susannah Wilkinson's husband served as
a soldier with the king's army. She came to New York with him upon the
evacuation of Philadelphia. Her husband had since died. She and her child,
"dangerously ill with smallpox," sought help.[9] Loyalist James M. Bath also
left Philadelphia in 1778. His wife had since died, and he needed assistance
to support his three children.[10] For refusing to take up arms against the

king, Thomas Griffin was obliged to leave his property of two thousand acres in South Carolina in June 1778. He needed employment in New York.[11] Georgia's governor, James Wright, left when the rebels judged him guilty of high treason and passed a bill of attainder against him. He hoped the British would send directions that all slaves belonging to friends of the British government should be delivered back to the attorneys of their rightful owners. Wright feared that more slaves would seek refuge with the British, following the example of those who had sailed away in king's transports in 1776.[12]

The influx of hundreds of common people in New York City alarmed loyalist leaders. In February, just six months after British rule, refugees from Pennsylvania and New Jersey had raised the city's population to eleven thousand. The rush of new arrivals threatened to undermine social order in the city further. In March 1777, the author of an anonymous letter written to Germain from New York complained about the nuisance of young male refugees who lacked means or occupation. If "we do not give [them] bread and encouragement," he explained, these men through sheer necessity would either "fight against us" or "plunder and rapine." In April, Smith hoped that the British administration would publish a proper and official statement to reunite the colonies with the mother country before the rebellion fell into the hands of the lower sort.[13]

The loyalist leaders believed they could reasonably negotiate an understanding with Parliament but would be helpless against the common people's anarchic potential if unleashed by the rebellion. Only "horror, distress, and confusion" would accompany rebel success. Smith insisted that the people "lose nothing by being obliged to elect men of Substance attached to territory." If the masses gained political power, the established social order would collapse and lead society to utter ruin.[14]

Like other loyalist spokesmen, Smith feared the potential power of the common people to overthrow the colonial political hierarchy in which propertied gentlemen governed society. Calling the common people the "unthinking ignorant multitude," Galloway had feared that the "licentousness" and "lawless ambition" of commoners would destroy the revered system of imperial government that provided checks and balances over arbitrary usurpation by demagogues. Reverend Inglis insisted that it was the "Duty of all Men" to accept their station in life. Another loyalist from Maryland, Jonathan Boucher, thought the common people "particularly unworthy and unamiable." They were also "wrongheaded, ignorant and prone to resist authority."[15]

The burgeoning population of loyalists in the city placed the British in a dire predicament. They confronted the dilemma of an expanding population of the king's friends that they could neither trust nor abandon. In January 1777, suspicious of the hundreds of refugees entering the city daily, Governor James Robertson had mandated that newcomers enter their names with British officials or face the consequences of being treated as "spies." Those who did not cooperate with British mandates were deemed "unworthy inhabitants" and had to move out of the city.[16]

The British displayed ambivalence toward the destitute refugees, especially women, who flocked into the city after Saratoga. In December 1777, the following announcement in the New-York Gazette and Weekly Mercury exemplifies British attempts at goodwill: "On Wednesday next being Christmas Eve, 40 poor Widows, Housekeepers, having Families in this City, will receive 40 lb. of fresh Beef, and a half Pack Loaf each, as a Certificate of their Necessity, signed by two Neighbors of Repute, which is to be delivered at the Rev'd Dr. Inglis's House in the Broadway, between 10 and 12 o'clock that day, who will give a Ticket for the above Donation."[17] Within the formula of Christmas charity, the British specified the military requirement that "neighbors of repute" authenticate the recipients' loyalty. Suspicious of the newcomers, the British wanted to certify that the rations went only to the loyal poor. The "ticket" accepted as proof of loyalty revealed the pressures the British faced as they sought to demonstrate benevolence to New Yorkers without endangering the security of the garrison.

The elite disposition of loyalist leaders contradicted and undermined their bid to win popular support from wavering colonists. The arrival of people of uncertain status raised leading loyalists' anxiety about the unorganized masses or, as Smith stated vividly, "the capricious Wantonness of the Multitude."[18] These refugees, the loyalist leaders warned, would commit crimes, abuse private property, and further jeopardize the loyalist haven. Theophylact Bache's observations on the refugees typify the elitist disdain. An Englishman who had immigrated to New York City in 1751 at the age of sixteen, Bache established himself by forming strong ties to New York merchants such as Leonard Lispenard and by marrying the wealthy daughter of Andrew Barclay, Ann Dorothy Barclay. By 1774, he was a member of the Marine Society and had served a two-year term as president of the city's Chamber of Commerce. Bache lamented the arrival of common refugees:

> There are no doubt at this very time a number of bad disaffected people who have come in, and reside in the city, who have no property there; and are more to be dreaded than an enemy without. They lurk there for no good purposes and some of them may be so hardened in inequity as to attempt the destruction of its remains and that at a time, when the loyal Inhabitants may be call'd out in its defense.[19]

He urged British officials to record the name, place of birth, business, and last place of residence of every newcomer in each ward in the city. At least two to three principal gentlemen in town should assist the British authorities in organizing these lists. If a person could not provide a satisfactory account, he or she should be "disposed in some secure place or sent out of town."[20] Bache sought help from British officials in keeping poor people out of the city. The political allegiance of the refugees was incidental in light of their poverty.

The elites resented the influx of needy loyalists just as they had opposed supporting the poor before the rebellion.. During the 1750s and 1760s, leading New Yorkers had complained about the high cost of immigration as evidenced by numerous laws setting forth regulations for legal residence. In addition to the seasonally employed seamen and cartmen, debtors, and war refugees, William Livingston worried about the newcomers who lacked skills and trades and burdened the community. Two and a half decades before Bache, Livingston complained about the high cost of "foreign invasions of beggary and idleness."[21]

The rebellion did not transform the mentality of New York's elites, who continued to measure poverty in moral terms. Bache worried about the high cost of supporting dependents in New York City after the rebellion came to an end. The benevolence of private individuals like Bache and the activities of charity groups had long supported paupers in New York. Bache's suggestion to round up vagrants and transport them out of the city followed the pattern New Yorkers had long established for dealing with poor outsiders. In the 1760s and 1770s, New Yorkers had faced a surge in poor-relief expenditures, which averaged £5,000 annually. Providing for the poor was the most serious and expensive social problem New Yorkers confronted. Bache did not want prominent New Yorkers to be burdened with the permanent expense of poor refugees.[22] Between 1778 and 1780, New York's vestrymen collected £64,862 from rents, licenses, and lotteries to assist the city's poor.[23]

Bache's pleas to monitor the poor refugees in New York City received a prompt, if partial, response. In December 1777, Robertson formally appointed nineteen prominent loyalists to solicit and receive donations for the relief of the poor "according to their several wants and necessities." The appointees included four former presidents of the New York City Chamber of Commerce: Theophylact Bache, William Walton, Isaac Low, and Elias Desbrosses. Robertson also named John Thompson to cut wood to meet the needs of the poor and set fixed prices for bushels of wheat, rye, and Indian corn. The latter, he explained, was necessary "to guard against the extortion of individuals who raise the necessaries of life, without which other parts of the community cannot subsist." It was "highly unreasonable" that many "in need of these articles" should be left to the mercy of the farmers, who possessed a "great deal" of grain.[24]

Between 1778 and 1781, General Clinton repeated General Howe's earlier offer of "free and unlimited pardon" to all rebel deserters who surrendered to any of His Majesty's troops. In addition, he offered European subjects, especially Irishmen, "a pardon for all the felonies and treasons (murder excepted) which they are heretofore guilty of," provided that they took up arms against His Majesty's enemies.[25] Yet, ironically, the pardons meant to shatter the core of the rebel army resulted in greater friction between New York loyalists and British military officials. The migration and settlement of a large white underclass seduced by British promises augmented loyalist anxiety. They complained that longtime rebels acquired, by a belated gesture of allegiance, all the privileges reserved for British subjects.

More critically, loyalist leaders feared that the flood of refugees would further destabilize the war-weary city. Some suspected that many of the so-called deserters were in fact spies, thieves, or opportunists. On July 28, 1779, in a letter addressed to James Rivington of the *Royal Gazette,* "A Real Lover of Constitutional Liberty" complained of a tavern owner, Mr. Marchalk, who nightly hosted a rebellious crew "notoriously disaffected to government." On February 21, 1780, another loyalist accused a rebel deserter of robbing a loyal civilian in the city. On March 22, a resident raged at British leniency toward Robert Neil of New Jersey who sought refuge in New York City. The loyalist railed that Neil had taken wood from loyalist lands, sold it to the rebels, and thereby amassed a large estate.[26]

The British officers and the leading loyalists had long feared that the suspicious newcomers posed a security hazard to the city. The covert rebel shared with the loyalist physical, linguistic, and cultural character-istics. The example of Peter Hally demonstrates how New York's refu-gees exploited the British confusion. When George Lent, a loyalist miller, accused Hally, a mulatto, of stealing a horse, three lambs, and a pig from his property, Hally offered an extraordinary explanation to the British in his defense. He said that "he was led to [the property] by a white man who told him they belonged to a rebel." Clearly, Hally suspected that stealing from a rebel would merit less severe punishment. Far from a criminal act, he framed the theft as an act of loyalty. Although his clever justification did not preclude his banishment, Hally understood well the civil war context of the conflict.[27]

In July 1779, William Tryon urged Sir Henry Clinton to establish an office of enquiry to procure intelligence and authenticate the loyalty of all persons entering into British lines. Tryon felt that the British would benefit from integrating military reconnaissance with loyalist intelligence. Tryon recommended two "gentlemen of the first abilities & every way qualified for so laborious a task": William Smith Jr. of New York and Lewis De Rosette of North Carolina. But Clinton did not see fit to establish an autonomous office manned by loyalist civilians because he wanted to retain military control over the city. Instead, Clinton entrusted intelligence to his aide-de-camp, Captain John Andre, and, after his untimely death in 1780, to Major Oliver DeLancey.[28]

New York's prominent loyalists accepted Clinton's partial compromise. They worked around Clinton's objection to an office of enquiry by estab-lishing themselves informally as gatekeepers of the garrison. They autho-rized the movement of ordinary refugees in and out of British lines. If they deemed a refugee as authentically loyal, they recommended the refugee to the military commandant, who granted official sanction. On August 15, 1779, when refugee John Cozens sought to return to Gloucester County, New Jersey, John Hinchman vouched for him: "I have been well acquainted with him for many years past, that he acted as a lieutenant in the militia of Greenwich township in said county." Daniel Coxe also authenticated Hinchman by swearing that he had held the reputable position as His Maj-esty's judge in the county of Gloucester and therefore asserting that "full faith and credit may be given to his certificate as above." On September 5, 1779, William Franklin endorsed the testimony of four refugees: William Peck, Darlen Welsley, Solomon Farris, and Edward Lockwood. Franklin certified that the subscribers were "loyal refugees from Connecticut and have been well recommended to me as men of good character." On November 22, 1779, when Charity Lee of Trenton, New Jersey, asked for sixty-one days' full rations for her voyage to Ireland, Daniel Coxe and New Jersey's Anglican clergyman George Panton testified for her.[29]

## Loyalist Tensions

Through the years of the war, the British army in New York City provided a haven for slaves who sought to escape their masters. In need of laborers, British authorities looked the other way when servants and slaves fled their masters—some of them loyalists—and sought employment with the British military. Although the British formally promoted the return of social order in the colonies, the confusion of military rule created social fissures.

The British explicit promise of freedom to slaves of rebel masters, designed to disrupt the business of rebel slave owners, infuriated New York's leading loyalists. They already worried that the overcrowded and disordered city—filled with large numbers of British soldiers as well as refugees, deserters, and homeless people—provided sufficient encouragement to the unruly elements in society. The loyalists realized that such explicit promises would further encourage their own slaves to take flight. Determined to guard their valuable investments, these loyalists dismissed the military potential of armed blacks. In July 1778, William Smith Jr. belittled Washington's army because it included many blacks, who were allowed to "mix, march, mess & sleep with the Whites."[30]

Within weeks after British rule, New Yorkers who had greeted the British as a shield against further losses came to view the administration as a threat to their property. Many demanded that the British return runaway slaves. In October 1776, Charles Arding offered an eight-dollar reward for a slave boy named York from Jamaica who spoke good English. Arding supposed he was "lurking about the camps or shipping." In November, Thomas Hepbburn offered a ten-dollar reward for the return of a creole named Will, age nineteen, who he suspected had "made for the camp." In December, Samuel Sackett advertised that a black man named Joe, a child about five months, and a twenty-four-year-old black woman with smallpox were all in the army. In January 1777, William Tongue advertised for the return of "Betty," who spoke both Dutch and English. In July, one resident noted that two black men who received payment as teamsters were actually his property. He demanded that the army remove them from the commissary's books or pay him forty shillings for each man.[31]

As early as October, 1777, a British census taker found 1,951 blacks living in New York City, 16 percent of the total civilian population of 12,408. As leading loyalists feared, slaves owned by loyalists and rebels alike embraced liberty by accepting the halting, often slippery British promises to exchange freedom for military service. Slaves owned by loyal New Yorkers, prominent merchants, and Anglican clergymen as well as those owned by newly arrived refugees exploited the confusion and turmoil of a garrisoned city to slip away from their masters. In nearby New Jersey, the runaway rate quadrupled as a more educated and urbanized black population took advantage of British proximity in New York City.[32] In September 1778, Gabriel H. Ludlow's slave, eighteen-year-old William, and Alexander Wallace's slave, sixteen-year-old Bet, ran away. Reverend Charles Inglis's slave, fourteen-year-old Pyrmis, fled in January 1779. On March 6, 1779, Moses from Rhode Island ran away. On December 3, a slave boy from South Carolina made his escape, and a month later the slave George from Virginia took his chances for freedom. On August 23, 1780, two Negro women, one from Charlestown and another from Virginia, remained missing. The blacks guarded their security vigilantly by harboring in regionally specific clusters within the city. On July 26, 1780, a black woman, Bina, disappeared to the "Virginia Negro houses" in the city. In October, a light-skinned black boy, Bill, fourteen years of age, joined the "Amboy refugees" in the city.[33]

Loyalist ads attempted to reclaim slave men, women, and children, but with little evidence of success, as many reappeared repeatedly in the papers. In May 1780, prominent loyalist and superior court judge Jonathan Fowler offered a five-dollar reward for "a Negro Boy named JACK, aged about 17 years, pitted with the small pox, stoops in his walk, talks much like a Guinea Negro, very black, about five feet four inches high." In December, a South Carolina refugee described his missing Richard as "about eighteen to twenty years of age, short and stout made, but active and nimble, of a very black complexion." In June 1781, upholstery-maker Elizabeth Evans hoped to locate a "Mulatto wench, Pamela, 18 years old, stout and well made." On September 1, 1781, the prominent Ludlow family offered a three-dollar reward to return a black slave boy named Jacob, around fourteen years old, to his "Mother Jenny."[34]

The runaway notices reveal the plethora of occupations within British administration available to slaves. They also indicate that many who ran away from rebel or loyalist masters did not settle into a single position in the British military infrastructure but maneuvered between jobs. Blacks served in the Virginia Company of Blacks, the New York Volunteers, the Horse Department of the Royal Artillery, and His Majesty's transports. They also worked in the General Hospital, swept chimneys, and drummed for a Hessian regiment. They labored in a separate "Negro Carpenters" group in the Engineer's Department.[35]

As New Yorkers had done before the war, the British employed blacks and whites side by side as cartmen, wagon drivers, and carpenters. Minimizing the distinction between black and white subjects, the British wished to satisfy urgent military requirements. But white loyalists reacted angrily, for some of the blacks employed in British lines were their escaped property.[36]

The British operations in New York City required the support of carpenters, wagon makers, wheelwrights, blacksmiths, stablemen, and others working in shipbuilding and ship maintenance. The quartermaster general, responsible for the care and maintenance of camp and field equipment of the army, employed over 1,100 civilians. The commissary department, which provided food to an average of 35,000 men and 4,000 horses, employed over 500 civilians. The barrack master general, who provisioned troops not campaigning in the field, employed over 750 civilians. The British also employed 921 laborers to build fortifications around New York City. In 1781, 120 blacks worked as laborers in the quartermaster general's department. Although blacks generally received less pay than their white counterparts, the wartime shortages in labor meant that they could command the same inflationary wages as whites. In 1780, the shortage of manpower led the British to pay laborers ten shillings per day, five times more than in prewar years.[37]

Blacks also worked alongside British and loyalist units in foraging excursions. In July 1779, Clinton designated the commissary of captured cattle to employ three cattle rangers with a party of ten mounted Negroes each.[38] Clinton established the commissary to meet the wartime shortage of fresh meat and to correct the inequitable distribution of meat among competing regiments. On June 24, 1780, loyalist refugee and former mayor

of Albany Abraham Cuyler employed black and white refugees in Bergen
Point, New Jersey, to cut wood for New York City. Cuyler's discriminating
stance toward the black refugees was apparent. He ordered that not more
than half the blacks "are to have arms and those that take best care must
have them."[39]

Although British military officers actively solicited black manpower,
they tried to restrict black families from entering British lines. They did not
want to waste precious resources on feeding and housing black women and
children. When the exploits of Colonel Tye and interracial guerrilla bands
posted in ferry landings in New Jersey encouraged black families to flee to
New York City, some British officials fumed. In May 1780, Major General
James Patterson wrote Cuyler that "not only male but female Negroes
with their children take advantage of your port in New Jersey to run away
from masters and come into the city where they must become a burden to
the town. . . . Be so good as to prevent their passing the North [Hudson]
River as far as it is in your power to do it."[40] Some officers explicitly forbade
black men to enter British lines with their families. On December 2, 1780,
Lieutenant Colonel John Simcoe of the Queen's Rangers issued a proclamation from his station in Oyster Bay, Long Island. Addressing the "able
bodied men slaves to those who are in arms against his Majesty's government," he announced that they "would have their liberty & be protected
by King George provided they come without their wives & children who
cannot be received or protected at present." In exchange for their own
freedom, Simcoe demanded that black men abandon their families to face
the rage of rebel masters.[41]

The British reliance on black manpower sometimes inclined them to
protect the fugitives in the garrison. In October 1779, when a drunken
British soldier forced himself into a cart driven by a black man in Bowery
Lane, a loyalist, Dr. Baily, interceded on the man's behalf. Baily led him
into a house and notified the British hospital of his miserable condition.
However, the British authorities regarded Baily's concern suspiciously.
Apparently, they suspected that Baily had seized the man in order to claim
or sell him as his own property. Sympathetic to the plight of a black man
who also served as cartman for the British administration, the British
commandant put Baily in jail. In disgust, Baily demanded satisfaction and
threatened to leave New York City for the rebel lines.[42]

The British suspected that arbitration between loyalists and slaves would result in cumbersome and time-consuming proceedings that would divert attention from planning military operations. Their minimal interference in disputes between masters and slaves sometimes worked to the advantage of the former. In November 1778, when Daniel Manson from Charlestown demanded that the British return his slave who served in the Black Pioneers because the slave "loves his master and would wish to go with him," General Clinton answered: "If the Negro wishes it, I have no objection."[43]

Holding the British to the promises they made to the slaves, some blacks pressed the British to protect them from the insults of white loyalists. On February 10, 1779, Judea Moore, a black refugee from Virginia, faced eviction when John Harrison and his journeyman offered to pay Moore's landlord, Mr. Brasier, fifteen pounds to get Moore removed. Moore had rented the cellar from Brasier for only eight pounds a year. When Moore complained to the mayor, David Mathews, the latter dismissed Moore as an annoyance. According to Moore, the mayor added that "it was a pity that we black folk from Virginia was not sent home to our Masters."[44] Clearly, Matthews found it tedious to deal with petty racial issues when more pressing military matters remained unresolved.

The British unwillingness to become involved in black and white disputes formalized the slave trade within New York. Because New Yorkers recognized that the British authorities would not unduly involve themselves in settling claims over slave ownership, they exchanged official documents that would demonstrate to the British their legal ownership of a slave. Slave owners found that they could only sell a slave if they possessed proof of legal title. In November 1778, a notice in the *New-York Gazette and Weekly Mercury* invited gentlemen, farmers, and others to purchase "Negroes of all kinds, with their age, size, and qualification." A year later, the growth in the black population had altered the situation dramatically. In December 1779, a notice for the sale of a Negro girl ended with the following: "Title to her is indisputable." In February 1780, an ad for the sale of a Negro woman emphasized that she was "bred in this city." The following month, another ad guaranteed that a "Negro wench" for sale was born on Long Island and therefore was "warranted" property. On June 19, 1781, a Negro sale notice by loyalist merchants Hugh and Alexander Dean promised a "good title" to the purchasers. Ironically, the New Yorkers' new demand for legal proof, intended to continue the business in slaves, may have prevented an exchange of runaway slaves because nobody possessed the proper documents to dispose of them. While formalizing the selling of some slaves, the requirement for titles may have reduced the overall slave trade in the city.[45]

Disgusted by British leniency toward black fugitives, New Yorkers clamored to change British policy. And as loyalist complaints escalated, British officials conciliated loyalist masters by restoring the city to its prewar racial hierarchy. In June 1781, the British authorities reneged on their commitment to the escaped slaves. They refused to distinguish between the slaves of rebels and the slaves of loyalists. They prohibited all Negroes, free and unfree, belonging to loyalists or rebels, from selling or buying goods without written permission from their owners. In demanding that blacks engage in business only under a loyalist owner, the British severely curtailed black participation and mobility within the city.[46]

## British Order

In May 1778, General Howe established the Office of Police to manage the influx of refugees after the British failure at Saratoga in October 1777. Howe appointed Andrew Elliot, customs port collector, as the superintendent general of the police. The British choice of Elliot as both police and port superintendent indicates their high regard for the Scot's ability to conciliate New York's merchants and to balance the conflicting needs of ordinary refugees. It also highlights that New York City was both a commercial port and a military garrison. Elliot headed the police with the help of two magistrates, former mayor David Mathews and Peter Dubois. Governor Tryon had appointed Mathews mayor in February 1776.[47] Imprisoned by the rebels in July 1776, Mathews remained a prisoner in Litchfield, Connecticut, until his escape to the city in December. A lawyer from Ulster County, New York, Dubois slipped away from rebel lines in New Jersey to serve as a spy for the British.[48]

The city police performed some of the functions previously conducted by the city's council. It had orders to suppress vice and licentiousness, to regulate supplies for the support of the poor, to enforce the nightly watch, and to monitor transactions in the markets that promoted "economy, peace, and good order" in the city.[49] Yet this office hardly represented a symbol of British commitment to civil governance. The civilian police held no authority over military movement, conduct, or administration.

Elliot could provide security for property and persons in the city only "as could be admitted of by the military government." Elliot could not admit civilians to the provost without authorization from the commandant. He could only fine civilians who refused to abide by the police regulations.[50]

Under Elliot's supervision, the Office of Police centralized and tightened control to minimize the threat of fire and to monitor suspicious activity in the city. Elliot received authorization to place administration in the hands of loyalist merchants, attorneys, and refugees who had actively demonstrated their loyalty to the Crown. In March 1777, the military commandant, Sir Robert Pigot had assigned six chimney inspectors in the city: John Norris, John Burt Lyng, John Burns, Dederick Heyer, David H. Mellows, and Richard Ebbetts. In November 1778, Elliot retained only John Norris, doorkeeper of the Chamber of Commerce, and David Henry Mellows.[51] In December 1778, Elliot appointed New York attorney John Roome to examine the stoves in the city. The "injudicious method of firing stoves and keeping ashes," Elliot feared, could endanger the city. In January 1777, James Robertson had established a city watch to protect the city against incendiaries and other suspicious people. He had appointed two to three New Yorkers to manage the city watch in each of its seven wards. In May 1779, Elliot replaced the sixteen directors of the city watch with two loyalists: businessman and vestryman Jeronymus Van Alstyne and John Amory, a refugee from Albany County who had served as a lieutenant in a loyalist regiment.[52]

The Office of Police could not contain the antagonisms that hampered civil order. By 1779, civilian-military relations had soured. Resentful of the presence of thousands of armed men in the city, New York's civilians complained about sharing their cramped quarters and precious necessities with the military.[53] British officials strove to pacify the soldiers' desire for alcohol while at the same time discouraging overconsumption, attempted to regulate the spiraling cost of necessities so the needy would not starve, struggled to provide firewood and shelter to both refugees and soldiers in the garrison, and tried to control the hygiene of the city to prevent an outbreak of disease. But a series of military orders and provisional offices could not contain the tension between civilians and soldiers or adjudicate between loyalists.

Rum, at great expense, comprised an important part of soldiers' diet. Between May 1777 and November 1781, the British shipped 2,865,782 gallons of rum to troops in the North American colonies. In May 1777, one brewery established by the British commissary in New York City employed eleven men and turned out 4,233 gallons every two days.[54]

In 1777, Robertson warned owners of public houses to disallow soldiers and sailors inside their taverns and to shut out fires and lights by 9:00 p.m. As the number of unknown persons grew, the British worried that taverns served as a hatching ground for plots against His Majesty's cause. In 1778, Elliot directed taverns and public houses to obtain an operating license from the police. Owners could obtain a license only if recommended by the "principal officers of the army and navy, merchants, and other respectable inhabitants" of the city. Without a license, the tavern owners faced one month's imprisonment or a fine of five pounds.[55]

The British feared that misconduct by soldiers and sailors would poison civilian-military relations.[56] By the summer of 1777, the increasing irregularities committed by soldiers in New York City compelled official attention. In a private letter written in July 1777, Clinton worried that "plundering" by troops had made the British "hateful" to the inhabitants. As troops "constantly moved" to different posts around the city, they seized vegetables, fruit, and provisions from inhabitants without offering compensation. When they lodged in city churches near residents' homes, they "were very noisy." They seized new hay from gardens to bring to camp to lie on.[57] They communicated "venereal complaints." They also alarmed residents when they shot firearms in the streets and beat the people employed in ferryboats between New York City and Brooklyn. In August, Colonel Stuart regretted that the "want of firmness" on the officers' part encouraged a "total relaxation of discipline" and led to many crimes.[58] Many officers not only condoned the depredations but added their own. They repeatedly used their authority to compel civilians to relinquish their wagon horses and then deployed them for "private business." They used inhabitants' pastures and fields to feed their horses. One inhabitant accused "some person" of leaving a horse attached to his garden fence from ten o'clock in the morning till nine at night. He demanded that the person "prove his property, pay expences and take him away."[59]

In 1779, the British curtailed the mobility of seamen and soldiers in an effort to limit indiscipline caused by drunkenness. Admiral George Collier issued a proclamation that demanded that captains deny seamen permission to leave their vessels after dark. Unable to fully control the mobility of the sailors, the British instead curtailed civilian freedom. In 1780, Major

General James Pattison denounced the "many evils" that arose from the unlimited number of taverns and restricted the number of taverns to two hundred. To enforce the new regulation, he appointed Thomas Bayeaux and Thomas Dolton to serve under Elliot and regulate licensing.[60]

But these restrictions did not have the desired effect. The British regulations had reduced the number of taverns but could not prevent illicit activity within the taverns. Tavern owners saw no reason to forgo hefty profits. In June 1780, Elliot specifically attacked licensed public houses that sold to patients in the General Hospital, to the "great detriment of their health and subversion of good order and regularity." Convalescents, henceforth, would wear the distinguishing mark of an "H" made of blue cloth sewed conspicuously on each arm. Those who sold to these patients would lose their licenses permanently.[61]

The British also struggled to manage the distribution of food in the cramped city. Between May 1777 and November 1781, British victuallers supplied 79,465 pounds of bread, flour, and rice to the soldiers stationed in the North American colonies. To avoid the transportation costs of shipping large quantities of provisions, often damaged in the three-month voyage to the colonies, the British Treasury encouraged the commissaries to procure food locally. But surrounded by the rebel-controlled hinterlands, the British found it difficult to provision the army, its dependents, and the refugees. In 1777, the British set an assize on bread to ensure that most of the inhabitants of the city could afford bread of a specified quality. The commandant specified that a loaf of bread of the finest flour, weighing three pounds four ounces, should sell for fourteen coppers. Any person who extracted a higher price would face arrest, and the bread in question would feed the poor.[62]

The delay in importing provisions in the winter of 1778–79 alarmed both the British and the loyalists. In January 1779, as Pastor Schaukirk awaited the fleet from Ireland, he hoped it would "render some articles, particularly flour, cheaper for the inhabitants, for the exorbitant prices charged caused distress." To regulate the spiraling cost of the bread caused by the shortage, Elliot specified that a two-pound loaf of bread should sell for no more than twenty-one coppers. To prevent fraud, he mandated further that every baker in the city should mark with "his christian name and sirname upon the loaf bread he shall expose to sale."[63]

However, irregularities persisted. Like tavern owners, bakers exploited the high demand. In February 1779, the police apprehended Dennis Carrol, who sold bread at a higher price than fixed by the last assize. Elliot fined Carrol five pounds. In April and in August, authorities received notice of persons who overcharged for flour. In March 1780, one inhabitant reported the innovative methods bakers used to maximize profit. He explained that bakers bought damaged flour sold cheaply at auctions and mixed it with one-third good flour. Not only that, the bakers sold the bread not fully baked so that it weighed more. The inhabitant ended by declaring New Yorkers should not be "obliged to eat bad bread." In January 1780, Elliot had appointed two loyalists to control the abuse related to the sale of liquor. In March, he appointed Jeronymus Van Alstyne, vestryman and codirector of the city watch, as inspector of bread in the city.[64]

The September 1776 fire and the influx of refugees combined to produce a scarcity of housing that inflamed relations between landlords and military tenants in the city. On August 24, 1778, Peter Cornell complained that the officers who lived in his home "take and get milk and every other necessary what they want without asking or thanking me for the same." In November 1779, some inhabitants petitioned to the commandant when British officers arrested civilian occupants of the household and sent them to the provost in the city. The civilians protested that the British officers had no authority to put them in jail without the commandant's explicit authorization. On February 5, 1780, Joshua Pell demanded compensation when officers billeted in his house broke open one of his rooms and killed poultry. In November 1780, another inhabitant complained that officers had introduced a greater number of servants and took up more room than specified in the billets.[65]

As evidenced by the court-martial trial held at the death of Reverend John Drummond, the British wanted to protect the king's loyal friends. But it was not easy to distinguish between true and pretending friends. In mid-1777, the British recognized the military services of Boston loyalist Captain Alexander Campbell by granting his family a house and farm in Jamaica, Long Island, which belonged to Parson Kettletas, who had fled to Connecticut. The loyalist Campbell had volunteered with the King's Troops in Bunker Hill in June 1775, and in Danbury, Connecticut, in April 1777. When Campbell left his new residence to serve with British troops in the South, he was "happy in the thoughts of being so comfortably settled." However, when he returned on the evening of July 8, 1778, after a year's absence, he found a Connecticut refugee, Reverend Drummond, sleeping in his bedroom while his wife lay in a back room with two servants and their six children. Led by British authorities, escorted by three soldiers, and accompanied by two oxen and two horses, Reverend Drummond had "fixed upon" the Campbell bedroom and family store room in early June. In a generous response to Drummond's petition of suffering and allegiance, the British had permitted, indeed protected, his entry into the Campbell home. Enraged at Drummond's usurpation, Campbell struck him with a cane. Two months later, the minister died.

In the absence of civil courts, a British military court convened to determine whether Drummond had died of bruises inflicted by Campbell or of dysentery.[66] The case of the two nonresident Scot loyalists invited interest and testimony from neighbors and bystanders. But what finally acquitted Campbell was not the many testimonies but the evidence of Drummond's cunning. During the trial, the British learned that Reverend Drummond lived "in the most familiar intimacy" with the rebel Parson Kettletas in Connecticut. In fact, Drummond, "by pretended sufferings," wanted "to get possession of Kettletas's house and take care of it for him."[67] In effect, the reverend had conspired to protect the Parson's property in New York City. His loyalty was clearly with Kettletas and not the British government.

Other loyalists resented the unilateral military authority exerted by appointed officials. John Thurman's case against Mayor David Mathews suggests the tensions between New York's proprietors and British administration over housing. A successful merchant and loyal member of New York's Chamber of Commerce, Thurman had been "out of lines" in 1776 when the mayor, Mathews, marked his house, standing on the wharf at the North River, for use by the British authorities. Thurman claimed that the loss of the house, "unrighteously detained from me by Mayor Mr. Mathews," amounted to more than a thousand pounds. Because Mathews refused him access to the lot, Thurman could not make urgent kitchen repairs. Because Thurman's property did not appear in the city's vestry list, Thurman did not receive any rent. Because Thurman could not get possession of the property, he could not sell it when a Henry Ludlam offered to buy it. Thurman believed Mathews could only be brought to justice "if ever law and civil authority takes place."[68]

Serving as mayor and as magistrate in the Office of Police, Mathews had earned an unsavory reputation. Although he insisted that his duty was to "serve government and to bring knaves to justice," other loyalists believed he exploited the possibilities in the garrison. In September 1779, fellow magistrate Peter Dubois spoke of Mathews as a "profligate and villain" who took advantage of his position by receiving stolen goods such as spoons, watches, and clothes and appropriated goods that should have gone to the poorhouse.[69]

Some New Yorkers supported Thurman because they worried about the adverse results of denying promised privileges to returning loyalists. Andrew Elliot believed payments should be made to proprietors who had "come in upon proclamation to preserve the faith of government." Like Elliot, Smith worried about the "evil reports and bad Spirit" that could be a consequence of British refusal to honor the promises of the proclamation. The British unwillingness to appease returning New Yorkers would serve as a weapon to rebels and as a deterrent to loyalists: "Neither friends nor foes ought to hear that Government would not or could not bear the expenses of the war."[70]

But British officials hesitated to set an example. Giving up some houses to "clamours" would open up additional demands from loyalist residents, which the British could not afford to satisfy. General Clinton observed that admitting one claim would "produce ten thousand more of a like nature which if admitted would cost millions and if refused after some payments had fixed precedents, would give cause to great complaints." Major General Robertson also preferred dealing with loyalist complaints informally because "written answers to each memorial would tend chiefly to increase the number of applications."[71]

Thurman's case was not unique, and British concern was well founded. In 1783, four New York proprietors requested rent for property occupied by British troops. They complained that residence without payment violated "every principle of the British government" and remained "repugnant to reason and justice." They ended by emphasizing that "several persons under similar circumstances" had received rents with approval from the commander in chief.[72]

Designed to prohibit illegal trade, British commercial regulations appeared unreasonable and inconsistent to some New York merchants. In July 1779, William Roscale of the Superintendent's Office accused Black of attempting shipment of four trunkloads and padlocks from New York City to Long Island without a permit from the commander in chief. Although Black had attained possession of these goods in a public bidding, he did not have permission to move them without an explicit permit. In defense, Black observed that Roscale had violated customary procedures because he had seized the casks on the wharf and not aboard a vessel.

Arguing that Roscale had assumed Black's guilt for his own profit, Black demanded: "Have you ever seized goods before they were on board like you did with me?" Roscale had not. But the lack of precedent did not matter, and Black lost the case. Bitterly he accused the British of behaving arbitrarily and unfairly. In explanation, one resident cynically observed that Black should have abided strictly with the proclamation of the commander in chief in a garrison town.[73]

The lack of suitable accommodations in the city frustrated both ordinary and elite refugees. In March 1779, Clinton authorized refugees to cultivate lands and erect temporary habitations upon lands previously owned by rebels. On July 17, 1780, Philip J. Livingston officially mediated the vying claims of the refugees. Sheriff of Dutchess County and nephew of the rebel governor of New Jersey, William Livingston, Philip J. Livingston parceled out land to distressed refugee families. But the lands, usually looted of everything of value including trees, meant little to refugees who lacked means to do more than subsist on the plots.[74]

In some cases, refugees competed unsuccessfully with New Yorkers to receive the benefits of British patronage. Richard Tomlinson from Bucks County, Pennsylvania, served as a spy in Philadelphia in 1777–78. After the British evacuated Philadelphia, he suffered imprisonment but finally escaped to New York City. In 1780, when he requested provisions from the commander in chief, he received a derelict farm, much as Alexander Campbell had in 1777. Before he could take over the farm, he received a November notification from Philip J. Livingston stating that Isaac Low with his family of seven children had taken possession of it until the spring of the following year. Low did not vacate the farm, and Tomlinson, despite "incessant applications for two years," received no redress. Tomlinson accused Livingston of favoring Low. He mourned that our "true state could never be known to those high enough in power to relieve us."[75] But upon closer examination, Tomlinson appears more fraud than victim. Tomlinson had already received half a house and forty acres of land in lieu of living on a farm from New York's commandant, Sir James Robertson. He coveted Low's farm only because of the many improvements since made. Robertson dismissed Tomlinson's complaints because they lacked precedent. Livingston, Robertson pointed out, had allocated more than a hundred farms and "no complaints ha[d] ever been offered against him but this."[76]

Other resentments festered as loyalists felt their expendability. In October 1779, many alienated New Yorkers resented the commandant's requisitioning of the Dutch Church for the quartering sick British soldiers. On August 3, eight hundred soldiers had arrived from England. Unknown to the British or the loyalists, these troops carried a virulent fever, which they spread in the cramped city. More than six thousand soldiers required hospitalization. Neither the affluent nor the poor inhabitants remained immune from the sickness. In September, William Smith lamented that "we are a hospital at this house." Loyalist merchant William Bayard wondered that "so sickly a season was never known in the memory of the oldest person."[77]

The congregation that worshipped in the Dutch Church fumed at the British usurpation. Some members called upon loyalist merchant and former New York Council member Hugh Wallace to protect them against British infringement. Yet when Wallace appealed to the British authorities, he was "harshly told the matter was compounded to their satisfaction, and if the person and key did not come soon he [would] send the provost for them." Wallace censured the "impolity of disobliging the Dutch people who adhered to their loyalty." As Smith observed the carpenters removing the pews from the church, he lamented the injustice. The commandant's high-handed behavior caused the inhabitants to "despise the police of this place."[78]

The cost and scarcity of wood in the city led New Yorkers to regard the British regulars with hostility. The British army required seventy thousand cords annually. Unlike flour, oats, candles, bedding, axes, and stoves that arrived from Britain, the army depended on the colonial hinterlands to procure the wood needed for cooking, baking, washing, and, most important, for staying warm. The army's rate of consumption had rapidly exhausted the limited timber available in areas safely held by British troops. In 1780, some British officials requested that Britain supply coal to make up the deficiency. But the British Treasury balked because of the high cost of coal along with the cost of transportation and the perennial shortage of ships.[79]

During the severe winter of 1779–80, both soldiers and civilians suffered from the scarcity of firewood. The British soldiers stationed in New York City received only half their usual rations of wood. In February 1779, Clinton granted farmers special permits to cut wood from the forests on the Long Island estates of absentee rebels such as William Floyd. Clinton hoped that the farmers would contribute the cordage toward the army's needs. But the woodcutters did not distinguish between rebel and loyalist estates. In December 1779, when William Tryon instructed Major General Francis Smith at Brooklyn to employ three hundred loggers, they violated British orders by cutting wood from loyalist estates.[80]

Loyalist families on Long Island and Staten Island resented the waste and devastation committed on their lands by the refugees. In December 1779, William Smith lamented that "these attacks upon private property greatly offend." Some loyalists "excoriate[d] the General, others the police and the barrackmaster." To appease the affluent loyalists, the British authorities issued a new proclamation in April 1780 warning inhabitants not to cut wood on any land "unless they have leave from the owner to do so."[81]

The British had to transport wood across Long Island Sound and the Hudson River because they had depleted wood within fifty miles of the city. The conveyors of wood, the cartmen and the boatmen, exploited the desperate demand by imposing high prices. Many inhabitants could ill afford the extraordinary prices for firewood. Between 1778 and 1780, the price of wood rose from thirty-five shillings to seventy-five shillings a cord. In November 1777, the commandant, Valentine Jones, offered warnings to boatmen who overcharged for the transportation of firewood from Long Island to New York City. In December, he appointed John Thompson of Brooklyn to employ people to cut wood on Long Island "in order that the poorer inhabitants of this city may receive some supplies of wood at a reasonable price." In January 1778, James Robertson regulated the rates for loading and unloading of cordage. But the warnings and stipulated prices had little effect on the shrewd cartmen. A year later, British authorities were concerned that inhabitants continued to pay "exorbitant prices" for firewood. Like tavern owners and bakers, some cartmen exploited the distressed condition of the city to reap grand profits. As a result, cartman Abraham Parcell, who did not have sufficient funds to qualify to vote as a freeholder in New York in 1769, left his heirs three houses in the city, £250, and a 600-acre farm in New Jersey.[82]

The human flux and confusion strained the primitive sanitation of the crowded in the city. Between 1777 and 1780, successive military commandants issued orders to keep the streets free from debris, as the piles of filth created a health hazard for the inhabitants and the soldiers and posed a security risk for the troops by rendering the roads impassable. In 1777, James Robertson warned inhabitants and soldiers to halt their "constant practice" of throwing "dirt and filth out of their house and yards, into the streets and lanes" of the city. In 1778, Major Valentine Jones issued another notice forbidding people to leave "filth, garbage, or dirt" near a freshwater pond, which would contaminate the city's drinking water. In 1780, General Pattison designated days for garbage collection within each of the wards: South Ward on Monday, Dock Ward on Tuesday, East Ward on Wednesday, Montgomery Ward on Thursday, North Ward on Friday, and West Ward on Saturday. Finally, in April, Pattison appointed a loyalist refugee, William Hill, to supervise the cleaning of the wards. In October 1777, Hill had supplied candles to British troops. His new position represented an increase in stature.[83]

But Hill could do little to prevent the persistent accumulation of filth in the city. In August 1780, Peter Dubois worried that the ill-regulated state of the town would promote disease.[84] In April 1781, the city's commandant, Lieutenant Colonel Samuel Birch, mandated that inhabitants not throw tubs of water out of windows, clean meat and fish on the streets, or throw broken glass or oyster or clam shells on the streets.[85] Birch's desperate proclamation reveals that the inhabitants had lost faith in creating an ordered and peaceful community inside the garrison.

Some loyalists took advantage of the taxed British administration to plot intrigue. In July, 1778, Sarah Willis's husband accused Thomas Gormon, a British mariner, of sexually assaulting his wife. After shouting "surround the house," Gormon "burst open the door" and searched to see if Sarah's husband was in the house. Although the neighbor, laborer Peter Leary, heard Gormon, he did not interfere because he feared that the British had arrived to impress Sarah's husband and would seize him as well. Finding her alone, Gormon "threw her upon the floor and absolutely entered her body against her inclination." But like Reverend Drummond, Sarah was not what she appeared. Instead of protecting a loyalist woman from a British mariner, the British court found itself involved in a liaison plotted by Sarah so she could enjoy an extramarital affair with Gormon. After careful cross-examination, British officials found that Sarah had told Gormon "to pretend he came with a press gang" so that if her husband happened to be home, "it would frighten him and make him run away." Having determined that Gormon "had previous carnal knowledge of her," the court acquitted him and left Sarah to deal with her husband.[86]

The British governed New York through a series of military commandants and the Office of Police. They issued proclamations intended to reassure New Yorkers that the military did not rule arbitrarily but uniformly protected the customary rights of the king's friends. However, they could not satisfy the white underclass who needed rations and wood, the blacks who wanted security from loyalist disdain, the early loyalists who demanded a higher priority because they had pledged allegiance sooner, and the later loyalists who asked that the British keep the promises offered to those outside the king's lines. An anonymous five-page letter addressed to the commander in chief argued that loyal colonists entering British lines merited "protection & in some degree adequate support," and if the means to meet the claimants remained inadequate, "uneasiness and complaints [would] doubtless continue."[87] As the needs of the military superseded loyalist shortages, the British alienated many supporters and divided leading loyalists.

# 7 ❦ "The Die Had Been Cast"

## Loyalist Divisions

> *When it is considered that they [loyalists] have resorted further from several rebellious colonies, which must necessarily create distinction & parties amongst them and which perhaps are subdivided by more local prejudices, & animosities, it may be found difficult to combine their force so as to render it efficient and usefull either to themselves or the public.*
>
> —Anonymous, "Cursory Observations on the Refugees . . ."

In the fall of 1779, New York's leading loyalists faced a legal death. On October 27, the rebel government of New York enacted confiscation legislation that declared that some loyalists who had joined the British army or who had moved to a British-held zone such as New York City automatically forfeited their property. The new act also declared that these tainted persons would suffer the death penalty if discovered within rebel lines.[1]

Between 1776 and 1778, rebel governments in Pennsylvania, Maryland, New Jersey, Massachusetts, and New Hampshire had passed laws to secure the property of those they termed variously "fugitives and offenders," "conspirators," and "absentees." They punished loyalists for joining the British army, for offenses against the state, for entering enemy lines, and for staying within enemy's lines. In addition to penalizing loyalists, the confiscation acts promised the rebel governments sufficient returns to prosecute the war and to rebuild each colony's faltering financial position. In December 1778, the New Jersey government attainted prominent New York refugees Daniel Coxe and David Ogden Jr. The 1778 Massachusetts confiscation act punished Abijah Willard, council member from Lancaster, Massachusetts, for his appointment as assistant commissary in the British military. A Maryland act outlawed the militant loyalist refugee Robert Alexander for treason.[2]

The New York Provincial Assembly declared fifty-nine persons guilty of felony and confiscated their property for the state. Those punished by the New York Confiscation Act included Frederick Philipse III from Westchester County; Abraham Cuyler from Albany; George Duncan Ludlow and Thomas Jones, two Supreme Court judges from New York City; and each living member of His Majesty's Council resident in New York City: Oliver DeLancey, John Watts, Roger Morris, William Axtell, Hugh Wallace, Henry White, and John Harris Cruger. In addition, the rebel government of New York confiscated the property of Governor William Tryon, commander in chief Henry Clinton, Mayor David Mathews, and Reverend Charles Inglis. Remarkably, it left unnamed three loyalists closely and undeniably associated with British government: William Smith Jr., James Robertson, and Andrew Elliot. Clearly, the moderate position adopted by these gentlemen protected them from the vengeance of the rebel government.[3]

Smith worried that his omission from the Confiscation Act aroused jealousy in the city and stretched the divide between loyalist hard-liners and moderates. In December, he feared the worst consequences: "Tory writers had now given up, for the most part, any attempt to convince the Whigs of their error. The die had been cast, and there was left nothing but recrimination, invective, direful prophecy, and terrible threats."[4] The personal attacks launched against powerful and influential militant loyalists further embittered the contest, and made reconciliation a receding dream. The Confiscation Act fueled the hard-liners' growing resentment against the rebels and distanced them from loyalist moderates. The hard-liners determined that their allegiance to the Crown had done nothing to protect their persons or their estates. In February 1780, "A Refugee" expressed the need for retribution in a letter addressed to Rivington in the *Royal Gazette:* "The late rebel act of confiscation . . . should rouse every loyalist of whatever rank or denomination to a serious consideration of what must be the consequence to them and their posterity should the rebels succeed in their diabolical purposes." In 1783, the youngest son of Lieutenant Governor Cadwallader Colden damned the rebel government that had condemned him without allowing him to appear on trial. David Colden wrote that the attainder took "a man's life for the express purpose of getting his estate."[5] The act violated the reverence that Anglo-Americans felt for the security of private property that once lay behind the rebellion over British taxes.

Since Washington's raid on Trenton, the garrison loyalists had tolerated various rebel depredations. Aware of the shortage of British troops and the unguarded state of the inhabitants, the rebels had increased their control over Long Island Sound. In April 1777, Hugh Gaine observed that inhabitants in Bergen County, New Jersey, were not only in a "dismal situation for want of every necessary" but required armed protection from the "insults of the Rebels."[6] In April, a party of rebels came from Connecticut to the house of Solomon Smith on Long Island and robbed him of all the "cloathing of his Family and some Household furniture." In May, Lord Howe's aide reported another group who came to Long Island to seize a captain and sixty of his recruits. They also set fire to several barns before escaping. He regretted that the British did not have "good spies" with intelligence that would protect the inhabitants.[7] In June, Gaine reported rebels from Elizabethtown, New Jersey, who raided Staten Island "in order to plunder." In August, rebel forces made simultaneous attacks on the British posts in eastern Long Island, at Kingsbridge, and on Staten Island. Gaine reported that the British "lost in killed, wounded and missing about 150." Although British and loyalists retaliated in kind, they could not put a stop to the raids. In August, Ewald Gustav Schaukirk concluded that although British troops had put up a "smart fight," they had "lost more than they own."[8]

With Howe in Philadelphia and Burgoyne defeated in the upper Highlands, New York City and its environs became the rebels' obvious target. In October and November 1777, rebel raids targeted British posts on Staten Island.[9] The British commander of Staten Island, Captain John Campbell, complained that the troops were "inadequate to its defense." In fact, he could not find even a wagon master to apply to in case of an emergency.[10] In November, in his report of rebel success, he echoed the widespread British derision of loyalist soldiers: "Rebels have retreated and escaped the Sound under cover of their cannon from this new redoubt. From what I can learn of the Provincial Troops this morning, I found what I always suspected that they can not be thoroughly depended upon, unless supported by British troops."[11]

After the fall of Saratoga, rebel raids became more organized and targeted prominent loyalists in New York. In November, a loyalist refugee from Boston, Ward Chipman, wrote that rebels arrived "every night" in small parties. One such attack captured a "Lieutenant Buskirk & a few men of Buskirk's corps" and carried them to New Jersey.[12] A loyalist from

New Jersey, Abraham Van Buskirk, commanded the 4th Battalion of the New Jersey Volunteers. Lieutenant Colonel Stephen Kemble reported a party of rebels who ransacked New York loyalist Brigadier General Oliver DeLancey's house in Bloomingdale, Long Island, "using his wife and daughter extremely ill."[13] In November 28, Clinton reported the incident to General Howe in Philadelphia: "At one o'clock yesterday morning about 12 or 14 rebels landed at Bloomingdale, drove the small Guard of Provincials left there to protect the house, forced the doors, robbed and pillaged it, set fire to it, and behaved in a most inhuman & barbarous manner to Mrs. DeLancey, her daughter, and family."[14]

From his vantage point in Kingsbridge, just northeast of New York City, Brigadier General Montfort Browne observed that the rebellious contingent had grown more violent. In January 1778, he noticed that the rebels "are so elated and puff'd up from their success, that they have dared to do the most unwarrantable acts." Browne deplored the rebel execution of Lieutenant Palmer, killed for carrying a British warrant for raising men. He also denounced the execution of a corporal who had gone to Connecticut to bring back his four sons into British lines. The sons had watched the father's execution.[15]

Rebel attacks persisted through the summer of 1778. In June, Kemble reported that a party of twenty men "with their faces blacked and otherwise disguised came into Flatbush [Long Island] and took off Major Moncrieffe and Mr. Bache." This rebel party also attempted to capture the mayor, David Mathews. Thomas Moncrieffe, in addition to being a major, was Theophylact Bache's brother-in-law.[16]

The Spanish entry into the war in June 1779, the consequent reduction of available British naval strength in the Atlantic, and the abandonment of the British naval base in Rhode Island in the fall provided a wider scope of action to rebel naval vessels, privateers, and whaleboats. Organized in groups ranging from three to thirty, rebel gangs from Connecticut rowed across in whaleboats to seize provisions from Long Island. They robbed and plundered to incite fear, to exact revenge on loyalists, to acquire hard currency, and to seize desperately needed clothing and wagons. In July 1779, three rebels murdered Morris Simmons, a refugee from Dutchess County, because he occupied the farm previously owned by a rebel. In addition to carrying off ten "respectable and loyal inhabitants from Musket Cove," another party of thirty rebels plundered the house of Stephen Thorne and his son, Edward, in Cow's Neck. When they found a refugee from Westchester County in Thorne's household, they robbed him of his clothing and his gold, silver, and New York currency. In November, they plundered the house of Thomas Jones and carried the junior judge of the supreme court off to Connecticut. In his letter to the Society for the Propagation of the Gospel in November 1779, Inglis lamented that Long Island "is infested by the Rebels who are constantly making incursions across the Sound . . . plundering the inhabitants, & carrying many of them off captives." No clergyman dared settle in the dangerous region. As the British failed to protect New Yorkers, gangs of robbers established themselves within the city. In January 1780, one seven-member gang even established a code called the "Articles for Robbing." Blackening their faces, the gang swore to target people purported to be rebels, to live like brothers, to shun strong drink when coming to action, and to "dive with each other to the last copper."[17]

New York City's leading loyalists hoped desperately to resolve their formidable problems through news of British victories. But during 1779 and 1780, the war around New York amounted to little more than a series of maneuvers and destructive raids, signifying no strategic gains for the British. In June 1779, the British captured the forts of Stony Point and Verplanck's Point, which projected from opposite sides of the Hudson and formed the southern threshold of the Highlands. However, as Clinton awaited reinforcements to seize West Point in the Hudson Highlands, the rebels retaliated. In July, within six weeks of the British conquest, General Anthony Wayne led rebel forces to recapture Stony Point and take 324 prisoners. In August, Major General Henry Lee, with 500 soldiers, attacked the British post across the Hudson at Paulus Hook, New Jersey, and took 150 prisoners.[18]

Although British troops recaptured Stony Point immediately and the rebel attack of Paulus Hook had no far-reaching military consequences, the rebels' boldness reminded New Yorkers of the lurking rebel threat just miles from the city. Many New Yorkers questioned the British prospects of suppressing the larger rebellion if the British had difficulty repelling rebel attacks immediately outside British headquarters. In August, William Smith remarked that soldiers as well as refuges grew "suspicious of the General, and the worst consequences must follow." The town, he lamented, grew "disgusted and dispirited." Colonel Charles Stuart noted that the rebel attacks at Stony Point and Paulus Hook "served to inspirit the rebels and gave a degree of venom to the General's enemies."[19]

On September 1, 1779, word reached New York that Spain had entered the war against Britain. Added to the military stalemate of the summer, the appearance of a new enemy further eroded loyalists' morale. Some worried that the Spanish threat preoccupied the British ministers to such an extent that they "neglected America." The intervention of another powerful Bourbon foe meant a further diversion of British resources. In June, a combined armada of French and Spanish ships had already made a serious bid against Britain in the English Channel. As French and Spanish privateers had raided the British waters and took hundreds of ships as prizes, British forces were stretched thinly to protect their overseas possessions. The rebellious colonies became a lesser concern, a buffer zone to protect the valuable British West Indian islands from Spanish and French attack.[20]

In the fall of 1779, Clinton prepared for his offensive in Charlestown, South Carolina. He abandoned Stony Point and Verplanck's Point and removed British troops from Rhode Island to create a combined force of twenty-five thousand troops. In September, Major Patrick Ferguson opposed abandoning the Highland posts after exerting half a campaign in seizing them. He lamented that the retreat "must hurt the King's cause by discouraging his friends, giving confidence to his enemy, and rendering the troops totally averse to future works." William Tryon also protested the evacuation of Rhode Island, for he believed that the British occupation of Rhode Island had kept rebels in New England under continual apprehension, provided a good harbor for the British fleet, and added to the security of Long Island. Most of all, Tryon feared that the evacuation meant "a damp [was] thrown on the minds of the numerous loyalists throughout the continent and the spirits of the rebels in proportion raised."[21] Clinton ignored Tryon's prescient concerns because he determined to consolidate requisite military resources to launch his next campaign in the South to the neglect of the North.

## Toward Militancy

In 1779, William Franklin intensified his efforts to lead an autonomous military organization of loyalist refugees. He criticized the loosely organized refugee groups that engaged in piecemeal depredatory incursions against rebel posts. On June 1, the *Royal Gazette* reported that forty refugees attacked the houses of "some notoriously violent Rebels" in Shoal Harbor, New Jersey, and brought back with them to New York "27 milch

cows, 7 horses, 2 waggons loaded with goods, &c." The refugees sold the
plunder at an auction.[22]

General Clinton's practice of limiting warrants to loyalist refugees who
performed ancillary duties on behalf of the garrison antagonized Franklin.
In early November, Clinton authorized the former mayor of Albany, Abraham Cuyler, to muster a battalion of six hundred loyal refugee volunteers
who would procure wood for the garrison. Franklin considered the ad hoc
groups wasted precious resources because "so little will be done by them
in that way as not to deserve attention." Franklin highlighted the importance of embodying the loyalist refugees under a single person in whom
the loyalists could "confide and to whom they have an attachment." He
hoped to establish a substantial loyalist corps that would conduct large-
scale campaigns to inflict permanent damage to rebel forces.[23]

Reverend Inglis and William Tryon supported Franklin. In December
1778, Inglis had hoped that the Refugees "may be empowerd to act against
the rebels this winter." In June 1779, Tryon embraced the idea of widening
the breach between the loyalists and the rebels by setting William Franklin
in direct opposition to Benjamin Franklin, placing the "the father and son
in open opposition to each other." He believed the zeal of the loyal refugees along with their "intimate and minute knowledge of the country"
would render them invaluable to the King. After all, the loyalists fought
not only to reclaim the land they had lost during the war but within a
landscape they understood better than British soldiers.[24]

Tryon resolved to help Franklin. On June 30, 1779, Tryon drafted an
ambitious twelve-article outline on behalf of Franklin and his refugees,
entitled "Proposal for embodying the loyalists within the British lines."
Tryon claimed that the "soundest policy" dictated that Franklin, under
the title of director general and commandant, lead the refugees. Franklin
alone could encourage the hundreds of loyalists willing to fight to suppress the rebellion. If provided with an initial £20,000 to £30,000, arms,
ammunition, and armed vessels, Franklin would set up an organization
that planned and directed enterprises for distressing the enemy from
Rhode Island, Long Island, Staten Island, and Sandy Hook, New Jersey. Of
fundamental importance to Tryon's plan was the stipulation that the refugees would have authority to imprison the rebels they seized and exchange
them for captured refugees. By holding their own rebel prisoners independently, the loyalists would have the critical leverage required to negotiate
on behalf of their imprisoned fellows.[25]

The British had neglected loyalist prisoners, whom the Continental Congress treated as traitors—common criminals—rather than legitimate prisoners of war. In contrast to their disregard for the imprisoned loyalists, the British had worked out a system by "composition" for the exchange of their own men, who they believed merited higher consideration. The British assigned each soldier's rank a value and negotiated with the congress to exchange soldiers of like rank. If the British could not exchange those of equal rank, they combined values of several to achieve equality.[26]

In the summer and fall of 1779, New York's hard-liners organized to influence British policy by corresponding directly with England and transacting other business "conducive to the interest of the whole." No intercolonial loyalist organization had previously formed on behalf of all the loyalists in the colonies. In order to create a unified group to speak for the whole, the loyalist spokesmen met with refugees from their own colonies. They hoped to encourage participation by inviting their constituents to meet and speak separately, without interference from loyalists in other colonies. In August, the *Royal Gazette* announced a meeting for the respectable people from the province of Pennsylvania and from New York. In October, the refugees from Maryland convened in Hick's Tavern, and in November, Massachusetts refugees met in Queen's Head Tavern. In December, refugees from New Jersey and Virginia arranged their own meetings.[27]

Coincidentally, as the refugees pressed for Clinton's sanction to form an autonomous military organization, Clinton received from his trusted officer Major John Andre a sixteen-page indictment of soldiers' excesses within the borders of New York City. In December 1779, Andre criticized the violence directed against civilians by British and loyalist soldiers. Andre rationalized that soldiers stole and killed cattle for want of a sufficient supply of fresh meat from the commissary. But the soldiers' rampant destruction of items with no utility disturbed Andre. He had seen "soldiers loaded with household utensils which they have taken for the wanton pleasures of spoil and which they have thrown aside an hour afterwards." The soldiers' conduct involved the king's friends in ruin and falsified the word of the general. Andre asked Clinton to construct some kind of a "check wheel" not only to "stop any further decline of discipline but even retrieve something of what has been lost." From Clinton's perspective, the loyalist hard-liners hardly seemed suitable to the purpose. Rather, their fervor threatened to intensify the civil war that raged on the city's borders.[28]

The militant refugees established an association, created a committee, elected Franklin as their president, and continued to demand official sanction. On November 29, they circulated their first public declaration. They assured their subservience to General Clinton and requested his patronage and encouragement, that is, funds and ammunition. But they stated unequivocally their separate stakes in fighting the rebellion. They explained that they found it beneficial to their "interests, families, and estates to have mutual intercourse with each other." In addition, through their example and influence, they wanted to "excite a spirit among His Majesty's loyal subjects." They emphasized a recourse to arms remained the "only effectual means to restore the public tranquility and or the authority of legal government."[29] The suppression of the unnatural rebellion now required previously unthinkable measures.

Clinton ignored the hard-liners' petition for fear that their intervention would impede his own ability to operate militarily around New York City. In November, he feared they would "alarm the enemy where he might wish to lull them to security, by carrying distress where he might wish to protect, by giving admission into & egress from our posts to various persons without his knowledge or consent." The refugees could operate successfully without hindering Clinton's army only if Clinton trusted Franklin sufficiently to share the details of British military objectives. Clinton could not countenance such a strategy. Clinton refused to trust Franklin for the same reasons he had earlier denied authorization of a loyalist office of inquiry. Not only could the loyalists interfere with his own plans, but their success could make his own command appear inadequate. As Joseph Galloway had complained about General William Howe's military strategy in the parliamentary inquiry of 1779, these loyalists could complain about him and thereby destroy both his reputation and his career. Determined to maintain sole control in New York City at all costs, Clinton refused to concede to the militants or the moderates.[30]

As Clinton balked at granting the refugees the funds and the military autonomy they demanded, the refugees went over Clinton's head. During the summer of 1780, they appealed directly to their contacts in London and to the British ministry there. Writing to Joseph Galloway, Daniel Coxe reflected that each colony contained "a few loyal active subjects who by disarming the disaffected, intimidating the wavering and driving the violent" could suppress the "wanton and languishing rebellion" and restore America to the king's authority.[31]

The refugees sent George Leonard to lobby Lord George Germain. A prominent merchant from Boston, Leonard had accompanied the British troops to Halifax in 1775 and followed them to New York City in 1776. During the summer of 1779, Leonard commanded a small fleet of privateers, and the captured prizes brought him more than £23,400.[32] General Thomas Gage had recommended him as one of the "Gentlemen who are sensible, remarkably firm and not to be intimidated."[33] The February 13, 1779, issue of the *Royal Gazette* circulated Leonard's petition on behalf of New York's refugees who suffered confiscation and banishment, the "two inhuman acts of the usurped government." Given the indignities they had endured, Leonard asserted that they considered themselves "fully justified by the laws of God and man, in making retaliations and reprisals." He concluded by inviting "all sincere friends of government who are predisposed to join full participation of all the privileges benefits and advantages . . . in this determined Band of Loyal Associators."[34]

Leonard articulated most clearly the vision of the hard-liners. He observed that a great number of zealous loyalists lacked the means to put their "zeal into practice." Generally of a rank in life superior to the common seaman or soldier, they owned large properties and came from several provinces. Averse to remaining "idle spectators" in the rebellion, these gentlemen prepared to employ loyalists, attack and distress rebel ports, and capture badly needed supplies. The refugees' efforts would lessen the financial burden on the British government and promote His Majesty's cause.[35]

In the fall of 1780, Lord Germain approved the refugees' request for a parallel and powerful loyalist-led organization because it focused so much on operations by sea—that is, on the raiding of rebel ports. Three years earlier, Germain had written Howe about the importance of a "warm diversion upon the coasts of Massachusetts Bay and New Hampshire" to place a "salutary check" on rebel privateering "as far as your intended plan will admit." In August, when Howe's operations toward Philadelphia precluded any diversions upon the coast of New England, Germain regretted the loss of the "great advantages [that] would certainly have arisen from that mode of alarming and distressing the enemy." Although he finally placed his faith in the success of military operations and not a naval blockade of rebel-controlled ports, Germain hoped that loyalists could assist the British efforts by hindering shipments from rebel ports.[36]

Indeed, Leonard's proposal appeared ideal. Germain envisioned an autonomous organization whose members received neither rank nor pay as military officers. He directed Clinton to grant the refugees' requests for funds and provisions and committed to providing each of the armed refugees two hundred acres of land in the colonies if they served until the end of the war. In April, Leonard triumphantly reported Germain's approval to Franklin.[37]

Germain's sanction compelled Clinton to heed the refugees' demands, but it did not require him to accommodate the terms they requested. With the assistance of William Smith and Andrew Elliot, Clinton gutted Franklin's plan. He relegated the refugees to occupy an inferior and ancillary position under British military command. The refugees could undertake no enterprise without Clinton's explicit permission. Clinton could issue unilaterally "other new Instructions altering enlarging or changing" the refugees' original powers "from time to time." Furthermore, the refugees had to describe each proposed operation in "minute" detail, allowing for no modification in plans. Most gallingly, Clinton denied the refugees any power to exchange rebel prisoners. He wanted to supervise any exchanges himself.[38] The refugees swallowed the revisions bitterly. Their common experience of exile had created, on one hand, an uncompromising tone in stating their case and, on the other, a deep disenchantment with the realization of their ultimate lack of power. In December 1780, the Associated Loyalists were formally organized under a board of directors.

Significantly, Clinton did not grant Franklin sole authority over the new organization. In addition to Franklin, nine other loyalists became codirectors. These men included Daniel Coxe from New Jersey, Josiah Martin from North Carolina, Robert Alexander and Anthony Stewart of Maryland, Timothy Ruggles and George Leonard of Massachusetts, George Rome from Rhode Island, Edward Lutwyche from New Hampshire, and George Duncan Ludlow from New York. Many of these leaders had suffered harshly for their allegiance to reunion.[39]

A member of the New Jersey Council under Governor Franklin, Daniel Coxe played an important role in British government during Sir William Howe's rule over Philadelphia. Whereas Joseph Galloway served as superintendent of police directly under Howe, Coxe, along with Philadelphia merchants John Potts and Samuel Shoemaker served as magistrates under Galloway, for which role they received £300 per annum.[40]

Coxe's inability to gain a respectable position within the British administration disappointed him. However, when he discovered that equivalent loyalist gentlemen benefitted while he suffered, his bitterness was palpable. In November 1779, he raged against the £400 warrant received by Andrew Allen, late attorney general of Pennsylvania.[41] Allowing the "indelicate" situation that compelled him to "hold a personal contrast between another Gentleman and myself," Coxe made his case. First, Coxe observed that Allen had not opposed independence "from the first" but only after the Declaration of Independence. The government needed to reward men like Coxe who had "exhibited unequivocal and constant proofs of attachment." Second, unlike Allen, Coxe had collected intelligence and formed under his own patronage the 250–man corps called the Jersey Volunteers.[42] Third, by fleeing to London in 1778, Allen had deserted his country and could in no way surpass Coxe's contributions of "early steady uniform loyalty, principle, conduct, active exertion, private influence, public character, or estate." Fourth, Allen merited less because William Penn had appointed him, whereas Coxe served in the executive and legislative council appointed "immediately by the King."[43]

Coxe maneuvered relentlessly to gain a higher footing than his fellow loyalists. On July 4, 1780, Coxe, Shoemaker, and Potts jointly petitioned General Clinton to use his "discretionary powers" to make provisions for their families in New York City. Fearing his appeal "must have sunk in a joint representation," Coxe distanced himself from the other two by submitting a second memorial: "Though equally intitled with me . . . [Potts and Shoemaker] are in many other essentials short of my pretensions, though in every other respect equally meritorious." Coxe may have felt his position on the New Jersey Council distinguished him from the merchants in Philadelphia who lacked direct political connections to the government.[44] His attempts at elevating his worth appear to have been successful. In August 1783 Clinton's replacement as commander in chief, Sir Guy Carleton, granted both Coxe and Shoemaker £100 annually. John Potts, however, received just half that amount.[45]

Born in Ireland and raised on the island of Antigua, Governor Josiah Martin had long benefited from the slave-trading interests of his father, Colonel Samuel Martin; his uncle Josiah Martin's standing as former councillor of New York colony; and his elder half brother Samuel's political connections as a member of Parliament.[46] Among the wealthiest on the island of Antigua, Colonel Martin's plantation of 605 acres, together with 304 slaves, sugar works, and livestock, was valued at £300,000 sterling. The colonel used the income from his sugar plantations to further his four sons' careers, to help them acquire "any genteel little post." Like William Franklin, Josiah Martin flourished under his father's scrupulous attention. He also benefited from his uncle's connections to General Thomas Gage and to Scottish merchant John Watts.[47] Martin disappointed his ambitious father by joining the military and marrying his cousin Betsey. The colonel had aspired to a high civil position and a more beneficial matrimonial union with "a Lady of Character and good fortune at New York, where there are many heiresses to vast Estates."[48] Fortunately for the colonel, ill-health caused Josiah Martin to sell his military commission, and Samuel Martin helped him gain an appointment as royal governor of North Carolina in 1771.

Occupying the North Carolina seat left vacant by his predecessor, William Tryon, Josiah Martin inherited the position at a time of turbulence. He faced many of the difficulties confronted by Governor Franklin of New Jersey and Governor Tryon of New York. Like Franklin, Martin tried but failed to prevent North Carolina from sending representatives to the Continental Congress in 1774. After the bloodshed at Lexington, Tryon found refuge on the *Dutchess of Gordon* for eleven months. Likewise, Martin hid on the *Cruizer* and other ships in the harbor of Wilmington for over fourteen months before escaping to New York City in January 1777. Like Tryon, Martin had hoped that British regiments would come to the assistance of the king's friends in time to put down the rebellion. As Tryon had petitioned on behalf of New Yorkers, Martin asked General Howe for funds on behalf of loyalist troops in North Carolina.[49] General Howe and General Clinton rejected both appeals. In 1779, the two men looked to the Associated Loyalists as a viable alternative.

Unlike Coxe and Martin, the Maryland representatives of the Associated Loyalists had no seat in the proprietary government of that province. Anthony Stewart, a merchant, and Robert Alexander, a Cecil County lawyer, followed different routes to New York. Born in Aberdeen, Scotland, Anthony Stewart came to Maryland in 1753 at the age of fifteen and within ten years had established himself as a merchant in Annapolis. Burned in effigy because of his opposition to nonimportation, Stewart fled to England in 1775 and arrived in New York in 1777 with a recommendation from Germain for a position in the British administration.[50] Unlike Stewart, Alexander came to oppose the rebellion slowly. He served as a delegate to the Second Continental Congress but refused to take an oath against the British government. He left Maryland for Philadelphia when British troops gained control of that city in September 1777, and he followed the regulars to New York City upon evacuation of Philadelphia in the summer of 1778. Drawing information from their contacts with key merchants in Maryland, Alexander and Stewart recommended that the British capture the peninsula between Delaware and Chesapeake Bays and utilize it as a base of operations and supply.[51] Trusted by the last British commander in chief, Sir Guy Carleton, Alexander served on a British-appointed board to handle loyalist claims in 1782. Stewart was paymaster for a loyalist regiment, the Maryland Loyalists.[52]

Along with George Leonard, Timothy Ruggles was a long-standing resident of Massachusetts and had risen to the highest levels. A graduate of Harvard College, Ruggles established a prestigious military and civil career. By 1758, he was brigadier general, and in 1762, he served as chief justice of the Worcester County court. His opposition to the rebellion led crowds to plunder his mansion and poison his horses. In 1775, Ruggles fled from Worcester to Boston and then left for Halifax with the British troops when they evacuated in March 1776. He accompanied the British troops to New York in June 1776 and commanded on Staten Island during the first battle between British regulars and Continental soldiers.[53]

Clinton made sure the Associated Loyalists posed no threat to British authority or strategy. Fundamentally, Clinton distrusted the organization and felt its potential to obstruct his own operations far outweighed any potential advantages. At every step, Clinton restricted the refugees' activities and limited their supplies of weapons, rations, ships, and supplies. In January 1781, when the directors asked to control their own munitions and weapons, Clinton refused. When they asked for blank commissions to add prospective members, Clinton balked. Deprived of Clinton's much-needed support, the Associated Loyalists never expanded to become a serious menace to rebel strongholds.[54]

By the end of January, the refugees amounted to no more than five hundred members. They operated off Long Island, in Kingsbridge, and at Paulus Hook along the coastline of New Jersey. The refugees harassed isolated regions and forced the inhabitants to remain on guard. The Long Island group became the most powerful and successful as it plundered the Connecticut shores with whaleboats. But their severely circumcised powers hindered the scale of their operations. One report typifies the limited reach of their raids. In July 1781, Lieutenant Colonel Joshua Upham, a refugee from Massachusetts commanding at Lloyd's Neck, Long Island, reported to Franklin that 38 men had marched five miles through enemy country and captured 50 men and 40 horses without the loss of a single man.[55] Franklin had envisioned much more.

## Toward Civil Rule

During the summer of 1779, the hard-liners' ardor and persistence gradually drew the attention and then the condemnation of moderate New Yorkers. Andrew Elliot worried about the "fatal consequences that must attend a separate command particularly in the hands of People heated by resentment."[56] On June 16, 1779, police magistrate Peter Dubois distanced himself from New Jersey's hard-line refugees. He called them a "parcel of murdering, robbing, thieving rascals." The refugees defended themselves immediately and publicly. In an essay in the *Royal Gazette,* one hardliner lamented that the British stigmatized the refugee as a "miscreant, a wretch, a plunderer," whereas a loyalist who "from a delicate sense of honor, and a tender regard to the dictates of conscience" refused to take up arms to protect his country's future received undue approbation.[57] The hard-liner accused the moderates of cowardice.

In 1776, General William Howe had suspended the civil authority of New York's governor, William Tryon. After three years of indecisive battle, Lord Germain returned these civil powers to Major General James Robertson in hopes of pacifying the colonists estranged by military governance. In July, as Tryon and Franklin clamored for greater loyalist military autonomy, some worried about General Robertson's delay. The violence proposed by the militants would destroy any chance of reconciliation. In December, Smith observed that the multitude expressed "ardent longing for General Robertson as the common father of the refugees."[58]

Smith supposed that some loyalists opposed the restoration of civil rule because they dreaded the loss of lucrative positions within the British military government. In August 1779, when William Bayard censured Robertson's appointment, Smith suspected that it rendered Bayard's plan "of engrossing the vendue business abortive." In September, Smith challenged David Mathews's objection to civil government on the same grounds. Mathews had accrued wealth by accepting bribes from loyalists who desired to protect their estates from refugees and soldiers. Since Mathews received many corrupt advantages from the distraught state of the city, Smith claimed, he "must dread the restoration of the peace in this country and the reestablishment of order."[59]

New York's moderates found new hope for their vision of civil government with the arrival of Robertson in March 1780. Robertson had served as military commandant of New York City between 1776 and 1778. In 1780, he considered his rank in North America only below that of General Henry Clinton and General Charles Cornwallis.[60]

A newly appointed council composed of Andrew Elliot, merchant John Harris Cruger, and former councillors Charles W. Apthorpe, William Axtell, Oliver DeLancey, Roger Morris, Hugh Wallace, and Henry White greeted Robertson. The councillors read Robertson's commission in a room opposite Tryon's bedroom, "fearing it would be too much" for Tryon to tolerate hearing the expansive powers granted to his replacement. Afterward, the councillors proceeded to the balcony of City Hall, waited for silence, and read aloud Robertson's commission.[61]

Like a minority of British military officials, Robertson favored the more moderate policy of potential reconciliation.[62] He bewailed the plundering disposition of the army, which, he complained to Smith, "is brave, but under no direction. There is neglect of everything. There is neither police within [n]or vigor without."[63] In 1776, Robertson advocated leniency as the best means to regain the allegiance of the deluded Americans. He condemned the seizure of private property of noncombatant rebels by British soldiers because he hoped to reconcile such colonists. In 1777, he devoted considerable time to reviewing, addressing, and praising loyalist regiments. He commended Massachusetts refugee Abijah Willard for forming a company to cooperate with the king's troops, which would "extirpate anarchy and overawe a rebellion." In 1778, he favored the restoration of civil government in at least one British-held colony to demonstrate the benefits of royal control.[64]

Robertson assumed that reconciliation between the rebellious colonies and the British Empire remained tenable. He sympathized with the plight of the New York loyalists, caught between rebel persecution and the constraints of British martial rule. He lamented the presence of those who, using the arts of "malice and faction," rejected the "ties of language, manners, laws, customs, habits, interests, religion, and blood" in favor of an "unnatural separation."[65] In the parliamentary inquiry against General Howe initiated by Germain in mid-1779, Robertson had testified to loyalist strength. Robertson still anticipated the "number and spirit of the Loyalists" in the colonies "would afford great Aid" and lead to British victory.[66]

New York's leading moderates expressed effusive support for Robertson. In May, members of the Chamber of Commerce congratulated Robertson on his appointment. They expressed satisfaction with the appointment of one who knew the province's "real Interests" and had proved "capable and desirous of promoting them."[67] In June, another group of prominent New York inhabitants, led by the mayor, David Mathews, formally welcomed Robertson. They commended the British administration for the "just and equitable Military Establishment" but hinted strongly at their desire for the restoration of civil government. In July, eleven inhabitants of King's County, led by Councillor William Axtell, expressed their support. One month later, seventeen Queen's County loyalists expressed trust in Robertson's competent administration.[68]

The loyalist addresses submitted to Robertson reveal the steadfast conviction and cohesion of the loyalist moderates. But the limited number of signatures hints at common loyalists' loss of hope. In 1776, almost four thousand New Yorkers had submitted proclamations in which they had expressed their loyalty and requested the restoration of civil government. In 1780, New York's leading loyalists could no longer summon the same thousands to declare effusive allegiance. The inhabitants determined that loyalist leaders lacked clout in shaping British strategy in New York.

In 1778, Lord George Germain had predicated the southern campaign on the rumored existence of loyalist sentiment in the southern colonies of Georgia, South Carolina, and North Carolina. The southern loyalist leaders insisted that thousands of loyalists would declare themselves once the British army defeated the local rebels. Organized into loyalist militia units, and led by experienced British officers, the loyalists could control substantial areas of the South, freeing the British regulars to expand operations northward into the Chesapeake Bay area.[69]

Dismissing the failure of an earlier expedition of 1776, the former governors of Georgia and the Carolinas emphasized the advantages of a renewed campaign in the South. In March 1776, British troops under Major General Henry Clinton had launched their first excursion in the southern colonies. Encouraged by the glowing reports of substantial loyalist support in North Carolina from former governors Josiah Martin and William Tryon, the ministry had sought to exploit the loyalist potential there before beginning the main campaign in New York City. However, Clinton's troops arrived too late. The loyalists in North Carolina had risen prematurely, and rebel forces impeded their efforts to join the British troops on the coast. Clinton's expedition suffered further when a much-anticipated

British fleet of forty-four vessels did not arrive in time to provision the British regulars who had landed on Cape Fear, North Carolina.[70]

In December 1778, Lieutenant Colonel Archibald Campbell captured Savannah, Georgia. The British hoped that the recovery of Georgia would protect East Florida and provide a base for future operations in the Carolinas. In May 1780, Clinton secured the most dramatic British victory of the revolution by capturing the major southern seaport of Charleston, South Carolina. Charleston would secure Georgia, and its harbor made it an ideal base for an army dependent on supply by sea. At Charleston, the rebels surrendered six thousand soldiers, four frigates, and over three hundred cannon. Confident of British victory in the South, Clinton returned to New York City in June 1780.[71]

During his first months in New York, Robertson optimistically assessed the state of affairs in the city. He viewed his long experience in the colonies as an appropriate prelude to his governorship. He mused that New Yorkers "have been looking for my Arrival." Encouraged by his appointment, many had begun to "repair and rebuild houses and to enclose and manure fields." In May, upon news of Clinton's victory in Charleston, Robertson became still more optimistic. This "single circumstance" convinced him that America and England would again unite. Robertson anticipated that Clinton's victory would "prodigiously encrease our friends and lessen the force of our enemies." His only regret, Robertson wrote admiringly to Clinton, is "that You have left us nothing to do."[72]

Robertson expected the restoration of civil government to reanimate loyalists by providing irrefutable proof His Majesty's commitment to their well-being. On March 29, 1780, Robertson asked Clinton to declare "such Parts of this Colony, as are within Our Lines, at the King's peace," as he could not "by meer military Exertions give Satisfaction to the Loyalists in these Islands." In April, Robertson anticipated a "complete re-Establishment" of civil government in New York province. The assembly would immediately declare a complete amnesty for those who had supported rebel leaders. Protected from "vindictive Rage of their own Countrymen," many would "throw down their Arms." The civil courts would enforce a "renewal of order and a respect for the laws." Administered by their entrusted leaders in the assembly and in the courts, many loyalists would aspire to become "better and happier Soldiers."[73]

Like Robertson, Smith also conceived that the restoration of civil government in New York would begin to heal the bitter wounds inflicted on the battlefield. In May, he declared that the colonists so cherished the "constitution ever dear to Englishmen" that they would remain forever "sullen under any other Government."[74] Smith believed staunchly that the civil government could act in harmony with the military without obstructing military operations. Prior to the formal opening of the courts, a loyalist-dominated assembly should structure laws to promote military and civilian cooperation. Smith anticipated the assembly would comprise four members from the four counties of Long Island and of Staten Island, four from New York City, and four from Westchester County. The sixteen members would constitute a quorum. Representatives from the northern counties of New York posed no threat, as loyal counties constituted a majority. At the very least, sending the writs for an assembly to upstate New York would divide the rebel faction. In August, Smith sent a copy of Robertson's proclamation to Livingston Manor in Dutchess County in hopes that it would persuade tenants to declare their loyalty to the Crown.[75]

But Clinton forcefully opposed the revival of civilian rule in New York. On July 1, he asserted that he would give up his command if "Civil government should take place in a province when military operations were carrying on."[76] In part, Clinton's objection to the resumption of civil government resulted from military necessity. Since the British occupation and subsequent evacuation of Philadelphia in 1778, the British had reclaimed no substantial territory in the northern colonies. Their attempts to gain command of the Hudson Highlands had failed. Almost a decade later, in 1790, Clinton recollected that the British never controlled sufficient regions in New York to guarantee a fair representation from each of the thirteen counties. Within the province of New York, the British only held Manhattan Island, Long Island, and Staten Island. Delegates from the northern counties could have added to the assembly's numbers, but the British commander did not know these loyalists and therefore distrusted them. They could establish laws that would adversely affect the British garrison.[77] Finally, despite Smith's optimistic claims, the British did not fully command Westchester County. And without representation from Westchester County, a quorum, and therefore, an assembly, remained impossible.[78]

Clinton especially worried that judicial power could restrain his military operations. The civil courts, Clinton feared, would place "clogs, destructions, and disappointments . . . in the way of our military proceedings." He wished therefore to avoid the "ills and inconveniencys that at this time would attend the opening of courts of law and the formal revival of civil government." The establishment of civilian courts staffed by loyalist judges who believed fiercely in the subordination of the military to the civil power would result in harsh sentences. Clinton dreaded civilian suits against conscientious officers who had only performed their duties.[79]

Clinton recognized that many New Yorkers would abuse him for withholding his consent to the revival of civil government. But his reasoning never wavered. When an area remained actively involved in the actual operations of war or stayed immediately threatened, civil restoration would prove "inexpedient." He asserted that "experience has proved that in all countries when the operations of war existed the martial law has always been found to be better adapted to the exigencies of such a state than the civil."[80] While the fate of the rebellion remained undecided, military rule had no parallel.

On the other hand, Admiral Mariot Arbuthnot supported the restoration of civil government. Frustrated by the army's plundering operations, he wanted civil courts to divide the spoils between the army and the navy. But Clinton detested the aged Arbuthnot and disregarded his views. He dismissed Arbuthnot as "an old woman," and in August 1780 demanded that the London ministry recall Arbuthnot. As intermediary between the two commanders, Robertson found their animosity inimical to the king's interests. He determined that the good repute of the British command in the colonies required a "Concealment of those Differences." In August 1780, Lord Germain settled the dispute between Clinton and Arbuthnot by reassuring Clinton that Arbuthnot could not authorize the revival of civil governance without Clinton's full consent.[81]

In July, Clinton consigned Robertson to serve as lieutenant governor of New York. Robertson determined to execute the spirit of the instructions he had received "under any name."[82] He tabled restoring civil government and focused on ameliorating what he called "military misrule." He promised to provide the inhabitants with all the advantages of civil government while remaining "free from the loss of time and the expense of lawsuits." He hoped that a "good police and good discipline may make the neighborhood of the army advantageous to its inhabitants, and the industry of these, being excited by security and order, useful to the state."[83] A return to security and protection would stand in favorable contrast to the "tyranny, taxes, and arbitrary cruelties" among the rebels. Reanimated by the orderly state of the city, the inhabitants would gratefully assist the British troops. The colonists who witnessed the munificence if not the constitutionalism of British governance in New York City would abandon rebel leaders. In September, he asserted: "As sure as men prefer ease to pain, so surely our government will be sought and the rebels shunned."[84]

Robertson sought to conciliate New Yorkers by appointing prominent civilians to key posts within British administration. Modeled on the office established in the city by Sir William Howe in May 1778, Robertson set up a second police office on Long Island in July 1780. He appointed a forty-six-year-old New York councillor, Gabriel Duncan Ludlow, as superintendent of police and as master of the rolls on Long Island. As master of the rolls, Ludlow would serve as the chief judge of the Court of Chancery and exercise broad jurisdiction over frauds, foreclosures, and trusts in the event that civil courts reopened.[85] Robertson believed it "more agreeable to the British constitution and [of] less offense to the people to be tryd and even punished by the judgments of their peers than by soldiers."[86] He also appointed Cadwallader Colden's son, David Colden, as assistant superintendent of police. In his September report to Germain, Robertson anticipated the salutary effects if gentlemen of known loyalty and high esteem would act as "magistrates or arbitrators, and prevent or settle all differences, without delay, fee, or expense."[87]

Predictably, Clinton balked at Ludlow's appointment. Robertson had extended the civilian infrastructure without Clinton's authorization. Clinton's hard-line stance frustrated those who had hoped for civil rule as a means to peaceful reconciliation. Smith saw no reason a competent military commander could not accommodate a civilian government. He contended that a wise general would "not suffer the laws to check the success of the Royal arms."[88]

## The Case of Colonel Roger Morris

Between December 1781 and January 1782, 356 loyalist refugees asked for the removal Colonel Roger Morris as inspector of refugees. In January 1779, in an effort to placate the loyalists, Clinton had appointed Morris, a former New York councillor, to examine loyalist memorials. The memorialists faulted Morris for two reasons. First, they argued that his "inhumanity" resulted "from his total ignorance of the characters of the refugees." When Hannah Watson, a widow from Dutchess County, applied for relief, Morris dismissed her memorial because it did not include signatures from known loyalists. He wrote that "there were no names of any consequence in it"; the names she mentioned may as well have been "cartmens' names."

Second, they resented his "austere manners." They concluded he was unfit for his task and inspired a "want of confidence" among the friends of government. Indeed, they asserted that his attitude suppressed the "ardor which if improv'd might be attended with the utmost beneficial effects." Thus, Morris's haughtiness revealed his alien status and suppressed the passions of those who could be loyal.[89]

Living in cramped and filthy conditions, hundreds of refugees submitted memorials to the British government in hopes of receiving some relief. This shift from the use of petitions in 1776 to the use of memorials by 1778 merits notice. Whereas the petitions expressed staunch confidence in the British government, the memorials, asking for necessities such as firewood, rations, and housing, displayed loyalist need. The petitioners had asked for constitutional justice; the memorialists vied for fair treatment under a military establishment.

Clinton worried about the numbers of refugees in need: "Amidst the multiplicity of business which pours in upon me from almost every part of this continent nothing distresses me so much as the application I hourly receive from great numbers of Refugees who crowd to this place from all quarters many of whom have been reduced from affluent circumstances to the utmost penury by their attachment to Government." He added, "Humanity and good policy requires that some attention should be paid to them."[90] Headquartered within a civilian community loyal to the king's cause, Clinton recognized that he could not completely neglect the loyalists' desperate situation. Waging a war to reconcile the rebellious within the imperial fold and to increase the number of king's friends in the colonies, he could not afford to alienate the refugees.

Yet Clinton's disdain for the plight of the common loyalists was apparent. He viewed them as troublemakers; they had potential only as information gatherers or as laborers for the military administration, useful when supervised by military officers. He instructed Morris to remain vigilant against those drawing provisions based on fraudulent claims. Only the "zealous friends of His Majesty's government," he warned Morris, should receive consideration. Furthermore, "no single able-bodied man used to labor or having a trade" was to draw rations except in case of sickness. Unsurprisingly, Clinton stipulated that "higher pay" be reserved for the loyalist elite, to "persons of order of life above labor and handicraft & trade."[91]

In their requests to the British, the loyalist refugees contrasted an image of rebel tyranny with the justice of British government. Their memorials followed a predictable three-part sequence: an appeal to British benevolence, a pledge of everlasting loyalty, and finally, a narrative of suffering. In 1780, Mary Donnelly of Philadelphia appealed directly to the British commander in chief as the "father of the people" who was "no stranger to the tender feelings of humanity." The memorialists highlighted their incapacitated situations, an illness or old age, which prevented them from securing employment. In 1781, George Defendorf, another refugee from Philadelphia, wrote that he and his wife "were old and destitute of the necessaries of life and in suffering condition." Most memorials ended vaguely, not requesting anything specific from the British government. In 1779, Mary Price, whose house was burned down in New Brunswick, New Jersey, left it to the commander in chief to "consider her situation and afford her such relief as you shall judge proper."[92]

Younger people did not merit the same compensation as elderly loyalists. They not only had to demonstrate an injury such as a wound or an amputation but needed authentication from a physician in the city. In May 1782, John Harlock from Bergen County explained that he had maintained his wife and six children until he lost his eyesight. Appended to his memorial was testimony from surgeon Sam Isaacs.[93]

Older men stated their age and named their dependents. In 1780, Connecticut's Samuel Jarvis explained that he and his wife were "upwards of sixty years of age" and their family consisted of "three daughters and one little son incapable of living in this distressed and unhappy situation." John Hitchcock, sixty-seven years old, explained that he "fell from a wagon and was now incapable of maintaining himself." In 1782, Isaac Yurex wrote that his own "age and infirmity" made him unable to support his family; his wife likewise was lame and unable to assist him.[94]

Most memorialists demonstrated they had dependents living in the city—a wife, children under thirteen years of age, servants, or slaves—before they submitted their appeals. The British expected older children to work: daughters as domestics and sons in British military employ. In his memorial of March 1782, Ariel Ketchum of Connecticut acknowledged that his two eldest daughters, seventeen and thirteen years of age, could earn wages, but he asked rations for his five younger children, who were incapable of service. Similarly, Patience Johnston from Rhode Island emphasized that she had children, "five of whom were under eight years of age." In July, when Jane Isabella Winslow asked for fuel and provisions, she emphasized that her daughter, twenty-three years of age, one of seven children, was "totally deprived of the use of her limbs." Apparently incapable of supporting herself, she remained dependent on British support.[95]

The memorials demonstrate loyalist cooperation with British military requirements. The New Yorkers followed British rules and asked only for what was justifiable. If the British expected children over thirteen to labor in the military, the loyalists did not dispute this: they only asked that crippled or lame children receive special consideration. If the British expected able-bodied young men to cut wood or serve as sailors, the loyalists did not argue against this: they only asked that blind men be exempt from this service. Widows appealed because they expected the British to reward their husband's service. In 1782, Sophia Terrell hoped her "distressed situation would be alleviated" if she received the same allowance made to other officers' widows.[96] The loyalist civilians presented themselves as ready to follow British military protocol if the British in turn behaved fairly with them. In this sense, the loyalists expected the British to honor their side of an implicit contractual agreement: "good policy" required it.

By focusing on their deprivation and linking it to their allegiance, and by emphasizing emotion over reason, the loyalists made it difficult for the British to quantify their loyalty and to compare different loyalists' sufferings. If the British refused a memorial, they would risk rejecting the loyalty—the passion and the pain—extended on behalf of the king's cause. Although the distraught and intense nature of the loyalists' appeals read as an affective blur, the very sentimentality of the memorials compelled British attention: in this respect, "humanity" required it.

But this softhearted—and also shrewd—form of self-representation illuminates only one aspect of the loyalists' relationship with the British. Of course, the loyalists adopted sentimentality to hold the British to their ideals of imperial conduct. But this deference does not represent adequately the loyalist-British relationship in New York City. The loyalist refugees used the same effusive language to take an uncompromising stance when they clashed with British administration.

Significantly, loyalist complaints against Colonel Morris reflect New Yorkers' earlier concerns about the role of vestrymen in pre-Revolutionary New York, and hence they articulated their sentiments about Morris in the same language they had used to express their resentment of the city's vestrymen before the rebellion.[97] They conceived of Morris as a vestryman who did not properly represent their concerns. Significantly, prewar New Yorkers believed the ideal vestryman was one of middling circumstances who resided in the ward he represented. Both the lower sort and the eminent were undesirable as vestryman candidates as they would be in a "hurry to be gone." Too preoccupied with the means of subsistence, the poor could not wholly attend to the city's concerns. Prone to expensive and extraneous distractions, the prominent would not respect the people's needs. Most important, New Yorkers advised against vestrymen of "proud and haughty temper" because they would deter poor individuals from applying for assistance. They observed the negative consequences of a "stern look": "If a man's necessities obliges him to apply to such a man for help he finds so much difficulty and ceremony to come at him and when in his presence, a stern look, which is the natural to those men and perhaps a surly answer cuts him to the heart that he chooses rather to perish under his trouble than apply a second time."[98]

It is not surprising that Morris's elitism failed to win loyalists' favor.[99] Indeed, he typified the stereotype of the wealthy and Crown-connected loyalist gentleman in New York City. He had served in the British establishment for thirty-eight years, most recently in the Seven Years' War and as councillor of New York province, where he served for a decade. Intolerant of the agitation promoted by the Sons of Liberty, Morris supported the British occupation of Boston: as recounted by a more moderate loyalist, "He was for letting the Disease cure itself and the Sons of Liberty get a Dressing."[100] At the close of the Seven Years' War, Morris expressed his preference for a future in the American colonies when he married the daughter of wealthy Hudson Valley landowner Frederick Philipse and established himself as a gentleman in the province. Morris was clearly ill-suited to serve as intermediary between the British, who desired to spend minimally on the refugees, and the loyalists, who in growing numbers appealed for support. What the loyalists regarded as justice Morris viewed as an unnecessary handout.

When British officials met to consider the memorial requesting Morris's removal, they were inclined to dismiss the loyalist allegations. They believed that the charges against Morris were "false and scandalous and malicious." But another loyalist—Governor William Franklin from New Jersey—pressed Clinton for another resolution. Franklin believed that the numerous complaints substantiated that Morris was "unhappy in his temper." Franklin urged that a person from each province serve as "pipe" to

Colonel Morris. Clinton, who had long hesitated to relinquish any authority over British headquarters, relented. He appointed a gentleman from
each province to serve with Colonel Morris, as "some amongst them
might be acquainted with [the refugees'] situation, better able to state
their claims." It seems that the common refugees, acting collectively, had
achieved a small victory.[101]

This reading situates Colonel Morris with the British military and not
with the loyalists. In addition, American-born William Franklin emerges
as a successful loyalist spokesperson—a middleman—for the ill-treated
refugees. It appears as a shining moment for the refugees, a victory against
military encroachment. But this is not the full story of the memorial.

The 1781–82 loyalist memorial did not merely signify loyalist unhap-
piness at the hands of a British-appointed military official. One of the
first signers of the memorial, English-born merchant Samuel Hake, pro-
vides a clue to another meaning of the memorial. According to New York
Councillor William Smith Jr., Hake had "very aspersive intimations" for
encouraging the refugees' signatures. Smith believed Hake exploited the
refugees' disappointments to oust Morris from his influential position in
New York. Smith accused Hake of "trying to graft something for his own
interest upon the zeal of some of the lower sort of the country loyalists."[102] In Smith's eyes, the memorial did not represent loyalist refugees'
resentment of Colonel Morris: it was a calculated attempt by a competing
loyalist faction—Franklin and Hake—to remove Morris with one of their
own leaders.

Indeed, it appears that Hake, like Franklin, also tried to create an autonomous loyalist unit. In the summer of 1781, Hake identified over 2,434
wealthy farmers prepared to fight for the king in the Hudson Highlands.
When General Clinton referred Hake to Morris, the inspector general of
refugees, Hake was offended. He believed Morris was an "improper dis-
penser of the royal bounty" because his "cool indifference" could result in
potentially fatal consequences for the loyalists. He further insinuated that
"there was neither policy nor enterprise to be found in any of the King's
generals."[103]

Unable to maintain or extend their authority through the restoration
of civil government, loyalist elites like Morris and Hake vied for a place
within the military establishment. In this case, William Franklin sided with
Hake, and William Smith with his fellow councillor Morris. Although representing opposing positions, Hake and Morris had remarkable similari-

ties. Hake was also English-born, had migrated to New York at the end of the Seven Years' War, and married into the prominent Livingston family. In addition to the acquisition of landed wealth through their wives, both loyalists benefited from New York's role in the expanding early modern British Empire, Hake from commercial connections and Morris from military ones. New York, after all, served as the main port of entry for British soldiers and material for the wars of the eighteenth century. Both men had turned their wartime gains into significant wealth. Both shared a vision of the American future nestled within the British Empire.[104]

This second reading of the Colonel Morris case explains why the many loyalist groupings in New York did not become interconnected organizations fueling the loyalist cause. Denied power by the rebels outside New York City and prevented from attaining the few lucrative posts within the city, the loyalist elites competed and collided. Had the British officials been inclined to empower the loyalists in New York City after 1778, they would have hesitated to antagonize the many by favoring any one person.

In 1779 and 1780, New York's loyalists demanded that the British treat them as equal partners in suppressing the rebellion. Both proposals—the hard-liners' appeal for an independent military organization and the moderates' clamor for the restoration of civil government—received sanction from London. Facing an international war dispersed over multiple continents, the London ministry found itself short of military and financial resources. Unwilling to abandon the colonies, Lord Germain actively tried to encourage and reward loyalist participation in suppression of the rebellion. In 1779, Germain sought to pacify New York's moderates by appointing Sir James Robertson as civil governor of New York. In 1780, Germain approved William Franklin's plan to associate New York's refugees as a separate military body, independent of British military command. Germain's support for both the moderate and hard-line loyalists reflects Britain's desperate attempts to contain and control the rebellion at all costs.

However, the same loyalists who won concessions from London failed to receive them from British military officials in New York City. In 1776, when loyalists shone with expectation and exuberance, Sir William Howe refused to trust them. In 1780, when loyalists expressed resentment and hostility, General Clinton distrusted them as allies against the rebellion. He would not sanction civil or military authority to disappointed and resentful civilians who could enact rules against military regulations, engage in criminal proceedings against soldiers, and hamper British military campaigns around New York City. Clinton regarded New Yorkers' demands for a share in strategic planning as a dangerous complication.

By the fall of 1780, New York's leading loyalists recognized their negligible role in British strategy. New York City would serve neither as a symbol of His Majesty's constitutional commitment to the colonies nor as a base for an intercolonial loyalist military organization. The New York loyalists saw bitterly that their future hinged on British victory in the South. Far from playing an integral role in British strategy, they would participate only as spectators.

# 8 ❧ "Look Yo Tory Crew, and See What George Your King Can Do"

*Loyalists Unprotected*

> *Those who were for independence at all events and in the beginning of the American disturbances were pushed forward and first took the lead are now greatly elated and intoxicated by the peace; they have cast off all appearance of a desire to be reconciled to the loyalists who remained among them; they are forming associations with all interested in not restoring to the loyalists their estates and property. . . . Almost all of those who have attempted to return to their homes have been exceedingly ill treated, many beaten, robbed of their money and clothing and sent back.*
>
> —Sir Guy Carleton, May 27, 1783

In September 1781, New York's loyalist leaders celebrated the visit of Prince William Henry, third son of the king and "patron of Liberty and the Protestant religion."[1] He served an apprenticeship as a midshipman with Admiral Robert Digby's fleet. At the behest of General Henry Clinton and New York's respectable inhabitants, the prince paraded with Clinton and his officers toward Queen Street. Pastor Ewald Schaukirk noted the "concourse of people, both old and young" that had gathered to welcome him.[2] The loyal inhabitants of New York City viewed his visit as a timely event that symbolized the affinity of the king to his loyal subjects in the colonies, and they used the occasion to pledge their loyalty to "Royal virtues." They imagined his auspicious arrival on the American shore would "sink" the rebellion. In October, the refugees at Bergen Neck similarly welcomed His Royal Highness, informed him of their sacrifices and active service "early in this unnatural contest," and hoped he would return "crowned with the laurels of victory to your [his] parents."[3]

New York's loyalist spokesmen awaited the results of the southern campaign. They reassured the anxious inhabitants that the British troops would return victoriously from the South. Numerous essays celebrated British strength. Loyalist writers asserted that the British "bid defiance to the combined fleets in the universe" because of their "superior bravery and discipline." The rebels in Virginia would receive soon a "British answer to all their impertinence." On October 31, as rumors of Major General Cornwallis's surrender in Yorktown, Virginia, trickled into the city, a notice in the *Royal Gazette* insisted boldly that the people had yet "no grounds" to feel disappointed. However, Adjutant General Frederick Mackenzie sensed the residents' desperation. "The anxiety of all ranks of people here at present is very great," he observed, as this was the "most critical period of the war."[4]

Major General Cornwallis had considerable freedom to pursue operations in the South. Like Clinton, Cornwallis had risen up the ranks with the advantages provided by a powerful family and friends. However, the personalities of the two commanders fundamentally differed and led to frustrations on both sides. Clinton remained unsure and greatly burdened by the responsibilities of command. In contrast, Cornwallis was a confident and gregarious man, filled with energy and prepared to act aggressively—even rashly. In January 1781, he spurned defensive measures, as they "would be the certain ruin to the affairs of Britain in the Southern colonies."[5] Added to this, Cornwallis was a peer, while Clinton, his superior, was not. Most critically, Cornwallis had a dormant commission to succeed Clinton as commander in chief in certain contingencies. Clinton therefore had to deal cautiously with his titled and favored subordinate, while Cornwallis could sidestep Clinton and make independent decisions.[6]

During 1780 and 1781, Cornwallis pushed his troops deep into the backcountry of South and North Carolina. The troops' distance from the sea jeopardized their supply line. Disadvantaged by its distance from the coast, the British army depended heavily on the assistance of powerful loyalist families. However, the loyalists in the South, many of them slave owners, worried that the proximity of British troops and the British promise of freedom to rebel-owned slaves could encourage their own slaves to revolt. Vastly outnumbered by the slave population, the white owners lived in perpetual fear of a slave uprising. Caught between their attachment to the Crown and their slaves worth thousands of pounds, these loyalists regarded the British presence suspiciously.[7]

The British military success in the southern colonies depended on containing rebel forces, inspiring and supporting loyalist military action, and protecting the lives and property of loyalist citizens. But by the summer of 1780, rebel gangs and militia launched a campaign of terror, characterized by wholesale destruction of livestock, provisions, and carriages. Rebel irregulars intimidated loyalists and neutrals and annoyed isolated British outposts. They murdered their loyalist neighbors or dispatched them to prison camps deep in the interior. The fighting and plundering devastated agricultural production. The consequent shortage of provisions resulted in the misery of all the inhabitants and fueled the vicious cycle of predatory excursions by both sides.[8]

The British commander in chief resisted depending on loyalist companies. In May 1780, Clinton asked Major Patrick Ferguson to recruit loyalist militia to fight in the southern colonies. Ferguson was to provide loyalists with a written certificate that guaranteed a limited period of service "to remove all distrust that they may entertain of being drawn into regular service without their consent." Yet Clinton doubted loyalists' military effectiveness. In the conclusion of the dispatch, Clinton instructed Ferguson "to derive as much advantage from their services at as little expense as may be."[9]

Bent on preserving the security of New York City, Clinton sent troops to the southern colonies in small detachments. In October 1780, 72 percent of all British troops in the rebellious colonies remained in New York, with only 28 percent in South Carolina and Georgia. Gradually, Clinton sent more troops to Cornwallis: in October 1780, he sent 2,500 troops to the Chesapeake under Major General Alexander Leslie; in December, another 1,900 went with Benedict Arnold; and in March, another 2,400 accompanied Major General William Phillips. Only by May 1781 did the distribution alter dramatically, with 41 percent in New York and 59 percent in Georgia, the Carolinas, and Virginia.[10]

During the summer of 1781, Cornwallis moved from North Carolina to the Chesapeake Bay area. In September 1780, he had moved to North Carolina because he did not believe he could effectively protect South Carolina without destroying rebel strongholds to the north. Not having met success in North Carolina, he hoped to avoid recrimination from Lord Germain by achieving victory in Virginia. Unwittingly, his march to Virginia allowed a combined attack of the French fleet and the rebel army. Unlike the distant port of Charleston, the Chesapeake stood accessible to

Washington's army on the Hudson and within close striking distance of the French squadron based in the West Indies. The British could neutralize this threat by blocking either the Continental army or the French fleet.[11]

Given Clinton's reluctance to remove the regulars from New York City to engage directly with the Continental troops, it became imperative for the British to contain the powerful French fleet in the West Indies and a smaller one in Rhode Island to prevent disastrous consequences in the South. The French fleet had occupied Newport, Rhode Island, in July 1780. The seven French ships of the line carried the French royal army of fifty-five hundred men under the experienced and competent general Comte Jean-Baptiste de Rochambeau. The French army posed a persistent threat to British troops in New York and around the Chesapeake.[12]

The antagonism between Clinton and Admiral Mariot Arbuthnot prevented combined operations against the French fleet. The British army and naval commanders wrangled over the distribution of spoils and over shortages in resources. Arbuthnot wanted soldiers to fill vacancies in ships, while Clinton clamored for frigates to carry the army's dispatches between British-held posts in New York and the Carolinas and along the Chesapeake. Each denied the requests of the other, and the refusals generated friction. According to historian William Willcox, both men remained petty, and "neither was able to understand the pettiness in the other." Until July 1781, when Germain recalled Arbuthnot and replaced him with Admiral Thomas Graves, the impasse between the two commanders persisted.[13]

In August 1781, General Washington exploited British inactivity and seized the initiative to capture Cornwallis in Virginia by marching the Franco-American armies from the Hudson to the Chesapeake. The French admiral, Comte de Grasse, had already arrived from the West Indies with twenty-eight men-of-war. The French and rebel troops trapped the British soldiers and sealed the fate of Cornwallis. On September 23, 1781, Cornwallis found himself in dire straits in Yorktown and wrote desperately to Clinton, "If you cannot relieve me very soon, you must be prepared to hear the worst."[14] But Clinton did not believe Cornwallis faced an urgent situation. Clinton's memorandum of September 17 reveals his analysis of the situation: "I do not say that [Lord Cornwallis's] misfortune might not finally lose us this Empire but that would not be so immediate." Clinton's troops reached the Chesapeake on October 24, too late to save Cornwallis, who had surrendered five days earlier.[15]

New Yorkers' response to Yorktown was divided. Some refused to accept the potentially grave consequences of Cornwallis's defeat in the South. They continued to hope that Great Britain would abandon neither the colonies nor the loyalists. They drew solace from the thirty thousand effective British troops still serving in America and the failing and mutinous state of the Continental army. Washington commanded a rebel army short of food, clothing, medical supplies, and ammunition. In May 1780, the Connecticut Line, stationed in Morristown, New Jersey, mutinied to protest short rations and the absence of pay for five months. In January 1781, short of pay, food, and clothes and seeking discharge, the Pennsylvania Line left Morristown and marched toward Philadelphia to seek redress from the Continental Congress. Representatives of the congress met these mutineers in Trenton and pacified them with pay, food, and clothing. During the same month, the New Jersey Brigade stationed at Pompton, New Jersey, abandoned its quarters and marched toward Trenton. To suppress further mutinies, General Washington sent a regiment of New Englanders against them and subsequently executed two of the ringleaders.[16]

Some British officers and loyalists believed the mutinies signaled the impending collapse of Washington's army. They hoped that war weariness would result in a schism within the rebel ranks and lead many to favor reconciliation. After hearing of the mutinies, Mackenzie did not think that the "rebellion [could] possibly exist much longer." He expressed the "most sanguine hopes that the loyalists in Maryland and other southern provinces . . . will immediately rise and declare themselves." William Smith Jr., insisted that the mutinies, along with Cornwallis's success in the South before Yorktown, marked the "concurrence of favorable circumstances."[17]

In late October, loyalists began to circulate personal letters written by the rebel agent of the Continental Congress to France, Silas Deane.[18] Deane repudiated the revolution, questioned the French alliance as dangerous, and urged rebel leaders to accept British terms of reconciliation. Believing the colonies incapable of effective self-government, Deane proposed that America had to choose not between independence and submission to Great Britain but between dependence on Great Britain and dependence on France, and of these two choices, he preferred the former. He asserted that independence would prove "rather a curse than a blessing" because, if the rebels demolished the "venerable fabric of the British empire," they would become tools for their Roman Catholic allies. By partnering with France, the colonies would become the "slaves" of a domineering nation.[19] Deane epitomized a rebel leader who converted to loyalism at the darkest and most desperate moment. Loyalists used him as an example to encourage other colonists to unite on behalf of ordered liberty within the empire. Deane provided them with the last glimmer of hope, the possibility that reasonable colonists would see the soundness of supporting the empire.[20]

In 1778, loyalist newspaper essays had accused rebels of committing treason by joining with Great Britain's historical foes. They had hoped to garner support from common people who dreaded popish intervention. After Yorktown, they again drew upon the heritage of British patriotism to dramatize the malign consequences of French domination. They warned the rebels of the dire consequences of aligning with a Catholic power. The loyalist writers portrayed the devastating impact of French government in the colonies. They painted a future of the colonies under a rapacious army, a set of ungrateful rebel upstarts exalted into sudden power, and an insidious popish ally. They assured the public that the whole Continental Army served Louis XVI and received French pay. Indeed, they claimed, every American soldier had now become "in every sense a Frenchman." Another loyalist writer warned that the rebels threatened the British constitution, the pride of their ancestors, in order to "encourage a religion which they held in abhorrence as idolatrous and tyrannical." And the French, the loyalists insisted, were only helping the rebels demolish the British Empire. Secretly, the loyalists claimed, the French held the rebels in extreme contempt and viewed the rebels as upstarts who had no social status and little political acumen.[21]

But leading New Yorkers' desperate faith in British strength and their dire predictions about French domination in the colonies did little to quell the inhabitants' alarm. Hugh Gaine's journal reveals the loyalists' disorientation. In October, when news of Cornwallis's surrender reached New York, Gaine observed that it was "not credited by some people." In November, Gaine heard that various reports circulated about future British initiatives but found "none of them the least consequence to anybody." In March, Gaine expressed "great joy" that a packet had finally arrived from Falmouth but then noted the people's disappointment as "nothing material more than the war is to be prosecuted here." On April 11, Gaine remarked that no news had arrived from England, and "we long wait for it."[22]

Meanwhile, loyalist hard-liners railed at the terms of Cornwallis's surrender. The tenth item in the Articles of Capitulation made a devastating distinction between loyalist soldiers and British regular troops. It specified that rebels could treat loyalist prisoners not as legitimate prisoners of war but as treasonous citizens. Thus the loyalists who surrendered in Yorktown and Gloucester would not merit treatment under the military codes of justice but could suffer civil punishment for having joined the British cause. Holding a low opinion of loyalists in general, and much disappointed at what he regarded as their military passivity, Cornwallis had accepted Washington's terms without securing the loyalists' safety. Although few loyalists suffered directly because of the terms of surrender, loyalist soldiers could not forget British willingness to abandon them.[23]

Indeed, the British officers could hardly miss loyalists' rage over the tenth article. On December 20, 1781, Lieutenant Colonel Alured Clarke feared the consequences of loyalist disillusionment in Savannah:

> I am sorry to inform your Excellency that the tenth article of the
> capitulation of Yorktown has made a very alarming impression on
> the minds of the people in general, and that I have just ground of
> apprehension that it will amount to so considerable a defection of
> the militia—if our situation should become more critical—as to
> leave us but very little hopes of any material assistance from them,
> many having already gone off.[24]

Fearing the harsh judgment of the victorious rebels, southern loyalists sought refuge in British-occupied Charleston. In January 1782, Lieutenant General Alexander Leslie reported that the loyalists "are daily coming in to us and seek that protection, though entailing a burden on ourselves, is not to be refused them." Hoping to pacify the embittered loyalists, Leslie explained that their "misery and helpless situation justifies our attention to them."[25]

The terms at Yorktown stunned the Associated Loyalists in New York City. Just as the British had abandoned loyalist soldiers in Yorktown, they could sacrifice the armed refugees in New York. In November 1781, Joshua Upham, commander of the Associated Loyalists at Lloyd's Neck, Long Island, expressed mortification. The tenth article, he wrote to William Franklin, "reaches the hearts of the unfortunate loyalists of this place. . . . I wish to know whether we too are to be sacrificed."[26] In his narrative of the revolution, Clinton recounted the "indignation, horror, and dismay" of the refugees in New York City on receiving news of the capitulation.

"Excluded from the same conditions of surrender with their fellow soldiers," they considered themselves "cruelly abandoned to the power of an
inveterate implacable enemy to be persecuted at the discretion of party
prejudice and resentment."[27]

William Franklin demanded that the British assert their commitment
to protecting the king's subjects in New York. In November 1781, he requested that Clinton circulate a proclamation that denounced the tenth
article and that pledged, in any future capitulation, the loyalists would
receive the same terms as regular troops. Franklin also wanted Clinton
to threaten the rebels with retaliation in kind for any harm inflicted on
any loyalist already captured. Hoping to compel Clinton to acquiesce to
his demands, Franklin appealed directly to Germain, demanding that the
British army forbid "discrimination between American and European loyalists." But Germain's political position had deteriorated after Yorktown,
and he could do nothing for Franklin.[28]

Clinton postponed responding to the loyalists' appeals. In March 1782,
Clinton explained to Germain that he had delayed the request of the Associated Loyalists until Cornwallis arrived in New York City. He hoped the
interval would "quiet the refugees in this quarter who began to be very
clamorous." However, when Cornwallis pleaded necessity as his explanation, the board expressed renewed anger.[29]

To pacify Franklin, Clinton agreed to his first request. Clinton issued
an order to the British army "directing them to pay the same attention
to all cases and in every event whatsoever to the interests and security of
the loyalists within their respective districts that they did to those of the
king's troops under their orders." Stubbornly, Clinton refused Franklin's
second request. He explained that the threat of British retaliation could
provoke rebels to treat imprisoned British regulars harshly. However, Clinton argued, if the board wanted power to retaliate against the rebels, he
would consider opening civil courts in New York City so civil judges could
mete out punishment to vindictive rebels. Driven to diffuse the hard-liners'
anger, Clinton finally considered restoring civil courts in the city. Determined to keep the British regulars from harm, Clinton became ready to
make concessions long demanded by loyalists. Holding both the military
rank of general and the civilian rank of peace commissioner, Clinton saw
himself finally as a military leader whose foremost responsibility entailed
protecting the lives and interests of his soldiers and not as a commissioner
responsible for protecting the well-being of all civilians.[30]

The humiliating terms at Yorktown and Clinton's tepid response led William Franklin to lose faith in the British. During the years of the war, numerous British proclamations had exhorted the loyalists to remain steadfast and promised them protection. Cornwallis's humiliating abandonment disillusioned loyalists within and outside British lines. Dismayed at the terms that would have "pernicious effects to His Majesty's interest," Franklin asked to leave the colonies. However, Clinton, rightly fearful that hard-liners would blame Franklin's departure on him and retaliate against the British army, denied authorization.[31]

Clinton's refusal to protect the captured loyalist soldiers may have triggered a much-publicized incident that further discredited the hard-liners in British eyes. On April 12, 1782, Captain Richard Lippincott, a loyalist officer in Franklin's organization, hanged Captain Joshua Huddy, an officer in the rebel militia of Monmouth County. In a surprise attack on the blockhouse at Toms River, New Jersey, loyalist raiders had captured Huddy and imprisoned him in New York City. Meanwhile, the Monmouth militia killed loyalist prisoner Philip White. To avenge White, Franklin tacitly approved the removal of Huddy from his prison cell. Lippincott took Huddy on a boat and, after landing at Gravelly Point near Sandy Hook, had him hung.[32]

Washington reacted precisely as Clinton had feared, by threatening to execute a prisoner, Captain Charles Asgill of the British army. Under pressure from Washington, Clinton brought Lippincott before a court-martial. However, he immediately encountered loyalists' hostility. In November 1781, they had demanded that Clinton protect loyalists unconditionally against rebel punishment. Instead, five months later, Clinton determined to prosecute a loyalist for just retribution against a rebel. Clinton recognized tacitly the helpless fury that had provoked the Associated Loyalists. He reasoned that "allowances should be made for the actions of men whose minds may have been roused to vengeance by repeated acts of cruelty committed by the enemy on their dearest friends and connections." Indeed, Clinton attributed Huddy's murder directly to his refusal to concede to Franklin's second request. These gentlemen, Clinton wrote, "appear to have taken this bold step for the purpose of forcing that measure." The court-martial trial acquitted Lippincott, who subsequently fled to Canada.[33]

The Huddy affair marked the only deliberate execution by the Associated Loyalists. In May 1782, the newly appointed commander in chief of the

British army, Sir Guy Carleton, forbade them publicly from any independent operations without a "particular order." His hopes for power gone,
Franklin disbanded the organization and left for London in August.[34]

## Loyalist Disbelief

Loyalists responded despondently to the news that arrived in New York
City on April 28, 1782. The British government had declared a cessation
of all military operations in the North American colonies. In June, Gaine
observed the disillusionment of the city's loyalist militia as they awaited
further news from London. They served but "to their great mortification
indeed." Not yet ready to relinquish their hopes, these loyalists waited
stubbornly for peace terms that would enable them to return with honor
to their former homes and lives. Sensing the growing anger of the inhabitants, Gaine predicted that loyalist fortitude "cannot last."[35]

In May 1782, New Yorkers widely welcomed Sir Guy Carleton to the city.
As reported in the *New-York Gazette and Weekly Mercury,* "the gentlemen of
the army, most of the respectable inhabitants of the city, and a numerous
concourse of people" greeted Carleton.[36] Another report acknowledged
his esteem among the colonists and lamented his late arrival to the colonies: "Had he come sooner they say he could have made Tories of them
all."[37] Carleton replaced Clinton, who had resigned his post as commander
of British land forces in North America. Bitter with the ministry, which
had never supported his requisitions, and eager to clear himself of responsibility for Yorktown, Clinton returned to England.[38]

Carleton had entered the British army in 1742 at the age of eighteen
and served as deputy quartermaster general in Quebec during the Seven
Years' War. Carleton became governor of Quebec in 1768 and planned to
integrate the French colony into the British empire. Since March 1780,
Carleton had served as head of the newly established Commission of
Public Accounts, where he kept track of military expenditures and un-
covered nefarious practices by which some officeholders enriched themselves with public money. Carleton's leadership in administering colonial
relations and policing expenses made him the ideal candidate for his new
command.[39]

The loyalists assumed that Carleton's appointment represented yet
another British attempt to negotiate with the colonists for reunion with
the empire. In an essay in the *Royal Gazette,* one loyalist suggested that
Carleton would propose terms "more advantageous" than any the Con-

tinental Congress could derive from a French alliance. Councillors Hugh Wallace and William Smith Jr. hoped that Carleton would reinstitute civil rule and govern the city "in a train less repugnant to the principles of the law than the present mode by police and military discretion."[40]

On May 11, six days after Carleton's arrival in the city, the news of Admiral Rodney's victory in the West Indies became another occasion for loyalist celebration. On April 12, Rodney had defeated a French battle fleet of thirty-three ships of the line in the Caribbean, thus terminating the French threat to the British colony of Jamaica. Rodney had captured the French commander, Admiral de Grasse, the same admiral who had facilitated the British defeat in Yorktown just six months previously.[41]

But Rodney's victory, like the capture of Charleston in 1780, did not change the status quo in New York City. Apprehensive about their fate, New York's loyalists appealed to Carleton for reassurance that the empire would not forsake them. Two 1782 petitions reveal the desperate uncertainty within the divided loyalist community. On May 27, 1782, the city's commercial leaders, headed by mayor David Mathews, congratulated Carleton, lamented the "wretched state" of the colonies so "wasted by the ravages of war," and expressed their desire for reconciliation "on equal and honorable terms." They promised to "hazard their lives" for reunion but begged assurance that their "persons and property" would receive every proper regard in a peace settlement. Six days later, a group of loyal refugees mimicked the petition submitted by the merchants of the city. They emphasized that the persecution, imprisonment, banishment, and "ignominious deaths" they had suffered for their uniform attachment to the British government. They also underlined their active service in defense of their king and constitution.[42]

On August 3, 1782, New Yorkers received the shocking confirmation that Britain planned to recognize American independence. Five days later, Beverly Robinson expressed eloquently the lament of the loyalist elite to Clinton: "Oh my dear Sir, what dreadful and distressing tidings . . . the Independence of America given up by the King without any condition whatsoever, the loyalist[s] of America to depend on the mercey of their Enemies for the restoration of their possessions, which we are well assured they will never grant, the Greatest part of the Estates that have been confiscated by them are already sold."[43] The few who fled immediately to London with flattering letters of introduction hoped the British government would provide them employment or a sufficient income. Lacking free land desired by common loyalists, England attracted primarily the well-to-do office seekers, pensioners, and those with well-placed friends. On August 7, 1782, Barrak Hays sold his goods, including a "very good house Negro wench," and announced his departure for Europe. In July 1780, Hays had solicited employment from Clinton because he had suffered "heavy losses in privateers and other misfortunes in trade" and therefore had difficulty supporting his wife, four children, and crippled brother. Hays asked for a recommendation from Clinton so he could receive some "gratuity or benefit" when he went to Great Britain.[44]

From the southern colonies, five thousand white loyalists and ten thousand slaves with their owners left when the British evacuated Savannah in July 1782 and Charleston in December 1782. On January 6, 1783, the *New-York Gazette and Weekly Mercury* reported officially that the Charleston evacuation "was effected with the greatest regularity and without the least interruption from the enemy." The formal and impersonal notice missed both the impatience of the British officers and the despair of the southerners compelled to forsake their homes. When southern refugees pleaded for adequate provisions upon leaving their homes, fearing that the authorized allocation of six months' provisions would not suffice, the British responded brusquely. Lieutenant General Leslie regarded them as self-serving and greedy. In November 1782, he complained to Carleton of "the unreasonable demands of all sorts of people" leaving Charleston. He also expressed frustration that some slaves, unwilling to return to "hard labor and severe punishment," exploited the evacuation to escape bondage. Apparently, some asked to accompany British officers as servants.[45]

The clearing of the loyal South made New York City the last bastion of loyalism in the rebel colonies. Loyalist regiments from evacuated cities returned to New York and brought with them many southerners, particularly black loyalists who chose not to settle in the Caribbean. Over five hundred Charleston refugees sailed with Lieutenant General Leslie to New York, swelling the throng of some forty thousand refugees who had accumulated in the city.[46]

Gaine recorded renewed despair by the common New Yorkers who feared that the British troops would abandon New York City and leave the loyalists to face the wrath of returning rebels. On August 26, he observed that "every body appears uneasy and Some think of an evacuation here."[47] Fearing for their lives, some loyalists asked for arms and ammunition to defend themselves.[48] Dreading rebel retaliation, others immediately deserted their posts. In May 1782, 350 white refugees and 100 blacks under Captain Thomas Ward in Bergen Point, New Jersey, supplied wood to the troops in the New York City garrison. By September, only forty-nine refugees remained at the post.[49]

Some New Yorkers realized their dependence on British goodwill for a favorable settlement. After receiving news of American independence, they urged their constituents to "suspend their opinion on the present important occasion" and await news of peace from Europe. They emphasized that the taxes contrived by the Congressional Congress had led to an "increasing abhorrence of war" in rebel-controlled areas and that the people in general distrusted the congress. They counseled the multitude to wait with "manly sturdiness" in order to "preserve" a claim to His Majesty's protection. Indeed, they asserted pragmatically, it would be "madness to forfeit" the "surest pledges of safety."[50]

Many refused to relinquish hope that the British government would negotiate an arrangement to compensate New York's devoted loyalists. They hoped that no peace treaty would take effect until the king had provided full security for the future personal safety of loyalists, for the restitution of their property, and for an asylum for those who could not remain in their homes. In November, one loyalist writer stressed that New York would not face the fate of Savannah; that is, Great Britain would not abandon New York "without terms."[51] The British had evacuated Savannah in July 1782 without offering any concessions to the loyalists in that city. Prominent New Yorkers realized the appalling consequences of American independence. Sensing New Yorker's tension, Andrew Elliot believed that disappointing peace terms would "make all the loyalists the inveterate foes of Great Britain."[52]

New Yorkers also hoped that loyalists in London would lobby on their behalf. On November 27, one loyalist expected that Franklin's representation of American affairs would convince the British nation that its "sun [would] truly set forever" if it yielded to the republican despotism of the American rebels. Three days later, another writer asserted that the "language of government runs highly in favour of the loyalists and their patron, Governor Franklin has been agreeably received in the Royal closet."[53]

But like that of other eminent gentlemen such as Joseph Galloway and Thomas Hutchinson, William Franklin's influence remained insignificant. Germain had promised Franklin that his sacrifices would merit reward.

But Germain had resigned from office, and Franklin had no connections with the new political circle headed by Lord Shelburne. Furthermore, by the time Franklin reached London, the American and British diplomats had already agreed to a provisional peace treaty.[54]

In February 1783, when Franklin, along with Georgia's governor, James Wright, and New Hampshire's governor, John Wentworth, appealed to the British Parliament for financial compensation, they received an impatient hearing. The members of Parliament believed that the British had sufficiently compensated the loyalists. During the war years, the British Isles had taken in up to seven thousand loyalists, and by 1782, the British government had spent over £40,000 each year in compensation for loyalist claims.[55]

Incredibly, some loyalists continued to propose the restoration of civil government in New York. In October 1782, "WB" insisted that the voice of Congressional Congress did not represent the American people. "WB" argued: "If a Civil Government within the British lines were to be pursued (tho' some particular circumstances may plead against it) it wou'd tend to soften the minds of many without the lines and they would begin to have some confidence in our restoration of happyness." By returning as subjects under the British government, the people would avoid the "hardships and heavy taxes" under the Congressional Congress and the "misery" of French demands.[56]

Three months later, an essay by "Homo Angliae Novae" circulated in the Royal Gazette presented the loyalists' ideal of the American future. The author began by assuring the British government of loyalists' steadfast and specific devotion to the British government but not to the British armed and naval forces. The British army's depredations compelled the loyalists "to shun coming under the power of [the British] Generals and Admiral." However, the troops' destruction had not alienated the loyalists from His Majesty. Just as they did not want the domination of the congress and General Washington, the loyalists would not tolerate continued military rule.[57]

"Homo Angliae Novae" echoed the constitutional arrangement proposed by William Smith Jr. at the beginning of the war. The loyalists wanted a constitution like that of Ireland, under which each colony retained its rights and jurisdiction under a Crown-appointed lieutenant governor. Every hundred years until 2500, the Crown would decide on a valuation, and each colony would pay its proper proportion of the national expense. Most important, Great Britain should restore to each loyalist his property and "make good his damages out of the estates of the rebels."[58]

Carleton had hoped to reunite the colonies with Great Britain, to succeed where Lord Germain had failed. Embarrassed by the ministry's decision to cease military operations in the American colonies, he asked to resign his command. Like the Carlisle commissioners who had arrived in Philadelphia at the brink of its evacuation in 1778, Carleton entered a city that would shortly be abandoned by the British government. He realized bitterly his negligible role in bringing the war to a conclusion.[59]

Carleton had underestimated the political sentiment against the war in Parliament. Antiwar sentiment climbed after Yorktown. The British government had long remained divided over the strategy to end the American rebellion. Although many British ministers, driven by the king, had determined to fight the rebellion, a substantial portion of Parliament had opposed the effort. The rising cost of the war, which exceeded £110,000,000 by 1781, united the opposition against the king and his ministers. The national debt had doubled since the beginning of the war. Tired of the king's adherence to bankrupt policies, the ministers wanted to grant American independence to free British resources for the war against France and Spain.[60]

The war had expanded from one aimed at suppressing a rebellion to a world war against France, Spain, and the Dutch Republic.[61] Between November 1781 and February 1782, the British Parliament received news of further British disasters—the loss of St. Eustatius, Nevis, St. Kitts, and Montserrat in the West Indies and Minorca on the Mediterranean. With each loss, the ministerial majority in the House of Commons declined. On February 27, the Commons approved General Henry Conway's motion condemning further offensive operations in America, calling for direct peace negotiations with the revolted colonies.[62]

George III had long opposed American independence. The king feared that if the colonies succeeded, their example would encourage rebellion in the West Indies and in Ireland and would soon "annihilate the empire."[63] As late as November 27, 1781, he asserted that a "vigorous and united exertion of the faculties and resources of my people" would "restore the blessings of a safe and honorable peace to all my dominions."[64] However, the king gradually realized that he could not control Parliament. In February

1782, he agreed to negotiate a separate treaty with the colonies in hopes of detaching them from an alliance with France.[65] In October, he conceded grudgingly that that the American colonies had become so intractable that "it may not be in the end an evil that they become aliens to this empire."[66]

In February, when the Commons disowned further coercion against the thirteen colonies, Germain resigned. His desire to hold the cities of New York, Charleston, and Savannah in order to guard British trade to the West Indies had received little support from Parliament. As he bitterly left his seat of power, he predicted a continuing connection between the United States and France followed by the loss of the British West Indies. Closely associated with British failure in the colonies, Lord North also left the ministry in March. Lord Rockingham replaced Lord North, and Lord Shelburne accepted the position of secretary of state for home, Irish, and colonial affairs.[67]

Between March 1782 and February 1783, Shelburne would hold the office of secretary of state for three months and then that of prime minister for the remaining eight months.[68] Appointed by the king, he had responsibility for the peace process with the rebellious colonies.[69] Shelburne conceived of the American negotiations as more than a concession of independence to Britain's former colonies. He hoped to establish a new and enduring relationship between the empire and the colonies, one that would preserve the essential unity of English-speaking people in the Old and New Worlds. Like Joseph Galloway and William Smith Jr., Shelburne hoped that the colonies and Great Britain could remain united under one king, in one empire, but each with its own sovereign Parliament. In July 1782, he explained his stance: "My private opinion would lead me to go a great way for Federal Union; but is either country ripe for it? If not, means must be left to advance it." Three months later, he wrote again: "If we are to regain the affection of America, to reunion in any shape or even to commerce and friendship, is it not of the last degree of consequence to retain every means to gratify America?" He advocated persistent economic links that would not only maintain an alliance between the United States and Great Britain but would ensure that the Franco-American alliance did not survive the coming of peace. Shelburne wanted to make sure that French power had no place in North America.[70]

To negotiate the peace treaty with rebel leaders, Shelburne chose Richard Oswald, a septuagenarian Scottish merchant. Oswald shared with Shelburne a determination to restrict American independence by maintaining a lingering commercial affiliation with the new nation. The new nation would retain its former role as a source of raw material for an industrializing Great Britain. In his diary in mid-June, Oswald predicted that both the increase in cultivation and the population growth in the American colonies would profit English commerce. As long as the American colonies had "an immense expansion of vacant Lands . . . they will never become Manufacturers." Hence, their high level of consumption would fuel the economy of the British Empire as long as Britain had "free and safe access to their ports."[71]

Oswald hoped the Americans would continue as subjects under the British government. He wished that Great Britain could impose a constitutional model on the United States, and under the guidance of a viceroy with a six- or eight-member council, preside over the entire continent. The council would discourage town meetings, supervise colleges—especially Harvard with its "government of fanatics and independents"—and disenfranchise all those who had served in the Continental Congress.[72]

Shelburne and Oswald determined to do everything possible to break the Franco-American alliance, to reestablish British-American peace, and to reestablish British economic dominance interrupted by the war. But they had underestimated the enmity caused by seven years of fighting. No magnanimous gesture could return the colonies to their previous relationship with Great Britain. Compelled to make considerable concessions, the British eventually sacrificed the interests of the American loyalists.[73]

In the spring of 1782, Shelburne had demanded that Oswald insist on a general amnesty and restoration of property for the loyalists. He informed Oswald that Britain would only concede the trans-Appalachian lands in exchange for loyalist restoration and protection. But as Oswald reported opposition from the American diplomats, Shelburne wavered. The American negotiators had strict instructions to resist any treaty stipulations in favor of the loyalists. Robert R. Livingston, the American secretary of foreign affairs, claimed that the loyalists would subvert the formation of a new government and constitution in the United States. In addition, the state legislatures had already disposed of loyalist lands and could not, therefore, return the properties to their original holders.[74]

In addition, Shelburne faced inveterate hostility from within Parliament. He understood that support from the fallen prime minister, Lord

North, could not sustain his political survival. His position remained linked to a peace settlement that both the country and the ministers would deem satisfactory, and he hoped to conclude a peace treaty before Parliament convened again in the closing months of the year.[75]

Shelburne also faced external turmoil that compelled him to settle the peace treaty quickly. British troubles in Ireland weakened Shelburne's already precarious position in Parliament. In April 1782, Henry Grattan led Ireland in demanding a sovereign Parliament in Ireland as free as that of England. Furthermore, the British preoccupation with defending the West Indies from the French, its Baltic trade from the Dutch, and Gibraltar from the Spanish also blunted Shelburne's resolution. Afraid to endanger the whole treaty, Shelburne did not press the Americans to make restitution or indemnification for loyalists' losses. The Americans would receive the vast area of the backcountry as a mark of goodwill. Later, the British might make a "plea" on behalf of the loyalist that a gratified America would grant. As other problems loomed large, the loyalists became more disposable.[76]

Essentially in agreement with Shelburne, Oswald emphasized the resources required to satisfy the large number of "loyal sufferers." In July, Oswald wrote that the British would find it difficult to allocate compensation to the loyalists because "they were so numerous and their cases so various."[77] Shelburne allowed Oswald to surrender the stipulations concerning loyalist indemnity although he expressed his "deep concern" for the separation of "countries united by blood, by principles, habits, and every tie short of territorial proximity." In his apologia to the Parliament that ousted him in February 1783, Shelburne rationalized that a part had to suffer to prevent the destruction of the whole. The generous boundaries granted to the United States would do no harm if North America (the whole) remained economically dependent upon Britain. And the betrayal of the loyalists (a part) would serve a greater purpose if the treaty severed the link between France and the United States.[78]

In November 1782, the American negotiators and the elderly Scot signed their names to the provisional peace treaty. Nine months later, the preliminary treaty became definitive. The colonies gained independence with generous boundaries that included the trans-Appalachian lands and the southern shores of the Great Lakes. In return, the American delegates accepted responsibility for repaying debts due to British subjects. Britain retained control in Canada to keep the United States free from the grip of France and to supply lumber and other raw materials to the West Indies, as the American colonies had formerly done.[79]

The fifth and sixth articles of the treaty dealt with the white loyalists, and the seventh article dealt with the black loyalists. The former two called upon the Continental Congress to recommend that the states engage in no further confiscation of loyalist estates, return seized property or give compensation for it, and provide no "lawful impediment" for the recovery of loyalist property. Article 5 stipulated that the American congress should "earnestly recommend" that the thirteen states restore the civil privileges and property of "real British subjects" and of all those who did not participate in the war as combatants. The combatant loyalists would wait for one year before they could return to their states to repurchase their forfeited property. Article 6 provided that the states should grant the loyalists a general amnesty; that is, they should stop the confiscation of loyalist property and free all imprisoned loyalists.[80]

The British statesmen may have assumed that congressional action would serve as the equivalent of a royal message to Parliament.[81] However, the Articles of Confederation, ratified by each of the thirteen colonies in 1781, sharply restricted the powers of the congress and reserved broad governing powers to the states. The congress could regulate foreign affairs, declare war, and administer relations with the Indians living outside state boundaries, but the states retained sovereignty over all other concerns.[82] Both of the loyalist-related articles of the peace treaty left the enactment of the resolves in the hands of the American states. On January 14, 1784, when the congress requested the states to restore all properties and rights of loyalists, the state legislatures refused to comply. The northern states cited war damages committed by British military forces, and southern states cited the failure of the British government to offer indemnification for slaves who went off with the British.[83]

As compensation for the disastrous and humiliating terms of the treaty, the British government offered to relocate the loyalists to the British West Indies or to the Canadian provinces. It set aside land for the loyalists and made arrangements to provision them until the loyalists established autonomy in their new homes. In response to pressure from distressed exiles in England, Parliament also appointed a commission to review loyalist claims. If a loyalist could demonstrate losses that resulted directly from their loyalty to the Crown and not from wartime exigencies, the Commission would make recommendations for appropriate compensation. The British deemed it cheaper to compensate the loyalists through pensions, donations, and land grants in Nova Scotia than to incur the cost of further war by demanding their reinstatement in the United States.[84]

The British saw obvious advantages in encouraging loyalist migration to Nova Scotia. In paying a debt of honor to its loyal subjects, they hoped to simultaneously create a loyal population with a vested interest in the imperial connection. A British province since the Treaty of Utrecht in 1713, Nova Scotia had twenty thousand people: a mix of French Acadians, New England settlers, and some German and Swiss settlers.[85] In mid-1783, Brook Watson expressed best the sentiments of the British ministry when he envisioned that the "good People of property carrying in their hearts the most settled love to the Constitution of England" would render Nova Scotia a shining example of British governance, the "prop of Great Britain in America."[86]

In the seventh article of the peace treaty, the British contravened the pledge of freedom made by the British commanders to the blacks who entered British lines. The seventh article promised that "his Brittanic Majesty shall, with all convenient speed and without causing any destruction or carrying away any Negroes or other property of the American inhabitants, withdraw all his Armies, Garrisons, and Fleets, from the said United States."[87] The mutual interests shared by Richard Oswald and Henry Laurens resulted in the special provision regarding blacks in the treaty. Oswald owned a slave-trading post on Bance Island in the Sierra Leone River and had made a fortune through his slave trade to the American colonies.[88] His slave trade to South Carolina relied on Laurens. Oswald paid Laurens a 10 percent commission on each cargo of slaves sold. In 1780, when the British captured Laurens and imprisoned him in the Tower of London, Oswald posted a bail of £50,000 for his release.[89]

Laurens authored the clause that dealt with the blacks. Before Laurens reached Paris on November 29, 1782, the last day of the conference, the negotiations had focused on boundaries, fisheries, and the collection of debts. Laurens claimed that he wanted to protect the slaves from the British who would sell them into a worst slavery in the West Indies.[90]

The seventh article of the peace treaty emboldened slave owners. Led by General Washington, who had several runaway slaves with the British in New York City, rebel slaveholders argued that the property clause in the peace treaty extended to their human chattel. They insisted that General Carleton strictly honor terms of the treaty and return the fugitives concealed in New York City. A black loyalist from South Carolina, Boston King, recalled the terror in the slave community when southern slaveholders arrived in New York City and tried to prevent the British from evacuating their property. King remembered that "for some days we lost our appetite for food, and sleep departed from our eyes." The very thought of going back to "cruel masters," he said, "embittered life for us."[91]

Fortunately for King and others in his situation, Carleton interpreted the seventh article to apply only to blacks outside British lines. He considered that the blacks already within British protection by November 1782 counted as free people and not as American property. He invited the black loyalists who had lived in New York City for the preceding year or longer to present themselves to General Samuel Birch to receive certificates authenticating their claim to freedom.[92] He reassured General Washington that this "open method of conducting business" would prevent fraud. If the British denied them permission to embark, the blacks would "have found various methods of quitting this place so the former owner would no longer have been able to trace them and would have lost in every way, all chance of compensation."[93]

As a conciliatory gesture to Washington, Carleton recorded the personal data of each of the free blacks who left New York for Nova Scotia in 1783. If British diplomats agreed to financial compensation for the slaves' former owners, Carleton reasoned, they would need to know who had owned each fugitive and have some idea of the value of the claimants. Of the 3,000 blacks listed in the "Book of Negroes," 1,336 were men, 914 women, and 750 children. Two-thirds had escaped from the South. Aside from the free blacks, an estimated 1,232 slaves accompanied their owners to Nova Scotia.[94] Other slaveholders sent slaves to plantation colonies to maximize their usefulness. In February 1784, former governor of New Hampshire John Wentworth sent his nineteen slaves to his cousin, Paul Wentworth, who managed his Surinam estate. The governor reported that the slaves "are all American born and well seasoned and all are perfectly stout, healthy, sober, industrious, and honest. . . . The Women are stout and able, and promise well to increase their numbers.[95]

Some New Yorkers who lost hope became frenzied. Between November 1782 and January 1783, in the pages of the *Royal Gazette*, they warned the British government of the dangers of American independence. They described ominously the fatal consequences to the empire if deprived of the American colonies. Acquiescence to American demands for full independence could incite rebellions in Ireland, Scotland, and Wales. The Americans would raise a navy to damage British commercial interests, and emigration to American would "half depopulate" Great Britain. The colonies would grow into a full-sized monster and reduce Great Britain to the condition of a province. Some ended on a menacing note, intimating, for example, that if the British government did not provide a means for the loyalists to survive the war, the sixty thousand loyalists would seek "safety and protection in the arms of France" and pose a threat to the British Empire.[96]

The loyalist writers frantically pressed officials of the empire not to shame them by "begging peace" from an "unprovoked, aggressive, and vanquished enemy." They highlighted the "unquestionable" fealty of the "loyal thousands."[97] In December 1782, Samuel Hake pleaded with the British "not to withdraw . . . royal protection from us," as such a measure would render the distress of the loyalists "absolutely insupportable, absolutely ineffable." The New Yorkers stressed that nine-tenths of the people would prefer the empire to independence if only Great Britain would let it be "publicly known" that she was ready to grant the privileges and exemptions that they had first requested.[98] These loyalists had forgotten that the rebels had long rejected the Carlisle Commission's overtures in 1778.

On April 5, 1783, a packet with the copy of the provisional treaty arrived in New York City. Three days later, Carleton read the treaty to an anxious public gathered in City Hall. The treaty sounded the death knell for the hope of thousands of supporters of the royal cause in America. Despite the British concessions already granted to the rebels, some had hoped for restitution. Until they had received final news of the terms, they had hoped that astute negotiations might yet make their exile unnecessary. One New Yorker described the "settled gloom" experienced by the multitude upon hearing the news.[99]

Governor James Robertson resigned and left governance of New York to Andrew Elliot. In his April letter to the new governor, Robertson lamented that "military law has prevailed here and must prevail." He had done his best to "supply the want of civil government" but his authority came ultimately from the commander in chief. Robertson acknowledged the artificiality of his title in his final advice to Elliot. He emphasized that Elliot's authority would derive not from his official position but from "his private character and the regard the people have for [his] person."[100]

Neither General Carleton nor Governor Elliot could alleviate New Yorkers' worsening predicament. Struggling with unemployment, bankruptcy, and high prices, the rebels showed an intense hatred toward the loyalists. They claimed that the loyalists, protected by the British military, had pillaged and plundered rebel neighborhoods. Collaborating with the British administration against their neighbors, loyalists had held prisoners and gained enormous wealth. With the help of New York's wartime rebel governor, George Clinton, the returning rebels resolved to enact a series of vigorous proscription acts that violated the spirit of the peace treaty.[101]

Governor Clinton had served as brigadier general of the New York rebel militia during 1776–77. He had recruited, organized, disciplined, provisioned, and finally trained a motley collection of men to act as a fighting force. His military record and patriotism along with his lack of aristocratic pretensions won him the seat as governor of New York State in 1777.[102] During his tenure as governor, he identified loyalists as traitors and dealt harshly with them.[103] Early in the war, he had asserted that the loyalists' conduct "was so daring and insolent that a sudden & severe example [was] absolutely necessary to deter others from the commission of like crimes." During the war, he authorized, through the Committees for Detecting and Defeating Conspiracies, the imprisonment and banishment of loyalists considered dangerous. In 1777, the rebel state legislature seized loyalist estates and rented them at moderate cost to rebels. In late 1779, the rebel government sought to suppress and pacify the loyalists by force and land confiscations. In March 1780, the legislature ordered the sale of the confiscated property. By 1782, the state had earned over £3,600,000 from the sales.[104]

In 1782, Governor Clinton responded prudently to the people's pent-up anger. He resolved to retain the support of his constituents, the freehold farmers who populated the rural counties of New York State. Unwilling to extend forgiveness to the loyalists, Governor Clinton guided the New York legislature to pass a variety of laws that boded a bleak future for loyalists. In 1782, New York debtors could cancel all debts owed to loyalists as long as they paid a fortieth part of the amount to the state. A palpable violation of Article 6 of the peace treaty, the Trespass Act of March 1783 allowed a citizen to sue anyone who occupied his property behind British lines even if the occupant had authorization from the British commander in chief. In effect, it permitted anyone who had fled from New York to recover damages in an action for trespass against any person who had taken possession of the premises. The defendant could not plead the justification of a military order.[105]

In violation of Article 5 of the 1783 peace treaty, New Yorkers not only refused to restore confiscated estates to loyalists but made it impossible for them to return to repurchase their property. Governor Clinton resolved that no compensation was necessary for the loyalists because Great Britain planned no commensurate compensation for Americans who had suffered from the destruction caused by the British and their allies. Indeed, New York would hold the confiscated property as remuneration for its wartime losses. In March 1783, Congressman William Floyd assured Governor Clinton that Article 5 meant nothing. Its insertion in the treaty had allowed the king and his ministers to tell the loyalists "that they had attended to their interest as far as Lay in their power on the settlement of a peace."[106]

Emboldened by the British recognition of American independence and Governor Clinton's hard-line stance, rebel communities precluded loyalists from returning to their former lives. The prominent gentlemen who had openly displayed allegiance to the Crown or had been employed in the British administration faced few options. Those without connections or influence in England, such as Pennsylvania's John Potts, New Hampshire's Edward Lutwyche, Maryland's Anthony Stewart, and Rhode Island's William Wanton, prepared for a future in Nova Scotia.[107] When Philip J. Livingston, superintendent of derelict property since 1780, realized his open allegiance to the British would result in his ruin, he also decided in favor of the "mild monarchy of Great Britain" in Nova Scotia.[108]

In 1782–83, loyalist soldiers who tried to return to their former homes faced humiliation. One New York resident observed that the "panic" upon the news of independence had "occasioned alarming desertions" in some loyalist regiments.[109] In September 1783, when John Pellet and James Aston of the 1st Battalion of New Jersey Volunteers tried to return to Sussex County, New Jersey, they faced hanging as a penalty for their allegiance. Both men had entered British lines in the spring of 1777. In 1783, Aston was given twenty-five strokes on his bare back, "a fresh hand [and] a new rod at every five strokes." Pellet received twenty-one lashes. The rebels tied straw ropes tied around their necks, cut off their hair in the presence of a crowd, and sent them back to Staten Island.[110]

Fourteen loyalist regiments petitioned to Sir Guy Carleton for relief. The officers lamented their dire circumstances: "Civil dissentions have been so heightened by the blood that has been shed in the contest that the parties can never be reconciled." They asked for grants of land in Nova Scotia; provisions for wounded soldiers, widows, and orphans; and half-pay upon reduction of their regiments.[111] Under orders from the London ministry, Carleton promised 5,000 acres of land to field officers, 3,000 acres to captains, 2,000 acres to subalterns, and 200 acres to privates. Each loyalist civilian household would receive a free grant of at least 100 acres, with an additional 50 acres for each member of the family, including servants and slaves. In addition to boards and timbers for house construction, the government would provide rations for the first three years of settlement.[112] In contrast, the Black Pioneers, reduced to less than forty soldiers by the winter of 1782, each received twenty acres of land in Canada but no pay or clothing.[113]

Regarded as traitors, loyalist civilians also received brutal treatment. In June 1783, when William Hunt tried to return to Westchester County, a Colonel Thomas accused him of stealing flour from him in 1777. Hunt insisted he had followed orders from commanding officers in the British service. When Thomas demanded immediate satisfaction, Hunt's father gave £100 and rescued his son. In September 1783, when David Bonnet went from New York City to his home in New Rochelle, Westchester County, Justice Benjamin Stevens told him he would tie him to a tree and lash him five hundred times if he dared return a second time. Stevens accused Bonnet of enticing his slave to join the king's service. Stevens had lost valuable property and determined to derive compensation by taking Bonnet's house and farm. When loyalist wagoner Joshua Booth of Ulster County went from New York City to his home in Wallkill to see his mother, about forty men on horseback stopped him. They ordered that he "be shorn close to his head, and his eyebrows shaved with a pen knife." They tarred and feathered him, hung a low bell around his neck, and affixed a paper on his head with the inscription "Look yo Tory Crew, and see what George your King can do." After parading him on horseback with drum beating, fife playing, and much mockery on the streets of Newburgh, they sent Booth aboard a sloop to New York City at midnight.[114]

Loyalists returning to neighboring colonies faced the same predicament as those going back to New York's hinterlands. On June 15, 1783, when Samuel Jarvis went to Danbury, Connecticut, he "was visited by the populace," who ordered him to leave the town by sunset.[115] In November, when Samuel Knowles tried to return to his home in King's County, renamed Washington County during the war, in Rhode Island, he found his estate sold. Confined in a dungeon for four months, he was placed on a sloop bound for New York.[116] Prominent Philadelphia merchant Joseph Stansbury discovered he could not live outside British lines. In 1779, he had hesitated to display his allegiance openly, for "he shou'd hold himself unjust to [his] family to hazard his all on the occasion and part with a certainty—potentially at least—for an uncertainty."[117] During 1779–80, Stansbury provided the British with intelligence information.[118] Arrested by the rebel government in November 1780, he escaped to New York in January 1781. In 1783, trying to escape the cost of maintaining his household in New York, Stansbury tried to move with his wife, sister, seven children, and two servants to Moorestown, New Jersey. However, within twenty days he was forced to return to New York City. Stansbury left his family behind hoping "their stay might perhaps be overlooked after his departure."[119] But in August, Stansbury gave up. Seeing no probability of recovering his property or returning to his former home, he asked for asylum in Nova Scotia.[120] William Terrill, employed in New York's Customs Office since 1777, hoped to return home with his wife and five children to New Jersey, but faced with the "violent and persecuting spirit of the people without the lines," he departed for Nova Scotia.[121]

Some New Yorkers who had accepted loyalist persecution as part of the peace settlement lamented the prevailing sentiments against the loyalists. On January 25, 1784, Robert R. Livingston regarded the rebel payback with suspicion. He believed that selfish interests drove the returnees to such violence: "In some few, it is a blind spirit of revenge & resentment, but in more it is the most sordid interest." Livingston wondered cynically whether most rebels exploited the wretched state of the loyalists to better their commercial prospects, to get rid of debts, or to reduce the price of living by "depopulating the town."[122]

The black loyalists sought to escape the claims of loyalist and rebel slaveholders and the opportunism of British authorities. Some loyalists who came to the superintendent of police to collect a slave provided no proof respecting the legitimacy of their claim. When pressed for proof, they stalled and disappeared.[123] Despite their official role as protectors, some employees in the British administration also exploited the slaves' desperate situation. They sought a quick profit by capturing and selling blacks who had sought refuge in New York City. In May 1783, Thomas Willis, employed in Andrew Elliot's police department, seized a black man named Caesar, tied his hands behind his back, and forced him through the public streets of the city by beating him with a stick. Willis hoped to return the runaway Caesar to Elizabethtown, New Jersey, for a "piece of gold coin." Having evidence that Caesar entered the lines legally, the British sentenced Willis to five hundred lashes but then revoked the sentence because his service otherwise displayed "good character." Instead, they mandated his transport out of the city to Europe or the West Indies.[124]

Generally neglectful of the plight of black loyalists, the authorities adopted a high moral tone when returning New Yorkers challenged British presence. Their benevolence helped some runaways avoid re-enslavement. In July 1783, the British found Jacob Duryee and three others forcefully carrying off Francis Griffin, a black man under the protection of the British government. In his defense, Duryee insisted that as a citizen of the United States of America, he had a "right to his property whenever he could find it." He infuriated Deputy Judge Advocate Stephen P. Adye, who reminded Duryee that a "general commanding an army in a hostile country possesses powers beyond what even His Majesty himself enjoys!" Furthermore, Adye asserted that proclamations functioned as laws, and they applied not only to His Majesty's loyal subjects but to anyone who entered the king's lines. Duryee was ordered out of British lines and fined fifty guineas.[125]

In other cases, however, the British authorities seemed to care less about slaves' misery than about restoring slaves to their "real owner[s]."[126] In September 1783, the British denied Judith Jackson transport out of slavery. At the onset of the revolution, Jackson's owner, loyalist John McLean, sold her to Jonathan Elbeck and fled to Great Britain. Judith escaped Elbeck and served the British army, washing and ironing clothes for Lord Dunmore and other officers. As Jackson prepared to embark with her child to Nova Scotia in 1783, Elbeck arrived in New York City and claimed her. In her memorial, Jackson protested that "he wanted to steal me back to Virginia and was not my master." Elbeck, she lamented, "stole my child from me and sent it to Virginia." The British determined that Jackson was not free and ordered her return to Elbeck.[127] Two months later, they prevented another black woman from Virginia, Peggy Gwym, from leaving for Canada with her husband, an employee of the British artillery. Gwym's marriage to a free black man did not protect her from enslavement. In answer to Gwym's claim that a "certain Mr. Gammon who want to detain me & deprive me of my liberty that I have enjoyed by virtue of the proclamation," the British answered: "As she is not a free woman she must be delivered up to her owner."[128]

As desperately as the black loyalists wanted to create a new home outside the United States, the white loyalists within New York tried to stay within it. But unrelenting rebel attacks prevented this alternative. The British heard countless complaints from loyalists hurt by rebel gangs who daringly entered less protected areas around the city. In March 1783, when a noted "Storey's gang" landed on Staten Island, beat and abused John Steel and stole his whaleboat, Steel wished the British would destroy the "sett of pickaroons," as "every craft moving by water is in eminent danger of being captured by them."[129] General Carleton pressed Admiral Digby to appoint guard ships to protect the inhabitants. Digby, however, answered unequivocally: "If your Excellency suspects these guard ships can prevent boats landing in and about New York all hours of the night, you will certainly be mistaken." Instead, Digby recommended that Carleton regulate the shore.[130]

In May 1783, Westchester County loyalists described their suffering from "lawless banditti" who attacked their houses with "disguised features" and committed the most "enormous villainy." A party of fifty men armed with swords, pistols, and clubs entered John Fowler's house, struck him violently, and carried off his effects. They called to him "to run to Halifax or to his damned King for that neither he nor one of his breed should be suffered to remain in the country."[131] Five men in the same rebel gang came on horseback to Arthur Orser's home, beat him with clubs, stole his mare and clothing, and took his money. They also attacked John and Joseph Orser, Bartow Underhill, and Robert Hunt. When some anonymous Westchester refugees pleaded "to meet such person or persons who may be directed to attend to our complaints," they received no response.[132]

Loyalists who had lived peacefully in the hinterlands during the rebellion faced persecution in 1782–83. In January 1782, the aged and infirm loyalist Peter John of Orange County sought help because he received a cruel beating without provocation.[133] Another Orange County loyalist, Ralph Maenair, lamented the "gross insults and personal abuse to which too many loyalists in all parts of the country have been exposed."[134] Charles Traver of Charlotte precinct in Dutchess County faced similar persecution. After serving for two months in Sir William Howe's army in White Plains,

Traver returned to his home. He had resided "unvexed" with his wife and eight children since 1777. However, in September 1783, he received notice to leave the county within four weeks. Fearing for his life, he appealed to the British authorities.[135] The British responded to these appeals in the same manner as they addressed thirty-three other refugees from Albany who begged assistance to leave for Canada: "It is not possible to assist them at present."[136]

Following Cornwallis's surrender, New York's tradesmen and retailers recognized the enormity of the British loss. Some closed out their affairs and booked passage on private ships going to England, Ireland, and the West Indies. In November, the proprietor of a grocery business, Henry Juncken, and hairdresser David Beveridge with his partner, Elizabeth Bryan, left for England. In December, John Cochran, Francis Murphy, Thomas Quin, and John Wily announced their intentions to leave for Ireland. Loyalists of lesser stature asked to serve as servants to gentlemen and their families leaving for England or Europe.[137]

Despite the partisan warfare in the city, most New Yorkers resisted abandoning their homes. They hoped to find a way to maintain their livelihood and secure their safety within the city. A few merchants circulated their declaration to dissolve their partnership or leave without actually doing so. They may have worried about a sudden evacuation and therefore sought to settle their accounts. In June 1783, a year after their declaration to dissolve their partnership, Scott and Allingham still advertised their wares. On May 1, 1782, Alexander Zuntz of 16 Water Street announced his intentions to leave for Europe. But a year later, on May 14, 1783, Zuntz continued to advertise his assortment of dry foods, Madeira, and cutlery. In 1783, he operated from his new location at 41 Hanover Square.[138]

So many New Yorkers delayed abandoning the city in 1783 that British captains grew frustrated. In June, one notice announced transports stood ready to receive them and urged "every person to be on board on Saturday next, without fail." In August, Joshua Knight and Caleb Barratt informed loyalists to board on time "or else they must expect to be excluded the benefit of the proclamation." If they did not embark on the transport, the British would refuse the expense of a later passage. Daniel Wright expressed disgust at the loyalists' postponement. In September, as he waited for loyalists to embark for Port Roseway, he remarked acridly that "it should not be expected that the ship should lye by the wharf for no other purpose than to indulge indolent people."[139]

Many loyalists tried to recuperate money from the British before the army left the city. Andrew Elliot reported the unprecedented number of applications made within just twenty-four hours, when British evacuation became a certainty.[140] Some expected payments for soldiers' provisions, while others tried to get rent on property occupied by British troops.[141] Two inhabitants, Herlitz and Blackwell, complained of Captain de Franck of the Regiment of Hesse Hanan, who owed £158 for clothing furnished to his company. The regiment prepared to leave New York, and Herlitz and Blackwell wanted their money before "a decree of a foreign judicature in Europe interposed between them and their just rights."[142] Joseph Orchard wanted 26,800 pounds of flour that was due to him from soldiers who had already left the city.[143] "Firmly attached to His Majesty's person and government since the commencement of the present horrid and unnatural war," Anthony Woodward and John Leonard of Trenton wanted pay for the twenty-six wagons and seventy-two horses they had procured for the British army in December 1776.[144] A Mr. Bartow of Westchester wanted compensation for a horse taken from him by British soldiers in 1779.[145] Four New York proprietors petitioned because they had not received rent from the British for two and a half years. They believed "it was contrary to every principle of British government as well as repugnant to reason and justice that a few individuals among them who are under the full protection of government should bear so unequal a burthen of the war." They emphasized that others in "similar circumstances" had received their rents.[146] Charles Roubalet, a tavern keeper, complained that the British held court martial trials in his house for three and a half years. Indeed, Jacob Duryee's trial in July 1783 was held at his tavern. The expenditure on wood alone amounted to over £250.[147] Herman Leroy wanted compensation for the losses on his father's property caused by a fire. As the British occupied the estate during the time of the fire, Leroy believed they were answerable for the damage.[148]

The British worried that satisfying only a minority of loyalists' appeals would fuel outrage. Andrew Elliot observed that distinctions would "create murmurs and complaints."[149] Setting a precedent would "produce ten thousands more of a like nature, which if admitted would cost millions and if refused after some payments had fixed precedents, would give cause for great complaints."[150] It would provoke suspicion of the British and lead to jealousy among loyalists. Proving compensation to all of the loyalists was out of the question.

As the British prepared to evacuate the city, they found new reason to doubt New Yorkers' allegiance. In 1782–83, they found the king's friends weakening the force of the king's army by assisting Hessian desertion. The Hessians wanted to abandon military life and live within a civilian community inside rebel lines. In August 1783, one officer observed the "intolerable desertion from the German troops." Almost every day, he noted, at least two to three and sometimes four to five "passed by." Towns such as Middleton, New Jersey, already had two hundred Hessians.[151]

Hired from the princes of various German principalities, the Hessians formed between a quarter and a third of the British army. Comprising men from the bottom ranks of society, the Hessians accommodated their princes' desire for currency by serving as rented soldiers in European wars. Hoping to drive a wedge between the Hessians and the British, rebel leaders openly accused British commanders of treating Hessians with "utter contempt" and of exposing them to the most dangerous posts to spare the lives of British-born troops. They exhorted Hessians to desert from a conflict that did not concern them and to cease attacking people who had done them no harm. If the Hessians deserted the British forces, they could enjoy the same cash and land bounties offered to rebel soldiers. Rebel leaders enjoined Hessians to become "brethren and inhabitants of America."[152]

The British had long worried about the loyalty of the Hessians. Rented soldiers with no ideological commitment to His Majesty's cause who faced a bleak future on their return home might pursue opportunities in colonies with abundant land. In November 1776, upon the return of Hessian soldiers from rebel detention in Philadelphia, James Robertson feared that the men "had been gained over by the Rebels" and they would now persuade others to desert. It would therefore be "prudent" to watch their movements to uncover a possible rebel plot.[153] One returning Hessian soldier recounted that Washington had offered to buy his loyalty. General Howe responded by offering him the same compensation. This disgusted the man's German commander, who ordered his flogging.[154]

In the winter of 1776–77, as rebel appeals to the Hessians escalated, British and Hessian officers could no longer refute the propaganda by appealing to the invincibility of the British Empire. Instead, they pointedly directed Hessians to observe that rebel soldiers did not receive "ordinary pay & provisions punctually."[155] They also praised the steadfast devotion of the Hessian who would never abandon his solemn vows to his ruler. In

November, William Tryon asserted that "not a Hesse would be seduced by the proclamation."[156] The reasons the "Prince, their master" had to enlist his troops on behalf of the British, a Hessian officer stationed at Kingsbridge asserted, "rests on stronger grounds of policy than a carpenter, butcher, farmer, or any other, who does not study the laws of states or of nation, can possibly conceive." Unlike common laborers, the Hessian soldiers were a "faithful and patient people" who would not betray their country for "base" motives. The few "villains" who had deserted were "strangers both to the Hessians and their country." The soldiers, he claimed, would never leave their prince, country, and honor for the "sake of a plantation."[157] Another Hessian officer echoed in German: "The German is constant and glorieth in being an honest man, who sticketh to his words and may safely be relyed upon." With "unalterable firmness, we will persevere with our friends, and with honor we will return to our native home."[158] In December 1777, a Hessian officer rallied his corps with an extravagant address to rebel leaders:

> This is the best time for your submission, since you may depend upon it, next spring there will be such a powerful army of Russians and Hanoverians come over to subdue you, as will make it impossible for you to resist, then it will be too late to implore mercy, you then must wait that dreadful punishment denounced against such who have obstinately persisted in their revolt against their parent state and lawfull sovereign.[159]

After Yorktown, desertion by both English and Hessian soldiers became an increasing concern. In May 1783, the British arrested inhabitant Henry Hawley for carrying five Hessians from Long Island to New England. In June, Johan Dunnakey carried five more to Newbury, Connecticut. In August, Thomas Lasey took Hessian deserters to the Jersey shore. The British police accused three other inhabitants of Long Island of transporting soldiers to New Jersey. In September, Aaron Gibson attempted to carry a Hessian soldier out of the lines. In November, the British arrested Stricker, a black man within the lines, for assisting deserters.[160]

The British officers had more faith in Hessian military competence than in their allegiance. In 1777, General Burgoyne had contemptuously noted a "strong[er] disposition in the Germans to be prisoners than to endure hard blows." Almost six years later, General Guy Carleton's disgust was unconcealed: "It is recommended to the soldiers of every British regiment and to the soldiers of every British American regiment to kick all such Rascals out of their quarters should they have the Impudence to come in among them." The British directed their frustration with Hessian runaways on the body of one Carl Broiske. A 1783 notice for the return of the forty-year-old paymaster of the Hessian Grenadiers who had stolen £340 sterling described Broiske as "rather fat," with "a round full and pale face, short neck, his head bending forward." It also mentioned his connection with a Miss Sally Bunn from Perth Amboy, a twenty-two-year-old woman of middle size, "her face & features rather large," last seen in a yellow silk gown.[161] However ungainly, Broiske was clearly in demand.

Having little faith in the British government and few connections to well-placed British statesmen, more than two-thirds of the loyalists found it more expedient to take their chances in the United States instead of living in exile.[162] Like Tench Coxe in June 1778, former chief justice of New Jersey Frederick Smyth turned away from the British in December. Pragmatically, he wrote, "I have seen our affairs year after year growing from bad to worse and little prospect of any amendment. I think it high time to terminate the war in this country." After thirty-one years in the printing business, Hugh Gaine stopped publishing the New-York Gazette and Weekly Mercury on November 10, 1783. He quietly brought down the Crown from his shop sign and continued his printing business "at the sign of the Bible" in Hanover Square. The former loyalist received business from the new political leadership in the city, testifying to his reinstatement in the community. He printed the Laws, Statutes, Ordinances and Constitutions of the City of New York in 1784, money for the state in 1788, and, the two-volume Laws of the State of New York in 1789.[163]

Like Frederick Smyth and Hugh Gaine, many New York merchants waited for the tempest to pass, hoping to reclaim their possessions and status. With his brother, Philip, Frederick Rhinelander enjoyed a flourishing business as the proprietor of a china, glass, and earthenware shop in New York City during British occupation. After Frederick escaped rebel imprisonment and returned to New York City in 1776, he celebrated his "good fortune" when he found "a considerable quantity of Goods which I had concealed in Cellars safe so I have now in the City Goods & produce to amount of upwards 2000 pounds." Once Governor Tryon attested to Rhinelander's loyalty, his suppliers in England continued to send him goods to sell in the city. Rhinelander provided tableware to military personnel from General William Howe to the barrack master, and to leading loyalists. Trusted by the British administration, Rhinelander served in the city's vestry, empowered to deal with city maintenance, housing, and poor relief.[164]

After Yorktown, Rhinelander wrote to his London contacts to reassure them that the military defeat would not affect his business. On November 12, 1781, he explained that "although the misfortune of Lord Cornwallis will naturally alarm your Merchants who have property here, we beg leave, however, to assure you that your interest in our hands is perfectly safe and that our remittances shall be as regular as usual and that no circumstances shall induce us to act otherwise." However, Rhinelander's hopes did not materialize. On July 23, 1783, the State of New York identified him as treasonous and confiscated his property. On August 30, after a suspicious robbery in his store on 168 Water Street that resulted in a loss of £1,000, Rhinelander changed his line of work. Instead of importing glass and ceramics, he entered the lumber business.[165] Like Gaine, Rhinelander adapted his work and extended his contacts to establish his place in the new nation.

The case of James Rivington, publisher of the *Royal Gazette*, illustrates the curtailed circumstances of those who stayed in the city. In February 1783, the Sons of Liberty demanded that Rivington discontinue his business in the city. The *New York Packet* had warned Rivington and others "that those who have been enriching themselves under the mild and wise government of George III, shall never live peaceably in New York." Yet Rivington continued resolutely to publish his paper. In November, he conceded to American demands by changing the name of his paper to *Rivington's New-York Gazette, and the Universal Advertiser*. Only in December 1783 after the Liberty Boys beat him in the city streets did Rivington cease publishing his newspaper. Rumors that Rivington had served as General Washington's spy during the last years of the war failed to protect him.[166] Rivington's loyalism, expressed early, ardently, and publicly, had no place in the new republic.

William Smith Jr., trusted advisor to at least two commanders in chief, also tried to remain in New York. He accepted the turn of events following Yorktown only grudgingly. In December 1781, he entreated Tryon to use his influence to propose greater military vigor in the colonies and to oppose the evacuation of New York. In September 1782, Smith insisted that Britain overrated the rebel power and "American affairs are still recoverable." He suggested that the ministry should "send authority to drive the compact here, and discontinue the negotiation at Paris." In April 1783, upon news of the provisional peace, Smith attacked Lord Shelburne as "the weakest or wickedest of men," who had "cast off" the loyalists. In May, Smith still imagined that the final treaty could nullify the provisional articles. In July, he anticipated that the thirteen colonies would reunite under a new king or beg for reunion with the British Empire. He urged Carleton to take advantage of the crisis and propose a way out.[167]

By August, however, Smith had given up on reconciliation with the British government and determined to act on his own behalf. He wrote to Dr. Samuel Johnson, his fellow student at Yale College, asking for "full and effective protection" in New Haven, Connecticut. He hoped Johnson could persuade the Connecticut assembly to provide him with asylum. But Johnson could offer no definite assurance. In December, Smith departed for England with his most recent and powerful patron, General Carleton.[168]

Lacking Smith's connections with British men of distinction in England, over thirty-five thousand loyalists sailed to British North America.[169] For seven years, the loyalists sacrificed their properties, reputations, and friendships for reunion with the empire. Unable to return to their homes, they found excuses to explain British behavior, to assuage their doubts, and to contain their desperation. They had suffered the disdain of the British, who found their complaints irritating and their military assistance superfluous. The loyalists tolerated their terrible predicament in New York City because the British promised them that steadfast attachment to the empire would reap proper rewards. They never suspected that their allegiance would lead to a permanent exile from their homes. Ironically, their exile, like nothing preceding it, demonstrated their allegiance to the empire and entitled them to the full rights of British citizens.

# CONCLUSION

## Loyalist Patriotism Exceeds Loyalist Power

British New York did not transform into loyalist New York. The British rejection of civil rule in 1776 and again in 1780 compelled the loyalists to confront a shocking realization: they found that they valued the symbols of the British Empire—legal protection of property and liberty, civil government, and constitutional processes—more deeply than the Crown's representatives in New York or in London. Ironically, they learned too late that they cherished a more perfect version of the British constitution than the Britons across the Atlantic.

In the fall of 1776, New York's loyalist leaders anticipated a partnership with the British to crush rebel hopes for an American republic and to restore New York City to civil governance. By promoting the city as an exemplary model of His Majesty's reign, the loyalists hoped to garner support from the wavering colonists behind rebel lines. They offered applause, petitions, homes, provisions, and military assistance. Pushed to the defensive by rebel pressure tactics, they looked to the British to value their allegiance, to esteem their courage, and to mobilize their vast potential. They saw themselves as allies in the imperial enterprise to destroy the unnatural rebellion. Based upon their understanding of the reciprocal obligations of the empire, New Yorkers anticipated that the British would uphold the loyalists' standard of imperial conduct and establish New York as a model of just constitutional governance.

The British confounded loyalists' expectations when they instituted martial law in the city and cast loyalist leaders aside. In exchange for their devotion and their deference, the loyalists endured neglect, suspicion, and derision. Inheriting the biases of the upper crust of English society, the British shunned the Americans as unpolished and socially inferior. Despite loyalists' repeated demands for the restoration of civil rule in the city, New

York remained under martial law for the duration of the war. Instead of becoming a working model of an expansive loyalist vision, it remained a military town governed by a series of British commandants and their multiplying proclamations.

The tension between British authorities' desire for control over the city and loyalists' hopes for active and equal participation created irreconcilable differences between the two groups despite their shared goal of reunifying the empire. The loyalists needed both military and ideological support from the British. Reconciling the colonies required winning the hearts and minds of undecided colonists as much as breaking the military strength of the rebels. But the British relegated ideological persuasions to a lower and later priority. They stubbornly regarded the rebellion as a family quarrel that could be resolved when elements of the rebel faction learned a military lesson. During the war, New Yorkers did not live in a city that beckoned others with its promise of constitutional liberties. Instead, contrary to their longing for the political rights promised to them as British subjects, the loyalists lived under prolonged martial rule at odds with the British constitution. The suspension of civil rule undermined loyalist ideals and frustrated loyalist potential.

The ever-present danger from rebels in the border regions justified British unwillingness to empower the New York loyalists in a military or civilian capacity. The large-scale arming of white loyalists risked the rise of local factions who would compete with British officers for military sway. Arming blacks risked alienating white subjects. And reviving a civilian assembly and court required trusting unfamiliar loyalists who could potentially weaken lines of military control and endanger the security of the garrison. The British valued loyalist devotion—but at a distance.

Within New York City, the issue of distinguishing between the loyal and the disloyal plagued British administration. The city was crowded with rented soldiers, escaped slaves, rebel deserters, and runaway seamen. Rebels and loyalists alike worshipped the same Protestant God and could not be distinguished by skin color or language. Opportunists posed as loyalists; distinguishing charlatans, adventurers, and speculators from true friends created insurmountable difficulties. Equally burdensome were the smaller numbers of elite who entered the British lines for "unselfish" motives.[1]

Alarmed by the growing and contradictory needs of their military and civilian subjects, the British imposed regulations to maximize military security and minimize civilian disorder. Under the supervision of the commander in chief, the Office of Police issued proclamations to monitor and regulate the number of civilians in the city. It set restrictions on bakers, cartmen, ferryboat proprietors, wagoners, tavern owners, soldiers, and sailors. Intended to bring order to the city, these rules burdened British resources and caused loyalist disaffection. They inflated the power of British military officials at the expense of the loyalist elite. Diminished of political significance, the loyalists scrambled for a footing within British administration. They resorted to competing with one another to attain desirable appointments, to receive provisions, and to secure housing and dependable compensation.

Entering British lines from diverse regions, at different moments during the rebellion, and with conflicting motives, the loyalists lacked unity. Upholding the British to their high constitutional standards, loyalist moderates continued to believe that the resumption of civil rule would exemplify the constitutionalism of British government and change the course of the war. In contrast, the hard-liners abandoned faith in British leadership and British leniency and advocated a militant approach to the war. They demanded authority to launch raids along rebel-controlled coastlines and take their own prisoners. Confronted with competing interests and agendas, the British in New York hesitated to empower either the moderates or the hard-liners. General Henry Clinton resented loyalist clamor in what he regarded primarily as a rebellion against the empire, not a civil war.

Between 1776 and 1783, the local conditions in and around New York City—the military government within and the rebel threat without—narrowed the loyalists' political reach. Successive British military setbacks diminished loyalists' faith in the British commanders. Yet, incredibly, whatever political ideals, convictions, calculations, or circumstances divided them, the loyalists maintained their abhorrence for the unnatural and unlawful rebellion. Their optimism waned after the British defeat at Saratoga in 1777 and with the British evacuation of Philadelphia eight months later. In November 1778, William Smith Jr. feared loyalist devotion could not overcome the difficulties that threatened the fragmentation of the empire. He lamented, "Our Patriotism exceeded our power to apply the means for preventing the evils which have overwhelmed these dispersions of the empire."[2] Smith's remark reflected the loyalist despondency that accompanied the Franco-American alliance and the failure of the British peace commissioners.

William Franklin's bitter response in 1781 to British terms following the battle of Yorktown bears testimony to loyalist mortification. He observed that loyalists stood "in no better light than as runaway slaves restored to their former masters."[3] Yet many loyalists still refused to believe that the empire's focus on the Caribbean and other regions represented a complete abandonment of the North American colonies. In 1782, they anticipated that the British would negotiate terms that would shield them from the vengeance of their rebel neighbors and compensate them for the lives they had surrendered. The 1783 peace terms, which offered no compensation for past losses or future protection of loyalist property, shattered the last remnants of loyalist deference.

New York City's loyalists endured many losses to preserve the liberty they associated with the empire: at great risk, they provided intelligence information that was disregarded; at great cost, they housed and fed soldiers who damaged their property and left the colonies without repaying them; they left land, cattle, and slaves for which they received no credit or compensation; they offered sons who served and died in the British forces, leaving widows and orphans to fend for themselves. They tolerated inflationary prices, shortages of rations and fuel, and the horrible uncertainty of the war because they opposed the unnatural rebellion and would do anything to stamp it out. They believed the British shared their absolute conviction.

Neither loyalist thought nor loyalist history ended in 1783. The majority who fled New York City sought a new home in British North America. Some exiles, such as Mrs. Nancy Cameron, saw the migration to the north as yet another sojourn within the British world: "We must," she wrote, "follow the old flag wherever it takes us." As loyal to the "Cameron men" as to the empire, she accepted that "wives and children must tread the hard road" again. Committed to making their new homes the "envy of all their Neighbors" to the south, New York's loyalists, many of them imbued with unfulfilled aspirations, became active participants in revising the terms of imperial governance.[4] They took with them the painful lessons learned from opposing their rebellious neighbors and allying with the authoritarian British. They cursed the rebels publicly and the British privately. Carrying with them an almost equal knowledge—and suspicion—of the United States and the British Empire, they vowed to avert an unnatural rebellion in Canada.

# NOTES

ABBREVIATIONS

AAS       American Antiquarian Society
CL        Clements Library
CMNY      City Museum of New York
DLAR      David Library of the American Revolution
GLS       Gilder Lehrman Society
NA        National Archives
NYHS      New York Historical Society
NYPL      New York Public Library
NYSL      New York State Library

INTRODUCTION

1. *New-York Gazette and Weekly Mercury,* October 21, 1776.
2. Jordan, "Familial Politics," 306; also see McConville, *The King's Three Faces.*
3. Quoted in Morris, "The American Revolution," 109.
4. John Dyke Ackland to Richard Howe, January 6, 1778, in Clinton Papers, CL.
5. The loyalists' "paranoic obsession" was not with diabolical Crown conspiracy but with the sudden and unnatural rebellion. See Wood, "Rhetoric and Reality," 25. Charles Royster also differentiates between the loyalist "rebellion" and the rebels' "revolution." See Royster, *Revolutionary People,* 14.
6. See Eustace, *Passion Is the Gale.* The merchants in New York complained of the "spirit of persecution which prevails in the country" ("Memorial of sundry Merchants," August 10, 1783, in Carleton Papers, NA). If the rebels began the war to stop the encroachment of power and to preserve virtue, they may have won the war by successfully transferring the authoritarian connotations associated with power to the passionate and sympathetic nuances associated with the patriot "spirit."
7. Jeffrey N. Nelson has suggested that loyalists' dread of tumult and violence and their preoccupation with civil order borrowed from the work of the seventeenth-century English philosopher Thomas Hobbes, who assumed the need for an artificial government that contained and channeled individual competitiveness. Without the reigning hand of government, confusion, disorder, and tumult would destroy not only the society but also the individual. Subjects had to forsake some of their rights in

order to assure the preservation of their society. By consenting to government, they granted government the authority to regulate the liberty of the subjects so it could, in turn, ensure the security of the public order. In return for government protection, the subjects were obliged to allegiance and should refuse to disobey the regime, even if an unlawful one. Nelson characterizes the writing of Massachusetts loyalist Thomas Hutchinson as "applied Hobbesianism." See Nelson, "Ideology in Search of a Context," 747, 749. Also see Skinner, *Visions of Politics,* 292; Gross, "Early Modern Emotion," 318; and Attie, "Re-Membering the Body Politic," 504.

8. William Smith to Lewis Moore, June 5, 1775, in Smith Papers, Box 3, NYPL.

9. Ibid. Smith walked the knife-edge of neutrality until 1778, when he could no longer avoid a decision.

10. Quoted in Flavell, "Lord North's Conciliatory Proposal," 315.

11. Charles Inglis to Reverend Richard Hind, October 31, 1776, in Lydekker, *Life and Letters of Charles Inglis,* 159.

12. Walzer, "On the Role of Symbolism," 191–204, 195. Janice Potter and Robert Calhoon note that Massachusetts loyalist Daniel Leonard rejected rebel rhetoric as expressive of "disaffection, petulance, ingratitude, and disloyalty." See "Character and Coherence of the Loyalist Press," 235.

13. Perhaps best known for this formulation is Massachusetts loyalist Peter Oliver, as he expressed his grief in 1781: "Your leaders know that they have plunged themselves into the bowels of the most wanton and unnatural rebellion that ever existed" ("An Address to the Soldiers," *Boston Weekly News-Letter,* January 11, 1776, in Adair and Schutz, *Peter Oliver's Origin and Progress of the American Rebellion,* 159. Also see "Benevolus" in *New-York Gazette and Weekly Mercury,* October 7, 1776; and Potter, *The Liberty We Seek,* 137. Stephen Conway notes that supporters of Lord North's ministry also widely used the phrase "unnatural rebellion." See Conway, "From Fellow-Nationals to Foreigners," 86n. As an example, he points to the loyalty expressed by the Beverley Corporation (Yorkshire). On September 27, 1775, it rejected the "present unnatural rebellion which now prevails in some of His Majesty's colonies in North America" (Macmahon, *Beverly Corporation Minute Books,* 55).

14. Quoted in Calhoon, *Dominion and Liberty,* 65.

15. *New-York Gazette and Weekly Mercury,* October 21, 1776.

16. *Royal Gazette,* June 6, 1778.

17. Mary Price, July 1779, in Carleton Papers, DLAR.

18. *Royal Gazette,* June 7, 1780.

19. Ibid., December 30, 1780.

20. Ibid., October 6, 1781.

21. John Huyek, July 30, 1783, in Carleton Papers, NA.

22. Some earlier examples of works on prominent loyalists include Bailyn, *The Ordeal of Thomas Hutchinson;* Calhoon, *The Loyalists in Revolutionary America;* Ferling, *Joseph Galloway and the American Revolution;* Zimmer, *Jonathan Boucher;* and Berkin, *Jonathan Sewall.* For a sketch of various loyalists throughout the mainland colonies, see Sabine, *Biographical Sketches;* and Rawlyk, "The Reverend John Stuart," 55–72. For one of the most recent and important study of ordinary loyalists, see Tiedemann, Fingerhut, and Venables, *The Other Loyalists.* See also Tiedemann and Fingerhut, *The Other New York.*

23. As Joseph Tiedemann and Eugene Fingerhut observe, "The Whigs saw the loyalists as an unremitting menace." See their introduction in *The Other New York*, 11.

24. Previous studies that have covered some aspect of the British-loyalist relationship in New York City and its environs during the war include Barck, *New York City during the War for Independence;* Polf, *Garrison Town;* Paul H. Smith, *Redcoats and Loyalists;* Van Buskirk, *Generous Enemies;* Papas, *Ever-Loyal Island;* Condon, "Marching to a Different Drummer"; Davies, "The Restoration of Civil Government"; Potter, *The Liberty We Seek;* and Tiedemann, "Patriots by Default."

25. Peter Onuf used this very useful concept of "civic capacity" in his commentary during a conference titled "Making Democracy: Violence, Politics, and the American Founding" held in Athens, Ohio, April 22–24, 2010.

# 1. Natural Rights and Natural Ties

1. Quoted in Greene, "New York and the Old Empire," 132.

2. Truxes, *Letterbook of Greg & Cunningham*, 7; Klein, *New York in the American Revolution*, xviii. Within the next decade, the packet service employed five boats on a monthly schedule between Falmouth, England, and New York City.

3. Quoted in Truxes, *Letterbook of Greg & Cunningham*, 8.

4. Egnal, *New World Economies*, 42; East, "The Business Entrepreneur in a Changing Economy," 19.

5. Dawson, *New York City during the American Revolution*, viii.

6. Kammen, *Colonial New York*, 153; Bonomi, *Factious People*, 159; Hoffman, *Edmund Burke*, 79.

7. Quoted in Hulsebosch, *Constituting Empire*, 71.

8. Kross, "Patronage," 205, 210, 216, 218, 221–22, 227. From 1691 to 1775, the New York Council consisted of twelve members; Kross also notes that between 1735 and 1776, 28 percent were lawyers (221).

9. Katz, "Between Scylla and Charybdis," 400–401; Bonomi, *Factious People*, 145, 138. Oliver DeLancey served as a New York City alderman in the early 1750s, as a member of the provincial assembly in the late 1750s, and finally, as a member of the provincial council from 1760 to 1776. Also see Nash, *Urban Crucible*, 363.

10. Tully, *Forming American Politics;* Potter, *The Liberty We Seek*, 177.

11. Hulsebosch, *Constituting Empire*, 50–55.

12. Klein, *The Politics of Diversity*, 23 (Klein notes that in 1768, at least 48 percent of the population was composed of freeholders); Champagne, "Liberty Boys and Mechanics of New York City," 126. Gronowicz notes that in the decades before the Revolution voting in New York "became the process of choosing, from a narrow predetermined family-based field, the man best perceived as advancing the economy" ("Political Radicalism," 101).

13. Edwards, *New York as an Eighteenth-Century Municipality*, 18–39. According to the 1771 census, 4,023 white males over twenty-one—about 68.6 percent of adult males in the city—possessed the right to vote. Also see Champagne, "Liberty Boys and Mechanics of New York City," 124–25; Nash, *Urban Crucible*, 363; Varga, "New York Government," 12; and Bonomi, *Factious People*, 282. Over 90 percent of the men elected to the assembly throughout the colonial era resided among their constituents,

which was rare in English practice (Bonomi, "Local Government in Colonial New York," 33). New Yorkers elected fewer men to municipal offices than Boston. In addition to electing selectmen, sheriffs, assessors, and constables, Bostonians also elected surveyors of hemp, informers about deer, purchasers of grain, hay wards, town criers, measurers of salt, scavengers, viewers of shingles, sheep reeves, hog reeves, sealers of leather, fence viewers, fire wards, cullers of stave hoops, auditors, and others. See Nash, *Race, Class, and Politics*, 146.

14. Mechanics included not only skilled artisans immediately under the category of merchants and lawyers but also unskilled laborers. See Lynd and Young, "After Carl Becker," 217–218, 224. Lynd and Young note that they were "economically heterogeneous, socially excluded, politically only partially enfranchised" (224).

15. Champagne, "Liberty Boys and Mechanics," 129.

16. Lepore, *New York Burning*, 23, 17; Rucker, *The River Flows On*, 24–25.

17. Lepore, *New York Burning*, 23.

18. Rucker, *The River Flows On*, 62.

19. Middleton, *From Privileges to Rights*, 101–14; Nash, *Urban Crucible*, 108.

20. Kammen, *Colonial New York*, 37; Rediker, *Between the Devil and Deep Blue Sea*, 69; Edwards, *New York as an Eighteenth-Century Municipality*, 113.

21. Colley, *Britons*, 117–32. Colley notes that the army and empire offered Scots openings denied to them in London.

22. Scots established landed dynasties in Antigua, St. Kitts, and Jamaica. Bowen, *Elites, Enterprise, and the Making of the British Overseas Empire*, 158.

23. Colden was careful to nurture his contacts with his old Scottish patron, the Marquis of Lothian, and his scientific correspondent, Peter Collinson. See Katz, "Between Scylla and Charybdis," 398; and Landsman, "The Legacy of British Union for the North American Colonies," 302. Colden generously contributed to his sons' success. He placed Alexander as surveyor general; John became the storekeeper at the fort at Albany and, a year later, a clerk of the peace and of the Court of Common Pleas for Albany; and a third son, David, got the office of private secretary and surrogate of the Prerogative Court. See Kross, "Patronage," 211–12.

24. Landsman, "The Legacy of British Union," 303.

25. Bauchman, "Charles Inglis, Loyalist," 51–52.

26. Ernst, "Andrew Elliot," 285–87. Elliot's father was Sir Gilbert Elliot, Baronet of Minto, who in 1763 would become lord justice clerk of Scotland, and his mother was Helen Stuart, daughter of the Baronet of Allanbrink. Elliot's brother was the treasurer to the Royal Navy.

27. Quoted in Ernst, "Andrew Elliot," 286.

28. Landsman, "The Legacy of British Union," 309, 316.

29. Bowen, *Elites, Enterprise, and the Making of the British Overseas Empire*, 158, 162.

30. Landsman, "The Legacy of British Union," 298–99, 301, 303.

31. Goodfriend, "Social Dimensions," 252–78, 262, 268.

32. Pointer, *Protestant Pluralism and the New York Experience*, 3.

33. Quoted in Kammen, *Colonial New York*, 217; Goodfriend, "Social Dimensions," 252–78, 262, 268.

34. Rosen, *Courts and Commerce*, 88. By the 1730s, the Walton family had established shipyards in New York, and the Bayard family had set up a sugar refinery. Market "day" in the city occurred six days a week in four public markets. See East, "The Business

Entrepreneur," 16–27, 20; Kammen, *Colonial New York*, 163, 169, 189; and Varga, "New York Government," 3.

35. Wilkenfeld, *Social and Economic Structure of the City of New York*, 141; Sosin, *Agents and Merchants*, 3; Matson, *Merchants and Empire*, 267; Kammen, *Colonial New York*, 364; Perkins, *The Economy of Colonial America*, 133; McCusker and Menard, *The Economy of British America*, 279–94; Lepore, *New York Burning*, 23.

36. Don R. Gerlach, *Philip Schuyler*, 92; quoted in Middleton, *From Privileges to Rights*, 2–3, 102; McCusker and Menard, *The Economy of British America*, 196–97; Truxes, *Letterbook of Gregg & Cunningham*, 8.

37. East, "The Business Entrepreneur," 18; Walter Stahr, *John Jay*, 1; Gipson, *The Coming of the Revolution*, 3.

38. Truxes, *Letterbook of Gregg & Cunningham*, 5.

39. Bushman, *King and People*, 162, xv; Nash, *Urban Crucible*, 257.

40. Rosen, *Courts and Commerce*, 88; Middleton, *From Privileges to Rights*, 101–14, 100; Nash, *Urban Crucible*, 108.

41. Abbott, "The Neighborhoods of New York," 39–40; Truxes, *Letterbook of Gregg & Cunningham*, 5; Cray, *Paupers and Poor Relief*, 46–47.

42. Kammen, *Colonial New York*, 288, 166, 281, 112, 179–80; Bonomi, *Factious People*, 32, 282. In 1756, the colony of New York had 97,000 people, in comparison with the colony of Pennsylvania, which had 220,000 (Kulikoff, *From British Peasants to Colonial American Farmers*, 156).

43. Quoted in Kross, "Patronage," 213.

44. O'Callaghan, *Documents*, 293.

45. Bonomi, *Factious People*, 60, 66, 68, 71; Tully, *Forming American Politics*, 224.

46. Bonomi, *Factious People*, 178. In the 1758 elections, four members of the Livingston family gained seats in the General Assembly; this marked the beginning of the landed Livingston party opposition to the merchant DeLancey majority (Kammen, *Colonial New York*, 132).

47. Tully, *Forming American Politics*, 219.

48. Nash, *Urban Crucible*, 35; Truxes, *Letterbook of Gregg & Cunningham*, 7.

49. O'Callaghan, *Calendar*, 48. For example, the entry for March 8, 1757, refers to a "contract between certain Merchants of the City of New York and Masters of Vessels belonging to other Ports with Lord Loudon for furnishing Vessels to be employed as Transports in the Service of the Government." Leder, "Military Victualing," 17–19, 24, 46.

50. Bridenbaugh, *Cities in Revolt*, 46; Nash, *Urban Crucible*, 236–38.

51. Truxes, *Letterbook of Gregg & Cunningham*, 32, 10–11, 13, 21–22, 43, 46, 50, 92.

52. Kammen, *Colonial New York*, 330–32; Matson, *Merchants and Empire*, 276–78; Bridenbaugh, *Cities in Revolt*, 68.

53. Countryman, *A People in Revolution*, 7. Two editions of the Ratzer map were published, one in 1770 and the second in 1776.

54. Nash, *Urban Crucible*, 239.

55. Fred Anderson, *Crucible of War*, 562, 720; Taylor, *American Colonies*, 439.

56. Varga, "New York Government," 7, 138.

57. Fred Anderson, *Crucible of War*, 562.

58. Matson, *Merchants and Empire*, 281; Kammen, *Colonial New York*, 344; Watts 1762 quote in Nash, *Urban Crucible*, 248; Watts 1764 quote in Egnal, *New World Economies*,

76. Kammen notes that "mechanics" referred to artisans, shopkeepers, and sometimes even sailors.

59. Quoted in Nash, *Urban Crucible,* 250; Egnal, "New York and Massachusetts, 1682–1776," 56.

60. Nash, *Urban Crucible,* 251.

61. Mohl, "Poverty in Colonial New York City," 66; Nash, *Race, Class, and Politics,* 196, 214, 223.

62. Quoted in Mohl, "Poverty in Colonial New York City," 70.

63. Nash, *Urban Crucible,* 254; Nash, *Race Class and Politics,* 196, 214, 223; Mohl, "Poverty in Colonial New York City," 72; Gronowicz, "Political Radicalism," 102.

64. Bushman, *King and People,* 181–82.

65. Quoted in Launitz-Schürer, *Loyal Whigs and Revolutionaries,* 25.

66. Burt, *Imperial Architects,* 12–13; Christie and Labaree, *Empire or Independence,* 55–58.

67. Tiedemann, *Reluctant Revolutionaries,* 60–68; Champagne, "New York's Radicals," 21–40. Champagne describes the Liberty Boys trio as "merchants of modest fortune and middle age" (21).

68. Quoted in Nash, *Urban Crucible,* 301.

69. Quoted in Bridenbaugh, *Cities in Revolt,* 223; Nash, *Urban Crucible,* 302.

70. Gronowicz, "Political Radicalism," 104; Maier, "The Beginnings of American Republicanism," 108. Richard Maxwell Brown notes that riots occurred between 1641 and 1759 because of economic troubles, intercolonial boundary disputes, religious controversies, elections, and the impressment of seamen. See Brown, *Strain of Violence,* 45–56.

71. Ashton, "Loyalist Experience," 37.

72. Bonomi, *Factious People,* 261.

73. Quoted in McAnear, "Politics in Provincial New York, 1689–1761," 998; Champagne, *Alexander McDougall,* 21–22; Launitz-Schürer, *Loyal Whigs and Revolutionaries,* 82.

74. Hoffman, *Edmund Burke,* 84, 82.

75. Shy, "American Society," 76; Nash, *Urban Crucible,* 319.

76. Shy, *Toward Lexington,* 279.

77. Nash, *Urban Crucible,* 371. Nash suggests that the opposition was also based on a "vigorous labor market rivalry." Tiedemann, *Reluctant Revolutionaries,* 109–11; Hoffman, *Edmund Burke,* 98; Kammen, *Colonial New York,* 350. Note that the Battle of Golden Hill preceded the Boston Massacre by almost seven weeks (Shy, *Toward Lexington,* 388).

78. Tiedemann, *Reluctant Revolutionaries,* 115, 170.

79. Ibid., 4.

80. Quoted in ibid., 167.

81. Quoted in Lee Friedman, "The First Chamber of Commerce," 138, 142; Becker, *The History of Political Parties,* 60. Of the 104 members of the Chamber of Commerce in 1775, 57 later became loyalists, 21 remained neutral, and only 26 supported colonial independence. See Wright, "The New York Loyalists," 81, 41.

82. Calhoon, "William Smith Jr.'s Alternative," 105–18, 107; Wertenbaker, *Father Knickerbocker Rebels,* 51.

83. Kammen, *Colonial New York,* 348.

84. Wright, "The New York Loyalists," 90; Nash, *Urban Crucible,* 366.

85. Kammen, *Colonial New York,* 348; Nash, *Urban Crucible,* 365, 371.

## 2. "UNCOMMON PHRENZY"

1. Quoted in Upton, *The Loyal Whig,* 89; Higgenbotham, *The War of American Independence,* 46; Shy, *People Numerous and Armed,* 174.

2. Quoted in Burt, *Imperial Architects,* 70. Also see Upton, *The Diary and Selected Papers of Chief Justice William Smith.*

3. Upton, "The Idea of the Confederation," 185–87.

4. Quoted in Boyd, *Anglo-American Union,* 39.

5. Joseph Galloway, September 28, 1774, in Smith, *Letters of Delegates,* 118. Galloway called for an election of grand council members every three years and a general meeting annually (Schuyler, "Galloway's Plan," 281).

6. Quoted in Burt, *Imperial Architects,* 66; Callahan, *Royal Raiders,* 97; Boyd, *Anglo-American Union,* 94.

7. Burt, *Imperial Architects,* 66. The colony of Georgia was not represented at this meeting.

8. William Franklin to Lord Dartmouth, quoted in Boyd, *Anglo-American Union,* 38; also see Hulsebosch, *Constituting Empire,* 149.

9. Quoted in Morris, "The American Revolution Comes to John Jay," 103.

10. Launitz-Schürer, *Loyal Whigs and Revolutionaries,* 119; Marston, *King and Congress,* 93.

11. Toscano, McCarthy, and Conser, "A Shift in Strategy," 423; Conser, McCarthy, and Toscano, "The American Independence Movement," 13; Benton, *Whig-Loyalism,* 138.

12. Tiedemann, *Reluctant Revolutionaries,* 205; Kenneth Scott, *Rivington's New York Newspaper,* 10; quotation on Case in Reed, "Loyalists, Patriots, and Trimmers," 129; Callahan, *Royal Raiders,* 62–63; Sterling, "American Prisoners of War," 377.

13. Quoted in Tidemann, *Reluctant Revolutionaries,* 219, 205.

14. Wright, "The New York Loyalists," 81, 41.

15. Potter, *The Liberty We Seek,* 3; Launitz-Schürer, *Loyal Whigs and Revolutionaries,* 130; Seabury quoted in Tiedemann, *Reluctant Revolutionaries,* 208–9, and from Seabury, *Letters of a Westchester Farmer,* 30.

16. Franklin and *New York Gazette* quoted in Toscano, McCarthy, and Conser, "A Shift in Strategy," 439.

17. Quoted in Conser, McCarthy, and Toscano, "The American Independence Movement," 13.

18. Quoted in Nash, *Unknown American Revolution,* 195; quoted in Jensen, *Historical and Political Reflections,* xxi.

19. Alden, "Why the March to Concord?" 447–48; Ferling, *Leap in the Dark,* 141.

20. Bushman, *King and People,* 212–14, 217, 222; Marston, *King and Congress,* 31.

21. Champagne, "New York's Radicals," 22.

22. Andrew Elliot to Sir Gilbert, July 5, 1775, quoted in Ernst, "Andrew Elliot," 298.

23. Quoted in Launitz-Schürer, *Loyal Whigs and Revolutionaries,* 157.

24. Quoted in ibid., 157.

25. Cadwallader Colden to Lord Dartmouth, June 5, 1775, in O'Callaghan, *Documents*, 582–83.

26. Crary, *The Price of Loyalty*, 45.

27. Quoted in Hulsebosch, *Constituting Empire*, 134.

28. Champagne, "New York's Radicals," 24; Countryman, *A People in Revolution*, 138.

29. Champagne, "New York's Radicals," 24–26; Becker, *The History of Political Parties*, 168n. Only sixteen members of the committee were mechanics.

30. Morris, "The American Revolution Comes to John Jay," 108–9.

31. Champagne, "New York's Radicals," 27.

32. Paul David Nelson, "William Tryon Confronts the American Revolution," 277; Champagne, "New York's Radicals," 29.

33. Quoted in Champagne, "New York's Radicals," 33.

34. Calhoon, "William Smith Jr.'s Alternative," 106–11; William Smith Jr., June 5, 1775, Smith Papers, Box 3, NYPL.

35. William Smith to Mr. Hamilton on the American Dispute, November 1775, Smith Papers, Box 2, NYPL.

36. Wright, "The New York Loyalists," 88; Upton, *The Loyal Whig*, 16.

37. Upton, *Diary and Papers of Chief Justice William Smith*, xvii; Upton, *The Loyal Whig*, 29, 112; Countryman, *A People in Revolution*, 88.

38. William Smith Jr., June 5, 1775, in Smith Papers, Box 3, NYPL.

39. Upton, *Diary and Papers of Chief Justice William Smith*, xxix; Hulsebosch, *Constituting Empire*, 141, 94; Burt, *Imperial Architects*, 69.

40. Calhoon, "William Smith Jr.'s Alternative," 111–18; William Smith to Mr. Hamilton on the American dispute, William Smith Papers, Box 2, November 1775, NYPL.

41. Champagne, "New York's Radicals," 31.

42. Botein, "The Anglo-American Book Trade before 1776," 78; Seabury, *Letters of a Westchester Farmer*, 18; Cullen, "Talking to a Whirlwind," 591.

43. Burt, *Imperial Architects*, 67.

44. Crary, *Price of Loyalty*, 100–102.

45. Quoted in Callahan, *Royal Raiders*, 43.

46. Toscano, McCarthy, and Conser, "A Shift in Strategy," 436; Champagne, "New York's Radicals," 25–26; Kwasny, *Washington's Partisan War*, 9, 26–28.

47. Quoted in Paul David Nelson, *William Tryon*, 128–29.

48. Quoted in Paul David Nelson, *William Tryon*, 130; O'Shaugnessy, "If Others Will Not Be Active," 1–46; Bushman, *King and People*, 219.

49. William Tryon to Lord George Germain, January 3, 1776, in Davies, *Documents*, 32; Paul David Nelson, *William Tryon*, 134–35, 99; Tiedemann, *Reluctant Revolutionaries*, 237.

50. Quoted in Duncan, *Citizens or Papists?* 36; Paine, *Common Sense*, 6, 17–18, 28.

51. Paine, *Common Sense*, 28.

52. Ibid., xiii, 20, 32, 38, 31, 41; Foner, *Tom Paine*, 80–90.

53. Inglis, "The True Interest," 151, 155, 157, 152.

54. Callahan, *Royal Raiders*, 141; Lydekker, *Life and Letters of Charles Inglis*, 152; quote in Tiedemann, *Reluctant Revolutionaries*, 246.

55. Shy, "Charles Lee," 26.

56. Quoted in Champagne, "New York's Radicals," 37; Montross, *The Reluctant Rebels*, 71.

57. Morris, "The American Revolution Comes to John Jay," 113.

58. Shy, *People Numerous and Armed*, 176–78, Lee quoted on 142; Kwasny, *Washington's Partisan War*, 36.

59. Quoted in Champagne, "New York's Radicals," 39.

60. Shy, "Charles Lee," 33–34.

61. Extract of Letter from New York, February 17, 1776, in Carleton Papers, DLAR.

62. Lord Dartmouth to General William Howe, September 3, 1775, in Carleton Papers, DLAR; Bridenbaugh, *Cities in Revolt*, 216; Callahan, *Royal Raiders*, 63. In September 1775, Tryon reported that "at least one third of the citizens had moved with their effects out of Town" (William Tryon to Lord Dartmouth, September 5, 1775, in O'Callaghan, *Documents*, 632).

63. Extract of Letter from New York, February 17, 1776, in Carleton Papers, DLAR; Johnston, *Campaign of 1776*, 105; Champagne, "New York Radicals," 38.

64. Extract of Letter from New York, February 17, 1776, in Carleton Papers, DLAR.

65. Thomas Gage to Lord Dartmouth, August 20 and October 1, 1775, in Carter, *Correspondence*, 413–14, 418–19; Kammen, *Colonial New York*, 369.

66. Wertenbaker, *Father Knickerbocker Rebels*, 82. A resolution passed by the Continental Congress in November 1775 had authorized the Continental Army to inflict the death penalty for mutiny.

67. Quoted in Nettels, "A Link in the Chain of Events," 40, 45.

68. Upton, *United Empire Loyalists*, 19–20.

69. Potter, *The Liberty We Seek*, 42–49.

70. Bauchman, "Charles Inglis, Loyalist," 56–57.

71. Quoted in Benton, "Peter Van Schaack," 47, and in Benton, "Whig-Loyalism," 165. Also see William H. Nelson, *The American Tory*, 121.

72. Understanding the value of patronage among the electorate, Watts distributed £70 among the "most indigent families" in the city after he won a seat in the assembly in 1752. See Mohl, "Poverty in Colonial New York City," 174; Nash, *Urban Crucible*, 237; Truxes, *Letterbook of Gregg & Cunningham*, 111.

73. Quoted in Bernard Friedman, "The Shaping of the Radical Consciousness," 787; Hulsebosch, *Constituting Empire*, 141.

74. O'Callaghan, *Documents*, 590; William Tryon to George Germain, September 24, 1776, in I. N. Stokes, *Iconography*, 1027.

75. *Dictionary of American Biography*, s.v. "Low, Isaac." The Committee of Fifty-One was established to oppose the Coercive Acts. The Committee of Sixty was established to implement the Continental Association. Both Low and Van Schaack were elected to the Committee of Fifty-One and also to the Committee of Sixty. Van Schaack was also on the Committee of Correspondence and Intelligence in 1775. See Becker, *The History of Political Parties*, 168n; Benton, "Peter Van Schaack," 47.

76. Quoted in Wertenbaker, *Father Knickerbocker Rebels*, 37.

77. Quoted in Duncan, *Citizens or Papists?* 35.

78. Stevens, *Colonial Records*, 103; Barck, *New York City*, 55; Ashton, "The Loyalist Congressmen," 106.

79. Countryman, *A People in Revolution*, 115.

80. Frederick Philipse, August 22, 1776, in Crary, *Price of Loyalty*, 144; Bonomi, *Factious People*, 62. See also Judd, "Frederick Philipse III of Westchester," 30–32; Countryman, *A People in Revolution*, 18, 150.

81. "List of People that Draw Pay for their Salaries," 1782, Carleton Papers, NA.

82. Stevens, *Colonial Records*, 25.

83. Wright, "Men with Two Countries," 157.

84. Cole, "The Problem of 'Nationalism' and 'Imperialism,'" 164–65; York, "The First Continental Congress," 378.

85. Cortlandt Skinner, December 1775, in Crary, *Price of Loyalty*, 114–16.

## 3. "QUICKEN OTHERS BY OUR EXAMPLE"

1. Bodle, *The Valley Forge Winter*, 15–16; Polf, *Garrison Town*, 6.

2. Colonel Charles Stuart to Lord Bute, September 26, 1776, in Wortley, *Prime Minister*, 85.

3. Hugh Earl Percy to Duke of Northumberland, September 1, 1776, in Bolton, *Letters of Hugh Earl Percy*, 69–70.

4. Sir Henry Clinton to Elizabeth Carter, September 23, 1776, in Clinton Papers, CL.

5. Intelligence to William Tryon from New York City, April 17, 1776, in Clinton Papers, CL.

6. William Smith Jr., October 18, 1776, in Sabine, *Historical Memoirs to 25 July 1778*, 18.

7. Reverend Inglis to Reverend Richard Hind, October 31, 1776, in Lydekker, *Life and Letters of Charles Inglis*, 167.

8. Archibald Robertson, July 4 and July 7, 1776, in Lydenberg, *Archibald Robertson*, 88.

9. Frederick Mackenzie, September 4, 1776, in Mackenzie, *Diary*, 1:38.

10. Colonel Charles Stuart to Lord Bute, July 9, 1776, in Wortley, *Prime Minister*, 82.

11. I. N. Stokes, *Iconography*, 1026.

12. Ambrose Serle, September 15 and September 16, 1776, in Tatum, *American Journal*, 104.

13. *New-York Gazette and Weekly Mercury*, November 14, November 25, November 28, and December 9, 1776.

14. Ambrose Serle, September 16, 1776, in Tatum, *American Journal*, 107.

15. I. N. Stokes, *Iconography*, 1015.

16. *New-York Gazette and Weekly Mercury*, September 30, 1776, and October 7, 1776.

17. Ambrose Serle, September 29, 1776, in Tatum, *American Journal*, 110.

18. *New-York Gazette and Weekly Mercury*, October 21, November 11, December 2, and December 16, 1776.

19. General William Howe to Lord George Germain, July 7, 1776, in Davies, *Documents*, 158.

20. Frederick Mackenzie, September 16, 1776 in Mackenzie, *Diary*, 1:56.

21. Ambrose Serle to Lord Dartmouth, July 25, 1776, in Dartmouth Papers, DLAR.

22. Sir Henry Clinton to Elizabeth Carter, September 23, 1776, in Clinton Papers, CL.

23. The proclamations stated that the British invited the allegiance of colonists "compelled" to abandon their duty. *New-York Gazette and Weekly Mercury,* September 30, October 7, and October 14, 1776; Gruber, *Howe Brothers,* 120.

24. Mackesy, *War for America,* 32.

25. Ibid., 35. Mackesy observes that the British aimed at reconciliation, not conquest. The pardons were clearly attempts at reconciliation. *New-York Gazette and Weekly Mercury,* October 7, 1776; Howe Orders, July 14, 1776, in Carleton Papers, DLAR; Proclamation no. 3, November 30, 1776, in Mackenzie Papers, Collection D, CL. The latter refers to the proclamations issued on July 14 and September 19, 1776. General Howe instructed his soldiers to preserve good order and "upon no account to molest or commit any depredations upon the inhabitants of the island" (quoted in Gruber, *Howe Brothers,* 126). Shy, "The Loyalist Problem," 8.

26. Howe Proclamation, August 23, 1776, in Carleton Papers, DLAR.

27. Proclamation, September 19, 1776, Mackenzie Papers, Collection D, CL.

28. Gruber, *Howe Brothers,* 365.

29. William Tryon to George Germain, January 3 and April 6, 1776, in Davies, *Documents,* 32, 98.

30. Stephen Kemble, November 25, 1777, in *Collections of the New York Historical Society,* 145; Willcox, *Portrait of a General,* 69; Skemp, *William Franklin,* 231.

31. Ambrose Serle, September 27, 1776, in Tatum, *American Journal,* 115.

32. Reverend Inglis to Reverend Richard Hind, October 31, 1776, in Lydekker, *Life and Letters of Charles Inglis,* 159–72.

33. Ambrose Serle, December 2, 1776, in Tatum, *American Journal,* 98.

34. The initial proclamations asked colonists to return to their duty within sixty days. However, subsequent proclamations kept extending the invitation. For example, the one of March 17, 1777, invited colonists to accept pardons till May 1, 1777. *New-York Gazette and Weekly Mercury,* September 30 and March 17, 1776.

35. William Smith Jr., November 1777, in Acton, "Diary," xlviii.

36. Frederick Mackenzie, September 5, 1776 in Mackenzie, *Diary,* 39, 1:113.

37. Johnston, *Campaign of 1776,* 123.

38. Frederick Mackenzie, November 17, 1776, in Mackenzie, *Diary,* 1:111.

39. Quoted in Troye Steele Anderson, *Howe Brothers,* 163.

40. Lord William Howe and Admiral Richard Howe to Lord George Germain, November 30, 1776, in Davies, *Documents,* 257.

41. William Smith Jr., January 23, 1777, in Sabine, *Historical Memoirs to 25 July 1778,* 74.

42. See Acton, "Diary," xxvi.

43. Pardons issued September 30, 1776, for sixty days, and November 30, 1776, for sixty more days, *New-York Gazette and Weekly Mercury,* September 30 and November 30, 1776; William Smith Jr., October 11, 1776, in Sabine, *Historical Memoirs to 25 July 1778,* 16.

44. Colonel Charles Stuart to Lord Bute, undated [probably mid-1777], in Wortley, *Prime Minister,* 92.

45. Weldon Brown, *Empire or Independence,* 328.

46. *New-York Gazette and Weekly Mercury,* September 30, 1776; Troye Steele Anderson, *Howe Brothers,* 159.

47. Acton, "Diary," xxi.

48. Larry R. Gerlach, *The American Revolution*, 86.

49. Ibid. Also see Potter, *The Liberty We Seek;* and Colley, *Britons*. Potter discusses loyalist ideology in New York and Massachusetts, and Colley describes the primary tenets—Protestantism, prosperity, and constitutionalism—that bound British subjects to the empire.

50. Joseph Galloway, letter to unknown person, March 28, 1777, in Dartmouth Papers, DLAR.

51. Joseph Galloway to Richard Jackson, March 20, 1777, in Dartmouth Papers, DLAR.

52. Ibid.

53. Ibid.

54. Kammen, *Colonial New York*, 131, 284.

55. Edwards, *New York as an Eighteenth-Century Municipality*, 18–39.

56. Edward Winslow to Colonel James Patterson, November 6, 1776, in Winslow Papers, DLAR. Winslow mentions that he would like to make an application to the Board of General Officers to acquire provisions for loyalist units but fears "incurring his lordship's displeasure."

57. Eyre Coote Orderly Book 2, September 16, 1776, CL; Polf, *Garrison Town*, 9.

58. Adye, Treatise on Courts Martial, AAS; Wiener, *Civilians under Military Justice*, 92–106; Banning, *Military Law*, 285. The judge-advocate was a legal assessor who advised the president. The London ministry suspended the writ of habeas corpus in February 1777.

59. Anonymous and undated letter to George Germain from New York, in *Detail and Conduct of the American War*, 49.

60. Allan Maclean to Alexander Cummings, February 19, 1777, in Wortley, *Prime Minister*, 104; Klein and Howard, *Twilight*, 34; Frederick Mackenzie, November 17, 1776, in Mackenzie, *Diary*, 111.

61. *Detail and Conduct of the American War*, 100, 103.

62. Ibid., 101; *New-York Gazette and Weekly Mercury*, October 7, 1776.

63. Otto Gerland, October 29, 1776, in *Diary of Hessian Chaplain In the American War*, CL. Some colonists also regarded Hessians distastefully. One soldier reported that the colonists "had been told that Hessians ate children and were all very hostile" (Ambrose Serle, September 17, 1776, in Tatum, *American Journal*, 108).

64. Loftus Cliffe to Bartholomew Cliffe, September 22, 1776, in Cliffe Papers, CL.

65. Frederick Mackenzie, October 2, 1776, in Mackenzie, *Diary*, 1:68; War Office Records (WO 71/82), September 3, 1776, NA.

66. John Peebles, December 24, 1776, in Gruber, *John Peebles' American War*, 74.

67. Stephen Kemble, October 3, 1776, October 7, 1776, and November 7, 1776, in *Collections of the New York Historical Society*, 91–92, 98. Also see Howe Orderly Book, July 1776, CL; Frederick Mackenzie, September 7, 1776, in Mackenzie, *Diary*, 1:40, CL.

68. Howe Orderly Book, CL; Loftus Cliffe to Bartholomew Cliffe, September 22, 1776, in Cliffe Papers, CL; I. N. Stokes, *Iconography*, 1040.

69. Colonel Charles Stuart to Lord Bute, February 4, 1777, in Wortley, *Prime Minister*, 99; Stephen Kemble, October 3 and November 7, 1776, in *Collections of the New York Historical Society*, 91, 98; William Tryon to Lord George Germain, September 25, 1776, in I. N. Stokes, *Iconography*, 1023. Tryon wrote: "The Hessians are continually plunder-

ing, and are countenanced by their General; and General Howe dares not punish them for fear of producing a general mutiny."

70. General William Howe to Lord George Germain, November 30, 1776, in Germain Papers, CL. But there was no reason for Germain to pay urgent attention to Howe's plea. Howe's request was an aside within a long letter that explained the British expedition to east New Jersey and that also asked for fifteen thousand additional troops and three hundred horses with saddles and accoutrements.

71. Proclamation from Sir Henry Clinton, December 23, 1776, in Clinton Papers, CL.

72. Frey, *The British Soldier,* 74.

73. *New-York Gazette and Weekly Mercury,* October 7, 1776.

74. Ibid., October 14, 1776.

75. Schwoerer, "Law, Liberty, and Jury 'Ideology,'" 35–36.

76. William Smith Jr., October 11, 1776, in Sabine, *Historical Memoirs to 25 July 1778,* 16.

77. *New-York Gazette and Weekly Mercury,* October 21, 1776.

78. Ibid., October 14, 1776.

79. Ibid., October 21, 1776.

80. Ibid. From the July 14 proclamation, the loyalists cited the sentence that stated that the king was "desirous" of restoring the colonies to protection and peace. From the September 19 proclamation, they cited the line in which the Howes requested to "confer" with "well-affected" subjects. The petition was sent by the county and city of New York. At this time, this area comprised Manhattan Island and the tip of the adjacent mainland known as Harlem. See McAnear, "Politics in Provincial New York," 7.

81. *New-York Gazette and Weekly Mercury,* November 4, 1776.

82. Ibid., October 21, 1776.

83. Ibid., November 11, November 25, and December 9, 1776; also see Suffolk County Address to Lord William Howe, October 1776, CMNY.

84. Some merchants signed multiple petitions. William Axtell signed both the New York City and the King's County petition.

85. *New-York Gazette and Weekly Mercury,* November 4, 1776; Palmer, *Bibliography of Loyalist Source Material.* Palmer presents a short biography of prominent loyalists in alphabetical order; the son of Lieutenant Governor Cadwallader Colden, David Colden of Flushing, Long Island, led the Queen's County petition. The trio of Richard Floyd, Thomas Fanning, and Frederick Hudson spoke for Suffolk County.

86. Those who remained loyal included Henry White, Charles Ward Apthorpe, William Bayard, Oliver DeLancey, and John Watts.

87. Significantly, some New Yorkers who lost contracts because of inadequate English influence such as Peter Van Brugh Livingston, Lewis Morris Jr., William Alexander, and Philip Schuyler chose the rebel position. Arguably, they felt disillusioned about a future within the empire. See Leder, "Military Victualing," 48; Shy, *Toward Lexington,* 341–42; and Steele, "Empire of Migrants," 509.

88. Condon, "Circuitous Career of Loyalist Plans," 183.

89. Hodges, *New York City Cartmen,* 51–64. The data have been gathered from the following sources: Palmer, *Bibliography of Loyalist Source Material;* Dawson, *New York City during the American Revolution;* and Kenneth Scott, *Rivington's New York Newspaper.*

90. Bushman, *King and People,* 40, 22.

91. Morgan, *Inventing the People*, 224, 220.

92. *New-York Gazette and Weekly Mercury*, November 4, 1776.

93. William Tryon to George Germain, November 26, 1776, in I. N. Stokes, *Iconography*, 1038.

94. Lord George Germain to William Tryon, January 14, 1777, in O'Callaghan, *Documents*, 698.

95. His Majesty's Commissioners to George Germain, November 30, 1776, in Davies, *Documents*, 257.

96. I. N. Stokes, *Iconography*, 1020.

97. Tiedemann, "Patriots by Default," 51.

98. I. N. Stokes, *Iconography*, 1027.

99. Charles Inglis to Richard Hind, October 31, 1776, in Lydekker, *Life and Letters of Charles Inglis*, 165.

100. William Tryon to Lord George Germain, September 21, 1776, in I. N. Stokes, *Iconography*, 1022.

101. "Major Baumeister's narrative of Capture of New York," in Johnston, *Campaign of 1776*, 98, and in I. N. Stokes, *Iconography*, 1026.

102. I. N. Stokes, *Iconography*, 1015.

103. Burgoyne, "Diary of Jakob Piel," 20; Lieutenant Hinrichs to Professor Schlozer, September 18, 1776 in Pettengill, *Letters from America*, 177; Ewald Gustav Schaukirk, August 28, 1776, in Schaukirk, *Occupation*, 3; *Journal from J.R.*, August 24, 1776, 6; Ashton, "Paths to Loyalism," 157–58.

104. William Tryon to George Germain, September 24, 1776, in Callaghan, *Colonial Documents*, 685. The five council members in the city included Oliver DeLancey, Henry White, Charles Ward Apthorpe, William Axtell, and John Harris Cruger (I. N. Stokes, *Iconography*, 1027).

105. John Peebles, January 22, 1777, in Gruber, *John Peebles' American War*, 82; Hugh Earl Percy to Henry Reveley, August 8, 1774, in Bolton, *Letters of Hugh Earl Percy*, 31; Willcox, *Portrait of a General*, 14.

106. Sir Henry Clinton, Notes, September 24, 1776, in Clinton Papers, CL; Frederick Mackenzie, September 24, 1776, in Mackenzie, *Diary*, 1:64, 68; Ambrose Serle, December 16, 1776, in Tatum, *American Journal*, 159; Ambrose Serle, November 4 and October 31, 1776, in Tatum, *American Journal*, 136 and 134. On December 2, 1776, Serle called the people's attachment "precarious" and stated that "no dependence is to be made on their subjection further than we have the power to command it" (Tatum, *American Journal*, 154). Mackesy argues that the low opinion of Americans held by the British was due to the Americans' military incompetence during the Seven Years' War (Mackesy, *War for America*, 32).

107. *New-York Gazette and Weekly Mercury*, September 30, 1776.

108. Frederick Mackenzie, September 16, 1776, in Mackenzie, *Diary*, 51.

109. Ambrose Serle, September 21 and October 31, 1776, in Tatum, *American Journal*, 112, 134.

110. Ewald Gustav Schaukirk, June 13, 1776, in Schaukirk, *Occupation*, 108.

111. *New-York Gazette and Weekly Mercury*, September 30, 1776; William Tryon to George Germain, September 24, 1776, in Davies, *Documents*, 231; Johnston, *Campaign of 1776*, 119.

112. William Tryon to George Germain, September 24, 1776, in Davies, *Documents*,

231; Ewald Gustav Schaukirk, September 16, 1776, quoted in Johnston, *Campaign of 1776*, 118.

113. Mancke, *Fault Lines of Empire*, introduction; Colley, *Captives*, 236; Conway, "From Fellow-Nationals," 98–100.

114. Commissioners to George Germain, December 22, 1776, in Davies, *Documents*, 274.

115. William Tryon to Lord George Germain, December 24, 1776, in Davies, *Documents*, 275; William Tryon to George Germain, January 20, 1777, in O'Callaghan, *Documents*, 696; Shy, "The Loyalist Problem," 5.

116. Gruber, *Howe Brothers*, 195; Ambrose Serle, October 7 1776, in Tatum, *American Journal*, 117; Ernst, "Andrew Elliot," 285–87. In a letter written on December 2, 1776, Elliot confidently claimed that British triumph was imminent (Ernst, "Andrew Elliot," 302).

117. Gruber, *John Peebles' American War*, 55.

118. William Tryon to Lord Germain, December 31, 1776, in O'Callaghan, *Documents* 694; Willcox, *Portrait of a General*, 132; *New-York Gazette and Weekly Mercury*, January 13 and February 3, 1777.

119. Joseph Galloway to Richard Jackson, March 20, 1777, in Dartmouth Papers, DLAR.

120. William Smith Jr., February 15 and January 18, 1777, in Sabine, *Historical Memoirs to 25 July 1778*, 83, 69.

121. William Howe to George Germain, January 20, 1777, in Davies, *Documents*, 33; Johnston, *Campaign of 1776*, 124.

122. Mackesy, *War for America*, 97; Fred Anderson, *Crucible of War*, 678.

123. Quoted in Johnston, *Campaign of 1776*, 124.

124. Commissioners to George Germain, March 25, 1777, and George Germain to William Howe, May 18, 1777, in Davies, *Documents*, 51, 84.

125. George Germain to William Howe, May 18, 1777, in Davies, *Documents*, 84.

126. William Tryon to Lord George Germain, November 28, 1776, in O'Callaghan, *Documents*, 693; anonymous from New York, January 3, 1777, in Auckland Papers, DLAR; William Smith Jr., December 7, 1776, in Sabine, *Historical Memoirs to 25 July 1778*, 53; Archibald Robertson, January 21, 1777, in Lydenberg, *Archibald Robertson*, 122.

127. Allan Maclean to Alexander Cummings, February 19, 1777, and Colonel Charles Stuart to Lord Bute, March 29, 1777, in Wortley, *Prime Minister*, 102, 107.

128. William Tryon to George Germain, December 24, 1776, in O'Callaghan, *Documents*, 693; William Smith Jr., December 7, 1776, in Sabine, *Historical Memoirs to 25 July 1778*, 53; William Howe to George Germain, November 30, 1776, in Germain Papers, CL.

129. Lord George Germain to General William Howe, June 21, 1776, in Carleton Papers, DLAR; Curtis, *Organization of British Army*, 100–102. By the end of 1776, New York Island (Manhattan) had 5,715 British, 6,305 Hessian, and 1,374 provincial troops. Staten Island had 1,693 British, 460 Hessian, and 537 provincial troops. Paulus Hook had 507 British troops. Long Island had 3,955 British and 1,217 provincials. The army alone numbered close to 21,000 near New York City (Wiener, *Civilians under Military Justice*, 104).

130. Unsigned letter from New York to William Eden, January 3, 1777, Auckland Papers, DLAR; William Smith Jr., November 15, 1776, in Sabine, *Historical Memoirs to*

*25 July 1778*, 44; Colonel Charles Stuart to Lord Bute, February 4, 1777, in Wortley, *Prime Minister*, 99; Ambrose Serle to Lord Dartmouth, March 20, 1777, in Dartmouth Papers, DLAR. Serle believed that the "ardor" of British troops had escalated in "proportion" to the "desperate" acts committed by the "madmen."

131. Colonel Charles Stuart to Lord Bute, February 4, 1777, in Wortley, *Prime Minister*, 99.

132. William Tryon to Lord George Germain, December 24, 1776, in Germain Papers, CL.

133. William Tryon to Earl of Dartmouth, January 5, 1777, in Dartmouth Papers, DLAR.

134. *New-York Gazette and Weekly Mercury*, December 30, November 25, and December 3, 1776, and January 20, 1777.

135. Ambrose Serle, September 19, 1776, in Tatum, *American Journal*, 109. Serle noted that "many loyal inhabitants were returning with goods to the town."

136. *New-York Gazette and Weekly Mercury*, October 28, 1776; I. N. Stokes, *Iconography*, 1039; Jackson, *With the British Army*, 3.

137. *New-York Gazette and Weekly Mercury*, December 30, 1776.

138. Loyalist petitions of James Hughston of Queen's County, New York, and of John Hill of Brooklyn, Long Island, in Loyalist Transcripts, NYPL.

139. I. N. Stokes, *Iconography*, 1031; *New-York Gazette and Weekly Mercury*, October 21, 1776.

140. Loyalist Transcripts, NYPL.

141. I. N. Stokes, *Iconography*, 1033; Barck, *New York City*, 121; *New-York Gazette and Weekly Mercury*, October 21, October 28, December 23, and December 9, 1776.

142. *New-York Gazette and Weekly Mercury*, January 6 and January 27, 1777; Royal Theatre, Attendance and Payments, NYHS.

## 4. "LORD PITY THIS POOR COUNTRY"

1. Hugh Gaine, October 4, 1777, in Ford, *Journals*, 2:50. Gaine did suffer a loss of status for his two-month sojourn in Newark. Although the British permitted him to return to New York City and to resume his printing operations, they did not allow him to return to his prior station: James Rivington would receive the appointment as king's printer when he returned to New York in October 1777. See Chopra, "Hugh Gaine."

2. *New-York Gazette and Weekly Mercury*, September 2, 1776. Gaine printed his last New York City paper before leaving for Newark on September 9, 1776.

3. Four papers circulated in the city during the Revolution: Hugh Gaine's *New-York Gazette and Weekly Mercury* (1776–83), James Rivington's *Royal Gazette* (1777–83), James Robertson's *Royal American Gazette* (1777–83), and William Lewis's *New-York Mercury; or General Advertiser* (1779–82). Hugh Gaine and James Rivington had the most long-standing association with the colonies. Until October 1777, when Rivington returned to the city after almost a two-year absence, Gaine's *New-York Gazette and Weekly Mercury* served as the sole loyalist newspaper in the city. To oversee all the pro-British papers, the British ministry appointed a licenser, whom they paid twenty shillings per day. See Wroth, *Colonial Printer*, 127.

4. Ambrose Serle, September 25, 1776, in Tatum, *American Journal*, 113.

5. Tatum, *"Ambrose Serle,"* 268; Boyd, *Anglo-American Union*, 55.

6. Charles Inglis, October 31, 1776, in Lydekker, *Life and Letters of Charles Inglis*, 162; Willcox, *Portrait of a General*, 69.

7. Gaine returned to New York City on November 1 and resumed publication of the *New-York Gazette and Weekly Mercury*, albeit under British supervision.

8. *New-York Gazette and Weekly Mercury*, October 7, 1776.

9. *New-York Gazette and Weekly Mercury*, Tryon letter; anonymous essay titled "Considerations on the present revolted state of America, addressed to its Inhabitants at large; and "Benevolus," both on October 7, 1776, and "Irenicus," October 28, 1776.

10. Quoted in Mackesy, *War for America*, 116.

11. *New-York Gazette and Weekly Mercury*, February 3, February 24, and March 24, January 6, January 20, and January 27, 1777; Cortlandt Skinner to Lord Hugh Percy, April 17, 1777, quoted in Gruber, *Howe Brothers*, 198–200.

12. Taeffe, *Philadelphia Campaign*, 13–14.

13. Colonel Charles Stuart, March 1777, in Wortley, *Prime Minister* 109; John Peebles, May 28, 1777, in Gruber, *John Peebles' American War*, 25.

14. Hugh Gaine, May 17, 1777, in Ford, *Journals*, 2:33.

15. Joseph Galloway to Richard Jackson, Esq., March 20, 1777, in Dartmouth Papers, DLAR; Howe, *Observations upon A Pamphlet*, 41. Howe would later claim that Galloway's ideas were "visionary, and his intelligence was too frequently either ill-founded or so much exaggerated, that it would have been unsafe to act upon it" (Howe, *Observations upon a Pamphlet*, 41).

16. William Smith Jr., March 24, 1777, in Sabine, *Historical Memoirs to 25 July 1778*, 96.

17. *New-York Gazette and Weekly Mercury*, February 10 through April 7, 1777. The essays seemed especially to target support from merchants and traders who feared the economic losses they would sustain with an independent United States (Lorenz, *Hugh Gaine*, 111).

18. "Benevolus," *New-York Gazette and Weekly Mercury*, October 7, 1776.

19. *New-York Gazette and Weekly Mercury*, September 19, October 14, October 7, October 14, October 28, December 2, October 7, and December 2, 1776.

20. Lorenz, *Hugh Gaine*, 111; *New-York Gazette and Weekly Mercury*, February 10, March 31, February 24, March 3, March 24, and March 10, 1777. One essay written on March 10, 1777, and signed by "Z" dramatically expressed that the rebel villains, "serpent-like, fascinate and devour," and would create social anarchy in the colonies.

21. Wood, "Rhetoric and Reality," 3–32. Wood's analysis of the paranoiac style of rebel rhetoric applies equally to loyalist rhetoric.

22. *New-York Gazette and Weekly Mercury*, April 7, 1777.

23. Taeffe, *Philadelphia Campaign*, 10.

24. Ambrose Serle to Lord Dartmouth, April 25, 1777, in Dartmouth Papers, DLAR.

25. Colonel Charles Stuart to Lord Bute, July 10, 1777, in Wortley, *Prime Minister*, 113.

26. Levin Friedrich Ernst von Muenchhausen, June 18, 1777, in von Muenchhausen, *At General Howe's Side*, 18; Hugh Gaine, June 23, 1777, in Ford, *Journals*, 37; Ewald Gustav Schaukirk, June 28 and July 3, 1777 in Schaukirk, *Occupation*, 127.

27. Pancake, *1777*, 87.

28. Martin, *Philadelphia Campaign*, 2–3, 15–16.

29. Willcox, "Too Many Cooks," 56–90. Howe does not in any way indicate the influence of Galloway or other loyalists in his letters to Germain.

30. Willcox, "Too Many Cooks," 56–90.

31. Sir Henry Clinton to Lord Hugh Percy, July 23, 1777, and Sir Henry Clinton to William Howe, July 13, 1777, both in Clinton Papers, CL; Mackesy, *War for America*, 137; Martin, *Philadelphia Campaign*, 5; Taeffe, *Philadelphia Campaign*, 80.

32. Sir Henry Clinton to Sir Hugh Earl Percy, July 23, 1777, in Clinton Papers, CL; Sir Henry Clinton, Memo, October, 1777, in Clinton Papers, CL.

33. Ewald Gustav Schaukirk, August 31, 1777, in Schaukirk, *Occupation*, 6–7; Hugh Gaine, September 2, 1777, in Ford, *Journals*, 2:46; Levin Friedrich Ernst von Muenchhausen, September 15, 1777, in von Muenchhausen, *At General Howe's Side*, 32.

34. Quoted in Willcox, "Too Many Cooks," 81; Middlekauff, *Glorious Cause*, 383.

35. Mackesy, *War for America*, 138; Middlekauff, *Glorious Cause*, 382; Willcox, "Too Many Cooks," 81.

36. Howe quoted in Mackesy, *War for America*, 144.

37. Quoted in Martin, *Philadelphia Campaign*, 66; Gerald Saxon Brown, *Reflections on a Pamphlet*, 3.

38. Anonymous letter to Lord Dartmouth, November 11, 1777, in Dartmouth Papers, DLAR; anonymous letter from New York, December 16, 1777, in *Detail and Conduct of the American War*, 30; Galloway in Billias, *Letters to a Nobleman*, 72; Jones quoted in De Lancey, *History of New York*, 240.

39. *Royal Gazette*, January 24, 1778.

40. Hugh Gaine, September 24, 1777, quoted in Kenneth Scott, *Rivington's New York Newspaper*, 18.

41. *Royal Gazette*, February 21, 1778, February 14, 1778; *New-York Gazette and Weekly Mercury*, February 23, 1778.

42. *Royal Gazette*, March 21 and February 21, 1778; *New-York Gazette and Weekly Mercury*, May 11, 1778.

43. *Royal Gazette*, February 28, 1778.

44. Colley, *Britons*, 147–49.

45. *Royal Gazette*, June 3, 1778.

46. *New-York Gazette and Weekly Mercury*, May 25, 1778; *Royal Gazette*, May 23, 1778; *New-York Gazette and Weekly Mercury*, December 9, 1776; William Smith Jr., January 18, February 15, March 2, April 8, and April 9, 1777, in Sabine, *Historical Memoirs to 25 July 1778*, 69, 81, 86, 108–9.

47. Middlekauff, *Glorious Cause*, 396–405.

48. *Royal Gazette*, December 1 and December 29, 1777, and March 21, 1778.

49. *Royal Gazette*, June 13 and August 22, 1778.

50. *Royal Gazette*, June 13, July 1, June 6, June 24, and August 22, 1778.

51. Print also popularized the Protestant Reformation, allowing its advocates to reach an otherwise inconceivable number of people. See Colley, *Britons*, 40, 6.

52. Intelligence from Duncan Drummond, October 1778, in Clinton Papers, CL; Isaac Ogden to Joseph Galloway, November 22, 1778, in "Letters to Joseph Galloway," *Historical Magazine* (November 1861): 337.

53. Peter Dubois, January 24, 1778, in Clinton Papers, CL; Intelligence to John Andre, March 12, 1778, in Clinton Papers, CL; General William Howe to George Germain, April 19, 1778, in Germain Papers, CL; John Williams to Beverly Robinson, November

28, 1778, in Clinton Papers, CL; New York resident, December 7, 1778, in I. N. Stokes, *Iconography*, 1079; Nash, *Unknown American Revolution*, 309; William Smith Jr., January 19, 1779, in Acton, "Diary," 106.

54. Charles Inglis to Joseph Galloway, December 12, 1778, in "Letters to Joseph Galloway," *Historical Magazine* (October 1861): 298–300.

55. George Germain to Sir Henry Clinton, March 8, 1778, in Davies, *Documents*, 158.

56. Weldon Brown, *Empire or Independence*, 230, 205, 217; Richard Howe to John Dyke Ackland, February 17, 1778, in Clinton Papers, CL; peace proposal quoted in Ritcheson, *British Politics*, 274.

57. Quoted in Gerald Saxon Brown, *The American Secretary*, 26.

58. Sir Henry Clinton, Memo, June 6, 1778, in Clinton Papers, CL.

59. Mackesy, *War for America*, 184. Between 1795 and 1808, the British established the first all-black slave regiments to protect their interests in the Caribbean. See Morgan and O'Shaugnessy, "Arming Slaves," 199.

60. George Germain to Sir Henry Clinton, March 21, 1778, in Davies, *Documents*, 74; Mackesy, *War for America*, 185–86; Martin, *Philadelphia Campaign*, 221.

61. William Smith Jr., April 24, 1778, in Sabine, *Historical Memoirs to 25 July 1778*, 356.

62. Ibid., May 19, 1778, 382.

63. Peter Van Schaack to John Jay, August 14, 1778, quoted in Larry R. Gerlach, *The American Revolution*, 54.

64. William Smith Jr., May 5, 1778, in Sabine, *Historical Memoirs to 25 July 1778*, 369.

65. Ibid., March 12, 1778, 321.

66. Ibid., March 14, 1778, 321.

67. Ibid., 323.

68. Ibid., April 1, 1778, 338.

69. Ibid., April 9, 1777, 109.

70. Ibid., April 27, 1778, 358.

71. Ibid., May 7, 1778, 372; Daniel Chamier to Sir Henry Clinton, April 17, 1778, in Clinton Papers, CL; Bowler, "Logistics," 64; William Smith Jr., May 10, 1778, in Sabine, *Historical Memoirs to 25 July 1778*, 377.

72. Quoted in Charles R. Ritcheson, *British Politics*, 275; Sir Henry Clinton, Memo, June 6, 1778, in Clinton Papers, CL.

73. Schecter, *Battle for New York*, 311, 321; Mackesy, *War for America*, 217.

74. Frederick Mackenzie, July 26, 1778, in Mackenzie, *Diary*, 2:318.

75. Sir Charles Blagden to Sir Joseph Banks, July 20, 1778, and Lord Carlisle to Lady Carlisle, July 21, 1778, both in I. N. Stokes, *Iconography*, 1071; Alan S. Brown, "William Eden," 138; Washington quoted in Schecter, *Battle for New York*, 313.

76. Willcox, *Portrait of a General*, 239; Isaac Ogden to Joseph Galloway, November 22, 1778, in Balch Papers, NYPL.

77. *Royal Gazette*, July 9, 1778.

78. Ritcheson, *British Politics*, 277.

79. Quoted in Davies, "The Restoration of Civil Government," 116.

80. *Royal Gazette*, August 5, August 26, and September 19, 1778; Schecter, *Battle for New York*, 317; *New-York Gazette and Weekly Mercury*, August 17 and August 24, 1778; Wilkenfeld, "Revolutionary New York, 1776," 65; Polf, *Garrison Town*, 45.

81. Joseph Galloway to Richard Jackson, Esq., March 28, 1777, in Dartmouth Papers,

DLAR; William Smith Jr., April 8, 1777, in Sabine, *Historical Memoirs to 25 July 1778*, 108.

82. Martin, *Philadelphia Campaign*, 89–97.

83. Joseph Galloway, June 17, 1778, "Reason Against Abandoning Philadelphia & the Province of Pennsylvania," Clinton Papers, CL.

84. Martin, *Philadelphia Campaign*, 251.

85. Quoted in Anthony Stokes, *View of the Constitution*, 123

86. Letters from New York, May 5 and May 18, 1778, in Anthony Stokes, *View of the Constitution*, 34, 37.

87. Chapin, "Colonial and Revolutionary Origins," 14.

88. Joseph Galloway, Andrew Allen, John Potts, Samuel Shoemaker, Daniel Coxe to the Earl of Carlisle, Sir Henry Clinton, and William Eden, October 4, 1778, in Clinton Papers, CL.

89. James Humphreys to Joseph Galloway, November 23, 1778, in Balch Papers, NYPL; Isaac Ogden to Joseph Galloway, November 22, 1778, in Balch Papers, NYPL; John Potts to Galloway, November 25, 1778, in "Letters to Joseph Galloway," *Historical Magazine* (October 1861): 296.

90. Charles Stewart to Galloway, December 1, 1778, "Letters to Joseph Galloway," *Historical Magazine* (October 1861): 296.

91. Daniel Coxe to Joseph Galloway, December 17, 1778, in Balch Papers, NYPL.

92. Undated [late 1777], Clinton Papers, CL. An anonymous loyalist plan of 1777 entitled "Proposal to Subdue Rebellion and a Sketch of Necessary rout for that purpose" urged the circulation of a British manifesto that enjoined colonists to bear arms against the rebels. If colonists refused to submit, they should be punished by "fire and sword."

93. Ferling, *The Loyalist Mind*, 54.

94. Quoted in Ferling, *The Loyalist Mind*, 53.

95. Intelligence from Peter Dubois, December 18, 1777, Clinton Papers, CL.

96. *Royal Gazette*, September 19, 1778.

97. Letter from New York, August 4, 1778, in I. N. Stokes, *Iconography*, 1072.

98. Sir Charles Blagden to Joseph Banks, September 12, 1778, in I. N. Stokes, *Iconography*, 1075.

99. *Royal Gazette*, October 10, 1778.

100. Ibid., January 6, 1779.

101. John Goodrich to Sir Henry Clinton, November 2, 1778, Clinton Papers, CL.

102. Edward Winslow to London, 1778, in Winslow Papers, DLAR.

103. *Royal Gazette*, April 11 and June 6, 1778.

104. Ibid., June 6, 1778. Tryon had had already urged Suffolk County residents in 1777 to raise money for loyalist troops. Any "apprehension," he warned, would be construed as a "lukewarmness" to the "king and the Old Constitution" (William Tryon, May 19, 1777, in Floyd Papers, CMNY.)

105. William Tryon to George Germain, September 5, 1778, in Davies, *Documents*, 198.

106. Ibid., December 24, 1778, 297.

107. Edward Winslow to London, 1778, in Winslow Papers, DLAR.

108. Daniel Coxe to Joseph Galloway, December 17, 1778, "Letters to Joseph Galloway," *Historical Magazine* (December 1861): 358.

109. Letter from affectionate friend to Joseph Galloway, November 17, 1778, in "Letters to Joseph Galloway," *Historical Magazine* (September 1861): 271.

110. John Potts to Joseph Galloway, December 17, 1778, in "Letters to Joseph Galloway," *Historical Magazine* (December 1861): 359. The same thought was echoed by Charles Inglis in his letter to Joseph Galloway, December 12, 1778, in "Letters to Joseph Galloway," *Historical Magazine* (October 1861): 298.

111. Frey, "British Armed Forces," 181.

112. Quoted in Conway, "Military-Civilian Crime," 150.

113. Patrick Ferguson to Sir Henry Clinton, August 1, 1778, in Clinton Papers, CL.

114. Sir Henry Clinton to Duke of Newcastle, winter 1778, in Clinton Papers, CL; Willcox, *Portrait of a General,* 271, 268, 242, 261.

115. Charles Inglis to Joseph Galloway, December 12, 1778, in "Letters to Joseph Galloway," *Historical Magazine* (October 1861): 298; James Humphreys Jr. to Joseph Galloway, November 28, 1778, in "Letters to Joseph Galloway," *Historical Magazine* (September 1861): 272; Patrick Ferguson to Sir Henry Clinton, November 9, 1778, in Clinton Papers, CL; J. A. D. to Joseph Galloway, December 22, 1778, in "Letters to Joseph Galloway," *Historical Magazine* (December 1861): 361.

116. Joseph Galloway, "Proposal for Covering and Reducing the Country as the British Army Shall Pass Through It," June 17, 1778, in Clinton Papers, CL; Isaac Ogden to Joseph Galloway, November 22, 1778, in Balch Papers, NYPL; Joseph Galloway, December 3, 1777, in Dartmouth Papers, DLAR.

117. *Royal Gazette,* September 19, 1778.

118. Letter from a Sincere friend to Galloway, November 22, 1778, in "Letters to Joseph Galloway," *Historical Magazine* (September 1861): 272; Isaac Ogden to Joseph Galloway, November 22, 1778, in Balch Papers, NYPL; William Smith Jr., February 18, 1779, in Acton, "Diary," 124.

119. William Smith Jr., November 7, 1778, in Acton, "Diary," 68; in William Tryon's hand from New York, November 30, 1778, in Clinton Papers, CL; *Royal Gazette,* March 24, and April 21, 1779.

## 5. "Diversity of Sentiments"

1. Isaac Ogden to Joseph Galloway, November 22, 1778, in Balch Papers, NYPL; Skemp, *William Franklin,* 234.

2. Quoted in Glenn H. Smith, "William Franklin," 60, 64, 68, 75.

3. Ibid., 71.

4. Isaac Ogden to Joseph Galloway, November 22, 1778, "Letters to Joseph Galloway," *Historical Magazine* (November 1861): 337; William Smith Jr., September 5, 1778, in Acton, "Diary," 18; William Franklin to George Germain, December 20, 1778, in Davies, *Documents,* 295.

5. William Franklin to George Germain, November 10, 1778, in Davies, *Documents,* 246.

6. William Franklin to George Germain, November 12, 1778, in Davies, *Documents,* 252.

7. Loyalists of New Jersey to William Howe, 1778, list of 351 subscribers, Clinton Papers, CL; William Franklin to George Germain, December 20, 1778, in Davies, *Documents,* 294; Skemp, *William Franklin,* 233.

8. Willcox, *American Rebellion*, 361.

9. William Smith Jr., October 2, 1778, in Acton, "Diary," 55.

10. Paul David Nelson, *William Tryon*, 165; Skemp, *William Franklin*, 236; Johnston, *Storming of Stony Point*, 57.

11. William Franklin to George Germain, November 12, 1778, in Davies, *Documents*, 249; Skemp, *William Franklin*, 234.

12. William Smith Jr., November 7, 1778, February 10 and March 1779, in Acton, "Diary," 68, 120–21, 128.

13. William Smith Jr., July 22, 1778, in Acton, "Diary," 423.

14. William Smith Jr., October 2, 1778, and March 1, 1779, in Acton, "Diary," 52, 130.

15. William Smith Jr., August 25, July 8, June 22, and September 10, 1779, in Acton, "Diary," 263, 213, 200, 273.

16. William Smith Jr., September 30, November 24, and December 21, 1778, in Acton, "Diary," 47–49, 78, 90.

17. Isaac Ogden to Joseph Galloway, December 16, 1778, in "Letters to Joseph Galloway," *Historical Magazine* (December 1861): 356.

18. Montfort Browne to Edward Winslow, June 18, 1778, in Winslow Papers, DLAR; *Royal Gazette*, November 30, 1778.

19. Howe, *Observations upon A Pamphlet*, 60, 42.

20. Ibid., 39, 50.

21. British officer quoted in Shy, *Toward Lexington*, 100; British surgeon quoted in Kwasny, *Washington's Partisan War*, 3; Fred Anderson, "Colonial New Englanders," 395, 404.

22. During the Seven Years' War, black enlistments were uncommon. Morgan and O'Shaugnessy note that more money was spent to control slaves than to arm them (*Arming Slaves*, 186).

23. Frey, "Between Slavery and Freedom," 152, 154, 156.

24. Ibid., 144.

25. Braisted, "Black Pioneers," 4, 9–10; Frey, "Between Slavery and Freedom," 143.

26. Quoted in Braisted, "Black Pioneers," 11.

27. Howe Orderly Book, March 22, 1778, in Clinton Papers, CL; Sir Henry Clinton to George Martin, May 10, 1776, quoted in Braisted, "Black Pioneers," 11–13.

28. Howe Orderly Book, March 22, 1778, in Clinton Papers, CL; Sir Henry Clinton to George Martin, May 10, 1776, quoted in Braisted, "Black Pioneers," 4, 11–13; Frey, "Between Slavery and Freedom," 153.

29. Sir Henry Clinton, June 30, 1779, in Clinton Papers, CL; Morris, "Class Struggle," 19.

30. Ryan, *New Jersey's Loyalists*, 4; Raymond, "Loyalists in Arms," 203.

31. Paul David Nelson, *William Tryon*, 149; Smith, *Loyalists and Redcoats*, 49.

32. Mackesy, *War for America*, 137.

33. *New-York Gazette and Weekly Mercury*, January 13 and March 3, 1777; Gruber, *Howe Brothers*, 197–98. The British were ready to consider any source of manpower, even Irish Catholics, who had not traditionally served in the British army. See Morgan and O'Shaugnessy, "Arming Slaves," 198. In addition, many British officials, including Major General Patrick Ferguson, believed that the core strength of George Wash-

ington's army came predominantly from Irishmen. In 1778, Clinton hoped that Irish deserters would weaken the rebel army and compensate for the dispersion of his troops, scattered in the West Indies, in the southern colonies, and in Halifax, Nova Scotia. See Patrick Ferguson, Memo, August 1, 1778, in Clinton Papers, CL. On British officials' view of the Irish, see Mackesy, *War for America,* 31; and Willcox, *Portrait of a General,* 56.

34. *New-York Gazette and Weekly Mercury,* February 17, February 24, March 3, and March 15, 1776.

35. Colonel Charles Stuart, March 1777, in Wortley, *Prime Minister,* 109; Hugh Gaine, March 31, 1777, in Ford, *Journals,* 2:25; John Peebles, March 28 and April 1, 1777, in Gruber, *John Peebles' American War,* 107; Hugh Gaine, April 13, April 17, and April 18, 1777, in Ford, *Journals,* 2:28; Levin Friedrich Ernst von Muenchhausen, April 17 and May 31, 1777, in von Muenchhausen, *At General Howe's Side,* 11–12; Hugh Gaine, May 7, 1777, in Ford, *Journals,* 2:31; Loftus Cliffe, March 5, 1777, in Cliffe Papers, CL; John Peebles, June 6, 1777, in Gruber, *John Peebles' American War,* 115; Hugh Gaine, July 10 and July 11, 1777, in Ford, *Journals,* 2:40.

36. Over thirty thousand blacks served the British during the American Revolution, representing about 4 percent of the British military war effort. Only about seven hundred served under arms and in uniform. See Morgan and O'Shaugnessy, "Arming Slaves," 198–99, 192.

37. Oliver De Lancey, "Great Britain Army in America," December 1, 1778, in Clinton Papers, CL. DeLancey presumably reported only the numbers of white loyalists. Joseph Galloway, March 14, 1778, in Dartmouth Papers, DLAR. In March 1778, Galloway urged the British to provide loyalists with arms "so they may give proof of their attachment to government and assist the Crown in putting an end to their own distress and oppression" (Isaac Ogden to Joseph Galloway, November 22, 1778, in Balch Papers, NYPL).

38. William Tryon to George Germain, December 24, 1778, in Davies, *Documents,* 297; Braisted, "Black Pioneers," 12; William Tryon, January 21, 1779, in Clinton Papers, CL.

39. Charles Inglis to Joseph Galloway, December 12, 1778, in "Letters to Joseph Galloway," *Historical Magazine* (October 1861): 298.

40. John Campbell to Sir Henry Clinton, March 31, 1778, in Clinton Papers, CL; Valentine Jones to Sir Henry Clinton, April 11, 1778, in Clinton Papers, CL; Richard Swanwick to Sir William Howe, May 14, 1778, in Clinton Papers, CL; John Chalmers to Sir Henry Clinton, September 12, 1778, in Clinton Papers, CL; Robert Cooke to Sir Henry Clinton, October 22, 1778, in Clinton Papers, CL.

41. Lord Rawdon to Montfort Browne, May 29, 1779, in Clinton Papers, CL.

42. Sir Henry Clinton to General Benjamin Carpenter, January 18, 1778, in Clinton Papers, CL.

43. Fred Anderson, "Colonial Background," 12; Clinton quoted in Willcox, *American Rebellion,* 128.

44. Edward Winslow, December 1778, in Winslow Papers, DLAR; Sir Henry Clinton to George Germain, October 8, 1778, in Davies, *Documents,* 210.

45. Stryker, *New Jersey Volunteers,* 4; Raymond, "Loyalists in Arms," 206; Mackenzie, *Diary,* 2:550.

46. Leach, *Roots of Conflict,* 107–9. Leach's observations about American soldiers

during the Seven Years' War also apply to loyalist soldiers during the American Revolution.

47. Ibid., 107–9.

48. William Smith Jr., February 26, 1778, in Sabine, *Historical Memoirs to 25 July 1778*, 310; Sir Henry Clinton to Sir William Howe, February 15, 1778, in Clinton Papers, CL; Sir Henry Clinton to George Germain, May 14, 1779, in Clinton Papers, CL; Sir Henry Clinton to Sir William Howe, February 28, 1778, in Clinton Papers, CL; Lord Rawdon to Alexander Innes, December 18, 1779, in Clinton Papers, CL.

49. Sir William Howe to Sir Henry Clinton, October 25, 1777, in Clinton Papers, CL.

50. Court-Martial Trial, Brooklyn, Long Island, July 24 to August 1, 1778, in War Office Records (WO 71/86), NA; Court-Martial Trial, Brooklyn, Long Island, August 4 to August 10, 1778, in War Office Records (WO 71/86), NA.

51. Court-Martial Trial, Jamaica, Long Island, May 4 to May 8, 1779, in War Office Records (WO 71/88), NA.

52. Court-Martial Trial, New York, October 2 to November 4, 1779, in War Office Records (WO 71/90), NA.

53. Henry Rooke to Sir Henry Clinton, "Report of Dissolution of Emmerick Chasseurs," September 1, 1780, in Clinton Papers, CL.

54. Valentine Jones to Sir Henry Clinton, March 3, 1778, in Clinton Papers, CL; Conway, "Military-Civilian Crime," 56.

55. Alexander Innes to Sir Henry Clinton, November 9, 1779, in Clinton Papers, CL.

56. Sir Henry Clinton to William Eden, September 1, 1780, in Willcox, *American Rebellion*, 456; Barck, *New York City*, 199; Sir Henry Clinton to Lord George Germain, August 30, 1780, in Willcox, *American Rebellion* 455. Smith lamented that Clinton paid no attention to the militia in New York, Staten Island, or Long Island (William Smith Jr., July 11, 1781, in I. N. Stokes, *Iconography*, 1132).

57. Montfort Browne to Lord Dartmouth, January 20, 1778, in Dartmouth Papers, DLAR.

58. *Detail and Conduct of the American War*, 108.

59. Ambrose Serle, October 24, 1776, in Tatum, *American Journal*, 128–29; Skemp, *William Franklin*, 144.

60. His Majesty's Commissioners to Lord George Germain, November 30, 1776, in Davies, *Documents*, 257.

61. Barck, *New York City*, 131.

62. Andrew Elliot, Memorandum, in Elliot Papers, Box 7, NYSL. The British worried about the scarcity of provisions in the city. Until December 1777, Elliot permitted the shipment of logwood and mahogany to Great Britain and the shipment of staves and hoops to Ireland and the West Indies. But General Howe disallowed this trade because he feared that some merchants, more interested in earning profits than satisfying the garrison's needs, would exploit the port to trade merchandise clandestinely with the rebels and create a shortage of necessary items in the city.

63. Cooke, "Tench Coxe," 54, 71, 70n.

64. Ibid., 88.

65. Ibid., 52, 55n; *New-York Gazette and Weekly Mercury*, November 9, 1778; Andrew Elliot to Sir Henry Clinton from Superintendent's office in New York, January 9, 1779,

in Clinton Papers, CL (Elliot introduced Jamieson to Clinton as a "man of good character"); Meeting on the rate of exchange in New York City, December 4, 1782, Carleton Papers, NA. Jamieson was not the only merchant to receive Elliot's patronage. In May 1778, Stephen Goold expressed gratification at the "genteel" behavior of Elliot, whom he described as "a good man and a good friend to me" (quoted in Cooke, "Tench Coxe," 55).

66. *Royal Gazette,* September 2, 1778; William Eden to Sir Henry Clinton, August 21, 1778, in Clinton Papers, CL; Alan S. Brown, "William Eden," 147; Barck, *New York City,* 125, 121, 126.

67. Memorial of Robert Alexander and John Miller, undated, in Treasury Board Papers (T1/528), NA.

68. Andrew Elliot, August 13, 1778, in Elliot Papers, Box 2, Folder 1, NYSL.

69. Andrew Elliot, undated [November 1778], in Elliot Papers, Box 1, Folder 14, NYSL.

70. William Eden to Sir Henry Clinton, September 1778, in Clinton Papers, CL; Earl of Carlisle and William Eden to George Germain, November 15, 1778, in Clinton Papers, CL; George Germain to Commissioners, November 4, 1778, in Clinton Papers, CL. See also Barck, *New York City,* 121.

71. Earl of Carlisle and William Eden to George Germain, November 15, 1778, in Clinton Papers, CL.

72. George Germain to William Tryon, August 5, 1778, in O'Callaghan, *Documents,* 748; Barck, *New York City,* 131; Isaac Ogden to Joseph Galloway, February 6, 1779, in Balch Papers, NYPL; William Tryon to George Germain, March 1, 1779, in I. N. Stokes, *Iconography,* 1083.

73. William Tryon to George Germain, September 5, 1778, in Davies, *Documents,* 198; Andrew Elliot, August 15, 1778, in Elliot Papers, Box 1, Folder 15, NYSL.

74. William Tryon to George Germain, February 5, 1779, and William Tryon, Proclamation, March 8, 1779, in I. N. Stokes, *Iconography,* 1082–83.

75. William Tryon, March 8, 1779, in I. N. Stokes, *Iconography,* 1083; Court-Martial Trial, New York, January 28 to February 12, 1779, in War Office Records (WO 71/88), NA. John Farren, Thomas Agnew, John Purdy, and George Fogwell were implicated in the stolen property scheme. Also see Lydon, *Pirates,* 275–80; and Palmer, *Biographical Sketches.*

76. Quoted in Alan S. Brown, "William Eden," 105; William Eden to Sir Henry Clinton, August 21, 1778, in Clinton Papers, CL; Barck, *New York City,* 125; *Royal Gazette,* November 14, 1778.

77. Abraham Van Buskirk, Isaac Allen, and others thanked Bayard for "the active and humane part you have taken to procure watch-coats for the Jersey volunteers demand our warmest acknowledgements. You will also please to return our thanks to the loyal inhabitants of New York whose generous and seasonable donations have contributed so much to the comfort of the troops under our command and the good of his majesty's service" (*New-York Gazette and Weekly Mercury,* February 2, 1778); Callahan, *Royal Raiders,* 79; Barck, *New York City,* 139. Also see Acton, "Diary," 263n; and Wilkenfeld, "Revolutionary New York," 49.

78. Proclamations, June 21, August 3, and July 10, 1779, in I. N. Stokes *Iconography,* 1088, 1091, 1090.

79. Barck, *New York City,* 131; DeLancey Orderly Book, March 8, 1778, 50, DLAR;

*Royal Gazette,* December 16, 1778; Court-Martial Trial, January 18 to February 12, 1779, in War Office Records (WO 71/88), NA.

80. *Royal Gazette,* October 10, 1778; William Smith Jr., December 17, 1778, in Acton, "Diary," 90; *Royal Gazette,* May 1, 1779.

81. *New-York Gazette and Weekly Mercury,* April 16, 1779.

82. Ibid., September 20, 1779.

83. *Royal American Gazette,* April 20, 1780.

84. Ibid., June 11, 1782.

85. Mackesy, *War for America,* 253.

86. William Eden to Sir Henry Clinton, October 15, 1778, in Alan S. Brown, "William Eden," 149; Commissioners to George Germain, July 26, 1778, in ibid., 139; William Eden to Alexander Wedderburn, October 23, 1778, in ibid., 157. Also see Ritcheson, *British Politics,* 278–79.

87. Commissioners to George Germain, November 27, 1778, in Clinton Papers, CL; Mackesy, *War for America,* 256, 254; Ritcheson, *British Politics,* 282.

88. George Germain to General Clinton, January 23, 1779, and Peter Dubois to General Clinton, January 24, 1778, both in Clinton Papers, CL.

89. Daniel Chamier to Robert Mackenzie, March 3, 1778, in Clinton Papers, CL.

90. William Smith Jr., November 24, October 2, and December 29, 1778, in Acton, "Diary," 77, 52, 98; Willcox, *Portrait of a General,* 250; William Smith Jr., March 1779 and December 12, 1778, in Acton, "Diary," 128, 88; Smith quoted in Mackesy, *War for America,* 256.

91. Mackesy, *War for America,* 111; Germain quoted in Smith, *Loyalists and Redcoats,* 45, 62; Fryer, *King's Men,* 14.

92. Shy, *Toward Lexington,* 15, 368; Fryer, *King's Men,* 15.

93. George Germain to Sir Henry Clinton, August 5, 1779, in Clinton Papers, CL; George Germain to Great Britain Commissioners, November 4, 1778, in Clinton Papers, CL; George Germain to Sir Henry Clinton, March 8, 1778, and June 2 and January 23, 1779, in Clinton Papers, CL.

94. Edward Winslow, December 1778, in Winslow Papers, DLAR; Court-Martial Trials, New York, August 6 to August 24, 1779, in War Office Records (WO 71/90), NA.

95. George Germain to Great Britain Commissioners, November 4, 1778, in Clinton Papers, CL; Mackesy, *War for America,* 256.

## 6. "A Certificate of Their Necessity"

1. Mary Beth Norton, *British-Americans,* 32.

2. Willcox, *American Rebellion,* 399, 237.

3. William Smith Jr., September 22, 1778, in I. N. Stokes, *Iconography,* 1075; Polf, *Garrison Town,* 10.

4. "Report of the Board Appointed under Carleton to Consider the Circumstances and Claims of the Refugees, from September 1782," in Carleton Papers, NA. The 1782 returns show 159 refugees from New York, 78 from New Jersey, 43 from Massachusetts, 40 from Connecticut, 29 from Pennsylvania, 22 from Rhode Island, 15 from Virginia, 11 from Maryland, and 6 together from North Carolina, Georgia and Florida.

5. Hugh Gaine, October 30, 1777, in Ford, *Journals,* 2:53.

6. *New-York Gazette and Weekly Mercury,* December 22, 1777.

7. Joshua Gidney of Dutchess County, May 1, 1779, in Carleton Papers, DLAR.

8. Memorial of Alida, wife of Jesse Armstrong, May 1779, in Carleton Papers, DLAR.

9. Susannah Wilkinson, April 9, 1779, in Carleton Papers, DLAR.

10. James M. Bath, April 10, 1779, in Carleton Papers, DLAR.

11. Thomas Griffiths, April 9, 1779, in Carleton Papers, DLAR.

12. James Wright, governor of Georgia, undated [1779], in Carleton Papers, DLAR.

13. Anonymous letter to Germain, March 18, 1777, in Germain Papers, CL; Mary Beth Norton, *British-Americans,* 32; William Smith Jr., April 9, 1777, in Sabine, *Historical Memoirs to 25 July 1778,* 109.

14. *New-York Gazette and Weekly Mercury,* March 24, 1777; William Smith Jr., October 14, 1776, in Sabine, *Historical Memoirs to 25 July 1778,* 18.

15. Quoted in Ferling, *The Loyalist Mind,* 75, 113–14.

16. *New-York Gazette and Weekly Mercury,* January 13, March 3, and November 24, 1777.

17. *New-York Gazette and Weekly Mercury,* December 22, 1777.

18. William Smith Jr., October 14, 1776, in Sabine, *Historical Memoirs to 25 July 1778,* 18.

19. Stevens, *Colonial Records,* 41–44; Theophylact Bache to Sir Henry Clinton, November 8, 1777, in Clinton Papers, CL.

20. Theophylact Bache to Sir Henry Clinton, November 8, 1777, in Clinton Papers, CL.

21. Quoted in Mohl, "Poverty," 71.

22. Mohl, "Poverty," 71–73. In eighteenth-century England, E. P. Thompson notes that the poor were seen as an inconvenience, not a menace. This could not be said about the poor refugees entering New York City during the rebellion. Thompson, "Patrician Society," 387.

23. Klein and Howard, *Twilight of British Rule,* 165n.

24. *Royal Gazette,* January 3, 1778; Stevens, *Colonial Records,* 27–100. Eight of these nineteen men had signed the October 1776 petition requesting a restoration of civil rule in the city. These included Elias Desbrosses, Hamilton Young, Theophylact Bache, Rem. Rapalje, Jeronymus Alstyn, Willet Taylor, William Ustick, and Peter Stuyvesant (*New-York Gazette and Weekly Mercury,* December 22 and December 27, 1777).

25. *New-York Gazette and Weekly Mercury,* January 1, 1781.

26. *Royal Gazette,* July 28, 1779; Conway, "Military-Civilian Crime," 80; *Royal Gazette,* March 22, 1780; William Smith Jr., January 19, 1779, in Acton, "Diary," 108.

27. Court-Martial Records, Brooklyn, Long Island, July 24 to August 1, 1778, in War Office Records (WO 71/86), NA. Hally may have picked up this excuse from previous cases. In September 1776, when some inhabitants accused John Kelly of the 27th Regiment of Foot of pillaging and plunder, he replied that some blacks had informed him that the orchard belonged to a rebel. Kelly nevertheless was given a thousand lashes. See Court-Martial Trial, Newtown, Long Island, September 3, 1776, in War Office Records (WO 71/82), NA.

28. *New-York Gazette and Weekly Mercury,* January 20, 1777; I. N. Stokes, *Iconography,* 1090; Kaplan, "The Hidden War," 126–27.

29. John Cozens to Sir Henry Clinton, August 15, 1779, in Clinton Papers, CL;

Joseph Vaughan and Daniel Smith to Sir Henry Clinton, September 5, 1779, in Clinton Papers, CL; Charity Lee to John Andre, November 22, 1779, in Clinton Papers, CL.

30. William Smith Jr., July 19, 1778, in Sabine, *Historical Memoirs to 25 July 1778*, 420.

31. *New-York Gazette and Weekly Mercury*, December 9, October 14, and November 11, 1776, and January 6 and July 7, 1777.

32. Black and white numbers noted in letter from William Axtell to Governor Tryon, October 17, 1777, in Andrew Elliot Papers, NYSL; Shama, *Rough Crossings*, 8; Hodges, "Black Revolt," 28.

33. *Royal Gazette*, September 16 and September 26, 1778, January 2 and March 6, 1779, and August 23, 1780; *New-York Gazette and Weekly Mercury*, July 26, 1779, and January 3 and October 2, 1780; *New-York Mercury; or General Advertiser*, December 3, 1779.

34. *Royal Gazette*, December 9, 1780, and June 27, 1781; Hodges and Brown, *"Pretends to Be Free,"* 248, 255; *Royal Gazette*, September 1, 1781.

35. *Royal Gazette*, July 10, 1780, February 6, May 5, and October 13, 1779, August 4, 1781, and March 27 and May 20, 1780; *New-York Gazette and Weekly Mercury*, July 23, 1781; abstract of several accounts of expenses incurred in the Engineer's Department, September 1 to September 30, 1782, in Carleton Papers, NA. The Negro Carpenters received £24.14.

36. Hodges, *Root and Branch*, 150; William Smith Jr., December 21, 1778, in Acton, "Diary," 90

37. Bowler, "Logistics and Operations," 10, 26, 32, 33, 37; Hodges, *Root and Branch*, 149; Conway, "Military-Civilian Crime," 61.

38. Sir Henry Clinton to Great Britain Commissioners, July 1779, in Clinton Papers, CL.

39. Abraham Cuyler to Thomas Ward, Philip Luke, David Babcock, and John Everet, June 24, 1780, in Clinton Papers, CL.

40. *Royal American Gazette*, April 20, 1780; Patterson quoted in Hodges, *Root and Branch*, 152.

41. John Simcoe, December 2, 1780, in Simcoe Papers, CL.

42. William Smith Jr., October 5, 1779, in Acton, "Diary," 289.

43. Quoted in Braisted, "Black Pioneers," 15.

44. Judea Moore to Sir Henry Clinton, February 10, 1779, in Clinton Papers, CL.

45. *New-York Gazette and Weekly Mercury*, November 16, 1778; also in I. N. Stokes, *Iconography*, 1078; *New-York Mercury; or General Advertiser*, December 10, 1779, January 19, 1781; *Royal Gazette*, February 26, 1780, March 15, 1780.

46. *New-York Gazette and Weekly Mercury*, June 4, 1781.

47. Andrew Elliot, undated, Elliot Papers, Box 3, Folder 5, Paper Book No. 5, NYSL; General William Howe, Proclamation, July 17, 1777, in Mackenzie Papers, Collection D, CL; *New-York Gazette and Weekly Mercury*, May 22, 1780.

48. *New-York Gazette and Weekly Mercury*, December 9, 1776. The paper reported the following: "On Last Monday Evening, David Mathews, Esq., our worthy mayor arrived late in Town having effected an Escape, with great Danger and Difficulty, from Litchfield in Connecticut where he had been confined since the 21st of July. He was first apprehended on the 22nd of June at Flatbush, and was dragged out of Bed at Midnight by an officer and twenty Men belonging to the Rebel Army. By order of the provincial Congress, he was committed to close Confinement in the common Jail

among the felons, during a month in the hottest time of year, and afterwards sent under Guard to the committee at Litchfield with an express order form the President of the said Congress to detain him in Prison" (Klein and Howard, *Twilight*, 117n).

49. *Royal Gazette*, May 4, 1778.

50. The use of fines attests to the significant number of nondestitute residents in New York City. Fines imply that criminals were sufficiently prosperous to pay them (Preyer, "Penal Measures," 350). Note also that General Howe, and later Clinton, permitted Elliot's committee to share limited judicial responsibilities previously reserved for the commandant. If disputes arose among civilians in the city, the commandant would refer loyalists' concerns to a newly created Board of Inquiry made up of three field officers and two magistrates of police. Only if the board failed to reach a compromise would the commandant issue a unilateral decision. See Elliot Papers, undated, Box 3, Folder 5, Paper Book No. 5, NYSL.

51. *New-York Gazette and Weekly Mercury*, March 3, 1777; *Royal Gazette*, November 18, 1778; Stevens, *Colonial Records*, 379.

52. *Royal Gazette*, December 2, 1778; *New-York Gazette and Weekly Mercury*, January 13, 1777. The men assigned were George Shaw and David H. Mallows for the Out Ward; Normand Tolmie, Daniel Aymar, and Francis Cooley for the Montgomery Ward; James Aymar and Martin Cregier for the North Ward; David Fenton and John Amory for the West Ward; Edward Nicoll for the South Ward; James Wells for the Dock Ward; and Jeronymus Alstyne, Thomas Brownejohn, Valentine Nutter, John Devan, Charles White, Peter McLean, and Stephen Reeves for the East Ward (*Royal Gazette*, May 22, 1779). Also see Palmer, *Biographical Sketches*.

53. For example, the orderly books repeatedly issued orders against drunkenness.

54. Bowler, *Logistics*, 8–9, 31.

55. *New-York Gazette and Weekly Mercury*, January 13, 1777, and December 7, 1778.

56. Although complaints from civilians far outnumbered compliments, the inhabitants of Herricks, Long Island, requested that the 23rd Regiment remain among them. They wrote that the replacement of these troops with another regiment "unacquainted with the people" might result in less satisfaction. See Inhabitants of Herricks in Queen's County, July 15, 1783, in Carleton Papers, NA.

57. Sir Henry Clinton to Edward Harvey, July 11, 1777, Clinton Papers, CL; Ewald Gustav Schaukirk, May 31, 1777, in Schaukirk, *Occupation*, 5; DeLancey Orderly Book, August 19, 1777, DLAR.

58. DeLancey Orderly Book, September 18, 1777, DLAR; *New-York Gazette and Weekly Mercury*, July 14, August 18, and September 22, 1777; Colonel Charles Stuart to Lord Bute, July 10 and August 31, 1777, in Wortley, *Prime Minister*, 116.

59. DeLancey Orderly Book, April 1 and September 11, 1777, DLAR; *New-York Gazette and Weekly Mercury*, February 24, 1777.

60. *New-York Gazette and Weekly Mercury*, July 26, 1779; *Royal Gazette*, January 5, 1780; *New-York Gazette and Weekly Mercury*, January 3, 1780.

61. *New-York Gazette and Weekly Mercury*, June 5, 1780. I found no record of New Yorkers losing their licenses for this reason.

62. *New-York Gazette and Weekly Mercury*, December 21, 1778; Bowler, *Logistics*, 8–9, 111; *New-York Gazette and Weekly Mercury*, January 13, 1777.

63. Ewald Gustav Schaukirk, January 12, 1779, in Schaukirk, *Occupation*, 9; *Royal Gazette*, January 27, 1779, January 30, 1779.

64. *Royal Gazette*, February 6, April 10, and August 14, 1779; *New-York Gazette and Weekly Mercury*, October 23, 1779, and March 20, 1780.

65. *New-York Gazette and Weekly Mercury*, September 30, 1776; Polf, *Garrison Town*, 4–5; Cornell quoted in Conway, "Military-Civilian Crime," 93; I. N. Stokes, *Iconography*, November 23, 1779, 1097; *New-York Gazette and Weekly Mercury*, November 13, 1780. In addition to the incivilities of their own soldiers, the British also heard the injuries committed by Continental soldiers. On October 23, 1777, a British official acknowledged, "I do hereby certify that the fence of the Rev. Mr. Munro's garden and lots of land have been pulled up and destroyed by the Continental troops." See Reverend Dr. Henry Munro letter, CMNY.

66. Court-Martial Records, New York, September 28 to October 3, 1778, in War Office Records (WO 71/87), NA.

67. Ibid.

68. Stevens, *Colonial Records*, 395, 208; Andrew Elliot to William Smith Jr., August 8, 1783, in Carleton Papers, NA; Henry Ludlam, August 30, 1783, in Carleton Papers, NA; John Thurman to James Robertson, August 20, 1780, in Carleton Papers, DLAR. Nicholas Jones also complained that Mathews had assigned his property to a Mr. Ryckman without his permission. See Mr. Nicholas Jones' Claim, February 17, 1783, in Carleton Papers, NA.

69. David Mathews to Major Murray, February 17, 1783, in Carleton Papers, NA. On November 17, 1769, Peter Dubois, along with John Hill and Abraham Hardenberg, was appointed the assistant judge of the Ulster County court. See O'Callaghan, *Calendar*, 76.

70. William Smith Jr., February 20, 1782, in Sabine, *Historical Memoirs, 1778 to 1783*, 485.

71. Andrew Elliot and David Mathews, March 10, 1783, in Carleton Papers, NA; New York Board of Commissioners for Settling and Adjusting Matters of Debt, August 25, 1783, in Carleton Papers, NA.

72. Peter Clopper, Cornelius Bogert, William Lowther, and William Deplaine petition, May 6, 1783, in Carleton Papers, NA.

73. Court-Martial Records, New York, June 21 to July 30, 1779, in War Office Records (WO 71/89), NA.

74. *Royal Gazette*, March 13, 1779; *New-York Gazette and Weekly Mercury*, July 17, 1780; Klein and Howard, *Twilight*, 101n, 137n; Bowler, *Logistics*, 88.

75. Richard Tomlinson, undated [1782], in Carleton Papers, NA.

76. Ibid.

77. Willcox, *Portrait of a General*, 284; William Smith Jr., October 5, 1779, in Acton, "Diary," 287; Ewald Gustav Schaukirk, September 30, 1779, in Schaukirk, *Occupation*, 11.

78. William Smith Jr., October 20 and October 21, 1779, in Acton, "Diary," 299, 301.

79. Bowler, *Logistics*, 77, 67, 61; James Robertson to Sir Henry Clinton, Mach 29, 1780, in Klein and Howard, *Twilight*, 87.

80. *New-York Gazette and Weekly Mercury*, February 8, 1779; *Royal Gazette*, February 6, 1779.

81. William Smith Jr., December 22, 1779, in Acton, "Diary," 332; *New-York Gazette and Weekly Mercury*, November 27, 1780; James Robertson, April 1, 1780, in Klein and Howard, *Twilight*, 91.

82. Bowler, *Logistics,* 157; *New-York Gazette and Weekly Mercury,* November 24 and December 22, 1777, and January 5 and December 7, 1778; Hodges, *New York City Cartmen,* 64.

83. *New-York Gazette and Weekly Mercury,* May 19, 1777, and April 10, 1780; *Royal Gazette,* August 4, 1778; Records, October 13, 1777, in Clinton Papers, vol. 250, CL.

84. William Smith Jr., August 1, 1779, in Acton, "Diary," 240.

85. *New-York Gazette and Weekly Mercury,* April 30, 1781.

86. Court-Martial Records, Brooklyn, Long Island, July 24 to August 1, 1778, in War Office Records (WO 71/86), NA.

87. "Cursory Observations on the Refugees . . . ," undated, in Clinton Papers, vol. 229, CL.

## 7. "The Die Had Been Cast"

1. The New York Act of Attainder, or Confiscation Act, 1779; Proclamation of the Forfeiture of Property of Loyalists with list of names, Box 13, NYHS; Jacobs, "The Treaty and the Tories," 10.

2. Kenneth Scott, "Tory Associators," 511; Ireland, "Ethnic-Religious Dimension," 429–30; "Special Legislation," 1359; Keesey, "Loyalism in Bergen County," 565; Richard D. Brown, "Confiscation and Disposition of Loyalists' Estates," 536–38; Daniel Coxe to Sir Henry Clinton, June 28, 1780, in Clinton Papers, CL; Memorial of David Ogden Jr., in Loyalist Transcripts, NYPL; Keesey, "Loyalism in Bergen County," 562; Dubeau, *New Brunswick Loyalists,* 156–57; Bowler, *Logistics,* 254; Johnson, *Robert Alexander,* 101; Nolan, "The Effect of the Revolution," 980.

3. De Lancey, *History of New York,* 151; Judd, "Frederick Philipse III," 36; Stevens, *Colonial Records,* 380; William Smith Jr., December 15, 1779, in Acton, "Diary," 323.

4. William Smith Jr., December 1, 1779, in I. N. Stokes, *Iconography,* 1098.

5. "A Refugee" to Mr. Rivington, *Royal Gazette,* February 2, 1780; David Colden, September 13, 1783, in E. Alfred Jones, "Letter of David Colden, Loyalist," 83–86.

6. *New-York Gazette and Weekly Mercury,* March 10, 1777. In March 1777, rebels attacked the home of a Mr. Stephens, collector of East Jersey, and forced his wife to move to Amboy (Hugh Gaine, April 3, 1777, in Ford, *Journals,* 2:26).

7. *New-York Gazette and Weekly Mercury,* April 7, 1777; Levin Friedrich Ernst von Muenchhausen, March 17, 1777, in von Muenchhausen, *At General Howe's Side,* 10.

8. Hugh Gaine, June 10, 1777, in Ford, *Journals,* 2:35; Hugh Gaine, March 31, 1777, in Ford, *Journals,* 2:25; Hugh Gaine, June 10 and July 7, 1777, in Ford, *Journals,* 2:35; William Tryon to Sir Henry Clinton, July 8, 1777, in Clinton Papers, CL; Hugh Gaine, August 22, 1777, in Ford, *Journals,* 2:44; Ewald Gustav Schaukirk, August 22, 1777, in Schaukirk, *Occupation,* 6.

9. Hugh Gaine, November 4, 1777, in Ford, *Journals,* 2:54. In October, an intelligence report by Peter Dubois warned that a "variety of circumstances induce us to think that an enterprise is in contemplation against Staten Island" (Peter Dubois, October 1777, in Clinton Papers, CL).

10. John Campbell to Sir Henry Clinton, November 6, 1777, in Clinton Papers, CL.

11. John Campbell to Sir Henry Clinton, November 27, 1777, in Clinton Papers, CL.

12. Ward Chipman to Edward Winslow, November 29, 1777, in Winslow Papers, DLAR. It is not clear from the letter where they captured Buskirk and his men.

13. Stephen Kemble, November 25, 1777, in *Collections of the New York Historical Society*, 145.

14. Sir Henry Clinton to William Howe, November 28, 1777, in Clinton Papers, CL.

15. Montfort Browne to Lord Dartmouth, January 28, 1778, in Dartmouth Papers, DLAR.

16. Stephen Kemble, June 14, 1778, in *Collections of the New York Historical Society*, 152; Stevens, *Colonial Records*, 47.

17. Bowler, *Logistics*, 97; *New-York Gazette and Weekly Mercury*, July 5, 1779; William Smith Jr., November 11, 1779, in Acton, "Diary," 306; Charles Inglis to Society for the Propagation of the Gospel, November 26, 1779, in Lydekker, *Life and Letters of Charles Inglis*, 195; *New-York Gazette and Weekly Mercury*, August 7, 1780. In August 1780, this gang robbed innkeeper John Houlroyd of several hundred pounds and seized a market wagon from a Mrs. Threddle (Court-Martial Trials, January 27, 1780, in War Office Records [WO 71/91], NA). The gang included David Carrol, Jesse Harding, John Gellin, John Mason, Joseph Waller, Catherine Waller, and Hilibel Pigot.

18. Schecter, *Battle for New York*, 324; Willcox, *Portrait of a General*, 277; Hugh Gaine, August 19, 1779, in Ford, *Journals*, 61.

19. William Smith Jr., August 19, 1779, in Acton, "Diary," 259; Colonel Charles Stuart to Lord Bute, August 1779, quoted in Willcox, *Portrait of a General*, 279.

20. Willcox, *Portrait of a General*, 295; William Smith Jr., August 8, 1779, in Acton, "Diary," 247; Mackesy, *War for America*, 266; King George III to Lord North, June 11, 1779, in Johnston, *Storming of Stony Point*, 106.

21. Patrick Ferguson to Sir Henry Clinton, September 27, 1779, in Clinton Papers, CL; William Tryon in B. J. Johnson's hand, September 15, 1779, in Clinton Papers, CL; Patrick Ferguson to Sir Henry Clinton, September 27, 1779, in Clinton Papers, CL.

22. *Royal Gazette*, June 5, June 10, June 16, and July 17, 1779; William Franklin to John Andre, November 10, 1779, in Clinton Papers, CL.

23. *Royal Gazette*, November 3, 1779; William Franklin to John Andre, November 10, 1779, in Clinton Papers, CL; William Franklin to John Andre, November 10, 1779, in Clinton Papers, CL.

24. Charles Inglis to Joseph Galloway, December 12, 1778, in "Letters to Joseph Galloway," *Historical Magazine* (October 1861): 301; William Smith Jr., June 26, 1779, in Acton, "Diary," 202; William Tryon to Sir Henry Clinton, July 20, 1779, in Clinton Papers, CL; William Smith Jr., June 22, 1779, in Acton, "Diary," 200.

25. William Tryon to Sir Henry Clinton, June 30, 1779, in Clinton Papers, CL.

26. Knight, "Prisoner Exchange," 203, 207; Skemp, *William Franklin*, 242–43; William Tryon to Sir Henry Clinton, June 30, 1779, in Clinton Papers, CL.

27. *Royal Gazette*, August 25, October 16, November 24, December 3, and December 29, 1779.

28. John Andre, December 1779, in Clinton Papers, CL; Bowler, *Logistics*, 67.

29. On December 17, 1778, Daniel Coxe had chosen not to "fly across the Atlantic" like Galloway (Daniel Coxe to Joseph Galloway, December 17, 1778, in Balch Papers, NYPL). *New-York Gazette and Weekly Mercury*, November 29, 1779; *Royal Gazette*, April

12, 1780; "Loyalist Refugees: Articles for Association," January 9, 1779, in Clinton Papers, CL.

30. Opinion of Clinton expressed in letter from John Andre to Henry Barry, November 13, 1779, in Clinton Papers, CL; Willcox, *Portrait of a General*, 295–97.

31. Daniel Coxe to Joseph Galloway, *New-York Gazette and Weekly Mercury*, July 31, 1780.

32. *New-York Gazette and Weekly Mercury*, July 31, 1780; Condon, *Dictionary of Canadian Biography*.

33. Thomas Gage to Lord Dartmouth, September 2, 1774, in Carter, *Correspondence*, 371.

34. *Royal Gazette*, February 13, 1779.

35. George Leonard, Memorial, late of Boston and New England, December 16, 1779, in Treasury Board Papers (T1/553), DLAR.

36. George Germain to William Howe, March 3 and August 6, 1777, in Carleton Papers, DLAR.

37. Skemp, *William Franklin*, 239.

38. Ibid., 243–45.

39. *Royal Gazette*, December 30, 1780. In 1782, Edward Lutwyche would serve as superintendent for His Majesty's Brewery (Curtis, *Organization of the British Army*, 110).

40. List of Warrants that have been granted by His Excellency for their support, May 2, 1782, in Carleton Papers, NA. In October 1778, Coxe, along with Potts and Shoemaker, had complained to the Carlisle Commission about the treatment and subsequent execution of Pennsylvania loyalists John Roberts, James Stevens, and Abraham Carlisle (Andrew Allen, Joseph Galloway, John Potts, Samuel Shoemaker, and Daniel Coxe to William Eden, October 4, 1778, in Clinton Papers, CL).

41. William Smith Jr., January 7, 1777, in Sabine, *Historical Memoirs to 25 July 1778*, 61–62.

42. Accounts of monies paid for secret services, May 24, 1778, in Clinton Papers, CL.

43. Daniel Coxe to Sir Henry Clinton, November 27, 1779, in Clinton Papers, CL.

44. Samuel Shoemaker, Daniel Coxe, and John Potts to Sir Henry Clinton, July 4, 1780, in Clinton Papers, CL; Daniel Coxe to Sir Henry Clinton, June 28, 1780, in Clinton Papers, CL. In November 1779, the Loyal Refugees under Coxe's leadership appointed gentlemen to represent the colonies in a committee. Since their "interests, families, and estates" coincided, these refugees committed themselves "to restore to this deluded country, the blessings of peace, order, and good government" (*New-York Gazette and Weekly Mercury*, November 29, 1779). This address is signed by "Daniel Coxe, President." The ten colonies mentioned in Coxe's address included New Hampshire, Massachusetts, Connecticut, New Jersey, Pennsylvania, Delaware, Maryland, Virginia, North Carolina, and South Carolina.

45. List of Expenses Extraordinaire granted by Carleton, within month of August 1783, in Carleton Papers, NA; Board to settle debts appointed, April 16, 1783, in Carleton Papers, CL; Intelligence to Daniel Coxe, June 5, 1779, in Clinton Papers, CL; Daniel Coxe to John Andre, October 21, 1779, in Clinton Papers, CL. Unlike Potts, Coxe continued to hold minor civil appointments in New York City. In addition to providing

intelligence, he served in a committee with fellow Loyalist Associator Robert Alexander to settle refugee debts.

46. The governor's uncle Josiah Martin served on New York's Council from 1759 to 1762. He also served as an aide to the governor of New York in 1757. See Sheridan, "West Indian Antecedents," 258.

47. Sheridan, "West Indian Antecedents," 253, 259, 262, 265.

48. Colonel Samuel Martin to Samuel Martin Jr., February 20, June 1, 1760, quoted in Sheridan, "West Indian Antecedents," 263.

49. Joshua Martin to the Lord Commissioners of His Majesty's Treasury, May 18, 1778, in Carleton Papers, DLAR; Sheridan, "West Indian Antecedents," 253–56. Martin's army of provincial loyalists was defeated at the Battle of Moore's Creek Bridge on February 26, 1776 (Sheridan, "West Indian Antecedents," 268).

50. George Germain to William Howe, June 12, 1777, in Carleton Papers, DLAR. Germain recommended Stewart to Howe's "Countenance & Protection." Also see Overfield, "The Loyalists of Maryland," 393.

51. Johnson, *Robert Alexander*, 72; Papenfuse, "Economic Analysis," 174; Nicholas Slubey to Robert Alexander, July 25, 1780, in Clinton Papers, CL.

52. *New-York Gazette and Weekly Mercury*, April 14, 1783; Johnson, *Robert Alexander*, 118. An undated [1783] document in the Carleton Papers (CL) lists Anthony Stewart of Water Street as paymaster of the Maryland Loyalists.

53. American National Biography Online.

54. Skemp, *William Franklin*, 248, 341.

55. Barck, *New York City*, 206; Tebbenhoff, "The Associated Loyalists," 138; *New-York Gazette and Weekly Mercury*, July 30, 1781.

56. Andrew Elliot, Memorandum, undated, in Elliot Papers, NYSL, Box 7; William Smith Jr., July 16, 1779, in Acton, "Diary," 222.

57. *Royal Gazette*, June 19, 1779.

58. William Smith Jr., July 27 and December 30, 1779, in Acton, "Diary," 234, 346.

59. William Smith Jr., August 25, 1779 in Acton, "Diary," 262; Palmer, *Biographical Sketches;* William Smith Jr., September 12, 1779, in Acton, "Diary," 276–77.

60. Klein and Howard, *Twilight*, 20, 26, 30.

61. Hugh Gaine, March 23, 1780, in Ford, *Journals,* 2:83; Klein and Howard, *Twilight,* 82.

62. Brigadier General Montfort Browne also believed that the British needed to restore colonists' confidence in government in order to counter rebel assertions that the British had come to "effect the most compleat and barbarous conquest of the country" (Montfort Browne, January 20, 1778, in Dartmouth Papers, DLAR).

63. William Smith Jr., September 4, 1778, in Acton, "Diary," 17.

64. James Robertson, July 27, 1778, in I. N. Stokes, *Iconography,* 1071; James Robertson to Abijah Willard, October 16, 1777, in Clinton Papers, CL.

65. Robertson, Proclamation of Civil Government, April 15, 1780, AAS.

66. James Robertson to William Knox, March 26, 1780, in Klein and Howard, *Twilight,* 83.

67. *New-York Gazette and Weekly Mercury*, May 15, 1780; James Robertson to Chamber of Commerce, May 11, 1780, in Klein and Howard, *Twilight,* 109.

68. *New-York Gazette and Weekly Mercury*, June 5, 1780; *Royal Gazette*, July 12 and August 12, 1780.

69. Gruber, "Britain's Southern Strategy," 218–19.

70. Willcox, *Portrait of a General*, 76; Gruber, "Britain's Southern Strategy," 213.

71. Gruber, "Britain's Southern Strategy," 221–23, 214, 227; Willcox, "British Road to Yorktown," 6.

72. Quoted in Klein and Howard, *Twilight*, 55; James Robertson to George Germain, May 18, 1780, in Klein and Howard, *Twilight*, 112; Sir James Robertson to Admiral Arbuthnot, May 30, 1780, in Klein and Howard, *Twilight*, 116; Sir James Robertson to Sir Henry Clinton, May 29, 1780, in Klein and Howard, *Twilight*, 113.

73. *Royal Gazette*, April 15, 1780; Sir James Robertson to Sir Henry Clinton, March 29, 1780, in Klein and Howard, *Twilight*, 88, 90; James Robertson to Lord Amherst, December 27, 1781, in Klein and Howard, *Twilight*, 234.

74. William Smith Jr., May 25, 1780, in "Notes whether any part of New York should be declared at peace," Smith Papers, Box 2, Lot 194 (3), NYPL.

75. The last New York Provincial Assembly comprised thirty-one members. See Klein and Howard, *Twilight*, 94n; Acton, "Diary," cv.

76. James Robertson to Lord Amherst, July 1, 1780, reporting Clinton's decision, in Klein and Howard, *Twilight*, 131.

77. Acton, "Diary," cx.

78. Sir Henry Clinton, Miscellaneous Letterbook, November 10, 1790, in Clinton Papers, CL; Acton, "Diary," cx.

79. Sir Henry Clinton, Memo, Miscellaneous Letterbook, quoted in Acton, "Diary," cxxxii.

80. Ibid.

81. Quoted in Acton, "Diary," cv. Also see Klein and Howard, *Twilight*, 54 55, 134, 149; and Lord George Germain to Sir Henry Clinton, August 3, 1780, in Clinton Papers, CL.

82. Klein and Howard, *Twilight*, 57, 123n; James Robertson to George Germain, July 1, 1780, in Klein and Howard, *Twilight*, 127; James Robertson to Jeffery Amherst, July 1, 1780, in Klein and Howard, *Twilight*, 131; James Robertson to Sir Henry Clinton, June 25, 1780, in Klein and Howard, *Twilight*, 122; James Robertson to Sir Henry Clinton, June 27, 1780, in Clinton Papers, CL.

83. James Robertson to George Germain, July 1, 1780, quoted in Davies, "The Restoration of Civil Government," 129.

84. James Robertson to William Eden, September 22, 1780, in Klein and Howard, *Twilight*, 154.

85. William Smith Jr., March 21, 1780, in Sabine, *Historical Memoirs, 1778 to 1783*, 242; Erwin C. Surrency, "The Courts in the American Colonies," 274.

86. "Observations on the Instructions Relative to Direlict Lands & Houses," November 25, 1783, in Carleton Papers (PRO 30/55/87), NA.

87. *Royal Gazette*, April 15, 1780. Ludlow had expected appointment as chief justice of the Supreme Court of New York. The post had gone to William Smith Jr. James Robertson to Judge Ludlow, July 7, 1780, in *Twilight*, 135; see also *Twilight*, 136n, 137n. Ludlow would "determine differences, prevent frauds, or punish them, by committing to prison, or turning out of our lines, those who are disobedient to Order" (James Robertson to George Germain, September 1, 780, in Klein and Howard, *Twilight*, 146).

88. Klein and Howard, *Twilight*, 137n, 53; Sir Henry Clinton to William Eden, July

3, 1779, in Johnston, *Storming of Stony Point,* 122; Willcox, *Portrait of a General,* x–xvi; Willcox, *American Rebellion,* xii, xvi; William Smith Jr., May 25, 1780, Smith Papers, Box 2, NYPL.

89. Memorial to Clinton, December 25, 1781, Carleton Papers, NA; Hannah Watson, December 21, 1781, in Carleton Papers, NA; Hannah Watson, January 22, 1782, in Clinton Papers, CL; Abraham Seller memorial(mentions 366 names), January 17, 1782, in Carleton Papers, NA; William Smith Jr., December 18, 1779, in Acton, "Diary," 325.

90. Sir Henry Clinton to George Germain, July 28, 1778, in Clinton Papers, vol. 255, CL.

91. "Instructions for the Inspector of Refugees," from Sir Henry Clinton to Colonel Roger Morris, undated [1782], in Carleton Papers, NA.

92. Mary Donnelly, 1780, in Carleton Papers, DLAR; George Defendorf, May 14, 1781, in Carleton Papers, NA; Mary Price, July 1779, in Carleton Papers, DLAR.

93. John Harlock, May 23, 1782, in Carleton Papers, NA.

94. John Hitchcock, December 28, 1780, in Carleton Papers, DLAR; Samuel Jarvis, a loyalist from Stamford, Connecticut, February 7, 1780, in Carleton Papers, DLAR; Isaac Yurex, March 26, 1782, in Carleton Papers, NA.

95. Ariel Ketchum, March 10, 1782, in Carleton Papers, NA; Patience Johnston, June 11, 1782, in Carleton Papers, NA; Jane Isabella Winslow, July 22 1782, in Carleton Papers, NA.

96. Sophia Terrell, December 1782, in Carleton Papers, NA.

97. Gilje, "Republican Rioting," 217.

98. Cray, *Paupers and Poor Relief,* 70; Early American Database, "A Guide to the Vestry," #5960. In 1747, the vestrymen of Manhattan issued a pamphlet designed "to show the duty and power of the vestrymen of the City of New York."

99. Wallace Brown, *The King's Friends,* 104. Morris was born in 1727 and lived until 1794. See Tilton, *Roger Morris, Jumel Mansion,* DLAR.

100. Quoted in Tiedemann, *Reluctant Revolutionaries,* 148.

101. Council Minutes, December 20, 1781, in Clinton Papers, CL; William Smith Jr., February 17, 1782, in Sabine, *Historical Memoirs, 1778 to 1783,* 484; Oliver DeLancey to William Franklin, February 21, 1782, in Clinton Papers, CL.

102. William Smith Jr., April 23, 1782, in Sabine, *Historical Memoirs, 1778 to 1783,* 498.

103. John Cook, Dutchess County, September 1783, in Carleton Papers, NA; Samuel Hake to Sir Guy Carleton, October 18, 1782, in Carleton Papers, NA; William Smith Jr., October 24, 1781 and December 20, 1781, in Sabine, *Historical Memoirs, 1778 to 1783,* 460, 470; Samuel Hake to General Henry Clinton, February 15, 1782, quoted in Wallace Brown, *The King's Friends,* 103.

104. Countryman, *A People in Revolution,* 113; Countryman, "Uses of Capital," 13–14; *New-York Gazette and Weekly Mercury,* August 5, 1777; New York Act of Attainder, or Confiscation Act, 1779.

## 8. "Look Yo Tory Crew"

1. *New-York Gazette and Weekly Mercury,* October 1, 1781.

2. Ewald Gustav Schaukirk, September 27, 1781, in Schaukirk, *Occupation,* 22.

3. *New-York Gazette and Weekly Mercury,* October 1 and October 8, 1781; *Royal Gazette,* October 6, 1781; Wallace Brown, *Good Americans,* 165.

NOTES TO PAGES 189–195    263

4. *Royal Gazette,* October 3 and October 13, 1781; *New-York Gazette and Weekly Mercury,* October 15, 1781; *Royal Gazette,* October 31, 1781; Frederick Mackenzie, September 15 and September 13, 1781, in Mackenzie, *Diary,* 2:633, 630.

5. Lord Charles Cornwallis to Lord Rawdon, January 25 and January 29, 1781; Rankin, "Charles Lord Cornwallis," 210.

6. Grainger, *Battle of Yorktown,* 16; Gruber, "Britain's Southern Strategy," 212; Evans, "View of Cornwallis's Surrender," 28–29.

7. Frey, *Water from the Rock,* 88.

8. Grainger, *Battle of Yorktown,* 16; Frey, *Water from the Rock,* 102, 141.

9. Gruber, "Britain's Southern Strategy," 229; Sir Henry Clinton to Major Patrick Ferguson, May 22, 1780, quoted in Willcox, *American Rebellion,* 441.

10. Gruber, "Britain's Southern Strategy," 232–33.

11. Willcox, "Rhode Island," 317; Mackesy, *War for America,* 345.

12. Willcox, "Rhode Island," 317; Grainger, *Battle of Yorktown,* 15–16.

13. Willcox, "Rhode Island," 306–7.

14. Ibid., 304, 329. General Charles Cornwallis to General Henry Clinton, September 23, 1781, quoted in Willcox, "Road to Yorktown," 29.

15. Sir Henry Clinton, memorandum, September 17, 1781, in Clinton Papers, CL; Schecter, *Battle for New York,* 359.

16. These troops were in New York, Charleston, Savannah, Halifax, and St. Augustine. Mackesy, *War for America,* 435; Klein and Howard, *Twilight,* 128n, 172n, 174n; Black, *Britain as a Military Power,* 169; Grainger, *Battle of Yorktown,* 18–19.

17. Frederick Mackenzie, January 7, 1781, in Mackenzie, *Diary,* 2:447; William Smith Jr., January 6, 1781, in Sabine, *Historical Memoirs, 1778 to 1783,* 374.

18. *Royal Gazette,* October 24, November 21, December 1, and December 22, 1781, and January 16, 1782.

19. *Royal Gazette,* November 24 and December 19, 1781; William H. Nelson, *American Tory,* 151.

20. James, *Silas Deane,* 98, 119; *Royal Gazette,* May 20, 1778. After seven years in exile, Silas Deane died on September 23, 1789, aboard a Boston packet bound for Connecticut.

21. *Royal Gazette,* March 20, 1782, November 3 and December 8, 1781, and January 2, 1782.

22. Hugh Gaine, October 27, 1781, in Ford, *Journals,* 2:135; Hugh Gaine, November 5, 1781, in Ford, *Journals,* 2:136; Hugh Gaine, March 5, 1782, in Ford, *Journals,* 2:144; Hugh Gaine, April 11, 1782, in Ford, *Journals,* 2:147.

23. Willcox, *American Rebellion,* 352n; Rankin, "Charles Lord Cornwallis," 222.

24. Lieutenant Colonel Alured Clarke to Sir Henry Clinton, December 20, 1781, in Willcox, *American Rebellion,* 591.

25. Lieutenant General Alexander Leslie to Sir Henry Clinton, January 29, 1782, in Willcox, *American Rebellion,* 594.

26. Joshua Upham to William Franklin, November 3, 1781, quoted in Tebbenhoff, "The Associated Loyalists," 141.

27. Sir Henry Clinton to William Eden, September 1, 1780, in Willcox, *American Rebellion,* 352.

28. William Smith Jr., reporting on George Germain's instructions to Sir Henry Clinton, March 11, 1782, in I. N. Stokes, *Iconography,* 1144.

29. Sir Henry Clinton to George Germain, March 14, 1782, in Willcox, *American Rebellion*, 597.

30. Willcox, *American Rebellion*, 353.

31. William Franklin to Sir Henry Clinton, November 12; 1781, in Clinton Papers, CL; William Smith Jr., November 8, 1781, in Sabine, *Historical Memoirs, 1778 to 1783*, 463.

32. Eldon Lewis Jones, "Sir Guy Carleton," 85; Ryan, *New Jersey's Loyalists*, 16–17.

33. Willcox, *American Rebellion*, 361; Eldon Lewis Jones, "Sir Guy Carleton," 16–17.

34. Board Minutes, May 2, 1782, quoted in Tebbenhoff, "The Associated Loyalists," 142; Skemp, *William Franklin*, 273, 265; Hugh Gaine, May 1, 1782, in Ford, *Journals*, 2:148.

35. Hugh Gaine, June 19, 1782, in Ford, *Journals*, 2:152.

36. *New-York Gazette and Weekly Mercury*, May 6, 1782.

37. Intelligence to Carleton by J. Michaeles, October 4, 1783, in Carleton Papers, NA.

38. Willcox, *Portrait of a General*, 444–50.

39. Eldon Lewis Jones, "Sir Guy Carleton," 12.

40. *Royal Gazette*, May 22, 1782; William Smith Jr., May 27, 1782, in I. N. Stokes, *Iconography*, 1147.

41. Paul H. Smith, "Sir Guy Carleton, Peace Negotiations," 253.

42. *New-York Gazette and Weekly Mercury*, May 27 and June 3, 1782.

43. Beverly Robinson to Sir Henry Clinton, August 8, 1782, quoted in Ernst, "A Tory-Eye View of the Evacuation," 379–80.

44. Barrak Hays to Sir Henry Clinton, July 6, 1780, in Clinton Papers, CL; *Royal Gazette*, August 7, 1782; Brown and Senior, *Victorious in Defeat*, 31; Moore, *The Loyalists*, 107.

45. Alexander Leslie to Sir Guy Carleton, November 18, 1782, quoted in Ritcheson, "Loyalist Influence on British Policy," 12; Alexander Leslie to Sir Henry Clinton, October 18, 1782, quoted in Wilson, *The Loyal Blacks*, 46.

46. Ernst, "A Tory-Eye View of the Evacuation," 393; Brown and Senior, *Victorious in Defeat*, 32.

47. Hugh Gaine records that Carleton announced the independence of America on August 3, 1782, in Ford, *Journals*, 2:155. British officer to friend in Cork, October 24, 1782, in I. N. Stokes, *Iconography*, 1154; New York officer, letter to London, August 9, 1782, in *Iconography*, 1151; Hugh Gaine, August 26 and September 10, 1782, in Ford, *Journals*, 2:156, 157; Eldon Lewis Jones, "Sir Guy Carleton," 227–28.

48. Spaulding, *New York in the Critical Period*, 122; *New York Packet*, August 29, 1782.

49. New Yorker to a friend in London, September 10, 1782, in I. N. Stokes, *Iconography*, 1152; Thomas Ward to Sir Guy Carleton, May 21, 1782, in Clinton Papers, CL; "Number of men in each Company of Loyal Refugees," September 5, 1782, in Clinton Papers, CL.

50. *New-York Gazette and Weekly Mercury*, August 7, 1782.

51. *Royal Gazette*, November 2, 1782.

52. Andrew Elliot to Sir Henry Clinton, November 17, 1782, in Clinton Papers, CL; Brown and Senior, *Victorious in Defeat*, 28; Frey, *Water from the Rock*, 174.

53. *Royal Gazette*, November 27 and November 30, 1782.

54. Brown and Senior, *Victorious in Defeat*, 31; Moore, *The Loyalists*, 107; Skemp, *William Franklin*, 264, 268; Mary Beth Norton, *British-Americans*, 173.

55. William Franklin to Sir Henry Clinton, January 15, 1782, in Clinton Papers, CL; William Franklin, *Royal Gazette*, December 21, 1782. In response to the loyalists' persistent efforts, Parliament appointed a five-member commission to examine refugee claims on a case-by-case basis. If the refugees could demonstrate that the property losses they had suffered resulted directly because of their allegiance to the Crown, the commission would review their cases and provide restitution.

56. "Proposition for Peace between Great Britain and the Colonies on the most certain and last foundation to Guy Carleton," signed WB, October 17 1782, in Carleton Papers, NA.

57. *Royal Gazette*, January 5, 1783.

58. Ibid.

59. Lord Shelburne to Sir Guy Carleton, April 4, 1782, quoted in Paul H. Smith, "Guy Carleton, Peace Negotiations," 255; Paul H. Smith, "Sir Guy Carleton, Peace Negotiations," 247–48.

60. Grainger, *Battle of Yorktown*, 8; Paul David Nelson, "British Conduct during the Revolutionary War," 624; Mackesy, *War for America*, 370.

61. Grainger, *Battle of Yorktown*, 185

62. Wright, "The British Objectives, 1780–1783," 9–10.

63. George III to Lord North, June 11, 1779, in Johnston, *Storming of Stony Point*, 106.

64. George III, Address, November 27, 1781, quoted in Russell, *American Revolution*, 302.

65. Wright, "The British Objectives," 11.

66. Quoted in Wrong, *Canada and the American Revolution*, 339.

67. Mackesy, *War for America*, 461.

68. Guttridge, "Lord George Germain," 42–43; Charles Stuart, "Lord Shelburne," 243.

69. H. M. Scott, *British Foreign Policy*, 324–28.

70. Quoted in Stuart, "Lord Shelburne," 245; Wright, "The British Objectives," 12; Charles Ritcheson, "The Earl of Shelburne," 322–45.

71. Richard Oswald, mid-1782, quoted in Wright, "The British Objectives," 15.

72. Quoted in Ritcheson, "Britain's Peacemakers," 81.

73. H. M. Scott, *British Foreign Policy*, 328–29; Ritcheson, "Britain's Peacemakers," 82.

74. Mary Beth Norton, *British-Americans*, 174.

75. Mackesy, *War for America*, 472–75.

76. Wrong, *Canada and the American Revolution*, 367; Norris, *Shelburne and Reform*, 342, 258–60; Ritcheson, "Britain's Peacemakers," 93.

77. Richard Oswald to Lord Shelburne, July 10, 1782, in Giunta, *Documents of the Emerging Nation*, 90.

78. Ritcheson, "Loyalist Influence," 2–3. When Charles Inglis, in 1776, accused Paine of "cutting off a leg because the toe happened to ache," he saw the rebels as the toe. Seven years later, Lord Shelburne came to regard the loyalists as the toe. See Inglis, "The True Interest," 157.

79. Hutson, "The Treaty of Paris," 11; Barber and Voss, *Blessed Are the Peacemakers*,

13; Wright, "The British Objectives," 26; Norris, *Shelburne and Reform,* 257–58; Wrong, *Canada and the American Revolution,* 357.

80. Pomerantz, *New York,* 78.

81. In November 1782, Henry Strachey explained, "My idea was and is that the Resolution of Congress to the different States concerning the Restitution of Property will be equivalent to a message from the King to Parliament and that it is not probable any refusal will be given except to a very few who are difficulties" (quoted in Ritcheson, "Britain's Peacemakers," 97).

82. Wright, "The British Objectives," 23.

83. Talman, *Loyalist Narratives,* xxxvii; Wright, "The British Objectives," 14–15, 23. However, Christopher Moore suggests that, for British readers, "it was possible to imagine that a Congressional 'recommendation' to the states would be binding in the same way that parliamentary 'advice' bound the British king. But in America, the clause was meaningless" (Moore, *The Loyalists,* 110). See also Ward, *War for Independence,* 48.

84. Egerton, *Royal Commission of the Losses,* xxxii.

85. Brown and Senior, *Victorious in Defeat,* 72; Moore, *The Loyalists,* 119; Bradley, *United Empire Loyalists,* 119. Wynn states that nine thousand people resided in the colony in 1763. See Wynn, "On the Margins of Empire," 189.

86. Brook Watson to Johsua Mauger, April 14 and June 17, 1783, in Mauger Papers, GLS. On September 28, 1783, William Smith Jr. commented on the "folly of the American committees who have opposed the closing with Great Britain and given her a powerful colony of loyalists in Nova Scotia" (in Sabine, *Historical Memoirs, 1778 to 1783,* 606).

87. Quoted in Clifford, *From Slavery to Freetown,* 34.

88. Wilson, *The Loyal Blacks,* 48.

89. Clifford, *From Slavery to Freetown,* 34; Wilson, *The Loyal Blacks,* 48.

90. *The Loyal Blacks,* 48.

91. George Washington to Commissioner Daniel Parker in New York City, April 28, 1783, quoted in Hodges, *The Black Loyalist Directory,* xvii; King quoted in Clifford, *From Slavery to Freetown,* 33–35.

92. Lord North to Sir Guy Carleton, August 8, 1783, quoted in Wilson, *The Loyal Blacks,* 56. Also see Wilson, *The Loyal Blacks,* 34; and *Royal Gazette,* April 26, 1783.

93. Sir Guy Carleton to George Washington, May 12, 1783, in Carleton Papers, NA.

94. Hodges, *Black Loyalist Directory,* 831; Clifford, *From Slavery to Freetown,* 37, 49.

95. John Wentworth, February 24, 1784, quoted in Walker, *The Black Loyalists,* 41; Grant, "Black Immigrants," 256n.

96. *Royal Gazette,* November 16, 1782, January 15, 1783, and November 2, 1782.

97. *Royal Gazette,* November 16 and December 14, 1782.

98. Memorial by American Loyalists, presented by Samuel Hake and Mr. Lydekker, December 18, 1782, in Carleton Papers, NA. Five hundred of the two thousand who had petitioned with Hake in 1781 requested provisions for Nova Scotia in 1783. See John Cook, Dutchess County, September 1783, in Carleton Papers, NA; *Royal Gazette,* December 11, 1782.

99. New Yorker to a friend in London, April 6, 1783, in I. N. Stokes, *Iconography,* 1158. The scarcity of ships may have been another reason loyalists waited until April 1783 to leave the city.

100. James Robertson to Andrew Elliot, April 14, 1783, in Carleton Papers, NA.

101. Sir Guy Carleton to Governor George Clinton, May 13, 1783, in Carleton Papers, NA.

102. Mushkat, *George Clinton,* 14–18.

103. Young, *The Democratic Republicans,* 67; Hastings, *Public Papers of George Clinton,* 99; Ward, *War for Independence,* 38. But by persecuting loyalists using committees, Governor George Clinton diminished the likelihood of mob behavior, which had earlier resulted in tarring and feathering, rail-riding, and destruction and theft of loyalist property.

104. Quoted in Kaminski, *George Clinton,* 77. Also see Spaulding, *New York in the Critical Period,* 115–21; and Kaminski, *George Clinton,* 78–81.

105. Jerome Gillen, "Political Thought," 185.

106. Quoted in Kaminski, *George Clinton,* 80; Spaulding, *New York in the Critical Period,* 130.

107. "Names of Persons who are forced to seek asylum in Nova Scotia by the unhappy termination of the war," July 22, 1783, in Carleton Papers, NA.

108. Philip J. Livingston, May 10, 1783, in Carleton Papers, NA.

109. New York gentleman to friend in London, October 2, 1782, in I. N. Stokes, *Iconography,* 1153.

110. John Pellet, recorded by William Smith Jr., September 15, 1783, in Carleton Papers, NA.

111. "Petition from Officers commanding His Majesty's Provincial Regiments," March 4, 1783, in Carleton Papers, NA. The fourteen signatories were B. Thompson, Thomas Menzies, Edward Winslow, Hale, Gabriel Ludlow, Beverly Robinson, Stephen DeLancey, John H. Cruger, Abraham Van Buskirk, George Turnbull, William Allen, Beverly Robmond Jr., James Chalmers, and Isaac Allen.

112. Officers of Provincial Line, March 15, 1783, in Carleton Papers, NA; Bradley, *United Empire Loyalists,* 119; Moore, *The Loyalists,* 123.

113. Black Pioneers, October 25 to December 24, 1782, in Carleton Papers, NA; Brook Watson to Major Frederick Mackenzie, October 19, 1783, in Carleton Papers, NA.

114. Information by David Bonnet, recorded by William Smith Jr., September 13, 1783, in Carleton Papers, NA; information by Joshua Booth, recorded by William Smith Jr., October 30, 1783, in Carleton Papers, NA.

115. Lieutenant Samuel Jarvis to Sir Guy Carleton, June 15, 1783, in Carleton Papers, NA.

116. Information by Samuel Knowles, recorded by William Smith Jr., November 19, 1783, in Carleton Papers, NA.

117. Joseph Stansbury to John Andre, August or September 1779, in Clinton Papers, CL.

118. Joseph Stansbury deposition and petition, July 10 and August 6, 1783, both in Carleton Papers, NA; Secret Services of Joseph Stansbury, August 23, 1782, in Carleton Papers, NA. Stansbury was paid £28.9.4 for services between May 1 and June 1782; Stansbury received British assistance from January 1781. General Clinton's certificate reads: "That on his arrival in New York, from imprisonment, in January 1781, with a wife and large family of Children, I ordered him Quarters, Rations, & a Stipend of two

Dollars per day in consideration of his Loyalty & Services" (Clinton Papers, undated, vol. 231, CL).

119. Joseph Stansbury, July 10, 1783, in Carleton Papers, NA.

120. Joseph Stansbury, August 6, 1783, in Carleton Papers, NA.

121. William Terrill, October 23, 1783, in Carleton Papers, NA.

122. Quoted in Kaminski, *George Clinton*, 79.

123. Major Frederick Mackenzie, Commandant's Office, September 19, 1783, in Carleton Papers, NA.

124. His Excellency Sir Guy Carleton's Orders, May 11, 1783, in Carleton Papers, NA.

125. His Excellency Sir Guy Carleton's Orders, July 18 and July 22, 1783, in Carleton Papers, NA.

126. Board of Commissioners for Adjusting Matters, Debt Accounts, August 1, 1783, in Carleton Papers, NA.

127. Judith Jackson, September 18, 1783, in Carleton Papers, NA; answer to Judith Jackson, September 20, 1783, in Carleton Papers, NA; Clifford, *From Slavery to Freetown*, 38, 49.

128. Peggy Gwym, a Negro woman formerly of Virginia, November 19, 1783, in Carleton Papers, NA.

129. John Steel to Sir Guy Carleton, March 5, 1783, in Carleton Papers, NA.

130. Sir Guy Carleton to Admiral Robert Digby, April 22, 1783, and his reply, in Carleton Papers, NA.

131. Oliver DeLancey, May 20, 1783, in Carleton Papers, NA.

132. Memorial from West Chester County, residing between the lines, undated, in Carleton Papers, NA.

133. Peter John, January 9, 1782, in Carleton Papers, NA; Rubin Coddington, February 17, 1782, in Carleton Papers, NA.

134. Ralph Maenair, May 27, 1782, in Carleton Papers, NA.

135. Information on Charles Traver, recorded by William Smith Jr., October 13, 1783, in Carleton Papers, NA.

136. List of Inhabitants in Albany & Tryon County, undated, in Carleton Papers, NA. Robert Bruce and Samuel Bagnall signed on behalf of themselves and other inhabitants of Albany.

137. *Royal Gazette*, November 3, November 7, December 8, and December 29, 1781.

138. Ibid., June 18, 1783, May 1, 1782, and May 14, 1783.

139. Ibid., June 25, August 16, and September 17, 1783.

140. Andrew Elliot to Morris Morgann, April 9, 1783, in Carleton Papers, NA.

141. Peter Paumier to Morris Morgann, October 1, 1782. In October 1782, Paumier complained of the insults he received from those clamouring for their just demands (Carmer's Petition, March 1, 1783, and Memorial to Board of General Officers, January 10, 1783, in Carleton Papers, NA).

142. Petition of Herlitz and Blackwell of the City of New York, undated, in Carleton Papers, NA.

143. Board of General Officers, January 10, 1783, in Carleton Papers, NA.

144. Anthony Woodward and John Leonard, April 17, 1783, in Carleton Papers, NA.

145. Claims made to the police, February 18, 1783, in Carleton Papers, NA.

146. Petition from proprietors of houses, stores, lots and other property, May 6, 1783, signed by Peter Clopper, Corn. Bogert, Wm. Lowther, and Wm. Deaplaine, in Carleton Papers, NA.

147. Charles Roubalet, November 4, 1783, in Carleton Papers, NA.

148. Jacob Leroy, July 3, 1783, in Carleton Papers, NA. Leroy pointed to the British proclamation of February 1783, which made persons occupying estates answerable to any damage.

149. Andrew Elliot to Morris Morgann, March 17, 1783, in Carleton Papers, NA.

150. Andrew Elliot and David Mathews, March 10, 1783, in Carleton Papers, NA. Almost five years earlier, Elliot had noted the difficulty of granting some claims over others: "Merchants and people in all lines will pursue either interest or friendship when the point can be carried by solicitations" (Andrew Elliot to General William Howe, January 1, 1778, in Carleton Papers, DLAR).

151. See Representation to Carleton, August 2, 1783, in Carleton Papers, NA.

152. Israel Putnam Proclamation, November 16, 1777, in Clinton Papers, CL; Taeffe, *Philadelphia Campaign*, 28.

153. Frederick Mackenzie, November 11, 1776, in Mackenzie, *Diary*, 1:102.

154. John Peebles, October 27, 1776, in Gruber, *John Peebles' American War*, 59.

155. Reply by Hessian corps encamp'd at Kingsbridge, November or December 1777, in Clinton Papers, CL.

156. William Tryon to Sir Henry Clinton, November 30, 1777, in Clinton Papers, CL.

157. Reply by Hessian corps encamp'd at Kingsbridge, November or December 1777, in Clinton Papers, CL.

158. Reply to Putnam's Proclamation of November 16 and December 8, 1777, in Clinton Papers, CL.

159. Reply by Hessian corps encamp'd at Kingsbridge, November or December 1777, in Clinton Papers, CL.

160. Report from Provost, May 12, 1783, in Carleton Papers, NA; State of the Provost, May 26 and August 4, 1783, in Carleton Papers, NA; War Office Papers, August 21, 1783, War Office Records (WO 28/9), NA. The three accused were J. Bennet, George Miller, and J. Van Pelt (State of the Provost, September 1 and November 3, 1783, in Carleton Papers, NA).

161. General John Burgoyne to General William Howe, October 20, 1777, in Carleton Papers, DLAR; His Excellency Sir Guy Carleton's Orders, May 14, 1783, in Carleton Papers, NA; Description of Carl Broiske, May 28, 1783, in War Office Records (WO 28/9), NA.

162. Alfred F. Young asserts that for every loyalist who left, two remained. See Young, *The Democratic Republicans*, 66.

163. Smyth quoted in Spaulding, *New York in the Critical Period*, 125; Lorenz, *Hugh Gaine*, 133–35.

164. Schwind, "Ceramic Imports," 21–36; Ryan, *New Jersey's Loyalists*, 24. Ryan names New Jersey merchant Andrew Bell as another example.

165. *Royal Gazette*, August 30, 1783; Rhinelander quoted in Schwind, "Ceramic Imports," 35.

166. *New York Packet*, February 27, 1783. Both Rivington and Gaine were indicted for "adhering to the enemies of the state" (Cullen, "Talking to a Whirlwind," 683).

167. William Smith Jr., December 10, 1781, in Sabine, *Historical Memoirs, 1778 to 1783*, 469; William Smith Jr., September 10, 1782, in I. N. Stokes, *Iconography*, 1152; William Smith Jr., April 22, May 24, and July 15, 1783, in Sabine, *Historical Memoirs, 1778 to 1783*, 583, 588, 597.

168. William Smith Jr., August 23, September 3, October 15, October 25, and November 13, 1783, in Sabine, *Historical Memoirs, 1778 to 1783*, 601, 602, 609–10, 612. His wife, Janet, stayed in New York City as his lawful attorney to watch over his considerable assets.

169. *New-York Gazette and Weekly Mercury*, September 15, 1783; Polf, *Garrison Town*, 54. On December 5, accompanied by the last British troops and a contingent of faithful loyalists, Carleton sailed for England. (Notice in the War Office Papers, November 20, 1783, in War Office Records [WO 28/9], NA). Just three days prior to the final evacuation, the British cautioned New Yorkers not to appear in the streets after 8:00 p.m. without lanterns. To the end, they wanted to preserve "good order, peace and regularity" in the garrison. See Proclamation, November 20, 1783, War Office Records (WO 28/9), NA.

## Conclusion

1. This question of loyalist motivation remained unresolved during the years of the rebellion. See Brigadier General John Campbell to General William Howe, November 7, 1777, in Carleton Papers, DLAR. In this note to Howe about a refugee with five young children, Campbell insists that her husband's attachment did not proceed "from selfish views (his property being large ample & extensive) but totally from his loyalty and principles."

2. William Smith Jr. [unsigned] to Mr. Eden from Bowery, New York, November 2, 1778, in Carleton Papers, DLAR.

3. Quoted in Tebbenhoff, "Associated Loyalists," 468.

4. Nancy Jean Cameron to Margaret MacPherson, May 15, 1785, Library and Archives Canada; Brook Watson to Joshua Mauger, July 1783, in Mauger Papers, GLS. Watson wrote that the Nova Scotia loyalists "will form a barrier against those of opposite principle, and become the envy of all their Neighbors."

# BIBLIOGRAPHY

## Archival Collections

*American Antiquarian Society (Worcester, MA)*
U.S. Revolution Collection

NEWSPAPERS

*The New-York Gazette and Weekly Mercury*
The Royal American Gazette
The Royal Gazette
The New-York Mercury; or General Advertiser

BROADSIDES

Adye, Stephen Payne. A Treatise on Courts Martial containing I. Remarks on Martial Law, and Court Martial in general and II. The manner of Proceeding against Offenders, to which is added An Essay on Military Punishments and Rewards. 1769.

The Alarm, or a Plan of Pacification with America, signed Cassandra. 1781.

Board of Associated Loyalists. A Declaration. 1780.

Letters of Papinian in which the Conduct, Present State and Prospects of the American Congress are examined. 1779.

Low, Isaac. To all Gallant Seamen. 1780.

*The New York Freeholder.* Vols. 1–7. 1781.

Robertson, James. Proclamation of Civil Government. April 15, 1780.

Ross, Robert. A Sermon in which the Union of the Colonies is Considered and Recommended; and the Bad Consequences of Divions are Represented delivered on the public thanksgiving. November 16, 1775.

ALMANACS

*Gaine's Universal Register, or American and British Kalendar.* 1777–1782.

Mills and Hicks's British and American Register, with an Almanac for 1779.

New York's Pocket Almanack for the year 1778.

*City Museum of New York (New York, NY)*
Floyd Papers. 1777.
Munro, Dr. Reverend Henry. Letter. 1777.
Suffolk County Address to General William Howe. October 1776.

*Clements Library (Ann Arbor, MI)*
Addison, Henry. Papers.
Adlum, John. Papers.
Asteroth, Valentin. Diary. Translated by Bruce E. Burgoyne (1989).
Cliffe, Loftus. Papers.
Clinton, Henry. Papers. 1776–1783.
Coote, Eyre. Orderly Books.
Gerland, Otto. *Diary of Hessian Chaplain In the American War.* Translated by
    Bruce E. Burgoyne.
Germain, George. Papers.
Great Britain Army. Regimental Orderly Book.
Howe, General Sir William. Orderly Book.
*Journal of Lieutenant Rueffer of Milsungen, 1 March 1776 to 28 December 1777.* Translated
    by Bruce E. Burgoyne.
*Journal of the Years 1776 to 1784 from J.R. (Hesse-Cassel Leib Regiment).* Translated by
    Bruce E. Burgoyne.
King's American Regimental Army Book.
Mackenzie, Frederick. Papers.
*Order Book of the von Mirbach Regiment, from 19th March, 1777 to 28th June 1780.* Trans-
    lated by Bruce E. Burgoyne. Lidgerwood Collection.
Piel, Jakob. *Diary of the Hessian Lieutenant (Jakob) Piel from 1776–1783.* Translated by
    Bruce E. Burgoyne (1986).
*Platte Grenadier Battalion Journal which sailed to America as the Koehler Grenadier bat-
    talion was later called the Graf Grenadier Battalion and finally the Platte Grenadier
    Battalion.* Translated by Bruce E. Burgoyne.
Reuber, Johannes. Diary.
Simcoe, John. Papers.
Steuernagel, Carl Philipp. *Kurze Beschreibung or A Brief Description (1776–1783).*
    Translated by Bruce E. Burgoyne (1982).
Von Feilitzsch, Lieutenant Heinrich Carl Philipp. *Diary, 1777–1778.* Translated by
    Bruce E. Burgoyne.
Waldeck, Johann Philipp Franz. *Diary of Johann Philipp Franz Waldeck, Field Chap-
    lain in the Prince of Waldeck's 3rd Regiment then in the service of Great Britain in
    America.* Translated by Bruce E. Burgoyne (1983).

*David Library of the American Revolution (Washington Crossing, PA)*
Auckland Papers. Microfilm.

Carleton, Sir Guy. Papers. (Also referred to as British Headquarters Papers.) Microfilm.

Dartmouth Papers. Microfilm.

DeLancey, Oliver. Orderly Books. Microfilm.

Great Britain Audit Office. Records of the American Loyalist Claims Commission, 1776–1783. Microfilm.

Tilton, John Kent. *Roger Morris, Jumel Mansion*. Pamphlet. Call no. 1236p. Undated.

Winslow, Edward. Papers. Microfilm.

*Gilder Lehrman Society*

Mauger, Joshua. Papers.

*Library and Archives Canada (Ottawa)*

Nancy Jean Cameron to Margaret MacPherson, May 15, 1785. MG23–HII19, R3682-0-5–E.

*National Archives (Kew, UK)*

Carleton, Sir Guy. Papers.

Treasury Board Papers (T1 Series).

War Office Records (WO28 and WO71 series).

*New York Historical Society (New York, NY)*

Buchanan, Thomas. Diary. 1780.

Livingston, R. R. Papers.

Proclamation of the Forfeiture of Property of Loyalists with list of names. Box 13.

Royal Theatre. Attendance and payments. 1779.

Smyth, John. Papers.

*New York Public Library (New York, NY)*

Balch Papers. Bancroft Collection.

Loyalist Transcripts.

Smith, William, Jr. Papers.

*New York State Library (Albany, NY)*

Elliot, Andrew. Papers.

## Published Primary Sources

Acton, Arthur James, ed. "The Diary of William Smith, August 26, 1778, to December 31, 1779." PhD diss., University of Michigan, 1970.

Adair, Douglass, and John A. Schutz, eds. *Peter Oliver's Origin and Progress of the American Rebellion: A Tory View*. San Marino: Huntington Library, 1961.

Billias, George Athan, ed. *Letters to a Nobleman, on the Conduct of the War in the Middle Colonies*. Boston: Gregg Press, 1972.

Bolton, Charles Knowles, ed. *Letters of Hugh Earl Percy from Boston and New York, 1774–1776*. Boston: Charles E. Godspeed, 1902.

Brown, Gerald Saxon, ed. *Reflections on a Pamphlet Intitled "A Letter to the Right Honble. Lord Vict. H——e."* Ann Arbor: University of Michigan Press, 1959.

Carter, Clarence Edwin, ed. *The Correspondence of General Thomas Gage with the Secretaries of State, and with the War Office and the Treasury.* Vol. 1. Hamden, CT: Archon Press, 1969.

*Collections of the New York Historical Society for the Year 1883.* New York: New York Historical Society, 1883.

Crary, Catherine S., ed. *The Price of Loyalty: Tory Writings from the Revolutionary Era.* New York: McGraw-Hill, 1973.

Davies, K. G., ed. *Documents of the American Revolution.* Vol. 12. Shannon: Irish University Press, 1976.

Dawson, Henry B., ed. *New York City during the American Revolution: Being a Collection of Original Papers from Manuscripts in the Possession of the Mercantile Library Association of New York City.* New York: Alvord, 1861.

De Lancey, Edward Floyd, ed. *History of New York during the Revolutionary War and of the Leading Events in the Other Colonies at That Period by Thomas Jones, Justice of the Supreme Court of the Province.* Vol. 1, part 1. New York: New York Historical Society, 1879.

*The Detail and Conduct of the American War under Generals Gage, Howe, Burgoyne and Vice Admiral Lord Howe with a very full and correct state of the whole of the evidence, as given before a Committee of the House of Commons, and the Celebrated Fugitive Pieces which are said to have given rise to the Important Enquiry.* London, 1780.

Early American Imprints Database. Series 1, Evans (1639–1800). NewsBank, Readex Division. http://www.newsbank.com/readex/product.cfm?product=22.

Egerton, Hugh Edward, ed. *Royal Commission of the Losses and Services of American Loyalists, 1783–1785.* New York: Arno Press, 1969.

Ford, Paul Leicester, ed. *The Journals of Hugh Gaine.* 2 vols. New York: Dodd, Mead & Co., 1902.

Galloway, Joseph. *Historical and Political Reflections on the Rise and Progress of the American Rebellion by Joseph Galloway.* Edited by Merrill Jensen. New York: Johnson Reprint Corporation, 1972.

Gruber Ira D., ed. *John Peebles' American War: The Diary of a Scottish Grenadier, 1776–1782.* Mechanicsburg, PA: Stackpole Books, 1998.

Hastings, Hugh, ed. *Public Papers of George Clinton, First Governor New York.* Vol. 1. New York: Wynkoop Hallenbeck Crawford, 1899.

Howe, William. *Observations upon A Pamphlet, &c.* 1779.

Inglis, Charles. "The True Interest of America Impartially Stated, in Certain Strictures on a Pamphlet Intitled Common Sense." In *Common Sense: Thomas Paine,* edited by Edward Larkin. Toronto: Broadview Editions, 2004.

Jones, E. Alfred. "Letter of David Colden, Loyalist, 1783." *American Historical Review* 25 (1919): 79–86.

Kelby, William, ed. *Orderly Book of the Three Battalions of Loyalists Commanded by Brigadier-General Oliver De Lancey 1776–1778.* . . . New York: New York Historical Society, 1917; reprint, Baltimore: Genealogical Publishing Co., 1972.

Klein, Milton M., and Ronald W. Howard, eds. *The Twilight of British Rule in Revolutionary America: The New York Letter Book of General James Robertson, 1780–1783.* Cooperstown: New York State Association, 1983.

"Letters to Joseph Galloway from Leading Tories in America." *Historical Magazine and Notes and Queries Concerning the Antiquities, History and Biography of America* 5 (September–December 1861).

Lydenberg, Harry Miller, ed. *Archibald Robertson His Diaries and Sketches in America, 1762–1780.* New York: New York Times & Arno Press, 1971.

Mackenzie, Frederick. *Diary of Frederick Mackenzie, Giving a Daily Narrative of His Military Service.* 2 vols. Cambridge, MA: Harvard University Press, 1930.

Macmahon, K. A., ed. *Beverly Corporation Minute Books (1707–1835).* Yorkshire Archaeological Society, Record Series, 122. London: Brown & Sons, 1958.

The New York Act of Attainder, or Confiscation Act, 1779.

O'Callaghan, Edmund B., ed. *Calendar of New York Colonial Commissions, 1680–1770.* New York: New York Historical Society, 1929.

———, ed. *Documents Relative to the Colonial History of the State of New York, Procured in Holland, England and France.* Vol. 8. Albany: Weeds Parson & Co., 1857.

Paine, Thomas. *Common Sense and Other Writings.* Edited by Gordon S. Wood. New York: Modern Library, 2003.

Palmer, Gregory, ed. *A Bibliography of Loyalist Source Material in the United States, Canada, and Great Britain.* Westport, CT: Meckler Publications, 1982.

Pettengill, Ray W., trans. *Letters from America, 1776–1779; Being Letters of Brunswick, Hessian, and Waldeck Officers with the British Armies during the Revolution.* Port Washington, NY: Kennikat Press, 1924; reprint, 1964.

Sabine, William H. W., ed. *Historical Memoirs from 12 July 1776 to 25 July 1778 of William Smith, Historian of the Province of New York, Member of the Governor's Council, and Last Chief Justice of That Province under the Crown; Chief Justice of Quebec.* New York: Colburn and Tugg, 1958.

———, ed. *Historical Memoirs of William Smith, 1778 to 1783.* New York: New York Times and Arno Press, 1971.

Schaukirk, Ewald Gustav. *Occupation of New York by the British.* New York: New York Times and Arno Press, 1969.

Scott, Kenneth, ed. *Rivington's New York Newspaper: Excerpts from a Loyalist Press, 1773–1783.* New York: New York Historical Society, 1973.

Seabury, Rev. Samuel. *Letters of a Westchester Farmer, 1774–1775 / by the Reverend Samuel Seabury, 1729–1796.* Edited by Charles H. Vance. White Plains, NY: Westchester Historical Society, 1930.

Smith, Paul H., ed. *Letters of Delegates to Congress, 1774–1789*. Washington: Library of Congress, 1976.

"Special Legislation Discriminating against Specified Individuals and Groups." *Yale Law Journal* 51 (1942): 1358–71.

Stevens, John A., Jr. *Colonial Records with Historiographical and Biographical Sketches of the New York Chamber of Commerce, 1768–1784*. New York: B. Franklin, 1971.

Stokes, Anthony. *A View of the Constitution of the British Colonies in North-America and the West Indies at the time the Civil War Broke out on the continent of America in which Notice is taken of such alterations as have happened since that Time down to the Present period, 1783*. London: Dawsons, 1969.

Stokes, I. N., ed. *The Iconography of Manhattan Island*. Vol. 5. New York: Arno Press, 1915.

Tatum, Edward H., Jr., ed. *The American Journal of Ambrose Serle, Secretary to Lord Howe, 1776–1778*. San Marino, CA: Huntington Library, 1940.

Truxes, Thomas M., ed. *Letterbook of Greg & Cunningham, 1756–57: Merchants of New York and Belfast*. Oxford: Oxford University Press, 2001.

Upton, L. F. S., ed. *The Diary and Selected Papers of Chief Justice William Smith, 1784–1793*. Vol. 1. Toronto: Chaplain Society, 1963.

Von Muenchhausen, Levin Friedrich Ernst. *At General Howe's Side, 1776–1778*. Edited by Ernst Kipling and Stelle Samuel Smith. Monmouth Beach, NJ: Philip Freneau Press, 1974.

Willcox, William B., ed. *The American Rebellion: Sir Henry Clinton's Narrative of His Campaigns, 1775–1782, With An Appendix of Original Documents*. New Haven, CT: Yale University Press, 1957.

## Secondary Sources

Abbott, Carl. "The Neighborhoods of New York, 1760–1775." *New York History* 55 (January 1974): 35–54.

Alden, John Richard. "Why the March to Concord?" *American Historical Review* 49 (April 1944): 446–54.

American National Biography Online. http://www.anb.org/.

Anderson, Fred. "The Colonial Background to the American Victory." In *The World Turned Upside Down: The American Victory in the War of Independence*, edited by John Ferling. New York: Greenwood Press, 1988.

———. *Crucible of War: The Seven Years' War and the Fate of Empire in British North America*. New York: Alfred Knopf, 2000.

———. "Why Did Colonial New Englanders Make Bad Soldiers? Contractual Principles and Military Conduct during the Seven Years' War." *William and Mary Quarterly* 38 (1981): 395–417.

Anderson, Troye Steele. *The Howe Brothers during the American Revolution*. New York: Octagon Books, 1972.

Ashton, Rick J. "The Loyalist Congressmen of New York." *New York Historical Society Quarterly* 60 (1976): 95–106.

———. "The Loyalist Experience: New York, 1763–1789." PhD diss., Northwestern University, 1973.

Attie, Katherine Bootle. "Re-Membering the Body Politic: Hobbes and the Construction of Civic Immortality." *ELH* 75 (2008): 497–530.

Bailyn, Bernard. *The Ordeal of Thomas Hutchinson*. Cambridge, MA: Harvard University Press, 1974.

Banning, Stephen Thomas. *Military Law*. Aldershot: Gale & Polden, 1943.

Barber, James G., and Frederick S. Voss. *Blessed Are the Peacemakers: A Commemoration of the 200th Anniversary of the Treaty of Paris*. Washington, DC: Smithsonian Institution Press, 1983.

Barck, Oscar Theodore. *New York City during the War for Independence, with Special Reference to the Period of British Occupation*. Port Washington, NY: I. J. Friedman, 1931.

Bauchman, Rosemary. "Charles Inglis, Loyalist." In *Loyalists in Nova Scotia*, edited by Donald Wetmore and Lester B. Sellick. Hantsport, NS: Lancelot Press, 1983.

Becker, Carl L. *The History of Political Parties in the Province of New York, 1760–1776*. Madison: University of Wisconsin Press, 1968.

Benton, William Allen. "Peter Van Schaack: The Conscience of a Loyalist." In *The Loyalist Americans: A Focus on Greater New York*, edited by Robert A. East and Jacob Judd. Tarrytown, NY: Sleepy Hollow Restorations, 1975.

———. *Whig-Loyalism: An Aspect of Political Ideology in the American Revolutionary Era*. Rutherford, NJ: Fairleigh Dickinson University Press, 1969.

Berkin, Carol. *Jonathan Sewall: Odyssey of an American Loyalist*. New York: Columbia University Press, 1974.

Black, Jeremy. *Britain as a Military Power, 1688–1815*. London: UCL Press, 1999.

Bodle, Wayne. *The Valley Forge Winter: Civilians and Soldiers in War*. University Park: Pennsylvania State University Press, 2004.

Bonomi, Patricia U. *A Factious People: Politics and Society in Colonial New York*. New York: Columbia University Press, 1971.

———. "Local Government in Colonial New York: A Base for Republicanism." In *Aspects of Early New York Society and Politics*, edited by Jacob Judd and Irwin H. Polishook. Tarrytown, NY: Sleepy Hollow Restorations, 1974.

Botein, Stephen. "The Anglo-American Book Trade before 1776: Personal Strategies." In *Printing and Society in Early America*, edited by William L. Joyce et al. Worcester, MA: American Antiquarian Society, 1983.

Bowen, H. V. *Elites, Enterprise, and the Making of the British Overseas Empire, 1688–1775*. New York: St. Martin's Press, 1996.

Bowler, P. Arthur. "Logistics and Operations in the American Revolution." In

*Reconsiderations of the Revolutionary War: Selected Essays,* edited by Don Higginbotham. London: Greenwood Press, 1978.

———. *Logistics and Operations in the American Revolution.* London: Greenwood Press, 1978.

Boyd, Julian P. *Anglo-American Union: Joseph Galloway's Plans to Preserve the British Empire, 1774–1788.* Philadelphia: University of Pennsylvania Press, 1941.

Bradley, Arthur Granville. *The United Empire Loyalists: Founders of British Canada.* London: Thornton Butterworth, 1932.

Braisted, Todd W. "The Black Pioneers and Others." In *Moving On: Black Loyalists in the Afro-Atlantic World,* edited by John W. Pulis. New York: Garland Publishing, 1999.

Bridenbaugh, Carl. *Cities in Revolt: Urban Life in America, 1743–1776.* New York: Alfred Knopf, 1955.

Brown, Alan S. "William Eden and the American Revolution." PhD diss., University of Michigan, 1953.

Brown, Gerald Saxon. *The American Secretary: The Colonial Policy of Lord George Germain, 1775–1778.* Ann Arbor: University of Michigan Press, 1963.

Brown, Richard D. "The Confiscation and Disposition of Loyalists' Estates in Suffolk County, Massachusetts." *William and Mary Quarterly* 21 (1964): 534–50.

Brown, Richard Maxwell. *Strain of Violence: Historical Studies of American Violence and Vigilantism.* New York: Oxford, 1975.

Brown, Wallace. *The Good Americans: The Loyalists in the American Revolution.* New York: William Morrow & Co., 1969.

———. *The King's Friends: The Composition and Motives of the American Loyalist Claimants.* Providence, RI: Brown University Press, 1965.

Brown, Wallace, and Hereward Senior. *Victorious in Defeat: The American Loyalists in Exile.* New York: Facts on File, 1984.

Brown, Weldon A. *Empire or Independence: A Struggle in the Failure of Reconciliation, 1774–1783.* Baton Rouge: Louisiana State University Press, 1941.

Burt, Alfred Leroy. *Imperial Architects, Being an Account of Proposals in the Direction of a Closer Imperial Union, Made Previous to the Opening of the First Colonial Conference of 1887.* New York: Oxford, 1913.

Bushman, Richard L. *King and People in Provincial Massachusetts.* Chapel Hill: University of North Carolina Press, 1985.

Calhoon, Robert M. *Dominion and Liberty: Ideology in the Anglo-American World, 1660–1801.* Arlington Heights, IL: Harlan Davidson, 1992.

———. *The Loyalists in Revolutionary America.* New York: Harcourt Brace Jovanovich, 1973.

———. "William Smith Jr.'s Alternative to the American Revolution." *William and Mary Quarterly* 22 (January 1965): 105–118.

Calhoon, Robert M., and Timothy Barnes. *The Loyalist Perception and Other Essays.* Columbia: University of South Carolina Press, 1989.

Callahan, North. *Royal Raiders: Tories of the American Revolution.* Indianapolis: Bobbs-Merrill, 1963.

Champagne, Roger J. *Alexander McDougall and the American Revolution in New York.* Schenectady, NY: Union College Press, 1975.

———. "Liberty Boys and Mechanics of New York City, 1764–1774." *Labor History* 8 (1967): 115–35.

———. "New York's Radicals and the Coming of Independence." *Journal of American History* 51 (June 1964): 21–40.

Chapin, Bradley. "Colonial and Revolutionary Origins of the American Law of Treason." *William and Mary Quarterly* 17 (1960): 4–21.

Chopra, Ruma. "Hugh Gaine Crosses and Re-Crosses the Hudson." *New York History* 90 (2009): 271–85.

Christie, Ian R., and Benjamin W. Labaree. *Empire or Independence, 1760–1766: A British-American Dialogue on the Coming of the American Revolution.* New York: W. W. Norton & Co., 1976.

Clifford, Mary Louise. *From Slavery to Freetown: Black Loyalists after the American Revolution.* Jefferson, NC: McFarland, 1999.

Cole, Douglas. "The Problem of 'Nationalism' and 'Imperialism' in British Settlement Colonies." *Journal of British Studies* 10 (1971): 160–82.

Colley, Linda. *Britons: Forging the Nation, 1707–1837.* New Haven, CT: Yale University Press, 1992.

———. *Captives.* New York: Random House, 2002.

Condon, Ann Gorman. "The Circuitous Career of Loyalist Plans for Colonial Union in America and Canada, 1754–1914." In *The Treaty of Paris (1783) in a Changing States System: Papers from a Conference, January 26–27, 1984,* edited by Prosser Gifford. Lanham, MD: University Press of America, 1985.

———. "Marching to a Different Drummer: The Political Philosophy of the American Loyalists." In *Red, White, and True Blue: The Loyalists in the Revolution,* edited by Esmond Wright. New York: AMS Press, 1976.

Conser, Walter H., Jr., Ronald M. McCarthy, and David J. Toscano. "The American Independence Movement, 1765–1775: A Decade of Nonviolent Struggles." In *Resistance, Politics, and the American Struggle,* edited by Walter H. Conser Jr. et al. Boulder, CO: L. Rienner Publishers, 1986.

Conway, Stephen. "From Fellow-Nationals to Foreigners: British Perceptions of the Americans, circa 1739–1783." *William and Mary Quarterly* 50 (January 2002): 65–100.

———. "Military-Civilian Crime and the British Army in North America, 1775–1781." PhD diss., University College, London, 1982.

Cooke, Jacob E. "Tench Coxe: Tory Merchant." *Pennsylvania Magazine of History and Biography* 96 (1972): 48–88.

Countryman, Edward. *A People in Revolution: The American Revolution and Political Society in New York, 1760–1790.* Baltimore: Johns Hopkins University Press, 1981.

———. "The Uses of Capital in Revolutionary America: The Case of the New York Loyalist Merchants." *William and Mary Quarterly* 49 (1992): 3–28.

Cray, Robert E., Jr. *Paupers and Poor Relief in New York City and Its Rural Environs: 1700–1830.* Philadelphia: Temple University Press, 1988.

Cullen, George Edward, Jr. "Talking to a Whirlwind: The Loyalist Printers in America, 1763–1783." PhD diss., West Virginia University, 1979.

Curtis, Edward E. *The Organization of the British Army in the American Revolution.* New York: AMS Press, 1969.

Davies, K. G. "The Restoration of Civil Government by the British in the War of Independence." In *Red, White, and True Blue: The Loyalists in the Revolution,* edited by Esmond Wright. New York: AMS Press, 1976.

Dawson, Henry. Introduction. In *Public Papers of George Clinton, First Governor of New York,* vol. 8. Albany: Oliver A. Quayle, 1904.

*Dictionary of Canadian Biography.* Toronto: University of Toronto Press, 1966.

Dubeau, Sharon. *New Brunswick Loyalists: A Bicentennial Tribute.* Agincourt, ON: Generation Press, 1983.

Duncan, Jason K. *Citizens or Papists? The Politics of Anti-Catholicism in New York, 1685–1821.* New York: Fordham University Press, 2005.

East, Robert A. "The Business Entrepreneur in a Changing Economy, 1763–1795." *Journal of Economic History* 6 (May 1946): 16–27.

Edwards, George William. *New York as an Eighteenth-Century Municipality, 1731–1776.* New York: AMS Press, 1968.

Egnal, Marc. *New World Economies: The Growth of the Thirteen Colonies and Early Canada.* New York: Oxford University Press, 1998.

———. "New York and Massachusetts, 1682–1776." In *Party and Political Faction in Revolutionary America,* edited by Patricia Bonomi. Tarrytown, NY: Sleepy Hollow Restorations, 1980.

Ernst, Robert. "Andrew Elliot, Forgotten Loyalist of Occupied New York." *New York History* 57 (July 1976): 285–320.

———. "A Tory-Eye View of the Evacuation of New York." *New York History* 64 (1983): 377–94.

Eustace, Nicole. *Passion Is the Gale: Emotion, Power, and the Coming of the American Revolution.* Chapel Hill: University of North Carolina Press, 2008.

Evans, Randolph G. "A View of Cornwallis's Surrender at Yorktown." *American Historical Review* 37 (1931): 25–49.

Ferling, John E. *Joseph Galloway and the American Revolution*. University Park: Pennsylvania State University Press, 1970.

———. *A Leap in the Dark: The Struggle to Create the American Republic*. New York: Oxford University Press, 2003.

———. *The Loyalist Mind: Joseph Galloway and the American Revolution*. University Park: Pennsylvania State University Press, 1977.

Fingerhut, Eugene. *Survivor: Cadwallader Colden II in Revolutionary America*. Los Angeles: California State University Press, 1983.

Flavell, Julie M. "Lord North's Conciliatory Proposal and the Patriots in London." *English Historical Review* 107 (April 1992): 302–22.

Foner, Eric. *Tom Paine and Revolutionary America*. New York: Oxford University Press, 2005.

Frey, Sylvia. "Between Slavery and Freedom: Virginia Blacks in the American Revolution." In *Slavery, Revolutionary America, and the New Nation*, edited by Paul Finkelman. New York: Garland Publishing, 1989.

———. "British Armed Forces and American Victory." In *The World Turned Upside Down: The American Victory in the War of Independence*, edited by John Ferling. New York: Greenwood Press, 1988.

———. *The British Soldier in America: A Social History of Military Life in the Revolutionary Period*. Austin: University of Texas Press, 1981.

———. *Water from the Rock: Black Resistance in a Revolutionary Age*. Princeton, NJ: Princeton University Press, 1991.

Friedman, Bernard. "The Shaping of the Radical Consciousness in Provincial New York." *Journal of American History* 56 (March 1970): 781–801.

Friedman, Lee M. "The First Chamber of Commerce in the United States." *Bulletin of the Business Historical Society* 21 (November 1947): 137–43.

Fryer, Mary Beacock. *King's Men: The Soldier Founders of Ontario*. Toronto: Dundurn Press, 1980.

Gerlach, Don R. *Philip Schuyler and the American Revolution in New York, 1733–1777*. Lincoln: University of Nebraska Press, 1964.

Gerlach, Larry R., ed. *The American Revolution: New York as a Case Study*. Belmont, CA: Wadsworth Publishing, 1972.

Gilje, Paul. "Republican Rioting." In *Authority and Resistance in Early New York*, edited by William Pencak and Conrad Edick Wright. New York: New York Historical Society, 1988.

Gillen, Jerome. "Political Thought in Revolutionary New York: 1763–1789." PhD diss., Lehigh University, 1972.

Gipson, Lawrence Henry. *The Coming of the Revolution, 1763–1775*. New York: Harper & Brothers, 1954.

Giunta, Mary A. *The Documents of the Emerging Nation: U.S. Foreign Relations: 1775–1789*. Wilmington, DE: Scholarly Resources, 1998.

Goodfriend, Joyce D. "The Social Dimensions of Congregational Life in Colonial New York City." *William and Mary Quarterly* 46 (April 1989): 252–78.

Grainger, John. *The Battle of Yorktown*. Woodbridge, UK: Boydell Press, 2005.

Grant, John N. "Black Immigrants into Nova Scotia." *Journal of Negro History* 58 (1973): 253–70.

Greene, Evarts B. Greene. "New York and the Old Empire." In *History of the State of New York*, vol. 3, *Whig and Tory*, edited by Alexander C. Flick. New York: New York State Historical Association, 1930.

Gronowicz, Anthony. "Political Radicalism in New York City's Revolutionary and Constitutional Eras." In *New York in the Age of the Constitution: 1775–1800*, edited by Paul Gilje and William Pencak. Cranbury, NJ: Associated University Press, 1992.

Gross, Daniel M. "Early Modern Emotion and the Economy of Scarcity." *Philosophy and Rhetoric* 34 (2001): 308–21.

Gruber, Ira D. "Britain's Southern Strategy." In *The Revolutionary War in the South: Power, Conflict, and Leadership*, edited by W. Robert Higgins. Durham, NC: Duke University Press, 1979.

———. *The Howe Brothers and the American Revolution*. New York: Atheneum, 1972.

Guttridge, George H. "Lord George Germain in Office, 1775–1782." *American Historical Review* 33 (1927): 23–43.

Higgenbotham, Don. *The War of American Independence: Military Attitudes, Policies, and Practice, 1763–1789*. Boston: Northeastern University Press, 1983.

Hodges, Graham Russell. *The Black Loyalist Directory: African Americans in Exile after the American Revolution*. New York: Garland Publishing, 1996.

———. "Black Revolt in New York City and the Neutral Zone, 1775–1783." In *New York in the Age of the Constitution, 1775–1800*, edited by Paul A. Gilje and William Pencak. Cranbury, NJ: Associated University Press, 1992.

———. *New York City Cartmen, 1667–1850*. New York: New York University Press, 1986.

———. *Root and Branch: African Americans in New York and East Jersey, 1613–1863*. Chapel Hill: University of North Carolina Press, 1999.

Hodges, Graham Russell, and Alan Edward Brown, eds. *"Pretends to Be Free": Runaway Slave Advertisements from New York and New Jersey*. New York: Garland Publications, 1994.

Hoffman, Ross J. S. *Edmund Burke, New York Agent, with His Letters to the New York Assembly and Intimate Correspondence with Charles O'Hara, 1761–1776*. Philadelphia: American Philosophical Society, 1956.

Hulsebosch, Daniel J. *Constituting Empire: New York and the Transformation of Constitutionalism in the Atlantic World, 1664–1830*. Chapel Hill: University of North Carolina Press, 2005.

Hutson, James H. "The Treaty of Paris and the International State System." In

*The Treaty of Paris (1783) in a Changing States System: Papers from a Conference, January 26–27, 1984,* edited by Prosser Gifford. Lanham, MD: University Press of America, 1985.

Ireland, Owen. "The Ethnic-Religious Dimension of Pennsylvania Politics, 1778–1779." *William and Mary Quarterly* 30 (1973): 423–48.

Jackson, John W. *With the British Army in Philadelphia, 1777–1778.* San Rafael, CA: Presidio Press, 1979.

Jacobs, Roberta Tansman. "The Treaty and the Tories: The Ideological Reaction to the Return of the Loyalists, 1783–1787." PhD diss., Cornell University, 1974.

James, Coy Hilton. *Silas Deane: Patriot or Traitor?* Ann Arbor: University of Michigan Press, 1975.

Johnson, Janet Basset. *Robert Alexander, Maryland Loyalist.* New York: G. P. Putnam, 1942.

Johnston, Henry P., ed. *The Campaign of 1776 around New York and Brooklyn.* New York: De Capo Press, 1971.

———. *The Storming of Stony Point on the Hudson.* New York: James T. White, 1900.

Jones, Eldon Lewis. "Sir Guy Carleton and the Close of American Independence, 1782–1783." PhD diss., Duke University, 1968.

Jordan, William D. "Familial Politics: Thomas Paine and the Killing of the King, 1776." *Journal of American History* 60 (September 1973): 294–308.

Judd, Jacob. "Frederick Philipse III of Westchester: A Reluctant Loyalist." In *The Loyalist Americans: A Focus on Greater New York,* edited by Robert A. East and Jacob Judd. Tarrytown, NY: Sleepy Hollow Restorations, 1975.

Kaminski, John P. *George Clinton: Yeoman Politician of the New Republic.* Madison, WI: Madison House, 1993.

Kammen, Michael G. *Colonial New York.* New York: Scribner, 1975.

Kaplan, Roger. "The Hidden War: British Intelligence Operations During the American Revolution." *William and Mary Quarterly* 47 (January 1990): 115–38.

Katz, Stanley N. "Between Scylla and Charybdis: James DeLancey and Anglo-American Politics in Early Eighteenth-Century New York." In *Anglo-American Political Relations, 1675–1775,* edited by Alison G. Olson and Richard M. Brown. New Brunswick, NJ: Rutgers University Press, 1970.

Keesey, Ruth M. "Loyalism in Bergen County, New Jersey." *William and Mary Quarterly* 18 (1961): 558–76.

Klein, Milton M. *New York in the American Revolution: A Bibliography.* Albany: New York State American Revolution Bicentennial Commission, 1974.

———. *The Politics of Diversity: Essays in the History of Colonial New York.* Port Washington, NY: Kennikat Press, 1974.

Knight, Betsy. "Prisoner Exchange and Parole in the American Revolution." *William and Mary Quarterly* 48 (1991): 201–22.

Kross, Jessica. " 'Patronage Most Ardently Sought': The New York Common Council, 1665–1775." In *Power and Status: Officeholding in Colonial America,* edited by Bruce C. Daniels. Middletown, CT: Wesleyan University Press, 1986.

Kulikoff, Alan. *From British Peasants to Colonial American Farmers.* Chapel Hill: University of North Carolina Press, 2000.

Kwasny, Mark V. *Washington's Partisan War, 1775–1783.* Kent, OH: Kent State University Press, 1996.

Landsman, Ned. "The Legacy of British Union for the North American Colonies: Provincial Elites and the Problem of Imperial Union." In *A Union for Empire: Political Thought and the British Union of 1707,* edited by John Robertson. Cambridge: Cambridge Press, 1995.

Launitz-Schürer, Leopold, Jr. *Loyal Whigs and Revolutionaries: The Making of Revolution in New York, 1765–1776.* New York: New York University Press, 1980.

Leach, Douglas. *Roots of Conflict: British Armed Forces and Colonial Americans, 1677–1763.* Chapel Hill: University of North Carolina Press, 1986.

Leder, Lawrence H. "Military Victualing in Colonial New York." In *Business Enterprise in Early New York,* edited by Joseph R. Frese and Jacob Judd. Tarrytown, NY: Sleepy Hollow Restorations, 1979.

Lepore, Jill. *New York Burning: Liberty, Slavery, and Conspiracy in Eighteenth-Century Manhattan.* New York City: Alfred Knopf, 2005.

Lorenz, Alfred Lawrence. *Hugh Gaine: A Colonial Printer-Editor's Odyssey to Loyalism.* Carbondale: Southern Illinois University Press, 1972.

Lydekker, John Wolfe, ed. *The Life and Letters of Charles Inglis: His Ministry in America and Consecration at First Colonial Bishop, from 1759 to 1787.* London: Society for Promoting Historical Knowledge, 1936.

Lydon, James. *Pirates, Privateers, and Profits.* Upper Saddle River, NJ: Gregg Press, 1970.

Lynd, Staughton, and Alfred Young. "After Carl Becker: The Mechanic and New York City Politics, 1774–1801." *Labor History* 5 (1964): 215–24.

Mackesy, Piers. *The War for America, 1775–1783.* Lincoln: University of Nebraska Press, 1964.

Maier, Pauline. "The Beginnings of American Republicanism, 1765–1776." In *The Development of a Revolutionary Mentality,* edited by Richard B. Morris. Washington, DC: Library of Congress, 1972.

Mancke, Elizabeth. *The Fault Lines of Empire: Political Differentiation in Massachusetts and Nova Scotia, ca. 1760–1830.* New York: Routledge, 2005.

Marston, Jerrilyn Greene. *King and Congress: The Transfer of Political Legitimacy, 1774–1776.* Princeton, NJ: Princeton University Press, 1987.

Martin, David G. *The Philadelphia Campaign: June 1777–July 1778.* Conshohocken, PA: Combined Books, 1993.

Matson, Cathy. *Merchants and Empire: Trading in Colonial New York*. Baltimore: Johns Hopkins University Press, 1998.

McAnear, Beverly. "Politics in Provincial New York, 1689–1761." PhD diss., Stanford University, 1935.

McConville, Brendan. *The King's Three Faces: The Rise and Fall of Royal America, 1688–1776*. Chapel Hill, NC: Institute of Early American History and Culture, 2006.

McCusker, John J., and Russell R. Menard. *The Economy of British America, 1607–1789*. Chapel Hill: University of North Carolina Press, 1985.

Middlekauff, Robert. *The Glorious Cause: The American Revolution, 1763–1789*. New York: Oxford University Press, 2005.

Middleton, Simon. *From Privileges to Rights: Work and Politics in Colonial New York City*. Philadelphia: University of Pennsylvania Press, 2006.

Mohl, Raymond A. "Poverty in Colonial New York City." In *Urban America in Historical Perspective*, edited by Raymond A. Mohl and Neil Betten. New York: Weybright & Talley, 1970.

Montross, Lynn. *The Reluctant Rebels: The Story of the Continental Congress, 1774–1789*. New York: Harper & Brothers, 1950.

Morgan, Philip D., and Andrew Jackson O'Shaugnessy. "Arming Slaves in the American Revolution." In *Arming Slaves: From Classical Times to the Modern Age*, ed. Christopher Leslie Brown and Philip D. Morgan. New Haven, CT: Yale University Press, 2006.

Moore, Christopher. *The Loyalists: Revolution, Exile, Settlement*. Toronto: Macmillan, 1984.

Morgan, Edmund. *Inventing the People: The Rise of Popular Sovereignty in England and America*. New York: W. W. Norton & Co., 1988.

Morris, Richard B. "The American Revolution Comes to John Jay." In *Aspects of Early New York and Politics*, edited by Jacob Judd and Irwin H. Polishook. Tarrytown, NY: Sleepy Hollow Restorations, 1974.

———. "Class Struggle and the American Revolution." *William and Mary Quarterly* 19 (January 1962): 4–29.

Mushkat Jerome. *George Clinton: New York Governor during Revolutionary Times*. Charlotteville, NY: SamHar Press, 1974.

Nash, Gary B. *Race, Class, and Politics: Essays on American Colonial and Revolutionary Society*. Urbana: University of Illinois Press, 1986.

———. *The Unknown American Revolution: The Unruly Birth of Democracy and the Struggle to Create America*. New York: Viking, 2005.

———. *The Urban Crucible: Social Change, Political Consciousness, and the Origins of the American Revolution*. Cambridge, MA: Harvard University Press, 1979.

Nelson, Jeffrey. "Ideology in Search of a Context: Eighteenth-Century British

Political Thought and the Loyalists of the American Revolution." *Historical Journal* 20 (September 1977): 741–49.

Nelson, Paul David. "British Conduct during the Revolutionary War: A Review of Interpretations." *Journal of American History* 65 (December 1978): 623–53.

———. *William Tryon and the Course of Empire: A Life in British Imperial Service.* Chapel Hill: University of North Carolina, 1990.

———. "William Tryon Confronts the American Revolution, 1771–1780." *Historian* 53 (1991): 267–84.

Nelson, William H. *The American Tory.* Oxford: Clarendon Press, 1961.

Nettels, Curtis. "A Link in the Chain of Events Leading to American Independence." *William and Mary Quarterly* 3 (January 1946): 36–47.

Nolan, Dennis R. "The Effect of the Revolution on the Bar: The Maryland Experience." *Virginia Law Review* 62 (1976): 969–97.

Norris, John. *Shelburne and Reform.* London: Macmillan, 1963.

Norton, Mary Beth. *The British-Americans: The Loyalist Exiles in England, 1774–1789.* Boston: Little, Brown, & Co., 1972.

O'Shaugnessy, Andrew Jackson. "'If Others Will Not Be Active, I Must Drive': George III and the American Revolution." *Early American Studies* 2 (Spring 2004): 1–46.

Overfield, Richard Arthur. "The Loyalists of Maryland during the American Revolution." PhD diss., University of Maryland, 1968.

Pancake, John S. *1777, The Year of the Hangman.* University: University of Alabama Press, 1977.

Papas, Phillip. *That Ever Loyal Island: Staten Island and the American Revolution.* New York: New York University Press, 2007.

Papenfuse, Edward C. "Economic Analysis and Loyalist Strategy during the American Revolution: Robert Alexander's Remarks on the Economy of the Peninsula or Eastern Shore of Maryland." *Maryland Historical Magazine* 68 (1973): 173–95.

Perkins, Edwin J. *The Economy of Colonial America.* New York: Columbia University Press, 1988.

Pointer, Richard P. *Protestant Pluralism and the New York Experience: A Study of Eighteenth-Century Religious Diversity.* Bloomington: Indiana University Press, 1988.

Polf, William A. *Garrison Town: The British Occupation of New York City, 1776–1783.* Albany: New York State American Revolution Bicentennial Commission, 1976.

Pomerantz, Sidney. *New York, an American City, 1783–1803: A Study of Urban Life.* New York: Columbia University Press, 1938.

Potter, Janice. *The Liberty We Seek: Loyalist Ideology in Colonial New York and Massachusetts.* Cambridge, MA: Harvard University Press, 1983.

Potter, Janice, and Robert M. Calhoon. "The Character and Coherence of the Loyalist Press." In *The Press and the American Revolution*, edited by Bernard Bailyn and John Hench. Worcester, MA: American Antiquarian Society, 1980.

Preyer, Katherine. "Penal Measures in the American Colonies: An Overview." *American Journal of Legal History* 26 (October 1982): 326–53.

Rankin, Hugh F. "Charles Lord Cornwallis: Study in Frustration." In *George Washington's Opponents: British Generals and Admirals in the American Revolution*, edited by George Athan Billias. New York: William Morrow & Co., 1969.

Rawlyk, G. A. "The Reverend John Stuart Mohawk Missionary and Reluctant Loyalist." In *Red, White, and True Blue: The Loyalists in the American Revolution*, edited by Esmond Wright. New York: AMS Press, 1976.

Raymond, W. O. "Loyalists in Arms." *New Brunswick Historical Society Collections* 5 (1904): 189–223.

Rediker, Marcus. *Between the Devil and the Deep Blue Sea: Merchant Seamen, Pirates, and the Anglo-American Maritime World, 1700–1750*. Cambridge: Cambridge University Press, 1987.

Reed, Patrick. "Loyalists, Patriots, and Trimmers: The Committee System in the American Revolution, 1774–1776." PhD diss., Cornell University, 1988.

Ritcheson, Charles R. "Britain's Peacemakers, 1782–1783: To an Astonishing Degree Unfit for the Task?" In *Peace and the Peacemakers: The Treaty of 1783*, edited by Ronald Hoffman and Peter J. Albert. Charlottesville: University Press of Virginia, 1986.

———. *British Politics and the American Revolution*. Norman: University of Oklahoma Press, 1954.

———. "The Earl of Shelburne and Peace with America, 1782–1783." *International History Review* 5 (1983): 322–45.

———. "Loyalist Influence on British Policy toward the United States after the American Revolution." *Eighteenth Century Studies* 7 (1973): 1–17.

Rosen, Deborah A. *Courts and Commerce: Gender, Law, and the Market Economy in Colonial New York*. Columbus: Ohio State University Press, 1997.

Royster, Charles. *A Revolutionary People at War: The Continental Army and American Character, 1775–1783*. Chapel Hill, NC: Institute of Early American History and Culture, 1979.

Rucker, Walter C. *The River Flows On: Black Resistance, Culture, and Identify Formation in Early America*. Baton Rouge: Louisiana State University Press, 2006.

Russell, David Lee. *The American Revolution in the Southern Colonies*. Jefferson, NC: McFarland & Co., 2000.

Ryan, Dennis B. *New Jersey's Loyalists*. Trenton: New Jersey Historical Commission, 1943.

Sabine, Lorenzo. *Biographical Sketches of Loyalists of the American Revolution*. Boston: Little, Brown, & Co. 1864.

Schecter, Barnet. *The Battle for New York: The City at the Heart of the American Revolution*. New York: Penguin Books, 2002.

Schuyler, Robert Livingston. "Galloway's Plan for Anglo-American Union." *Political Science Quarterly* 57 (June 1942): 281–85.

Schwind, Arlene Palmer. "The Ceramic Imports of Frederick Rhinelander." *Winterthur Portfolio* 19 (1984): 21–36.

Schwoerer, Lois G. "Law, Liberty, and Jury 'Ideology': English Transatlantic Revolutionary Traditions." In *Revolutionary Currents: Nation Building in the Transatlantic World*, edited by Michael A. Morrison and Melinda Zook. Lanahm, MD: Rowman & Littlefield, 2004.

Scott, H. M. *British Foreign Policy in the Age of the American Revolution*. Oxford: Clarendon Press, 1990.

Scott, Kenneth. "Tory Associators of Portsmouth." *William and Mary Quarterly* 17 (1960): 507–15.

Shama, Simon. *Rough Crossings: Britain, the Slaves, and the American Revolution*. New York: Ecco Press, 2006.

Sheridan, Richard. "The West Indian Antecedents of Josiah Martin, Last Royal Governor of North Carolina." *North Carolina Historical Review* 54 (1977): 252–70.

Shy, John. "American Society and Its War for Independence." In *Reconsiderations of the Revolutionary War: Selected Essays*, edited by Don Higginbotham. London: Greenwood Press, 1978.

———. "Charles Lee: The Soldier as Radical." In *George Washington's Generals*, edited by George Athan Billias. New York: William Morrow & Co., 1964.

———. "The Loyalist Problem in the Lower Hudson Valley: The British Perspective." In *Loyalist Americans: A Focus on Greater New York*, edited by Robert A. East and Jacob Judd. Tarrytown, NY: Sleepy Hollow Restorations, 1975.

———. *A People Numerous and Armed: Reflections on the Military Struggle for American Independence*. Ann Arbor: University of Michigan Press, 1990.

———. *Toward Lexington: The Role of the British Army in the Coming of the American Revolution*. Princeton, NJ: Princeton University Press, 1965.

Skemp, Sheila L. *William Franklin: Son of a Patriot, Servant of a King*. New York: Oxford University Press, 1990.

Skinner, Quentin. *Visions of Politics*. Vol. 3, *Hobbes and Civil Science*. Cambridge: Cambridge University Press, 2002.

Smith, Glenn H. "William Franklin: Expedient Loyalist." *North Dakota Quarterly* 52 (1974): 57–75.

Smith, Paul H. *Redcoats and Loyalists: A Study in British Revolutionary Policy*. Chapel Hill: University of North Carolina Press, 1964.

———. "Sir Guy Carleton, Peace Negotiations, and the Evacuation of New York." *Canadian Historical Review* 50 (1969): 245–64.

Sosin, Jack M. *Agents and Merchants: British Colonial Policy and the Origins of the American Revolution, 1763–1775*. Lincoln: University of Nebraska Press, 1965.

Spaulding, Ernest Wilder. *New York in the Critical Period, 1783–1789*. New York: Columbia University Press, 1932.

Stahr, Walter. *John Jay: Founding Father*. New York: R. R. Donnelley & Sons Co., 2005.

Steele, Ian K. "Empire of Migrants and Consumers: Some Current Atlantic Approaches to the History of Colonial Virginia." *Virginia Magazine of History and Biography* 99 (1991): 489–512.

Sterling, David L. "American Prisoners of War in New York: A Report by Elias Boudinot." *William and Mary Quarterly* 13 (July 1956): 376–393.

Stryker, William. *The New Jersey Volunteers (Loyalists) in the Revolutionary War*. Trenton, NJ: Naar, Day & Naar, 1887.

Stuart, Charles. "Lord Shelburne." In *History and Imagination: Essays in Honour of H. R. Trevor-Roper*, edited by Hugh Lloyd-Jones, Valerie Pearl, and Blair Worden. London: Duckworth, 1980.

Surrency, Erwin C. "The Courts in the American Colonies." *American Journal of Legal History* 11 (1967): 253–76.

Taeffe, Stephen R. *The Philadelphia Campaign, 1777–1778*. Lawrence: University Press of Kansas, 2003.

Talman, James J. *Loyalist Narratives of Upper Canada*. Toronto: Chaplain Society, 1946.

Tatum, Edward H., Jr. "Ambrose Serle, Secretary to Lord Howe, 1776–1778." *Huntington Library Quarterly* 2 (1939): 265–84.

Taylor, Alan. *American Colonies*. New York: Viking, 2001.

Tebbenhoff, Edward H. "The Associated Loyalists: An Aspect of Militant Loyalism." In *Patriots, Redcoats, and Loyalists*, edited by Peter S. Onuf. New York: Garland Publishing, 1991.

Thompson, E. P. "Patrician Society, Plebian Culture." *Journal of Social History* 7 (1974): 382–405.

Tiedemann, Joseph S. "Patriots by Default: Queens County, New York, and the British Army, 1776–1783." *William and Mary Quarterly* 43 (1986): 35–63.

———. *Reluctant Revolutionaries: New York City and the Road to Independence, 1763–1776*. Ithaca, NY: Cornell University Press, 1997.

Tidemann, Joseph S., and Eugene R. Fingerhut, eds. *The Other New York: The American Revolution beyond New York City, 1763–1787*. Albany: State University of New York Press, 2005.

Tiedemann, Joseph S., Eugene R. Fingerhut, and Robert W. Venables, eds. *The Other Loyalists: Ordinary People, Royalism, and the Revolution in the Middle Colonies, 1763–1787*. Albany: State University of New York Press, 2009.

Toscano, David J., Ronald M. McCarthy, and Walter H. Conser Jr. "A Shift in Strategy: The Organization of the Military Struggle." In *Resistance, Politics, and the American Struggle for Independence, 1765–1775,* edited by Walter H. Conser Jr. et al. Boulder, CO: Lynne Rienner Publishers, 1986.

Tully, Alan. *Forming American Politics: Ideas, Interests, and Institutions in Colonial New York and Pennsylvania.* Baltimore: Johns Hopkins University Press, 1994.

Upton, L. F. S. "The Idea of the Confederation, 1754–1858." In *The Shield of Achilles: Aspects of Canada in the Victorian Age,* edited by W. L. Morton. Toronto: McClelland and Stewart, 1968.

———. *The Loyal Whig: William Smith of New York & Quebec.* Toronto: University of Toronto Press, 1969.

———. *The United Empire Loyalists: Men and Myths.* Toronto: Copp Clark Publishing, 1967.

Van Buskirk, Judith. *Generous Enemies: Patriots and Loyalists in Revolutionary New York.* Philadelphia: University of Pennsylvania Press, 2002.

Varga, Nicholas. "New York Government and Politics during the Mid-Eighteenth Century." PhD diss., Fordham University, 1960.

Walett, Francis G. *Patriots, Loyalists, and Printers: Bicentennial Articles on the American Revolution.* Worcester, MA: American Antiquarian Society, 1976.

Walzer, Michael. "On the Role of Symbolism in Political Thought." *Political Science Quarterly* 82 (June 1967): 191–204.

Ward, Harry M. *The War for Independence and the Transformation of American Society.* London: UCL Press, 1999.

Weiner, Frederick Bernays. *Civilians under Military Justice: The British Practice since 1689 Especially in North America.* Chicago: University of Chicago Press, 1967.

Wertenbaker, Thomas Jefferson. *Father Knickerbocker Rebels: New York City during the Revolution.* New York: Scribner's Sons, 1948.

White, John Todd. "Standing Armies in Time of War: Republican Theory and Military Practice during the American Revolution." PhD diss., George Washington University, 1978.

Willcox, William B. "The British Road to Yorktown: A Study in Divided Command." *American Historical Review* 52 (1946): 1–35.

———. "British Strategy in America, 1778." *Journal of Modern History* 19 (1947): 97–121.

———. *Portrait of a General: Sir Henry Clinton in the War for Independence.* New York: Alfred Knopf, 1964.

———. "Rhode Island in British Strategy, 1780–1781." *Journal of Modern History* 17 (December 1945): 304–31.

———. "Too Many Cooks: British Planning before Saratoga." *Journal of British Studies* 2 (1962): 56–90.

Wilkenfeld, Bruce. "Revolutionary New York, 1776." In *New York: Centennial Years, 1576–1976*, edited by Milton Klein. Port Washington, NY: Kennikat Press, 1976.

———. *The Social and Economic Structure of the City of New York*. New York: Arno Press, 1978.

Wilson, Ellen Gibson. *The Loyal Blacks*. New York: Capricorn Books, 1976.

Wood, Gordon S. "Conspiracy and the Paranoid Style: Causality and Deceit in the Eighteenth Century." *William and Mary Quarterly* 39 (July 1982): 402–41.

———. "Rhetoric and Reality in the American Revolution." *William and Mary Quarterly* 23 (January 1966): 4–32.

Wortley, E. Stuart, ed. *A Prime Minister and His Son*. New York: E. P. Dutton, 1925.

Wright, Esmond. "The British Objectives, 1780–1783: 'If Not Dominion Then Trade.'" In *Peace and the Peacemakers: The Treaty of 1783*, edited by Ronald Hoffman and Peter J. Albert. Charlottesville: University Press of Virginia, 1986.

———. "Men with Two Countries." In *The Development of a Revolutionary Mentality*, edited by Robert B. Morris. Washington, DC: Library of Congress, 1972.

———. "The New York Loyalists: A Cross-Section of Colonial Society." In *The Loyalist Americans: A Focus on Greater New York*, edited by Robert A. East and Jacob Judd. Tarrytown, NY: Sleepy Hollow Restorations, 1975.

Wrong, George McKinnon. *Canada and the American Revolution: The Disruption of the First British Empire*. New York: Cooper Square Publishers, 1968.

Wroth, Lawrence C. *The Colonial Printer*. Charlottesville: University Press of Virginia, 1964.

Wynn, Grame. "On the Margins of Empire." In *The Illustrated History of Canada*. Toronto: Key Porter Square, 2002.

York, Neil L. "The First Continental Congress and the Problem of American Rights." *Pennsylvania Magazine of History and Biography* 122 (1998): 353–83.

Young, Alfred. *The Democratic Republicans of New York: The Origins, 1763–1797*. Chapel Hill, NC: Institute of Early American History and Culture, 1967.

Zimmer, Anne Y. *Jonathan Boucher, Loyalist Exile*. Detroit: Wayne State University Press, 1978.

# INDEX

New York Supreme Court, 10, 11
Nova Scotia, loyalists' relocation to, 206–7, 208, 211, 212, 213, 226, 266n86, 270n4

occupations: of blacks in military, 114–15, 143, 145–46, 212, 214, 245n59, 249n36; of landholders, 11, 16; of lawyers, 10, 38–41, 229n8; of loyalist petition signees, 66–67; of mechanics, 11, 27, 230n14, 232n58; of middling people, 15; of ship carpenters, 18–19. *See also* merchants
office of inquiry, 142
Office of Police (British): fines levied by, 149, 255n50; food distribution and, 151–52; function of, 148–49, 225; Long Island version of, 180; tavern licensing by, 150–51
Ogden, Isaac, 94, 101–2, 106, 108, 109, 112, 117, 127
Olive Branch Petition, 37–39
Oliver, Peter, 228n13
optimism of loyalists: with bleak conditions of Washington's army, 94; with British troops' arrival, 51–52; with Carleton's arrival, 197–98; in Deane's letters, 192–93; in December 1776, 73; with mutinies in Washington's army, 194; with peace commissioners, 96–97; with Robertson's arrival, 175, 176–77; in spring of 1777, 83–86; in winter of 1777–78, 90–91. *See also* disappointment of loyalists
Oswald, Richard, 203–6, 207

Paine, Thomas, 1, 43–44, 265n78
Parliament: antiwar sentiment in, 202; duties repealed (except on tea), 25; Howe questioned in, 112–13; lack of representation of colonies in, 21–22; loyalist hopes for political compromise with, 56–57, 58–60; loyalists' claims to, 201, 265n55; on paper money in colonies, 23–24; Shelburne's position in, 204–5. *See also* British ministry; *specific acts*
peace treaty. *See* Treaty of Paris (1783)
Pennsylvania: attitudes toward British troops in, 99–100; loyalist support in, 87, 88; population of, 231n42. *See also* Philadelphia
Percy, Hugh, 51, 70, 88
petitions and memorials: British response

to loyalist, 68–71; divisions concerning, 180–81, 183–85; for loyalist relief, 198; of merchants, 66–67, 239n84; for return to civil institutions, 64–69, 239n80, 253n24
Philadelphia: accusations about Howe's treatment of loyalists in, 112–13; British campaign for, 86, 87–88, 89–90; British evacuation of, 96, 97, 99–100, 106, 110; commercial activities during British rule of, 124–25; loyalists executed in, 100–101; military vs. civil rule in, 132; tournament and celebration in, 91; trade activities of, 8, 14; voting in, 11. *See also* Galloway, Joseph
Philipse, Frederick, III, 49, 161
police. *See* Office of Police (British)
political solutions: civil rule (proposed and opposed), 174–75; civil rule under Robertson, 176–78; Clinton on civil rule, 178–79; merchants on, 122–25; militants on, 42, 103–4, 109–11, 165–66, 168; moderates on, 60, 131–32, 142; office of inquiry, 142; peace commissioners on, 131; proposals in 1782, 201; revised constitution, 31, 40, 59
Potter, Janice, 228n12, 238n49
printers. *See* Gaine, Hugh; Rivington, James
prisoners: escape from rebels, 148, 254–55n48; prisoner exchange issue, 166–67, 170; rebel treatment of, 70, 100–101, 109–10, 155, 196, 210
privateering: before war, 18, 20; during war, 127–28; effects on navy, 129–30; French and Spanish against British, 165
Prohibitory Act: rationale for and effects of, 68, 122–24, 125–26; suspension of, 126–27
Protestantism, meanings for loyalists, 93–94, 238n49
punishment: of loyalist civilians, 212–13, 215; of loyalist soldiers, 210–11. *See also* Continental Association

Quartering Act, 23–24

rebels: actions against defeated loyalists, 160–62, 210–16; allegiances understood by, 4–5; boycott compliance enforced by, 32–34, 48–49; British assumptions about,

JEFFERSONIAN AMERICA